Praise for *Moral Triumph: The Public Face o*

"In this thoughtful and original study, Zhibin Xie brings his extensive knowledge of ethics and public theology into relationship with social and religious life in contemporary China. Western readers will learn a great deal about the complex realities of Chinese society, but they will also discover new ways to see their own social experience."

Robin W. Lovin
Cary Maguire University Professor of Ethics *emeritus*,
Southern Methodist University

"Based on a profound understanding of issues related to the relationships between Christianity, Chinese culture, and contemporary China, as well as Western and Asian voices in public theology, Xie has made a significant contribution to Chinese public theology and the moral engagement of Christianity in China."

Francis Ching-Wah Yip
Director, Divinity School of Chung Chi College,
The Chinese University of Hong Kong

"Few frontiers of world Christianity are more controversial and promising than those in mainland China today. And few scholars are more adept than Professor Zhibin Xie in negotiating the complex dialectics between Western and Chinese Christianity, traditional teachings and modern challenges, flourishing Christian communities and indigenous forms and forums of faith and politics. In this volume, Professor Xie continues to lay important groundwork for a distinct Chinese political theology that skillfully blends Chinese and Western teachings, and speaks powerfully and prophetically to fundamental issues of love, justice, rights, freedom, and legal and political reform. This volume deserves wide readership throughout the world."

John Witte Jr.
Robert W. Woodruff Professor of Law, Emory University

"Zhibin Xie is an inspirational pioneer in public theology and ethics in China. His work exemplifies a willingness to think both globally and contextually about the public face of Christian faith and values. Drawing on a rich and diverse range of Western and Chinese scholarship, he offers a nuanced and insightful intercultural analysis. Anyone interested in the public role that Christianity and theology could play in Chinese society should read this book."

David Tombs
Howard Paterson Chair of Theology and Public Issues, and
Director of the Centre for Theology and Public Issues,
University of Otago, New Zealand

"Zhibin Xie argues that Chinese Christianity can contribute to the public life of Chinese people through its 'moral accomplishments.' He believes that Christian moral values can help Chinese Christianity to redefine its public role and offer Chinese society a Christian analysis of social problems. This book is an authentic theological reflection for a Christian public life in China."

Wai Luen Kwok
Associate Professor, Department of Religion and Philosophy,
and Associate Director, Centre for Sino-Christian Studies,
Hong Kong Baptist University

"A Chinese philosopher by training, and joining with this heritage the life and thought of preeminent Dutch public theologian Abraham Kuyper, interpreted through the invigorating lens of Princeton Theological Seminary's Max Stackhouse and other notable reformers, Dr. Zhibin Xie brings his one-of-a-kind, cross-cultural learning to address the challenge of offering the gifts of Christian faith into today's vast transformation of China's 5,000-year-old ways of living. From exploring what vocabulary to engage and what methods to employ to articulating well-defined proposals for Christian contributions to Chinese public life, Dr. Xie skillfully reviews important Chinese and Western scholarship as he calls his readers to focus on the moral life of the Chinese people: its charitable roots and its institutional reconstruction today. Connecting with Chinese Christian theology's best—when it attends to the daily well-being of the people—Dr. Xie's analyses, critiques, and positive recommendations, interweaving Confucian and reformed Christian themes, provide indispensable reading and necessary guidance for the next generation, who must stand on the shoulders of those who have come before to view with yet greater precision China's still-emerging new 'public square.' *Moral Triumph* illumines a clear path forward!"

Diane Obenchain
Director, Chinese Studies Center, and Senior
Professor of Religion, Fuller Theological Seminary

MORAL
TRIUMPH

MORAL TRIUMPH

The Public Face of Christianity in China

Zhibin Xie

FORTRESS PRESS
MINNEAPOLIS

MORAL TRIUMPH
The Public Face of Christianity in China

Cover image: Cathedral of the Sacred Heart the main Catholic church of Dali, Yunnan, China. Dali, Yunnan, China—November, 2018.
Cover design: Savanah N. Landerholm

Print ISBN: 978-1-5064-8680-2
eBook ISBN: 978-1-5064-8681-9

For
Sophia, Yannah, and Lucien

CONTENTS

PREFACE AND ACKNOWLEDGMENTS

My intellectual interest in the public roles of religion in China can be traced back about twenty years ago to my doctoral studies at the University of Hong Kong, where I explored religious interaction with politics in China from the perspective of political philosophy. The revised version of my dissertation entitled *Religious Diversity and Public Religion in China* was published by Ashgate in 2006. After that, I became interested in the theological approach to public life and in 2006 visited Princeton Theological Seminary, where I studied the thought of public theology with Max L. Stackhouse (1935–2016), a well-known public theologian, with special attention to the global context of public theology. The project turned out to be a Chinese volume entitled *Public Theology and Globalization: A Study in Max L. Stackhouse's Christian Ethics* published by Religious Culture Press in Beijing in 2008. I have made some efforts to introduce public theology to the Chinese academia and church. In working in this field, I am deeply grateful to Max for all his guidance and support in various ways. It is also Max who encouraged me to think about the possibility of public theology in the Chinese context.

In these studies, I have moved to the issue of theological understanding of public life in China and started to write and present various articles on different occasions regarding the methodology of public theology and the theological engagement with different public issues in China. This book is an output from these works. My early political philosophical thinking about political and public life in China assists me in engaging philosophical and social scientific resources about what Chinese society is and ought to be while I undertake public theological thinking. This interdisciplinary method creates a wider possibility for me to activate theological involvement in public discourse as I hold on to specific Christian views of the world and humanity. Another issue persistent in my studies about religion and public life in China from the perspectives of political philosophy and Christian public theology is religious diversity and the place of Christianity against that background in China.

During my work on this book, I have presented some of its ideas in various conferences, including the conference on "Religions in Asian Public Life," organized by the United Board for Christian Higher Education in Asia in Hong Kong in 2012; the conference on "Church and Academy," organized by the Abraham Kuyper Center for Public Theology at Princeton Theological Seminary in 2013; the international symposium on "Religion-State Relationship in the Chinese Context: A Case Study of Christianity with Interdisciplinary Integration," organized by the Institute of Sino-Christian Studies in Hong Kong in 2016; the "Routledge International Conference: Religion and Nationalism in Asia," organized by the Department of Philosophy (Zhuhai) at Sun Yat-Sen University in 2016; the International Reformed Theological Institute (IRTI) "12th International Conference on Public Theology in Plural Contexts" in Hong Kong in 2017; and the international symposium on "Human Nature, Justice, and Society: Reinhold Niebuhr in the Chinese Context," co-organized by the Institute of Sino-Christian Studies and the Center for Christian Studies at The Chinese University of Hong Kong in 2019.

My work has appeared in various journals and book chapters, including *Asia Journal of Theology*,[1] *Archivio Theologico Torinese*,[2] *International Journal of Public Theology*,[3] *Political Theology*,[4] *Theology Today*,[5] *Journal of Church and State*,[6] the Routledge volume *Religion and Nationalism in Asia* (edited by Giorgio Shani and Takashi Kibe [@2019], reprinted by permission of Taylor & Francis Group), the Springer volume *Human*

---

1 Zhibin Xie, "The Possibility of Contextual Sino-Christian Ethics: with a Focus on Christian Public Significance," *Asia Journal of Theology* 27, no. 1 (2013): 3–20.

2 Zhibin Xie, "Christian Encounter with Religious Plurality and Public Life in the Chinese Context: A Contribution of Abraham Kuyper's Common Grace," *Archivio Theologico Torinese* 1 (2019): 147–57.

3 Zhibin Xie, "Why Public and Theological? The Problem of Public Theology in the Chinese Context," *International Journal of Public Theology* 11, no. 4 (2017): 381–404; Pan-chiu Lai and Zhibin Xie, "Guest Editorial: Public Theology in the Chinese Context," *International Journal of Public Theology* 11, no. 4 (2017): 375–80. (Published by Brill.)

4 Zhibin Xie, "Human Rights in China: A Social-Constructive Theological Approach," *Political Theology* 20, no. 5–6 (2019): 424–36. (Published by Taylor & Francis.)

5 Zhibin Xie, "Guest Editorial: Human Nature, Justice, and Society: Reinhold Niebuhr in the Chinese Context," *Theology Today* 77, no. 3 (2020): 233–42, https://doi.org/10.1177/0040573620926243; Zhibin Xiie, "The Dynamic between Love and Justice: A Confucian Engagement with Reinhold Niebuhr in the Chinese Context," *Theology Today* 77, no. 3 (2020): 269–84, https://doi.org/10.1177/0040573620947048. (Published by Sage.)

6 Zhibin Xie, "Religion and State in China: A Theological Appraisal," *Journal of Church and State* 63, no. 1 (2021): 1–22. (Published by Oxford University Press.)

Dignity, Human Rights, and Social Justice: A Chinese Interdisciplinary Dialogue with Global Perspective (edited by Zhibin Xie, Pauline Kollontai, and Sebastian Kim [@2020], reprinted by permission of Springer Nature), the *Routledge Companion to Christian Ethics* (edited by D. Stephen Long and Rebekah L. Miles [@2022], reprinted by permission of Routledge), the LIT Verlag volume *Space and Place as a Topic for Public Theologies* (edited by Thomas Wabel, Katharina Eberlein-Braun, and Torben Stamer [@2022], reprinted by permission of LIT Verlag), and the Mohk Siebeck volume *Faith, Freedom, and Family* (by John Witte Jr. [@2021], reprinted by permission of John Witte Jr.). I am grateful for the kind permission from the publishers or authors of the above journals and books to reuse the materials from these sources. I have additionally updated and rewritten them.

To conduct my work, I have also benefited from my discussions with several scholars, including Sebastian Kim, Lap-yan Kung, Pan-chiu Lai, Robin W. Lovin, James W. Skillen, Diane Obenchain, and John Witte Jr. I owe many thanks to them for their inspiring ideas and helpful suggestions. I am indebted to Daniel Yeung, director of the Institute of Sino-Christian Studies in Hong Kong, for his continuous support of my study of public theology in China over the years. Thanks also to Jesudas M. Athyal, acquiring editor at Fortress Press, for his encouragement and patience in various editorial matters since my initial contact with Fortress, and to Steven Hall and his colleagues, for their production work.

INTRODUCTION

Public Theology and Christianity in China

Through the centuries, Christianity in China has experienced many struggles with Chinese culture, society, and politics. Those struggles have derived from both the character of Christianity itself and the special features of the Chinese cultural and social structure. The term *public* has been increasingly used or addressed in the study of Christianity in China, either in the sense of theology or in practical aspects such as the problem of church-state relationship, civil society, social activism, and the rule of law. The practical aspects are thoroughly considered from social scientific perspectives such as political science, sociology, and law. Within academia, a group of ideas has been raised about Christianity and public life in China, including the "domination-negotiation" model[1] and "authoritarian containment"[2] of the church-state relationship, the ideas of civil virtue, civil engagement and citizenship regarding Christianity and civil society,[3] the issues of human rights, religious freedom, democratization regarding social activism,[4] and the ideas of nationalism, Christian love,

---

[1] See Carsten Vala, *The Politics of Protestant Churches and the Party-State in China: God above Party?* (London: Routledge, 2018).

[2] See Marie-Eve Reny, *Authoritarian Containment: Public Security Bureaus and Protestant House Churches in Urban China* (New York: Oxford University Press, 2018).

[3] About Christianity and civil society in China and beyond, see Shun-hing Chan and Jonathan W. Johnson, eds., *Citizens of Two Kingdoms: Civil Society and Christian Religion in Greater China* (Leiden: Brill, 2021); Joel A. Carpenter and Kevin R. den Dulk, eds., *Christianity in Chinese Public Life: Religion, Society, and the Rule of Law* (New York: Palgrave Macmillan, 2014); and Francis Khek Gee Lim, ed., *Christianity in Contemporary China: Socio-cultural Perspectives* (New York: Routledge, 2013).

[4] See Chris White and Fenggang Yang, eds., *Christian Social Activism and Rule of Law in Chinese Societies* (Bethlehem: Lehigh University Press, 2021).

and charity.[5] These ideas are reflected in Chinese Christian life and their practices toward society and state. Although they provide a foundation, they deserve further theological and ethical analysis to understand their deeper implications for both Chinese Christians and Chinese public life.

On the other hand, theological aspects are less developed regarding the public dimension of Christianity in China. Gerda Wielander attaches the idea of Christian love when she studies charitable projects in China while pointing out the "particular emphasis on love in Chinese Christian theology,"[6] even though it is not her primary concern to elucidate Christian love and Chinese society theologically. Chloë Starr emphasizes the theology underlining the church-state relationship in China as she approaches modern Chinese theology.[7] There are also biblical and theological reflections on social protests in Hong Kong, including the ideas of sin, crucifixion, suffering, and freedom in the midst of violence, injustice, and dehumanization.[8]

An outstanding book about the development of public theology in the Chinese context is *Chinese Public Theology: Generational Shifts and Confucian Imagination in Chinese Christianity*, by Alexander Chow. Chow aims to show that "both Confucianism and Christianity are indispensable for the Chinse public space,"[9] in which the Confucianism concept of divine-human unity plays an important role. After a historical exploration of the Confucian tradition of public intellectualism and the early Chinese Christian intellectuals, he demonstrates how the three major generations engage the various publics in different ways, including the leaders of the Three-Self Patriotic Movement of the Protestant Churches in China and the China Christian Council, the younger generation of Christian intellectuals who participate in the movement of Sino-Christian theology, and the urban Christian intellectuals who are obviously driven by Calvinism. His concern is "how Confucian understandings have influenced Chinese Christian intellectuals,"[10] including in their public engagement and perception, to help shape Chinese public theology. In Chow's view, both

---

5   See Li Ma and Jin Li, *Surviving the State, Remaking the Church: A Sociological Portrait of Christians in Mainland China* (Eugene: Pickwick, 2018), and Gerda Wielander, *Christian Values in Communist China* (New York: Routledge, 2013).

6   Wielander, *Christian Values in Communist China*, 48.

7   Chloë Starr, *Chinese Theology: Text and Context* (New Haven: Yale University Press, 2016).

8   Kwok Pui-lan and Francis Ching-wah Yip, eds., *The Hong Kong Protests and Political Theology* (Lanham: Rowman & Littlefield, 2021), especially part II.

9   Alexander Chow, *Chinese Public Theology: Generational Shifts and Confucian Imagination in Chinese Christianity* (Oxford: Oxford University Press, 2018), 120.

10   Chow, *Chinese Public Theology*, 16.

"foreign" Christianity and "indigenous" Confucianism have engaged together to shape the public face of Chinese Christianity.

My study in this book regarding the public face of Christianity in China[11] is theological and ethical-centered. I further study the theological implications of some of the issues raised about Christianity and society and state in China. I agree with Gerda Wielander's proposal about the role of Christian thought in terms of morality and love without confining itself in the overriding concern with human rights and dissent. According to Wielander, "The framing of the religious question in China through the lens of political repression, human rights violation and dissent, especially in the context of Christianity, has perhaps resulted in the wrong questions which have misled us in our quest to better understand the role and function of Christianity in China today."[12] Although I focus on the interactions between Christian moral values and society and state in China, I do so constructively in the hope of a just and healthy Chinese public life.

With regard to public theology itself, I move from the generational development regarding Christian public theology in China, as Chow does, and turn to the methodological and constructive approach to public theology, including the meanings of *public* and *theological* in defining public theology; the distinction and correlation between civil religion, political theology, and public theology in China; and the Christian constructive proposal for public issues such as social justice and human rights in China. In this respect, I refer to E. Harold Breitenberg Jr.'s definition of *public theology* in three forms: descriptive and interpretive with respect to the Christian tradition, including accounts of theologians; methodological with respect to what public theology is and how it ought to be; and constructive efforts and normative proposals with respect to the issues, institutions, and processes of public life.[13] I rely on the methodological and constructive approaches together to define the meaning of *public theology* while making theological efforts to engage in public issues in the Chinese context. Even though I study and draw from such public theologians as Abraham Kuyper, Reinhold Niebuhr, and Nicholas Wolterstorff to develop my thinking on public theology in China, I often integrate their theological and ethical ideas with my thinking about public theology in China in terms of its methodology and constructive efforts in

---

11   With the term *China*, I include the social and political context of mainland China shown in parts I and II, whereas Chinese traditions such as Confucianism are interwoven into part II.

12   Wielander, *Christian Values in Communist China*, 166–67.

13   E. Harold Breitenberg Jr., "What Is Public Theology?" in *Public Theology for a Global Society: Essays in Honor of Max L. Stackhouse*, eds. Deirdre King Hainsworth and Scott R. Paeth (Grand Rapids: Eerdmands, 2010), 10–13.

the Chinese context. Besides the Western Christian public theologians, I extensively refer to Chinese resources such as Christian thinkers, philosophers (including Confucian aspects), and social scientists to enhance my understanding of public theology in China.

Through methodological and constructive approaches, this book attempts to activate Christian ethical resources in response to moral problems in China. The term *moral triumph* in this book's title is taken from Kuyper to highlight Christianity's moral impact on the state and civil society. Kuyper writes:

> In a nutshell: what we want is a strong confessional church but not a confessional civil society nor a confessional state. . . . This secularization of state and society is one of the most basic ideas of Calvinism, though it does not succeed in immediately and completely working out this idea in pure form. . . . Calvinism from its own root produced the conviction that the church of Christ cannot be a national church because it had to be rigorously confessional and maintain Christian principle, and that the Christian character of society therefore cannot be secured by the baptism of the whole citizenry but is to be found in the influence that the church of Christ exerts upon the whole organization of national life. By its influence on the state and civil society the church of Christ aims only at a moral triumph, not at the imposition of confessional bonds nor at the exercise of authoritarian control.[14]

Despite its Calvinist roots, the idea of moral triumph is prominently necessary against the background of Chinese religious and political life. At first glance, it seems nothing new for Chinese Christians: such values as Christian love and charity have been highlighted in China. Yet I would like to stress a few points regarding the implications of Kuyper's statement in the Chinese context. Here is the idea of secularization of state and society: without national church, without baptism of the whole citizenry, but with the church's organic influence on society and state in its moral power. That pushes me to think about how Christianity and theology can play a public role in Chinese society. On the one hand, the Christian view of the secular character of state without any church or other religious group's dominance will more likely transform the influential view in China that Christianity is often seen as an opposition to the state; on the other hand, any evangelical enthusiasm for Chinese society and culture is conditioned not to be too optimistic, because it must take into account both seriously diverse religious traditions and political circumstances in the Chinese context. Secularization of both state and society will contribute to Christian distinctive moral significance in China.

---

14 Abraham Kuyper, "Common Grace," in *Abraham Kuyper: A Centennial Reader*, ed. James D. Bratt (Grand Rapids: Eerdmans, 1998), 197.

To this end, I investigate the public implications of Christian ideas of human nature, love, forgiveness and humility, sin, social and political order, and so forth in China. Although recognizing the relativity of these Christian positions, I attempt to keep an open mind toward followers of other diverse faiths, along with atheists who operate the policy toward religious practice. This new formulation of Christian public theology in China desires to engage with Chinese experiences, struggles, traditions, and ideology when investigating moral responses to public issues.

This public moral engagement will address the issues regarding Christianity in China, including Christian social participation and its religious spirit;[15] Christian identity in social and political ministry;[16] "sinification of Christianity";[17] individualist tendency or evangelical enthusiasm such as the advocacy of the "evangelization of China," "kingdomizing church," and "Christianization of culture";[18] and the moral aspects underlined in various social and political programs.[19] As a matter of fact, both the Chinese government and society at large have recognized high standards of moral behavior among many Chinese Christians performing as citizens and as professional workers. Particularly, we have reason to expect that Christian moral values of love and charitable works by Christian communities can be accommodated in the official effort of constructing core values such as fraternity and harmony. Even among Christian scholars, there has been strong consensus on the conjuncture between Christian ethics and Confucian ethics as well as other traditional Chinese resources.[20]

C. K. Yang rightly points out that, in China, "religious groups generally tried to justify their social existence by proclaiming their objective as the 'promotion of moral virtues.'"[21] Christianity is not an exception. In general, the major contribution of Christianity to Chinese society lies in its moral values. In engaging these discussions, I attempt to distinguish my concern with moral implications of Christianity in China from the commonly held view about the survival of Christianity in its moral accommodation and service in the concrete Chinese context. I intend to be morally constructive toward public life. In this way, it is my hope that this moral construction of Chinese public life will alter C. K. Yang's

---

[15] See chapter 3.
[16] See chapter 5.
[17] See chapter 4.
[18] See chapter 2.
[19] See chapters 7 and 8.
[20] See chapter 6.
[21] C. K. Yang, *Religion in Chinese Society: A Study of Contemporary Social Functions of Religion and Some of Their Historical Facts* (Berkeley: University of California Press, 1961), 278.

anxiety about the absence of independent moral status of religion in traditional Chinese society.[22]

In support of these theological and moral concerns about Christianity in China, I employ the approach of public theology, which aims to "illuminate the urgent moral questions of our time through explicit use of the great symbols and doctrines of the Christian faith"[23] and concentrates on the "moral accomplishments," including in social and cultural life rooted in Calvinism.[24] This type of pubic theology is "ethical" in nature in its "guidance to the structures and policies of public life."[25] As Jürgen Moltmann understands it, "Society can expect the theological faculties to have in view the moral values of the social ethos, and not to look merely to their own Christian morality and the ethics of their own religious community."[26] Indeed, a "social-ethical"[27] driver in public theology contributes to reconstructing the public role of Christianity in China.

In light of this new view, it is time to reconsider the problem of Christianity and its relationship with culture, state, and society in China from a different angle. The moral triumph for Christianity in China proposed in this book is to redefine the public role of Christianity itself and identify the moral problems in Chinese society from a Christian perspective.

THEMES AND STRUCTURE

Based on the above considerations, this book addresses the issue of the public face of Christianity in China through methodological and constructive approaches. At its center, this book attempts to answer the following questions: How does Christianity, with its moral and spiritual resources, engage in and contribute to public life in China? How does Christianity operate amid a background of religious diversity, cultural and social dynamics, and political realities?

---

[22] C. K. Yang says, "Religion functioned as a part of the traditional moral order, but it did not occupy the status of a dominant, independent moral institution." Yang, *Religion in Chinese Society*, 278.

[23] David Hollenbach, "Public Theology in America: Some Questions for Catholicism after John Courtney Murray," *Theological Studies* 37, no. 2 (1976), 299.

[24] H. Henry Meeter, *The Basic Ideas of Calvinism*, 6th ed., rev. Paul A. Marshall (Grand Rapids: Baker, 1990), 48.

[25] Max L. Stackhouse, *Public Theology and Political Economy: Christian Stewardship in Modern Society* (Grand Rapids: Eerdmans, 1987), xi.

[26] Jürgen Moltmann, *God for a Secular Society: The Public Relevance of Theology*, trans. Margaret Kohl (London: SCM Press, 1999), 256–57.

[27] James Haire, "The Place of Public Theology between Theology and Public Policy," in *Contextuality and Intercontextuality in Public Theology*, eds. Henrich Bedord-Strohm, Florian Hohne, and Tobias Reimeier (Munster: LIT Verlag, 2013), 49.

In the Chinese context, Christians need to engage with predominantly non-Christian communities in cultural, social, and economic life. Additionally, Christian engagement must interact in a dynamic fashion with public issues while it takes seriously state-society/church-state structures as well as the increasing social pluralism in China. A further question to explore in this book is: How can Christian engagement be justified and encouraged? In other words, how much space does social reality allow for Christian and other religious/nonreligious values to coexist for advancing the moral aspect of public life? The distinctive contribution of this book is that it moves beyond simple description and evaluation of what is happening in Chinese Christianity toward a constructive theology for the distinctive realities of Chinese culture, society, and politics.

In this book, I consider three major factors regarding the public face of Christianity in China: (1) the cultural issue of Christianity as a minority religion, (2) the religious and theological issues of how to orient toward a "public" that includes many non-Christians and the wider public life beyond the church, and (3) the issue of economic, social, and political change in the country more generally, which has raised moral problems in contemporary China. These factors call for a Christian public responsibility—"a moral vocabulary for public life," in Robin W. Lovin's words[28]—for Christians to identify the moral problems in Chinese public life while enhancing their own public image.

Overall, this book aims to develop a public understanding of Christianity in China theologically and ethically. For this purpose, it contains two major parts to conceive of the moral implications of Christianity in China. Part I, "Methodological Approach: Christianity, Religious Diversity, and Public Theology in China," presents a theological methodology regarding Christianity in Chinese public life, accounting for dimensions such as religious diversity and state-society structure and identifying the *public/theological* meanings. The main task of this part is to deal with the two methodological problems concerning the development of public theology in the Chinese context, namely, the public/theological problem and its distinction from civil religion and political theology based on Confucianism. It also explores the relevance of Kuyper and Niebuhr's public theological ideas to the public problems of Christianity in China, addressing such issues as Christian cooperation with non-Christians in public life and Christian engagement within an increasingly plural social structure in China. As a case study, this part devotes a chapter to analyzing the challenges of a desire to form a "Chinese Christianity" (shown in the

---

[28] Words by Robin W. Lovin; see Jeremy L. Sabella, *An American Conscience: The Reinhold Niebuhr Story* (Grand Rapids: Eerdmans, 2017), 125.

movement of "sinification of Christianity") from a public theological perspective. In this way, it proposes Chinese public theology as publicly responsible, theologically engaged, and politically critical.

Part II, "Constructive Approach: Christianity and Public Issues in China," provides case studies of Christian constructive engagement in the public discourse in the Chinese context, which focuses on the moral problem of public issues. One premise here is that the construction of social order consists of "the basic interweaving of culture and social structure," as sociologist Shmuel N. Eisenstadt suggests.[29] In this view, Christian moral engagement in Chinese public life should be undertaken through serious philosophical and social-scientific inquiries and insights regarding social structure in China. Starting with the background of studies of Sino-Christian ethics touching on public issues in China, this part examines social justice,[30] human rights, and religious freedom, taking into account the "rights" dimension of justice—emphasized by Wolterstorff[31]—and religious freedom as an outstanding exemplar of human rights in China. It explores these issues from the Christian perspectives of human nature, love, justice, sphere sovereignty, two kingdoms, and so forth. In addition, this part examines the social and political realities in China, engaging with the philosophical, political, legal, and sociological discourse on those issues and constructing a theological proposal with reference to Confucian and socialist perspectives. A Christian co-construction with

---

[29] Shmuel N. Eisenstadt, "The Protestant Ethic and Modernity—Comparative Analysis with and beyond Weber," in *Soziale Ungleichheit, Kulturelle Unterschiede: Verhandlungen des 32. Kongresses der Deutschen Gesellschaft für Soziologie in München. Teilbd. 1 und 2*, ed. Karl-Siegbert Rehberg (Frankfurt: Campus Verl, 2006), 181.

[30] The topic of social justice has been considered one that public theology must address. Nicholas Sagovsky claims, "Since the end of the Second World War, one crucial task for public theology has been to support the institutions and political practice of democratic states publicly committed to social justice. A key task for public theology today is to articulate in a secular public sphere the fundamental Christian commitment to the struggle for social justice." Nicholas Sagovsky, "Public Theology, the Public Sphere and the Struggle for Social Justice," in *A Companion to Public Theology*, eds. Sabastian Kim and Katie Day (Leiden: Brill, 2015), 251.

[31] Nicholas Wolterstorff cites "justice as grounded ultimately on inherent rights," as his main concern is "to speak for the wronged of the world . . . to see the faces and hear the voices of those who are wronged." Nicholas Wolterstorff, *Justice: Rights and Wrongs* (Princeton: Princeton University Press, 2008), 21, ix. Also See Zhibin Xie (interviewer), "World-Formative Christianity: Wonder and Grief, Love and Justice: An Interview with Nicholas Wolterstorff" (see appendix 1), where he says, "Justice consists of rendering to each person what is their due or right. I think of justice as grounded in rights."

philosophical and social-scientific perspectives on public life will lead to the modification of moral vocabulary in Chinese public life. This renewed vision of cooperation across disciplines and belief systems even suggests a co-construction of my research question about Christianity in Chinese public life. I refer to this position as the *social-theological construction of public life* in the Chinese context.

The appendix presents the materials on reformed public theology and Christianity in China from an interview project involving three leading American Christian public intellectuals: Nicholas Wolterstorff, James W. Skillen, and John Witte Jr. The interviews' themes and ideas help inform the different chapters in this book; for example, chapter 7, "The Dynamic between Love and Justice," reflects on some ideas from the interview with Wolterstorff; chapter 8, "Human Rights in China," engages Witte; and chapter 9, "The Structural Problem of Religious Freedom in China," addresses Skillen. The dialogue in this section provides resources and further reflections on the challenges and contributions of Christian public engagement in China in a broader global context.

PART I

METHODOLOGICAL APPROACH: CHRISTIANITY, RELIGIOUS DIVERSITY, AND PUBLIC THEOLOGY IN CHINA

1

CHRISTIAN ENCOUNTERS WITH RELIGIOUS DIVERSITY IN CHINA

China has a long history of struggle regarding various religions, a fact that has deep roots in its cultural and political heritage. To consider the role of Christianity in public life in China, it is imperative to locate Christianity in the country's diverse religious context. This chapter presents this diversity in its various forms such as plurality of different religions rather than different denominations within a common religion, harmony among the three major religions (Confucianism, Buddhism, and Taoism), and the mixed practice of various religions (syncretism). This feature raises social and political issues more than epistemological issues, the latter concerning which religion is valid for salvation. The social and political issues considered here include governmental attitudes toward and treatment of different religions, especially Christianity and Islam; the so-called religious ecology, describing the unbalanced development between Christianity and traditional Chinese religions; and, finally, religious struggle with political authority.

Historically speaking, it is widely acknowledged that there has been peaceful coexistence among a variety of religions in most periods of Chinese history. Compared to the religious tensions in the West, as Judith A. Berling points out, "the dominant story of religious pluralism in China was one of tolerance of all teachings in the realm under heaven"; she further suggests an "inclusivist approach to religious difference" in Chinese religious life.[1] Gregor Paul offers a fine account of religious diversity in Chinese history in terms of the idea of a heavenly lord or godlike heaven, the Daoist religions, Huang-Lao traditions, belief in the Jade Emperor, religious "Confucian" movements, Buddhist religions,

---

[1]   Judith A. Berling, *A Pilgrim in Chinese Culture: Negotiating Religious Diversity* (Maryknoll: Orbis Books, 1997), 9.

13

syncretistic religions, folk or minority religions, Christian religions (including Nestorian), Manichaeism, Islam, Judaism, and so forth.[2] As André Laliberté sees it, "Chinese culture does have all the moorings to allow for the flourishing of a society that could celebrate diversity in all kinds of beliefs and rituals, including atheism."[3]

Randall L. Nadeau also asserts the diversity of religious practices in their ideas of divinity: "Through all of its historical and cultural change, the Chinese conception of divinity is actively expressed in the veneration of ancestors, in the worship of gods and spirits, and in intellectual speculation about the cosmos and the natural world."[4] Another factor contributing to religious diversity and toleration in China is "harmonious syncretism."[5]

Religious diversity is still obvious in today's China. There are five officially recognized religions in contemporary China, namely Buddhism, Taoism, Islam, Catholicism, and Protestantism; some other religions also exist in Chinese society today such as different kinds of folk religions, the Orthodox Church, and other new religious movements. In 2014 the Pew Research Center produced an index that ranks each country by its level of religious diversity, in which Singapore is listed first, Taiwan second, mainland China ninth, and Hong Kong tenth. Here we see that Chinese societies have high levels of religious diversity, and the Asia-Pacific region has the highest level of religious diversity. Specifically, in mainland China, the percentage of followers of major religions are: Muslim 1.8 percent, Christian 5.1 percent, Buddhist 18.2 percent, folk religion 21.9 percent, and 52.2 percent identified as "unaffiliated."[6]

---

[2] See Gregor Paul, "China and Religious Diversity: Some Critical Reflections," in *Religious Diversity in the Chinese Thought*, eds. Perry Schmidt-Leukel and Joachim Gentz (New York: Palgrave Macmillan, 2013), 40–44.

[3] André Laliberté, "Managing Religious Diversity in China: Contradictions of Imperial and Foreign Legacies," *Studies in Religion/Sciences Religieuses* 45, no. 4 (2016): 496.

[4] Randall L. Nadeau, "Divinity," in *The Wiley-Blackwell Companion to Chinese Religions*, ed. Randall L. Nadeau (West Sussex: Wiley-Blackwell, 2012), 394.

[5] See Stefania Travagni, "A Harmonious Plurality of 'Religious' Expressions: Theories and Case Studies from the Chinese Practice of (Religious) Diversity," in *The Critical Analysis of Religious Diversity*, eds. Lene Kühle, William Hoverd, and Jorn Borup (Leiden: Brill, 2018), 150–51.

[6] See "Table: Religious Diversity Index Scores by Country," Pew Research Center, accessed January 2, 2022, https://tinyurl.com/ywfphb9d.

THE CHALLENGE OF CHRISTIANITY IN THE CHINESE CONTEXT OF RELIGIOUS DIVERSITY

We must acknowledge that Christianity has always been a minority religion in China, and it has brought about tension and even conflict with other religions in China, deserving careful examination. Many people have observed that the Chinese struggle with Christianity lies largely in the dogma of Christian exclusivism as the Chinese often grow out of and make sense of their own traditions, including religious beliefs.[7] On the other hand, as Pan-chiu Lai points out, when Chinese people become Christians, many of them, particularly at the grassroots level, "take a very exclusivist attitude towards Chinese religions."[8] However, Christian encounters with Chinese religions are still problematic, and the counter-exclusivist does not mean all. Rather, many educated Chinese Christians are concerned with "theological indigenization and cultural identities"[9]: "The educated Chinese Christians found themselves caught between their need to affirm their Chinese identity by following the customs mandated in the classics and their beliefs as Christians."[10]

This provides the possibility for an inclusivist approach among the typology of exclusivism, inclusivism, and pluralism regarding religious diversity, and the salvation purpose to be acknowledged by Chinese Christians. As Pan-chiu Lai suggests, the inclusivist approach "may allow Chinese Christians to uphold their religious (Christian) and cultural (Chinese) identities at the same time. On the one hand, this approach allows Chinese Christians to accept the value of their cultural heritage or at least part of it. On the other hand, this can help them to affirm why they are Christians."[11]

---

[7] See Qi Duan's 段琦 analysis in "Zongjiao shiheng yu zhongguo jidujiao fazhan" 宗教失衡與中國基督教發展 [The Outbalance of Religious Ecology and Development of Christianity in China], in *Sanshinian lai zhongguo jidujiao xianzhuang yanjiu lunzhu xuan* 三十年來中國基督教現狀研究論著選 [Selected Works on Situation of Christianity in China for Thirty Years], ed. Huawei Li 李華偉 (Beijing: Shehui kexue wenxian chubanshe 社會科學文獻出版社, 2016), 497.

[8] Pan-chiu Lai, "Chinese Religions: Negotiating Cultural and Religious Identities," in *Christian Approaches to Other Faith: An Introduction*, eds. Alan Race and Paul Hedges (London: SCM, 2008), 282.

[9] Lai, "Chinese Religions," 282.

[10] Judith A. Berling, "Why Chinese Thought on Religious Diversity Is Important," in *Religious Diversity in the Chinese Thought*, eds. Perry Schmidt-Leukel and Joachim Gentz, 34.

[11] Lai, "Chinese Religions," 284.

Chinese Christians' pursuit of their identities often shapes their attitudes toward other cultural and religious traditions in China. The challenge of Christian encounters with diverse religions in China also arises from the state's involvement in different religions, even though the Chinese state may affirm the "multiplicity of religious groups and practices."[12] As Kim-kwong Chan and Graeme Lang rightly point out, "In contrast to its attitude to Christianity, the state's perspective on 'native' religions such as Buddhism, Taoism (i.e. the officially registered and accepted Chinese versions of Buddhism and Taoism), Confucianism, and 'folk religion' is not so burdened with suspicions about foreign infiltration."[13] In other words, there is "diverse implementation of state policies on religion" in China between "native" religions and "foreign" religions (including Christianity), which accounts for the status of Christianity in Chinese society and politics.

This state's different implementation of diverse religions in China is used by some scholars in terms of *religious ecology* to describe the relatively rapid development of Christianity in contemporary China. This theory ascribes the growth of Christianity since the 1980s to a governmental repressive policy toward folk religions and associated Taoism and their decline after 1949, which resulted in one kind of outbalance of religious ecology and growing Christianity. For some of those who maintain religious ecology, the rapid growth of Christianity, especially in rural China, challenges and threatens traditional Chinese values. Accordingly, there is a tendency to encourage Chinese folk religions, Buddhism, Taoism, and even Confucian religion, either from the government or from the people, to counterweight Christian influence and even strengthen Chinese nationality of religious beliefs.[14] As a Confucian scholar, Qing Jiang 蔣慶 says, "Only with the revival of Confucian religion, can we resist the spread of Christianity in China" and maintain a "Confucian China."[15]

---

12 Berling, *A Pilgrim in Chinese Culture*, 43.

13 Kim-kwong Chan and Graeme Lang, "Religious Diversity and the State in China," in *The Politics and Practice of Religious Diversity: National Contexts, Global Issues*, ed. Andrew Dawson (New York: Routledge, 2016), 93.

14 See Qi Duan, "Zongjiao shiheng and zhongguo jidujiao fazhan," 492–503, and Xiangping Li 李向平, "'Zongjiao shengtai' haishi 'quanli shengtai'—cong dangdai zhongguo de 'zongjiao shengtailun' sichao tanqi" 宗教生態還是'權力生態'—從當代中國的'宗教生態論'思潮談起 ["Religious Ecology" or "Power Ecology": To Begin with the Trend of the Theory of 'Religious Ecology'"], *Shanghai daxue xuebao* (shehui kexue ban) 上海大學學報 (社會科學版) [*Journal of Shanghai University* (Social Sciences Edition)] 18, no. 1 (2011): 124–40.

15 Qing Jiang, "Guanyu Chongjian zhongguo rujiao de gouxiang" 關於重建中國儒教的構想 ["Some Thoughts on Reconstructing Confucian Religion in China"], Xin fajia 新法家 [*The New Legalist*], accessed January 5, 2022, https://tinyurl.com/bdevxeyj. My translation.

Even though there are critical reflections on this theory of religious ecology,[16] on which I will not go into detail here, I would like to introduce Philip Clart's evaluation of this theory by suggesting Christianity as a cultural participant in China. He states that "the religious ecology approach holds the promise of conceptualizing the role of Christianity in China not just as that of an eternal misfit, but as a participant in a larger cultural system. As such it may still stand in tension (or competition) with other participants, but it may also engage in more complex relationships with them."[17] Bin Chen 陳彬 and Shining Gao 高師寧 describe this tension as "cultural anxiety."[18] Despite the opposing and even hostile attitude to Christianity we learn from religious ecology's understanding of the relationships (either conflict or balanced) among religions in China, this approach is a good reminder about what role Christianity may play in Chinese culture and society and how it relates to other religions in China.

POLITICS OF RELIGIOUS DIVERSITY IN CHINA

Religious diversity as a cultural fact in China is also conditioned by political struggle. The coexistence of Confucianism, Buddhism, and Taoism is related to the Confucian idea of religious freedom. According to John Berthrong, Confucians usually take positive views of other religions such as Daoism, Buddhism, Christianity, and Judaism, "often both tolerant and respectful of the religious convictions and practices of other religious communities."[19] This tolerance can also be understood from the fact that Confucians often have associations with Daoists and Buddhists in advancing state interests in Chinese history, provided that Daoists and Buddhists make accommodations for the state ideology supported by Confucianism. Berthrong further suggests that "Confucian-influenced cultures have been remarkably tolerant of the diversity of human religious traditions throughout the East Asian region."[20]

This inclusion and tolerance of religions also means that different religions must struggle for their adaption to the dominant religions,

---

16 See Bin Chen and Shining Gao, "Dui 'zongjiao shengtai lun' de huigu yu fansi" 對'宗教生態論'的回顧與反思 ["Review and Reflection on the So-Called Theory of Religious Ecology"], *Daofeng jidujiao wenhua pinglun* 道風基督教文化評論 [*Logos and Pneuma: Chinese Journal of Theology*], no. 35 (2011): 317–35.

17 Philip Clart, "'Religious Ecology' as a New Model for the Study of Religious Diversity in China," in *Religious Diversity in the Chinese Thought*, eds. Perry Schmidt-Leukel and Joachim Gentz, 195.

18 Chen and Gao, "Dui 'zongjiao shengtai lun' de huigu yu fansi," 335.

19 John Berthrong, "Confucianism," in *Encyclopedia of Religious Freedom*, ed. Catherine Cookson (London: Routledge, 2003), 71.

20 Berthrong, "Confucianism," 72.

doctrinally and institutionally: "Major religions in China adopted some of the most strategic Confucian ethical values or made compromises with them."[21] In many occasions throughout Chinese history and up to the present day, religions have been forced to adapt to Chinese society.[22] In other words, they must pursue their own theological and practical strategy to counter the ideology and political authority to locate themselves appropriately and exert their influence in Chinese society.

Historically, religion was officially recognized insofar as it reinforced the total order, strengthened public morality, and benefited state stability and collective prosperity[23]: "In such a highly centralized political country as China, religion has had little chance to become independent of the state."[24] It is likely that religion has to encounter the state, which does not tend to lose its dominant position over religion and other civil affairs. As C. K. Yang wrote, "Political control of the voluntary types of religion was a consistent pattern in Chinese history."[25]

In this sense, the political nature of religious diversity in China can be understood as religious obligations for political purpose or religions subject to political control. Yet the governing policy of religious affairs also contributes to the development of religious diversity in China to some extent. Robert Weller explains that "the current system of state control forms a kind of governance by hypocrisy: much of the newly elastic religious sector lies outside the law yet is tolerated because officials act as if they cannot see . . . this kind of one-eyed governance can provide a medium for the growth of pluralism and diversity over relatively long periods of time."[26]

Furthermore, debates about the persistence of religious diversity and religious toleration in China need to consider how the cultural and religious aspects of Chinese society (polytheism and syncretism in particular) impact the state's attitude toward religious practice. This raises the

---

[21] Yang, *Religion in Chinese Society*, 280.

[22] See "China's Policies and Practices on Protecting Freedom of Religious Belief" (white paper), The State Council Information Office of the People's Republic of China, accessed December 19, 2019, https://tinyurl.com/y6n7s58y. Released in April 2018, this while paper states that "religions in China must be Chinese in orientation and provide active guidance to religions so that they can adapt themselves to the socialist society."

[23] See Jacques Gernet, *China and the Christian Impact*, trans. Janet Lloyd (Cambridge: Cambridge University Press, 1985), 109.

[24] Xinzhong Yao and Yanxia Zhao, *Chinese Religion: A Contextual Approach* (London: Continuum, 2010), 128.

[25] Yang, *Religion in Chinese Society*, 211.

[26] Robert P. Weller, "The Politics of Increasing Religious Diversity in China," *Daedalus* 143, no. 2 (2014): 136.

question of which factor is most determinative regarding the existence and practice of various religions in China, whether the shape of religion has determined how the state has responded to it or whether the shape of the state has determined the character of religion.

It is often said that the coexistence of various religions in the history of China without severe tension and war among religions should be attributed to the polytheistic and syncretistic nature of religious life in China. As C. K. Yang affirms, "There was the polytheistic and syncretic traditions that tended to tolerate religious differences and accept the coexistence of varying faiths. Consequently, no one religion dominated."[27] Based on this assumption, many suggest that there is a tradition of religious tolerance in China. According to Jian Zhang 張踐, the traditional Confucian idea of "revering yet staying away from gods and ghosts" (*Jing guishen er yuanzhi* 敬鬼神而遠之) contributed much to this tradition of religious tolerance: "Even though Confucius has suspicions about the existence of gods and ghosts, he neither denies them nor talks about them from distance. This position practically contributes to the toleration of various religious beliefs among peoples, which leads to China as a country of co-existence of various religions."[28] The traditional Chinese society made space for unity among diversity in Chinese religious life, grounded both in religious doctrines and pragmatic realities.

Although there were some tensions among Confucianism, Buddhism, and Taoism and between Confucianism and Christianity in traditional China, the tendency was toward peaceful coexistence of religions insofar as they adapted themselves to imperial political culture to assist political governance and cultivate the people. In this way, they were tolerated by the traditional Chinese government. However, was this real religious tolerance? Chinese scholar Shida Wang 王世達 questioned this assumption that we can find a spirit of religious tolerance in China on the basis of characteristics of Chinese culture. Instead, Wang contends that religious tolerance must be considered within a systemic structure, including toleration of personality, thought, and nationalities, as well as political and social tolerance, and that this structure must have institutional support.[29] Perez

27   Yang, *Religion in Chinese Society*, 215.

28   Jian Zhang, *Zhongguo gudai zhengjiao guanxii shi* (*xia ce*) 中國古代政教關係史下冊 ["A History of Religion and State Relationship in Ancient China, Vol. 2"] (Beijing: Zhongguuo shehui kexue chubanshe 中國社會科學出版社, 2012), 1207. My translation.

29   Shida Wang, "Zongjiao kuanrong: yizhong guanyu zhongguo gudai zongjiao de wudu" 宗教寬容: 一種關於中國古代宗教的誤讀 ["Religious Toleration: A Misinterpretation of Ancient Religion in China"], *Shijie zongjiao wenhua* 世界宗教文化 [*World Religious Culture*], no. 2 (2010): 57–61.

Zagorin's idea of the Enlightenment's secularization of the concept of toleration contributes to further understanding of the place of religious tolerance in a wider setting in the West. According to Zagorin, the dedication to "enlightenment and the sovereignty of reason pointed nevertheless in the direction of a humane and liberal society based on freedom of thought, the dissolution of orthodox religion as a coercive power, the rule of law, and political and religious liberty."[30] In this way, "toleration and freedom of the religious conscience also came to be more and more justified during the Enlightenment primarily as a natural right associated with other natural rights. These developments infused the idea of toleration with an increasingly secular character."[31] Wang suggests that what is mistakenly seen as religious toleration in China is really a sort of religious inclusion in that it is simply a coexistence of gods in religious life among people, without being woven into the chain of related values and institutional support.

In any case, it is undeniable that the coexistence and survival of various religions in China depend on the subjugation of religious authority to political authority. The conjuncture of religious authority and political authority leads to a basic issue regarding religious freedom or, more generally, religion and politics—that is, the relationship between the spiritual and the temporal or the sacred and the profane. Here we find an encounter between Chinese ideas of cosmic and imperial order and Western ideas of Christianity.

As Jacques Gernet observes, "It was through its close relations with the cosmic forces that the imperial power derived an essential part of its legitimacy and prestige. . . . The Chinese emperors combined, in their persons, functions and aspects in which the profane and the sacred were indistinguishable: the Chinese concept of universal order was a global one which tolerated no divisions."[32] In other words, the Chinese idea of a mandate from heaven and other religious or quasi-religious ideas are utilized for maintaining secular order and governmental rules. In Xinzhong Yao's words, "The Confucian Heaven functions as the Ultimate or Ultimate Reality, to which human beings are answerable with respect to fulfilling their destiny. . . . The diverse spiritual, ethical and natural meanings of heaven establish the Way of Heaven as the foundation of Confucian views of the world, the universe, and human society."[33] In this sense, Confucian heaven also accounts for religion, politics, and ethics in Chinese society.

---

[30] Perez Zagorin, *How the Idea of Religious Toleration Came to the West* (Princeton: Princeton University Press, 2003), 292.
[31] Zagorin, *How the Idea of Religious Toleration Came to the West*, 293.
[32] Gernet, *China and the Christian Impact*, 105.
[33] Xinzhong Yao, *An Introduction to Confucianism* (Cambridge: Cambridge University Press, 2000), 142.

C. K. Yang points out that "many of the religious influences in Chinese political life stemmed from the basic concept of heaven and its subordinate system of deities as a supernatural force that predetermined the course of all events in the universe, including political events."[34] The sanction from heaven manifests itself both in the endorsement of the supremacy of the central political power and common people's confidence in the governing authority. To some extent, Confucian heaven serves as a fundamental idea to shape the Chinese order of politics, religion, nature, and cosmos.

In recent years, there has been rigorous discourse in Chinese academia on the Chinese concept of "all under heaven" (*Tianxia* 天下). Tingyang Zhao, one of its important proponents, believes that "the all-inclusiveness concept of Tianxia must be viewed as a transcendental concept for a political world. It interprets an ideal state of the world as being an integrated entity that has no externalities and transcendentally acknowledges the world as common interests and common resources for all mankind."[35] The earthly order, including political order, must be symmetrical with the order of heaven. This encourages diversity, cooperation, and peaceful relationship in the world. In general, this concept sees the order of things in terms of totality and wholeness, I suppose, including the divine and worldly affairs. Religious, political, and moral affairs are placed together in the total order of heaven.

In the eyes of many Chinese, religions may be allowed because of the integration of the supernatural forces and the worldly order. By contrast, the Christian tradition distinguishes the spiritual and the temporal. The world depends on the monotheistic God as Creator, but it does not have the same integration: "By placing itself outside and above the sociopolitical order instead of combining with it and reinforcing it as the established cults did, Christianity threatened to destroy that order."[36] This way of distinguishing the sacred and the worldly challenges Chinese thinking on religion and the world in ways that may empower the meaning of religious practice in China.

As Richard Madsen claims, "Unlike liberal democratic governments, which for the most part purport to be neutral towards religion, making religion a private matter beyond the reach of the state, the Chinese government has an active policy toward religion."[37] On the one hand,

---

[34]   Yang, *Religion in Chinese Society*, 127.

[35]   Tingyang Zhao, *Redefining a Philosophy for World Governance* (Singapore: Springer Singapore, 2019), 18.

[36]   Gernet, *China and the Christian Impact*, 105.

[37]   Richard Madsen, "Back to the Future: Pre-Modern Religious Policy in Post-Secular China," Foreign Policy Research Institute, accessed June 11, 2012, https://tinyurl.com/54vbaxur.

Chinese authorities intend to make religious belief solely a private affair without getting involved in the public domain except for some social service and work. On the other hand, in practice, it never exists as purely private, becoming a "public" issue in terms of governmental management of, sensitivity to, and different attitudes toward religions and religious struggle with political authority.

The Chinese model of the space of religious beliefs and practices associated with the state's attitude and regulations is what Gregor Paul terms as "Chinese secularism." It occurs by "subjugating religions and churches to secular constitutions and laws," which contributes to "preventing, or at least curtailing or limiting, religious violence in Sino-Asia."[38] However, this subjugating should "abide by human rights norms," the rules of human dignity in particular.[39]

Gregor Paul explains that religious practice in China "can be found more in the control of the religions by the state than in the religions themselves."[40] Even though this control creates certain space to tolerate the relatively peaceful coexistence of a variety of religions in China, this tolerance should be further expounded toward religious freedom. As James E. Wood puts it, "Tolerance does require, however, respect for religious differences and a person's right to one's own religious identity. To be sure, religious tolerance is prerequisite to religious freedom, but falls far short of what is conveyed in the use of the term religious freedom, which connotes that beyond mere permissibility that religion is a basic human right that waits upon the voluntary will of the individual."[41]

To sum up this chapter, it is my intention to show the nature and challenge of Christianity in the Chinese context of religious diversity. Religion in China wrestled with both the impact of religious ideas on religious practice and the power of the state over religious affairs. The continuing religious diversity in China lies in the interface between religious roots themselves and the religious struggle with political authority.

---

[38] Paul, "China and Religious Diversity," 46.
[39] Paul, "China and Religious Diversity," 47.
[40] Paul, "China and Religious Diversity," 46.
[41] James E. Wood, *Church and State in Historical Perspective* (Westport: Praeger, 2005), 61.

2

ABRAHAM KUYPER, REINHOLD NIEBUHR, AND CHRISTIANITY IN CHINA

The religious and political background of Christianity in China, presented in chapter 1, locates Christianity itself and its interaction with public life. This chapter further proposes the relevance of Abraham Kuyper and Reinhold Niebuhr, two prominent public theologians, to the public problems raised in China, with a focus on the idea of human nature (human sinfulness in particular), social institutions, and morality of public life. Eric Patterson suggests the alignment of both neo-Calvinists (such as Kuyper) and Christian realists (such as Niebuhr) with regard to some common issues, including institutions, groups, self-interest, and power-balancing, despite the differences between them.[1] This chapter borrows this alignment of Kuyper and Niebuhr to explore the problems of Christianity in China.

According to the recent summary on the Niebuhr legacy by Jeremy L. Sabella, Niebuhr's major contribution lies in three areas—politics, society, and religion—particularly pointing to the questions of "how to ethically wield power, especially the power of governments," of "how the categories of love and justice shape human relation," and of "how humans find meaning in life."[2] Accordingly, we further probe the problems arising from the three areas in the Chinese context and see how both Niebuhr's and Kuyper's thinking can raise implications regarding these issues.

---

[1] Eric Patterson, "The Enduring Value of Christian Realism," *Philosophia Reformata* 80, no. 1 (2015), 39.

[2] Jeremy L. Sabella, *An American Conscience: The Reinhold Niebuhr Story* (Grand Rapids: Eerdmans, 2017), 119.

PROBLEMS: CHRISTIANITY IN CHINA

As seen from the last chapter, a notable phenomenon in China is its diversity of religious life and social life. Even though the percentage of Christians in China is estimated at 5.1 percent by Pew Research (i.e., more than sixty-five million Christians, including fifty-eight million Protestants and nine million Catholics),[3] the number is still controversial. Some may still expect considerable growth in the number of Christians in China in the future. Despite this, it is of some importance to seriously consider the intersection of the high level of religious diversity in China when we assess Christian interaction with Chinese cultural and social life in general.

This diversity is further demonstrated in Chinese social life. As Bingzhong Gao 高丙中 observes, "The theoretical models of social sphere, political sphere and economic sphere distinguished from each other can be effectively applied to the current stage of China."[4] The "social" category (in contrast to the state and the collective) has manifested itself in contemporary China in two layers: the differentiated spheres of social life and the emergence of various social organizations. Since the 1980s, together with launching a market economy, China has seen the emergence of different and dynamic social spheres, rather than a unified model of these spheres, such as agriculture, industry, business, trade, transportation, communications, architecture, arts, and media. These spheres have gained relatively independent status and flourished in diverse forms. Social life in China has become more and more dynamic.

Alongside the diversified social spheres, we can witness the emergence and development of various kinds of organizations in contemporary China, ranging from those approved by the Chinese government to those that are more independent, including unregistered grassroots organizations from nonprofit urban organizations to rural communities. These come in a multitude of forms, with nonprofit urban organizations, including the likes of professional associations, business associations, trade associations, academic associations, social service organizations, sports and entertainment organizations, public affairs organizations such

---

[3]   See "Table: Religious Diversity Index Scores by Country," Pew Research Center, accessed January 2, 2022, https://tinyurl.com/ywfphb9d. There are different estimates of the numbers of Christians in China, ranging from twenty million to seventy million or more. I will not go deeper into the controversial numbers, although I see Christianity as a minority religion that survives among a variety of religions in China.

[4]   Bingzhong Gao, "'Gongmin shehui' gainian yu zhongguo xianshi" 公民社會"概念與中國現實 ["The Concept of 'Civil Society' and Realities in China"], *Sixiang zhanxian* 思想戰線 [*Ideological Front*], no. 1 (2012): 30. My translation.

as environmental protection groups, social services, and charity organizations, whereas rural communities manifest themselves in various religious groups, kinship organizations, community schools, and the like.[5] It has been reported that there were more than nine hundred thousand social organizations in China by 2021.[6] Many of the organizations are associated with diversified social spheres.

Despite the rise of "society" and the social-plural tendency in contemporary China, the basic model remains "state-led civil society."[7] However, there are increasing demands for more autonomy of social spheres and institutions as many social organizations (religious and nonreligious alike) tend to be quasi-governmental.[8] Despite the problems of diverse social organizations and their relationship to the government, these organizations continue to be an important part of pluralistic social life in China while they "negotiate narrow political, economic, and personal opportunities."[9] In Jessica C. Teets's view, an "interactive and dynamic process" between government and civil society can "build a new state-society model that emphasizes both pluralism and control" instead of political liberation.[10] In addition, there are also problems of social justice arising from the various areas in Chinese society. In this regard, some emphasize institutional transformation, including constitutionalism, whereas others are more concerned with the moral aspect, especially the issue of humanity.[11]

In these cultural, social, and political settings, among many other aspects of Christianity in China, there coexists the ongoing movement of "sinification of Christianity," the quest for "evangelization of China,"

---

[5] For a detailed description and analysis of Chinese mass organizations, see Andrew Watson, "Civil Society in a Transitional State: The Rise of Association in China," in *Associations and the Chinese State: Contested Spaces*, ed. Jonathan Unger (New York: Routledge, 2015), 14–47.

[6] See "Shisiwu shehui zuzhi fazhan guihua" 十四五社會組織發展規劃 ["The 14th Five-Year Plan for Social Organization Development"], Zhongguo shehui zuzhi zhengwu fuwu pingdai 中國社會組織政務服務平台 [Service Platform of China Social Organization Affairs], accessed January 3, 2022, https://tinyurl.com/2p87y4vf.

[7] See B. Michael Frolic, "State-Led Civil Society," in *Civil Society in China*, eds. Timothy Brook and B. Michael Frolic (London: ME Sharpe, 1997), 46–67.

[8] See chapter 8.

[9] Timothy Hildebrandt, *Social Organizations and the Authoritarian State in China* (New York: Cambridge University Press, 2013), xii.

[10] Jessica C. Teets, *Civil Society under Authoritarianism: The China Model* (New York: Cambridge University Press, 2014), 2.

[11] See more details about the problem of social justice in China in chapter 7.

"kingdomizing church," and the "Christianization of culture."[12] It seems to me that Christians in China have always wrestled with the issues of being "toward the public" and "toward non-Christians." Some are too individualist and politically passive; others are too limited in social services; still, some do not show full respect for social and cultural achievements by non-Christians as there is a division between Christians and non-Christians not only on the matter of faith but also in their social life. There are also a number of Christian communities (both registered and nonregistered) that strive for the right to Christian practice, struggle for more freedom and autonomy, are linked with social and political activism, and engage in public disobedience.[13] There are Christian intellectuals linked with emerging urban churches in China who are practicing along the lines of Calvinist tradition and striving for a connection between Christianity and modernity, including church-state interactions.[14] There is also growing interaction between Christianity and the state and society, or the publicity of this, in contemporary China.[15]

From the above observations, the place of Christianity in Chinese culture and society will have to elucidate the following factors: (1) characteristic religious diversity; (2) the relationship between Christianity and Chinese culture; (3) relations between Christian communities, the state, and other spheres of social life in China, where Christians can cooperate with large non-Christian communities in cultural, social, and economic life; (4) the increasing influence of Calvinism among Chinese Christians; and (5) Christian dynamic engagement with social justice in respect to its own state-society/church-state structure and the increasing social pluralism in China. From my point of view, encouraging Christian public responsibility in China and expanding Christian moral vision beyond

---

[12]   These ideas were originally proposed by Chinese churchman Tian-en Zhao (1938–2004) and adopted by some unregistered churches in China. In general, these ideas encourage the wide spread, vast growth, and far-reaching cultural impact of Christians in China. See recent discourses on these ideas and the related idea of "Christianization of China" in Yucheng Bai, "One Foot above Liberalism: Wang Yi's Search for Civil Society," in *Christian Social Activism and Rule of Law in Chinese Societies*, eds. Chris White and Fenggang Yang (Bethlehem: Lehigh University Press, 2021), 271–72, and Bob Fu, "Baorong Duoyuan: A Proposal for Religious Freedom in China," in *Christian Social Activism and Rule of Law in Chinese*, eds. White and Yang, 337–38.

[13]   See White and Yang, eds., *Christian Social Activism and Rule of Law in Chinese Societies*; Kwok and Yip, eds., *The Hong Kong Protests and Political Theology*.

[14]   See Alexander Chow, "Calvinist Public Theology in Urban China Today," *International Journal of Public Theology* 8, no. 2 (2014): 158–75.

[15]   An example of the development, issues, and problems of Christianity in Chinese public life can be found in *International Journal of Public Theology* (Special Issue "Public Theology in the Chinese Context") 11, no. 4 (2017).

church boundaries departs from otherworldly Christianity. It is thus necessary to consider three factors:

(1) State: With recognition of religious (including Christian) moral competence, the state is supposed to become more open to social spheres for the engagement of religious groups in economic, political, and cultural life, even if their particular religious identity is disclosed.

(2) Church: Among Christian communities, besides philanthropy work, there are demands for more concern with and engagement in public issues such as public morality, business ethics, education equality, and ecological issues. These are pressing issues in contemporary Chinese public life and may certainly affect the lives of Christians.

(3) Academia: It becomes a responsibility for Chinese Christian scholarship to articulate the fullness of Christian faith in its public moral relevance, provide theological foundation for Christian social and cultural engagement for the common good of society at large, and elaborate moral analysis and response to public issues.

In current political-social circumstances, even though there are other programs that strive for more freedom to practice, the public significance of Christianity (and theology) in China lies in its moral power in different spheres of life and its spiritual resources for public life, as Kuyper suggests. It is struggling, yet it is demanding and promising.

RELEVANCE OF COMMON GRACE AND SPHERE SOVEREIGNTY IN ABRAHAM KUYPER IN THE CHINESE CONTEXT

To advance the moral significance of Christianity in China, it is crucial to understand the relationship of Christians to the general Chinese (non-Christian in particular) and the wider public life. At this point, Kuyper's doctrine of common grace in provoking Christian public responsibility and cultural engagement may become a resource for Chinese Christians' affirmative attitude to and reception of non-Christians, including their cultural achievements. The doctrine also calls for Chinese Christians to engage in social and cultural activities. In this way, it broadens our understanding of the relationship between Christianity and public life in the Chinese context.

In Kuyper's words, *common grace* means "temporal restraining grace, which holds back and blocks the effect of sin . . . [and] is extended to the whole of our human life," whereas *special grace* only extends to the elect: "a saving grace, which in the end abolishes and completely undoes it consequences . . . is in the nature of the case special and restricted to God's elect."[16] Furthermore, Kuyper specifies the interior and exterior aspects of the work of common grace: "The former is operative wherever civil virtue, a sense of domesticity, natural love, the practice of human virtue, the improvement of the public conscience, integrity, mutually loyalty among people, and a feeling for piety leaven life. The latter is in evidence when human power over nature increases, when invention upon invention enriches life, when international communication is improved, the arts flourish, the sciences increase our understanding, the conveniences and joys of life multiply, all expressions of life become more vital and radiant, forms become more refined, and the general image of life becomes more winsome."[17]

S. U. Zuidema understands the effect of common grace in terms of "doing the good" and "progress": it works in the realm of "the temporal and the visible," "enables people to do the good, the moral good, the civil good, opening up the possibility of progress in the life of creation," and "operates for 'progress'"; "it serves and promotes cultural development and progress, and makes these possible."[18] It was Kuyper who articulated the doctrine of common grace to an outstanding place, developing the Calvinist view of culture, which celebrates human development, cultural formation, civilization, enlightenment, and progress. As Henry R. Van Til describes, there are both negative and positive aspects to Kuyper's doctrine of common grace: "Common grace has a negative, constant influence in restraining sin and has its effects both in man and in the universe; but also has a positive action which is progressive. It functions as a culture-forming and activating power in history, in which man is both instrument and co-worker with God."[19] Vincent E. Bacote understands common grace in light of "faithful Christian engagement," stating, "God's sustaining work in creation encourages us to participate in the various area of life, striving to discern the best ways to pursue education, art, politics, and business as we participate within these domains. Faithful Christian engagement means the pursuit of the fullness of human life in the totality of God's created order. . . . We can be encouraged that God by common grace has

---

[16]   Kuyper, "Common Grace," 168.
[17]   Kuyper, "Common Grace," 181.
[18]   S. U. Zuidema, "Common Grace and Christian Action in Abraham Kuyper," in *On Kuyper: A Collection of Readings on the Life, Work and Legacy of Abraham Kuyper*, eds. Steve Bishop and John H. Kok (Sioux Center: Dordt College Press, 2013), 258.
[19]   Henry R. Van Til, *The Calvinistic Concept of Culture* (Grand Rapids: Baker, 2001), 120.

made it possible for us to participate in the public realm in multiple ways that contribute to the flourishing of the created order."[20]

Kuyper talked about China in his Stone Lectures on Calvinism[21] and elsewhere, even though at the time, China probably knew nothing about him. It is not easy to know why Kuyper was interested in China except that the achievements of civilization there attracted him. Yet, today, more and more Chinese, especially Christians, have become aware of and influenced by him. His *Lectures on Calvinism* and other texts are available in Chinese,[22] and his ideas have been studied by Chinese academics.[23]

Richard J. Mouw explains that in Kuyper, the doctrine of common grace is "a comprehensive theology of 'commonness,'" "a perspective that could provide a helpful framework of encountering and enabling Christians to benefit from the efforts of unbelievers."[24] Therefore, it calls for "openness to accepting truth, goodness, beauty, and justice wherever

---

[20]   Vincent E. Bacote, introduction to *Wisdom and Wonder: Common Grace in Science and Art*, by Abraham Kuyper, eds. Jordan J. Ballor and Stephen J. Grabill, trans. Nelson D. Kloosterman (Grand Rapids: Christian's Library Press, 2011), 29.

[21]   For example, Kuyper says, "In China it can be asserted with equal right that Confucianism has produced a form of its own for life in a given circle . . . But what has China done for humanity in general, and for the steady development of our race?" See Abraham Kuyper, *Lectures on Calvinism* (Grand Rapids: Eerdmans, 1931), 32. He also says, "In India, in Babylon, in Egypt, in Persia, in China and elsewhere, like periods of vigorous growth that have been succeeded by times of spiritual decadence; and yet in not one of these lands has the downward course finally resolved itself in a movement towards higher things" (Kuyper, *Lectures on Calvinism*, 174.)

[22]   Translated works by Abraham Kuyper in Chinese include *Lectures on Calvinism* (Beijing: Huaxia chubanshe 華夏出版社, 2014) and "The Anti-Revolutionary Program" in *Zhengzhi zhixu yu duoyuan de shehui jiegou* 政治秩序與多元的社會結構 [*Political Order and the Plural Structure of Society*], eds. James W. Skillen and Rockne M. McCarthy, trans. Yong Fang 方永 (Hong Kong: Logos and Pneuma Press 道風書社, 2013).

[23]   For example, see Zhibin Xie 謝志斌, *Gonggong shenxue yu quanqiuhua: sitakehaosi de jidujiao lunli yanjiu* 公共神學與全球化: 斯塔克豪思的基督教倫理研究 [*Public Theology and Globalization: A Study on Max L. Stackhouse's Christian Ethics*] (Beijing: Zongjiao wenhua chubanshe 宗教文化出版社, 2008), which includes one chapter on Kuyper: "Common Grace and Sphere Sovereignty," and Zhibin Xie 謝志斌, "Endian, wenhua yu fazhan—yizhong jiaerwen zhuyi wenhuaguan de quanshi" 恩典, 文化與發展—一種加爾文主義文化觀的闡釋 ["Grace, Culture and Development—An Interpretation of Calvinist Culture"], *Shijie zongjiao wenhua* 世界宗教文化 [*World Religious Culture*], no. 5 (2012): 80–83.

[24]   Richard J. Mouw, "Kuyper on Common Grace: A Comprehensive Theology of 'Commonness,'" in *Common Grace Vol. 1: The Historical Section*, by Abraham Kuyper, eds. Jordan J. Ballor and Stephen J. Grabill, trans. Nelson D. Kloosterman and Ed M. van der Maas (Grand Rapids: Christian's Library Press, 2014), x.

we find it."[25] He even suggests, "Common grace operates mysteriously in the life of, say, a Chinese government official or an unbelieving artist to harness their created talents to prepare the creation for the full coming of the kingdom."[26] As we have seen, there are many believers of other religions and nonbelievers today in China; many of them are working together with Christians toward economic and social progress, along with cultural development and flourishing in contemporary China. It is indeed the responsibility of Christians to work together with others of various religious and nonreligious backgrounds in the areas of education, business, politics, and culture.

To encourage Christian engagement and responsibility in various spheres of social life and the development of social institutions, Kuyper and other Calvinists rely on the idea of sphere sovereignty. The principle of sphere sovereignty forms the basic relationship between individuals, social institutions, and organizations and the state.[27] The question of autonomy of religious groups, alongside other social organizations, raises the question of the identity structure of these social institutions: the origin of the diversity of social life, the spheres' independent characters, their internal law structure, and, finally, their relationship to the state. At its root, it calls for understanding the plural social structure, particularly so as not to dissolve this diversity into the political whole. This theological idea of sphere sovereignty by Calvinists may not be foreign to many Chinese Christians. It has a significance regarding the state-society relationship and bears implications for religious and nonreligious groups to seek their appropriate relationship with the state. As Patterson affirms, "Sphere sovereignty also provides a way forward for arguing that moral issues should be defined by Christianity rather than the state."[28]

RELEVANCE OF REINHOLD NIEBUHR'S CHRISTIAN REALISM IN THE CHINESE CONTEXT

The problems in China inspired by Kuyper may be seen from another perspective in light of Niebuhr. I thus further explore how Niebuhr's insights are relevant to the religious, social, and political context in China and examine the place of Christianity in that context.

Niebuhr addresses the pluralism of religious life and social organization. For Niebuhr, religious and cultural diversity is "possible within the

---

[25]   Mouw, "Kuyper on Common Grace," xxx.

[26]   Mouw, "Kuyper on Common Grace," xxv.

[27]   About the Calvinist idea of "sphere sovereignty," see a more detailed analysis in chapter 9.

[28]   Patterson, "The Enduring Value of Christian Realism," 38.

presuppositions of a free society, without destroying the religious depth of culture," and "it demands that each religion, or each version of a single faith, seeks to proclaim its highest insights while yet preserving a humble and contrite recognition of the fact that all actual expressions of religious faith are subject to historical contingency and relativity."[29] He endorses religious diversity while demanding religious commitment and relativity. Wilfred M. McClay suggests, "He is envisioning the cultivation of religious toleration not merely as a process of bracketing one's own religious beliefs in the encounter with others, but as itself the product of redoubled religious intensity, as a kind of ascetic spiritual discipline leading to an ever higher form of religious commitment."[30]

Niebuhr also appraises the diversity of social organizations, saying, "The realists know that history is not a simple rational process but a vital one. All human societies are organizations of diverse vitalities and interests. Some balance of power is the basis of whatever justice is achieved in human relations."[31] However, as Eric Patterson shows, Niebuhr tends to see "institutions as tools of individual and/or collective self-interest, but realized that these institutions could check one another's power if they had sufficient resources for balancing the other."[32]

Niebuhr urges to "bear our Christian witness in the cause of justice"[33] and makes "continuous effort to find proximate solutions for the perennial problems of public life" in politics.[34] The cultural, religious, and social diversity further locates the background of Niebuhr's ideas of justice and democracy. Robin W. Lovin proposes, "Niebuhr's focus on the human capacity for justice and the political necessity of democracy will have to be integrated with a pluralism that makes a more complete statement about the human good and thus provides broader guidance in relation to the broader questions of our time."[35] The quest for justice and democracy informed by Christian insights in the contemporary context must be attentive to diverse ideas of the human good, including religious ideas and diversified or even conflicting interests of social organizations.

---

[29] Reinhold Niebuhr, *The Children of Light and the Children of Darkness* (Chicago: University of Chicago Press, 2011), 134.

[30] Wilfred M. McClay, "Reinhold Niebuhr and the Problem of Religious Pluralism," in *Reinhold Niebuhr and Contemporary Politics: God and Power*, eds. Richard Harries and Stephen Platten (Oxford: Oxford University Press, 2010), 222.

[31] Larry Rasmussen, ed., *Reinhold Niebuhr: Theologian of Public Life* (Minneapolis: Fortress Press, 1991), 121.

[32] Patterson, "The Enduring Value of Christian Realism," 39.

[33] Rasmussen, ed., *Reinhold Niebuhr*, 127.

[34] Larry Rasmussen, introduction to *Reinhold Niebuhr*, ed. Rasmussen, 17.

[35] Robin W. Lovin, *Christian Realism and the New Realities* (New York: Cambridge University Press, 2008), 83.

The central problem arises regarding Niebuhr's engagement in politics, society, and religion: the meaning of life offered by religions, which "ethically wield power," and "approximate justice," motivated and transformed by love. Starting with the possibilities and limits of human nature, Lovin develops Niebuhr's idea of the tensions and conflicts between impossible ideals (religious ideas in particular) and proximate solutions as essential to democracy. Lovin proposes a version of "realistic pluralism" that can accommodate realistic goals as "multiple, limited, and situated in a particular context" and a "religious humility" in politics under conditions of religious and political pluralism.[36]

As Lovin proposes, the crucial question is, again, how the biblical understanding of human nature requires both impossible ideals and proximate solutions in a functioning society in light of Niebuhr. Yet Niebuhr's Christian realism demands modification in different cultures, traditions, and politics in a new global reality, although we may find a possible analogy regarding human nature, ideals, and solutions in other traditions. This means "bringing the impossible ideal to bear on the recurrent task of creating a new proximate solution to insoluble problems."[37]

In my view, Niebuhr's idea of religious humility and religious toleration is relevant to the Chinese context of religious diversity. It provides a theological account for Christians to be as committed to their faith as they wish while humbly recognizing their own relativity with an open mind toward other followers of diverse faiths and even atheists, including in their engagement with Chinese traditions such as Confucianism and Taoism and contemporary ideology such as communism, when they address public issues. Christians in China may still attach much importance to aspects of human nature such as human sinfulness, which Niebuhr emphasizes, and show concern for the political and public expression of such values as love, compassion, forgiveness, and humility, either from Christian or Confucian roots. On the one hand, it would be stimulating for Chinese philosophers and social scientists who study Chinese politics and public life to recognize the meaning of moral ideals, either religious or secular, in facing social and political issues such as justice and democracy. On the other hand, it would be beneficial for Chinese Christian scholarship to enhance Christian moral ideals' relevance to public issues and seek proximate solutions in their own concrete situations.

---

[36] Robin W. Lovin, "Reinhold Niebuhr's Realistic Pluralism," *Theology Today* 77, no. 3 (2020): 304.

[37] Lovin, "Reinhold Niebuhr's Realistic Pluralism," 309.

AN ADVENTURE: KUYPER, NIEBUHR, AND
CHRISTIANITY IN CHINA

After exploring Kuyper and Niebuhr's relevance, in their own ways, to the Chinese context, I examine their possible commonality, along with their divergence, when it comes to the contextual problems in China. We may find that both Kuyper and Niebuhr attempt to understand human activities and responsibilities in the world in light of God. For Niebuhr, "his attention was to the relation of this God to the self and to history, to what the relationship means for human possibilities and how it sets the direction for relevant public action."[38] With particular reference to biblical understanding of humans being made in the image of God and being sinful as well, he is attentive to the drama of human experience and is directed to human responsibility. As for Kuyper, he forms his Christian worldview in terms of the relationships among God, human beings, and the world, upon which both human direct confrontation with God and Christian engagement in the world are established. Kuyper states:

> Calvinism has a sharply-defined starting-point of its own for the three fundamental relations of all human existence: viz., our relation to *God*, to man to the world. For our relation to God: an immediate fellowship of man with the Eternal, independently of priest and church. . . . And for your relation to *the world*: the recognition that in the whole world the curse is restrained by grace, that the life of the world is to be honored in its independence, and that we must, in every domain, discover the treasures and develop the potencies hidden by God in nature and in human life.[39]

This can be seen from their strong criticism and distancing to the Enlightenment and the French Revolution. Kuyper himself helped to establish an antirevolutionary party and attacked the principles of the revolution, saying it "annihilated all relation to God" in its manifestations in various parts of social and political life.[40] In a similar tone, Niebuhr disagrees with the Enlightenment's destructive power toward the relationship of human beings and God: "the process we have described has been the gradual extrication of our thought from the baneful effects of heresies about man and God which have infected it ever since the French Enlightenment."[41] For him, the danger is "if the secular part of our culture derived grave errors from its worship of reason and nature, rather than

---

38 Rasmussen, introduction to *Reinhold Niebuhr*, 5.

39 Kuyper, *Lectures on Calvinism*, 31.

40 Kuyper, *Lectures on Calvinism*, 23.

41 Reinhold Niebuhr, "Theology and Political Thought in the Western World," *Ecumenical Review* 9, no. 3 (1957): 256.

the worship of God, it compounded those errors by its extreme volun-
tarism, which was blind to the workings of providence in history and
thought that men could create both governments and communities by the
'social contract.'"[42]

In restoring human relationship and history to God, both Kuyper and
Niebuhr assure moral power in public life, either in the form of Christian
moral influence on the state and society, and its effect on non-Christians
in cultural engagement (in Kuyper), or the moral grounding and transformation of social and political justice (in Niebuhr).

In this train of thought, both Kuyper and Niebuhr take human sinfulness seriously, although they take different directions. Kuyper emphasizes
common grace as one form of checking sin while encouraging development and progress in various aspects of social life. Kuyper's distinction
between common grace and special grace provides a basis for Christian
cultural engagement, guides constructive social witness, opens a space
to appraise and elevate civil life as well as human cultural achievement
even by non-Christians, and reflects the purpose of cultural activities. At
this point, Kuyper's vision of public theology deriving from the doctrine
of common grace illuminates Chinese Christians' public responsibility, including more openness to non-Christians in terms of common
cultural development. It is common grace that unfolds God's sovereignty
in cultural and social development. I suggest this vision is applied to the
case of Christianity and society in China, which is to consider the characteristic persistent coexistence of Christianity and other religions in the
Chinese context.

For Kuyper, this temporary progress by common grace serves special
grace in the end. In his view, special grace is higher than common grace,
and common grace will ultimately serve special grace. Yet in the Chinese
context, from a historical perspective and regarding today's situation, I
would propose to expand Kuyper's vision of common grace to help the
Chinese seek the source of human virtue, the root of moral life; develop
cultural, economic, and political areas among people of various religious
backgrounds; contribute to the common benefit of humankind; and
responsibly construct public life.

When the doctrine of God's redemption to elect is hard to understand
and exercise in a particular context, we may recognize the exercise of
common grace as a good means for special grace. This is a more urgent
and significant work for Christianity in China today. Of course, as Mouw
states, "All of this will be revealed in the end of time as counting towards

---

42   Niebuhr, "Theology and Political Thought in the Western World," 260.

the coming of his kingdom."[43] At this point, we still expect something higher than the presence of common grace in China: together with the growth of Chinese Christians and the public moral impact of Christian churches, we may see the elevation of civil life and the enhancement of cultural and social achievements beyond solely human efforts and political expediency. Then we may reevaluate Kuyper's teachings about common grace and special grace in China, particularly about the influence of special grace.

To widely acknowledge God's grace in various life spheres and upon humanity and the world tends to be a good means for the Chinese to come to a full knowledge and acceptance of God, including, finally, God's special grace. It seemingly bears more immediate implications to expand Kuyper's vision of common grace than to focus on God's saving purpose solely among the Chinese.

For Niebuhr, human nature, as with human sinfulness and human worth, serves as a starting point to recognize the needs and limitations of human groups in the case of choices of self-interest: "This Christian faith is mediated to the community by sinful men and that our sins frequently obscure the wisdom of the Gospel and interfere with the course of God's grace to men."[44] Actually, Niebuhr has an account of common grace. He acknowledges "the efficacy of common grace and its superior efficacy in comparison with a religiously motivated life" as "the church is both an institution of saving and of common grace."[45] He also recognizes the limitations of common grace as it does not raise "the ultimate issue" and "a community of grace insofar as word and sacrament penetrate through the complacencies and contradictions of the realm of common grace."[46] This understanding leads to his emphasis that "the obligation to fulfill the possibilities of life and upon the limitations and corruptions in all historical realizations, implies that history is a meaningful process but is incapable of fulfilling itself and therefore points beyond itself to the judgment and mercy of God for its fulfilment."[47]

---

[43] Mouw, "Kuyper on Common Grace," xxvii. On this point, S. U. Zuidema states, "Common grace, after all, is 'only' common grace, some day it will end. There is something higher than common grace: there is particular grace. That is the grace that counts. That is the one thing needful." See S. U. Zuidema, "Common Grace and Christian Action in Abraham Kuyper," in *On Kuyper: A Collection of Readings on the Life, Work and Legacy of Abraham Kuyper*, eds. Bishop and Kok, 262.

[44] Niebuhr, "Theology and Political Thought in the Western World," 262.

[45] Reinhold Niebuhr, "The Relation between Common and Saving Grace," in *Archive Collection: Reinhold Niebuhr Papers (1907–1990)*, Archive: Manuscript Division, Library of Congress, United States.

[46] Niebuhr, "The Relation between Common and Saving Grace."

[47] Rasmussen, ed., *Reinhold Niebuhr*, 172.

Niebuhr recognizes common grace and human sinfulness at once. As Kuyper locates common grace in the realization of special grace, Niebuhr expects relative and progressive justice to be elevated by love and fulfilled in the light of the kingdom of God. Unlike Kuyper, Niebuhr does not give high regard to "civil virtue" as "bourgeois" individualism may occur, affecting the "trans-historical dignity of the person," which he calls the "fragmentary character of civil virtue."[48]

The issue of pluralism, either religious or social, is another domain where Kuyper and Niebuhr meet. As John Witte Jr. summarizes, Kuyper appraises the American principle of religious liberty and religious pluralism, ecclesiastical liberty and confessional pluralism, associational liberty and social pluralism, and political liberty and political pluralism.[49] Kuyper shows respect for the cultural achievements by non-Christians and encourages Christians to partner with other believers (even nonbelievers) in various spheres of social life to develop their own potentials and capacities. In this way, he endorses religious and social pluralism.

Niebuhr affirms cultural, religious, and social diversity while emphasizing religious humility and power-balancing among groups. Although he recognizes the vitalities and diversities of social organizations, Niebuhr ascribes self-interest among human groups to human selfness ("institutional pride") and asks for "the balance of power" among groups. This constraint can be demonstrated in the practice of social organization; as Lovin states, "For Niebuhr, the most difficult problems lie not between the Gospel profession and present practice, but between what the ethics of Jesus demands and any possible social organization."[50]

Patterson contrasts Kuyper and Niebuhr on the institutional problem. He suggests that, unlike Kuyper, who sees institutions as places to develop personal capacities and vocations, Niebuhr is more concerned with human groups "as checks on other power collectives":[51] "Where Kuyper focused on the benevolent family, church, and businesses, Niebuhr stressed that institutions are flawed by individual human sin and have often obscured their mundane will-to-power under various idealistic slogans."[52] Indeed, Niebuhr does not undermine developing a person's various potentials in

---

48 Niebuhr, "Theology and Political Thought in the Western World," 258, 262.
49 See John Witte Jr., "The Biography and Biology of Liberty: Abraham Kuyper and the American Experiment," in *Religion, Pluralism, and Public Life: Abraham Kuyper's Legacy for the 21st Century*, ed. Luis E. Lugo (Grand Rapids: Eerdmans, 2000), 243–62.
50 Robin W. Lovin, *Reinhold Niebuhr and Christian Realism* (Cambridge: Cambridge University Press, 1995), 5.
51 Patterson, "The Enduring Value of Christian Realism," 39.
52 Patterson, "The Enduring Value of Christian Realism," 38.

human groups, but he is well aware of the fact that "natural institutions of society may be nationalistic, exclusivist, and arrogant in ways more insidious than possible for an individual."[53]

We may be inclined to see that as Niebuhr regards human nature as both human worth and limitations, he tends to direct human abilities and creativity to seek proximate solutions in public life (in politics in particular), in light of impossible religious ideals, by checking self-interest in individual and group life. He also urges Christian responsibility to cooperate with non-Christians to strive for justice, yet with a sense of corrective transformation:

> We have an obligation as Christians to establish and extend community and justice as far as lies within our power. We must obey the law of love under conditions and within limits which make no simple application possible. It is not possible because the sins of men, the persistence of individual and collective self-interest, force us to maintain order by coercion and may make resistance and war a necessity of justice. We assume our responsibilities in this community with many other citizens who do not share our faith.[54]

On the other side, Kuyper affirms the commonality between Christians and non-Christians and appraises Christian cultural engagement as well as non-Christians' cultural achievements.

Through the above investigations, we have seen the commonality and divergence between Kuyper and Niebuhr. When we consider both of them in the Chinese context, there is a convergence despite their differences. I do not intend to simply combine Kuyper and Niebuhr in the Chinese context; rather, it is my experience and observation of Christianity in Chinese society that impel me to think about what kind of theological resources may be appropriate in China in respect to its own religious, social, and political realities. At the same time, I read public theologians such as Kuyper and Niebuhr, among others, and gradually recognize that both of them can inform Christianity in China.

The morality of public life, which Christianity can address, is an existing issue in China that contains various aspects. Whereas many Chinese Christians are conservative and fundamentalist, Kuyper's doctrine of common grace contributes to civil virtue not only for Christians but also for the appraisal of non-Christians' virtue in China's pluralistic setting. That could also include Christians developing their potential in different areas with an awareness of working together with many other citizens in cultural and social life. The problems of social

---

53   Patterson, "The Enduring Value of Christian Realism," 38.
54   Niebhur, "Theology and Political Thought in the Western World," 261–62.

37

organizations in China often emerge from their relationships to the state, within the organization, and with other organizations, which require power-balancing. In this sense, the ideas of both Kuyper and Niebuhr regarding social institutions are relevant.

In a general sense, the relevance of Kuyper and Niebuhr to Christianity in China is that both agree with Christian moral implications for political and public life. This can be done through Christian cultural engagement, the dynamic relationship between love and justice, and the relationship between impossible ideas and proximate solutions in immediate realities. This process shows respect for the relatively independent functions of state, religious, and other social institutions, either in their non-Christian forms or their secular efforts toward justice. This is also an important lesson we learn from Niebuhr, who claims, "We have now come to the fairly general conclusion that there is no 'Christian' economic or political system. But there is a Christian attitude toward all systems and schemes of justice."[55]

As Lovin reminds us, "Christian realism for the twenty-first century may need to focus attention on different questions or shift the emphasis between different aspects of human nature, but the basic Niebuhrian framework serves us well, provided that we are prepared to use it critically and not merely to replicate it."[56] He also clarifies, "Christian realists are reluctant to make predictions, but eager for understanding."[57] In this sense, this chapter may serve as a realist and critical understanding of the moral implications of Christianity for public life in China. Against the background of the interactions among Christianity, Chinese culture (including diverse religious life), society, and politics, this chapter suggests the relevance of both Kuyper and Niebuhr to the public problems of Christianity raised in China. Although both focus on the ideas of sin, social institutions, and balance of power, they also agree that Christianity offers deep moral teachings and implications for political and public life, either in the form of Christian moral influence on the state and society (in Kuyper) or the moral grounding and transformation of social and political justice (in Niebuhr). This chapter also addresses such issues as Christian cooperation with non-Christians in public life and Christian engagement with diverse social institutions in China. It is a starting point for the next chapter's further investigations into the methodological problems of public theology in the Chinese context.

---

[55] Niebuhr, "Theology and Political Thought in the Western World," 253.

[56] Robin W. Lovin, "Christian Realism for the Twenty-First Century," *Journal of Religious Ethics* 37, no. 4 (2009): 677.

[57] Lovin, *Christian Realism and the New Realities*, 16.

3

BEING PUBLIC AND THEOLOGICAL

Developing Public Theology in China

At a time when the topic of public theology is receiving increasing attention from academic and church circles in China and beyond, it is a legitimate undertaking to ask a number of questions. Those inquiries concern the particular understanding of what is meant by the concept of *the public* in the Chinese context, the theological as well as other problems involved in Christianity's engagement in public life in China, and how these issues may shape the Chinese understanding of a public theology.[1] Generally speaking, the discourses on public theology by Chinese academics and church groups are tangled up in the problematic nature intrinsic to the categories of both the public and theology and how they relate to one another. Here, there is a struggle between the private and public dimension of theology and faith as well as disputes over how theology is and should be regarded as a public enterprise. In its review of work already done on public theology evident in the Chinese context, this chapter explores the meaning of the term *public* in the Chinese intellectual and social tradition, as well as the tradition of public theology in China, and considers the particular public and theological issues that a public theology must deal with in the Chinese context. There is an underlying and encompassing major concern here. In a country like China, the government exercises much power over the social spheres, including religious life. How can Christian communities, together with Christian studies, shape public life in China through their reacting to and reflecting on public issues?

---

[1]   I acknowledge there are various resources and types of public theology; this
       chapter is primarily concerned with Protestant public theology with reference to
       Protestant Christians and churches in the Chinese context.

CONCEPT OF *PUBLIC* IN CHINESE INTELLECTUAL
AND SOCIAL TRADITION

Chinese thought is rich in its public tradition, which can serve as an inspiration for understanding the development of a public theology in the Chinese context. Jo-shui Chen 陳弱水, in his article "The Concept of 'Public' in Chinese History and Its Modern Deformations,"[2] provides a comprehensive analysis of the connotation of the public (*gong* 公). He describes five discrete types of public thought in Chinese history: (1) The original meaning of *public* refers to the court, the government, the ruler, or governmental affairs, from which the category of public affairs is derived; (2) During the late Warring States period, *the public* became a normative concept with a moral connotation, referring to that which is universal and concerns the whole. This rendering is related to such ideas as "all under heaven" (*tianxia* 天下) and the universe. It is that which is in opposition to what is deemed to be private; (3) In the neo-Confucianism of the Song Dynasty, now with a connotation of the good, *the public* refers to the fundamental principle of the world. It is here associated with ideas of righteousness (*yi* 義), that which is fair (*zheng* 正), in addition to the principle of heaven (*tian li* 天理) advocated by Confucian ethics; (4) Reflection on the discernment of the private, sentiment, and human desire in the late Ming Dynasty led the concept of the public becoming associated with a reasonable realization of the private; (5) Deriving from the guildhall, with a descriptive meaning of *common*, *together*, and *all*, the idea of *the public* can refer to public discussion or public opinion in politics in a way that is analogous to the discussions on imperial court affairs or common affairs in the family or clan. There are then derivative expressions like the *public court* (*gong tang* 公堂), *public land* (*gong tian* 公田), and a *professional public association* (*gong hui* 公會) or a *public corporation* (*gong tuan* 公團). It is only in and through the sense of a professional association or a public corporation that the concept of *the public* is related to social life.[3]

Analysis by Jo-shui Chen demonstrates some of the key characteristics of the Chinese understanding of the category of *public*. On the one hand, it is strongly connected with ethics, norms, and states of mind, especially in the expression of opposition between public and private; on the other hand, it is particularly prominent in the governmental sphere but not the

---

[2]   Jo-shui Chen, "Zhongguo lishi shang 'gong' de guannian jiqi xiandai bianxing" 中國歷史上"公"的觀念及其變形 ["The Concept of 'Public' in Chinese History and Its Modern Deformations"], in *Gonggongxing yu gongminguan* 公共性與公民觀 [*Publicness and Citizenship*], ed. Jilin Xu 許紀霖 (Nanjing: Jiangsu renmin chubanshe 江蘇人民出版社, 2006), 3–39.

[3]   Chen, "Zhongguo lishi shang 'gong' de guannian jiqi xiandai bianxing," 25–6.

other spheres. It rarely features in social life. Seen from this perspective, the constant connotation of *the public* refers to that which is official or pertains to the government—as in the assumption that public affairs are the responsibilities of the government.[4]

In a similar vein, the Japanese scholar Yuzo Mizoguchi points out two further characteristics of how the public is used in Chinese thought. The first has to do with the way in which the public emphasizes distributing equally to ensure equitable living for the common good. The other is concerned with how the concept of that which is public in China implies an understanding of heaven. For example, "in the Taoist system, thinkers used the word 'public' to indicate no deviation from the Heaven, the Way, the natural state. This kind of 'public' was called 'public of the Heaven.'"[5]

Of course, there are some variations to this typological model. William T. Rowe has emphasized the emergence of the nongovernmental civil or public sphere in his case study of Hankow (Hankou 漢口) in nineteenth-century China; here, the meaning of *public* (*gong* 公) "moved away from the sense of 'governmental' and closer to that of 'collective' or 'communal.'"[6] Rowe further suggested a tripartite categorization of responsibility embracing social activities such as river conservancy and urban street maintenance. The threefold division became that which was official (*guan*, or *kuan* 官), the private (*si*, or *ssu* 私), and the popular (*min* 民), "where the central category between *kuan* and *ssu* was now clearly labeled 'public' (*kung*)."[7] The ever-expanding role of the public sphere was sanctioned by the state; later, "an expanded governmental sphere merged with (or captured) the already much-expanded extra-bureaucratic public sphere."[8] Furthermore, in his study on Hongmou Chen 陳宏謀 (1696–1771), an influential officer in the Qing dynasty, Rowe identified the significance of public opinion (*gong lun* 公論) in guiding the formation of policy and evaluating individual official performance. Rowe

---

4   Chen, "Zhongguo lishi shang 'gong' de guannian jiqi xiandai bianxing," 29.

5   Yuzo Mizoguchi, "Zhongguo sixiang zhong de gong yu si" 中國思想中的公與私 ["Public and Private in Chinese Intellectual History"], in *Gong yu si de sixiang shi* 公與私的思想史[*Public and Private in Comparative Intellectual Histories*], eds. Sasaki Takeshi and Kim Tea-Chang, trans. Wenzhu Liu 劉文柱 (Beijing: Renmin chubanshe 人民出版社, 2009), 42. My translation.

6   William T. Rowe, *Hankow: Conflict and Community in a Chinese City, 1796–1895* (Stanford: Stanford University Press, 1989), 183.

7   Rowe, *Hankow*, 184.

8   Rowe, *Hankow*, 185. He points out this problem in the Qing dynasty elsewhere: "Like a variety of twentieth-century Chinese regimes, one might say, Yongzheng 雍正 was attempting at least in part to governmentalize an active and existing 'public sphere.'" See William T. Rowe, *Saving the World: Chen Hongmou and Elite Consciousness in Eighteenth-Century China* (Stanford: Stanford University Press, 2001), 365.

theorized, "To a certain (albeit limited) extent, then, the preoccupation with *gonglun/renqing* that we see in Chen and many of his contemporary political actors in the eighteenth-century Qing empire parallels the rising importance of the notion of public opinion in early modern Europe."[9]

Alongside the emerging nongovernmental public sphere in Chinese history, we may observe certain prevailing meanings of *public* in the Chinese intellectual and social tradition. The list of these characteristics must include a vague awareness of the multiplicity of spheres, the fragile existence of social life, and the intermingling between the public and officials, as well as the prominent place occupied by the government in public affairs. Now we are in a better position to understand Jilin Xu's judgment on the formation of public spheres in modern China and its limitations:

> unlike the European public spheres with bourgeois individuals as the basic members which are based on civil society, the shape of public spheres of modern China is remote from civil society but related to political issues such as founding of national states and social reforms.

Further,

> the threat to the development of Chinese public spheres is not the soft in-filtration of power and money of late capitalism analyzed by Habermas, but that it is impossible to get stable institutionalization and legitimacy within the social system, and difficult to maintain the independence and non-partisanship of its publicness due to the increasing influence of partisan struggle.[10]

Of course, *the public* in a more general sense has a broader set of meanings. Foreign discourses on publicness, public spheres, and public philosophy have attracted the attention of Chinese scholars, most notably Jilin Xu,[11]

---

9   Rowe, *Saving the World*, 375. Also see Mary Backus Rankin, "'Public Opinion' and Political Power: Qingyi in Late Nineteenth-Century China," *Journal of Asian Studies* 41, no. 3 (1982): 453–84.

10   Jilin Xu, "Jindai zhongguo de gonggong lingyu: xingtai, gongneng yu ziwo lijie: yi Shanghai weili" 近代中國的公共領域: 形態、功能與自我理解:以上海為例 ["Public Sphere in Modern China: Its Pattern, Function, and Self-Understanding: Taking Shanghai as an Example"], *Shi lin* 史林 [*Historical Review*], no. 2 (2003): 89. My translation.

11   Jilin Xu is general editor of *Zhishi fenzi luncong* 知識分子論叢 [*Forum of Intellectuals*], a book series published by Jiangsu renmin chubanshe 江蘇人民出版社. The series includes *Gonggongxing yu gonggong zhishi fenzi* 公共性與公共知識分子 [*Publicity and Public Intellectuals*] (edited by Jilin Xu), *Gonggongxing yu gongminguan* 公共性與公民觀 [*The Concept of "Public" and Citizenship in Comparative Perspectives*] (edited by Qing Liu 劉擎), and *Gonggong kongjian zhong de zhishi fenzi* 公共空間中的知識分子 [*Intellectuals in the Public Sphere*] (edited by Jilin Xu).

Yan Wang 王炎,[12] Hui Wang 汪暉, and Yangu Chen 陳燕谷. The volume entitled *Culture and Publicness* collects the major writings of Western thinkers on public issues, such as Hannah Arendt, Jürgen Habermas, Charles Taylor, John Rawls, and Michel Foucault.[13] These publications will undoubtedly facilitate discussions on the concept of publicness and reflections on the development and construction of public spheres in the Chinese context.

Yi-huah Jiang 江宜樺 highlights the significance of this kind of discourse on the concept of *publicity* or *publicness* in the Chinese-speaking world. He argues that it is necessary to adhere to the principle of "rationality of willingness to communicate." He writes that "the formation of public space must presume that people are willing to communicate among themselves and use the language each other may understand. Although this kind of communication is not necessarily to ensure that all parties can reach consensus, it is the basis of creating space for discourse on public philosophy."[14]

Moreover, this kind of communication and discussion is concerned with a wide range of public affairs: "In terms of the theme of public philosophy, as long as public affairs are attended to by everyone or issues are not realized by the general public, which in fact has profound influence, intellectuals have the responsibilities to expound them so that these issues could receive due attention. These issues include constitutional system, economic development, security and human rights, educational reform, financial control, homeland planning, ecological preservation, rights of

---

[12] Yan Wang is the general editor of *Gonggong luncong* 公共論叢 [*Res Publica*], a book series published by Shanlian shudian 三聯書店, which includes *Shichang shehui yu gonggong zhixu* 市場社會與公共秩序 [*Market Society and Public Order*] (edited by Junning Liu 劉軍寧), *Jingji minzhu yu jingji ziyou* 經濟民主與經濟自由 [*Economic Democracy and Economic Freedom*] (edited/authored by Junning Liu, Yan Wang, and Weifang He 賀衛方), *Ziyou yu shequn* 自由與社群 [*Freedom and Community*] (authored by Junning Liu, etc.), and *Xianzheng zhuyi yu xiandai guojia* 憲政主義與現代國家 [*Constitutionalism and Modern Country*] (edited by Yan Wang).

[13] Hui Wang and Yangu Chen, eds., *Wenhua yu gonggong xing* 文化與公共性 [*Culture and Publicness*] (Beijing: Sanlian shudian 三聯書店, 2005).

[14] Yi-huah Jiang, "Huaren shijie fazhan gonggong zhexue de yiyi" 華人世界發展公共哲學的意義 ["The Significance of Developing Public Philosophy in the Chinese-Speaking World"], in *Gongsi lingyu xintan: dongya yu xifang guandian zhi bijiao* 公私領域新探: 東亞與西方觀點之比較 [*A New Exploration of the Public and Private Spheres: A Comparison between East Asian and Western Perspectives*], eds. Chun-chieh Huang 黃俊傑 and Yi-huah Jiang (Shanghai: Huadong shifan daxue chubanshe 華東師範大學出版社, 2008), 52. My translation.

vulnerable groups, life education, issues from global perspectives, etc., and all of these are closely related to public wellbeing."[15]

The formation of the public sphere can thus be promoted if attention is paid to the rational communication of public welfare. That the Chinese-speaking world attaches importance to the general problems and principles of this understanding of *public* will undoubtedly provide a good academic background and theoretical basis for the involvement of philosophical and religious perspectives in public affairs. The way in which the concept of *the public* is used in the Chinese intellectual and social tradition also casts light on the problems to be taken into account in this kind of discourse.

The Tradition of Public Theology in the Chinese Context and Its "Theological" Problem

In his introduction to a book series on Chinese Christian public theology, Ken-pa Chin (曾慶豹) noted that the National Christian Council of China held a National Convention on Christian Economic Relations in Shanghai in August 1927. That convention bore witness to the opportunity for a Christian involvement in various aspects of modern public life, most notably issues to do with industry, rural economy, labor, and women. It could be said to have been "the most imposing public theology convention in the history of Christianity in China."[16] Ken-pa Chin further asserted that it was during the period of the Republic of China that the actual idea of a public theology first appeared in Chinese Christian thought and became extremely dynamic: "As Christianity draws particular attention to social participation and activities, it is most likely to become the target of public criticism. From Confucianism to freedom of belief, from nonreligious to anti-Christian, from recovering the right to education to abolishing unequal treaties, from imperialist aggression to the movement of indigenization, Christianity in China has always been in the public debate."[17]

---

[15]   Yi-huah Jiang, "Huaren shijie fazhan gonggong zhexue de yiyi," 52. My translation.

[16]   Ken-pa Chin, "Zhongguo jidujiao gonggong shenxue wenxuan xilie zongxu" 中國基督教公共神學文選總序 ["General Introduction to Anthology of Christian Public Theology in China"], in *Zhongguo Jidu jiao gonggong shenxue wenxuan, yi, shehui sixiang pian* 中國基督教公共神學文選一:思想篇 [*Collected Essays on the Public Theology of Chinese Christianity, I, Volume on Social Thought*], ed. Ken-pa Chin (Hong Kong: Center for Advanced Biblical Studies and Application 研道社, 2012), xiii. My translation.

[17]   Chin, "Zhongguo jidujiao gonggong shenxue wenxuan xilie zongxu," xxiii. My translation.

The volume on social thought in this series is comprised of essays having to do with Chinese Christians' views on Christianity and revolution; the social ideals of Jesus; Christianity and socialism; and Christianity and communism. Of particular significance is the essay *"Jidujiao de shehuixing"* ["Sociality of Christianity"] by T. C. Chao (Zichen Zhao, 1888–1979) 趙紫宸. T. C. Chao argued that God acts in the cosmos and within history. The latter is the platform within which the sociality of Christianity is manifested: "The human being can succeed only with a higher level of entity falling on him or her. In the same way, society must have a higher social entity so as to be consolidated and developed. Therefore, God is necessary for both human beings and society."[18] This position establishes a theological ground for supporting the public theology we talk about today. It is due to the necessity of God for society that we can affirm the relevance of theology to public life.

T. C. Chao recognized the possibility of two kinds of counterarguments. The first is the sole focus on personal salvation, and thus faith, in practice, becomes "indifferent to various social and national issues," but this is "against the purpose of Christianity, concealing the essence of Christianity, and destroying the spirit of Christianity." The second contrary position is to be overly involved in "social transformation and economic revolution, yet neglecting the religious basis of Christianity, such as the relationship between human beings and God and the unity of human beings and church."[19] In T. C. Chao's view, Christianity should focus on the unity of individuals and society: "She (namely Christianity) really pays attention to society as well as individuals so that she entreats God's spirit to fall upon the hearts of human beings and on society as well while both individuals and society strive towards God. Christianity is the only key to solve social problems, the only way to create society; because Christianity tells us that human beings need God and society needs God too."[20]

Due to the sociopolitical changes and turbulence in China in the first half of the twentieth century, it was inevitable that Christianity also became deeply involved in emerging sociopolitical issues. Its theological thinking was often related to these topics. According to Wing-hung Lam 林榮洪, "These fifty years of Chinese theology centered on one theme: saving the nation and reconstructing the country. This theme covers the religious experience, rational thinking, moral struggle, and consistent

---

[18] T. C. Chao, "Jidujiao de shehuixing" 基督教的社會性 ["Sociality of Christianity"], in *Zhongguo jidujiao gonggong shenxue wenxuan*, ed. Chin, 184–85. My translation.

[19] Chao, "Jidujiao de shehuixing," 192. My translation.

[20] Chao, "Jidujiao de shehuixing," 192. My translation.

choice among Chinese Christian believers for half of the century."[21] One example of such thinking is an article by Fu-ya Hsieh (Fuya Xie, 1892–1991) 謝扶雅 published in 1935. Here, he claimed quite openly that "the mission of Christianity in China is to contribute to a great revolutionary movement—national revolution, social revolution, and spiritual revolution."[22] Such active participation of Christianity in social reconstruction nevertheless also underscores the problem of lacking a "religious foundation"—as, indeed, T. C. Chao warned.

It seems as if the history of Christianity in China before the twentieth century was concerned mostly with ideological struggles or missionary efforts. In the first half of that century, there emerged a series of interactions between Christianity and the Chinese society at large. The Christian impact on China began to turn toward an active participation in social action. As Lee Ming Ng 吳利明 pointed out during the 1920s and 1930s, "Whether Christianity in China will be accepted in China or not does not depend on its relationship with the Chinese traditional culture but the specific contribution it can provide for the reconstruction of the Chinese society."[23] These "specific and effective contributions" to the Chinese society were activities in the fields of education, medicine, and social work. The best example of such was the work of the Chinese Christian Movement of Rural Construction during the 1920s–1930s.

From a theological perspective, this Movement of Rural Construction was deeply influenced by the American social gospel. It was seen to be a representation of the gospel that sought to addresses the salvation of both the individual and society in its desire to achieve the "Christianization of the social order." The leaders of this movement "integrated various doctrines of Christianity and Chinese folk social life in order to inculturate the Christian gospel in the local Chinese society. It did so by means of engaging with secular life, thereby exerting an influence on the thought

---

[21] Wing-hung Lam, *Zhonghua shenxue wushi nian* 中華神學五十年 [*Fifty Years of Chinese Theology: 1900–1949*] (Hong Kong: China Graduate School of Theology 中國神學研究院, 1998), 2. My translation.

[22] Fu-ya Hsieh, "Jidujiao dui jinri zhongguo de shiming" 基督教對今日中國的使命 ["The Mission of Christianity in China Today"], in *Ershi shiji zhongguo jidujiao wenti* 二十世紀中國基督教問題 [*The Problems of Chinese Christianity in the 20th Century*], ed. Yu-ming Shaw 邵玉銘 (Taipei: Cheng Chung 正中書局, 1980), 516. My translation.

[23] Lee Ming Ng, *Jidujiao yu zhongguo shehui bianqian* 基督教與中國社會變遷 [*Christianity and Social Change in China*] (Hong Kong: Chinese Christian Literature Council 基督教文藝出版社, 1997), 3. My translation.

and behavior of the Chinese people at the level of daily life rather than at the level of elites."[24]

The criticism leveled at such an approach should not take us by surprise: "They do not promote social gospel with church as the starting point, nor are they eager to develop followers, but they rush to construct a service system oriented to the most urgent needs of the villagers. . . . To value entering into the world rather than detaching from it and to value daily life rather than sermons had become a common consensus among intellectuals involving Christian rural construction at that time."[25] These practices improved living conditions in some social fields in different ways; they did so "at the cost of increasing decline of religiosity,"[26] and they tended to be indifferent to the pursuit of religious spirit.

The theological positions of the leaders of this movement were derived from their knowledge of the social problems at that time. The leaders were "determined by their own social position, and then they attempted to defend these positions in a Christian category."[27] In other words, their Christian social practices were based on a "social theory in the name of Christianity."[28] Generally speaking, the efforts of Chinese Christian intellectuals in nation-building during the 1920s had gradually tempered tensions between Christianity and the Chinese ideological tradition. As a consequence, they acquired a degree of social acceptance in a time of nation-building. In some ways, there was a shift away from focusing on culture and philosophy to a focus on social practice, and the price of such a shift was obvious. Apart from the influence of the social gospel, the relevance of Christianity to Chinese society was far from adequate. It failed to show the particularity of Christian doctrines and to distinguish clearly its links from the Western political powers. However, a new trend of Christian social practice emerged in the first half of the twentieth century. Departing from the individualistic tendency of its religious heritage, the Christian faith had begun to show that it could be involved in and influence social life.

---

[24] Nianqun Yang 楊念群, "Shehui fuyin yu zhongguo jidujiao xiangcun jianse yundong de lilun yu zuzhi jizhu" 社會福音與中國基督教鄉村建設運動的理論與組織基礎 ["'Social Gospel' and Theoretical and Organizational Foundation of the Chinese Christian Movement of Rural Construction"], *Daofeng jidujiao wenhua pinglun* 基督教文化評論 [*Logos and Pneuma: Chinese Journal of Theology*] no. 8 (1998): 253. My translation.

[25] Yang, "Shehui fuyin yu zhongguo jidujiao xiangcun jianse yundong de lilun yu zuzhi jizhu," 278. My translation.

[26] Yang, "Shehui fuyin yu zhongguo jidujiao xiangcun jianse yundong de lilun yu zuzhi jizhu," 281. My translation.

[27] Wu, *Jidujiao yu zhongguo shehui bianqian*, 277–78. My translation.

[28] Wu, *Jidujiao yu zhongguo shehui bianqian*, 278. My translation.

This effort and its inherent weakness lead us to consider the problems underlying the relationship between Christianity and its theology with Chinese society. The overriding concern is how to achieve the shift from a particular social position to an authentic Christian position while participating in social activities and the construction of the common good. This history of how Christians were able to act out their faith in the social and public life of China during the first half of the twentieth century anticipates questions having to do with the theological nature of public theology that we discuss nowadays.

Although public theology is theology by name, debate about its precise theological nature or status continues in both Chinese academia and the church. The debate in China is mainly focused on Max L. Stackhouse's idea of public theology. Accompanying the publication of works on Stackhouse,[29] some Chinese scholars have raised serious criticisms regarding his method and understanding of a public theology.[30] Andres S. Tang 鄧紹光, writing in his "Public Theology, What Theology? Some Radical Reflections," has examined "the priority of the public" in Stackhouse's public theology: "Even though it uses the term 'theology,' Stackhouse's public theology defines God and the God-world relationship in terms of the public spheres of life and public discourse, not vice versa."[31]

Andres S. Tang has suggested that the theological contents of this sort of public theology are so weak that it should be replaced by the theological method proposed by John Webster. It assumes, "Only God makes Godself knowable; only returning to God can guarantee that our knowledge of God is appropriate and thus define the nature and purpose of theology."[32] For Andres S. Tang, knowledge of God and relevant doctrines define the nature of the public. He has claimed that the space and publicness of theology must be defined by the church itself. The comparison is

---

[29] For example, Xie, *Gonggong shenxue yu quanqiuhua*, and Deidre King Hainsworth and Scott R. Paeth, eds., *Quanqiu shehui de gonggong shenxue: xiang makesi sita kehaosi zhijing* 全球社會的公共神學:向斯塔克豪思致敬 [*Public Theology for a Global Society: In Honor of Max L. Stackhouse*], Chinese translation edited by Philip Chia 謝品然 and Zhibin Xie (Hong Kong: Center for Advanced Biblical Studies and Application 研道社, 2012).

[30] *Shandao qikan* 山道期刊 [*Hill Road*], an orginal journal of Hong Kong Baptist Theological Seminary, published a special issue on public theology in 2013.

[31] Andres S. Tang, "Gonggong shenxue, shenmeyang de shenxue? yixie genbenxing de fansi" 公共神學，什麼樣的神學？一些根本性的反思 ["Public Theology, What Theology? Some Radical Reflections"], *Shandao qikan* 16, no. 1 (2013): 20. My translation.

[32] Tang, "Gonggong shenxue, shenmeyang de shenxue? yixie genbenxing de fansi," 21. My translation.

made with Stackhouse's public theology, which is concerned with "the public outside the church." Andres S. Tang has thus argued, "Being the real public, the church's discourse and living must be theological and Christological. That means that the church is public in its own ways, and Christian theology is public by itself too. In this sense, a Christian public theology is Christological-ecclesiastical."[33]

In a similar way, in his "Public Theology: Whose 'Public'? How 'Theological'?" Freeman Chi-wai Huen 禤智偉 has criticized the "theological inadequacy" and "absence of ecclesiology" in the kind of public theology represented by Stackhouse: "The public turn of theology may contribute to theology's position in humanities, but it does not construct the church. Public theology may gain publicity or reception in an academic way, but may lose its 'theological' nature."[34] Freeman Chi-wai Huen likewise has affirmed that the real public lies in the church: "It is not that the church becomes the church by being 'public'; rather, only when the church is to be the church, is the church becoming public/political."[35]

The criticisms made by Andres S. Tang and Freeman Chi-wai Huen against the public theology represented by Stackhouse elicited responses from other Chinese scholars. Ken-pa Chin pointed out, "Both Andres S. Tang and Freeman Chi-wai Huen deny any form of progressive or radical public theology on the grounds of the doctrines of God or ecclesiology so as to highlight a theology for the church; they think that serving as witness to God, a real public theology can be solely produced by the church."[36]

---

[33] Tang, "Gonggong shenxue, shenmeyang de shenxue? yixie genbenxing de fansi," 30. My translation.

[34] Chi W. Huen, "Gonggong shenxue: shui de gonggong? You ji shenxue?" 公共神 學: 誰的公共? 有几神學? ["Public Theology: Whose 'Public'? How 'Theological'?"], *Shandao qikan* 16, no. 1 (2013): 59.

[35] Huen, "Gonggong shenxue: shui de gonggong? you ji shenxue?" 62. In fact, some other Chinese Christian scholars also express their concerns about the theological nature of public theology. For example, Lap-yan Kung 龔立人 expresses this worry in terms of "anti-theological public theology": "For attempting to enter social publicness, anti-theological public theology gradually gives up its own language and tradition and replaces the value of faith by public values . . . as a result, theology does not bring creativity to society but is absorbed in society." See Lap-yan Kung, "Gonggong, jiaohui yu xianggang shehui: gonggong shenxue de xushixing" 公共、教會與香港社會: 公共神學的敘事性 ["The Public, Church, and Hong Kong: The Narrative Nature of Public Theology"], *Daofeng jidujiao wenhua pinglun* 道風基督教文化評論 [*Logos and Pneuma: Chinese Journal of Theology*], no. 32 (2010): 90–91.

[36] Ken-pa Chin, "Shi shui ba gonggong shenxue yange zuo 'gonggong shenxue" 是誰把公共神學閹割做 "公公神學" [*Who Emasculates Public Theology into*

For Ken-pa Chin, theology is by its very nature public, so there is no theology of church that is separate from the public. By questioning the pursuit of a pure theology, he argued that it is the emerging responsibility of the church to engage in public issues.

According to Pan-chiu Lai 賴品超, the debate among Chinese Christians is focused on the methodological questions having to do with whether there is and how to retain theological purity in public theology. As Pan-chiu Lai asserts, "Theological purity relates apparently to the question concerning theology's faithfulness to God's revelation but the most crucial issue is not merely whether the discourse of public theology cites only scriptures and theological works by the church fathers without mentioning any theory from non-theological disciplines, but also whether public theology is of the church, by the church and for the church."[37] In other words, the relevance of public theology to both the Christian tradition and theories from other disciplines is an unavoidable issue; moreover, an interpretation of social and public affairs as well as their practical implications should also be taken into account in public theological discourse. For Pan-chiu Lai, "Apart from theological purity, political effectiveness is another criterion for evaluating various approaches to public theology."[38] This criterion is more important in public theology than in systematic theology or dogmatic theology. To achieve the goal of political effectiveness, public theology must engage itself in cultural criticism and negotiation in various publics:

> In confronting some public values and their interpretations, Christianity may respond with acceptance, refusal, negotiation, or a combination of these. To realize effective cultural criticism and negotiation, Christianity must not only clarify its own positions and tradition in the first place so as not to lose its identity but also understand the dynamics of cultural change and consider strategies accordingly. In other words, theological discourse on public issues must not only interpret the Christian tradition and revelation correctly and profoundly but also work out effective strategies flexibly according to real circumstances.[39]

'Eunuch Theology'?"], *Shidai luntan* 時代論壇 [*Christian Times*], September 18, 2013, https://tinyurl.com/yckj5rjs and September 25, 2013, https://tinyurl.com/mr3repxh.

[37] Pan-chiu Lai, *Guangchang shang de hanyu shenxue: cong shenxue dao jidu zongjiao yanji* 廣場上的漢語神學:從神學到基督宗教研究 [*Sino-Christian Theology in the Public Square: From Theology to Christian Studies*] (Hong Kong: Logos and Pneuma Press 道風書社, 2014), 331. My translation.

[38] Lai, *Guangchang shang de hanyu shenxue*, 337. My translation.

[39] Lai, *Guangchang shang de hanyu shenxue*, 337–38. My translation.

These discussions among Chinese scholars cover various issues regarding the nature, method, and purpose of public theology. I will not make further assessment on all their divergent views here. There is nevertheless a need to make a general response to Andres S. Tang's statement that in Stackhouse's public theology, "criteria and evidence are detached from confessional and dogmatic theology and adopt public discourse instead"[40] and Freeman Chi-wai Huen's claim that "in their public theology, the church is absent."[41] The case must be made for public theology in general (including Stackhouse's definition of *public theology*) having its own theological appeal. Its construction cannot be separated from its engagement with the church. In other words, it is the mission of the church to develop a public theology, and that particular mission demands an understanding of how the church accepts responsibility from the wider public sphere. In this vision, a Christian responsibility in public life does not necessarily contradict religious faithfulness; rather, an authentic reading of what it means to be a church consists of integrating both. Stackhouse himself has argued:

> We find it both necessary and possible to develop a 'public theology'. Such a theology addresses public issues: it makes sense in public discourse beyond the privileged insights of our confessional communions; and it offers answers of compelling substance to those perennial and universal questions that must be addressed in every age by every religion, philosophy, or metaphysical-moral worldview. The basic themes of Christianity—Creation, Liberation, Vocation, Covenant, Moral law, Sin, Freedom, Church, Trinity, and Christology—constitute the core concepts of a viable 'science of the divine' as it bears on public life. These themes carry rich resources of guiding society, and the stewardship of these themes is the primacy public responsibility of the church. These themes also drive us to ethical engagement.[42]

In other words, to develop a public theology derived from scripture, tradition, reason, and experience is our stewardship of the Word. Stackhouse asserted that "the chief task of Christian stewardship is the cultivation of a new public theology, rooted in disciplined but diverse communities of faith and service."[43] The public theologians' public concern constitutes their

---

40 Tang, "Gonggong shenxue, shenmeyang de shenxue? yixie genbenxing de fansi," 11. My translation.
41 Huen, "Gonggong shenxue: shui de gonggong? you ji shenxue?," 62. He also writes on the same page, "When public theology concerns only the citizenship of believers, it ignores their discipleship and the necessary conflict between the two loyalties." My translation.
42 Max L. Stackhouse, *Public Theology and Political Economy: Christian Stewardship in Modern Society* (Grand Rapids: Eerdmans., 1987), 94.
43 Stackhouse, *Public Theology and Political Economy*, 176.

theology. As David Tracy has declared, "Every theologian provides both interpretations of a religious tradition and interpretations of the religious dimension of the contemporary situation."[44] Furthermore, the "theological concern with the 'publics' of society and academy cannot be dismissed as extra-theological . . . they must continue the drive to reinterpret or retrieve the classical resources of the church tradition in genuinely new applications for the present day."[45] For me, the public concern of theology and the theological nature of public concern are like two sides of the same coin.

PUBLIC CIRCUMSTANCES AND SPECIFIC ISSUES OF PUBLIC THEOLOGY IN THE CHINESE CONTEXT

The concept of *the public* in the Chinese intellectual and social tradition, the public dimension of the Christian tradition, and the problem of its theological nature form the current discussion on public theology in the Chinese context. This section continues to explore some specific issues arising from these public circumstances. It concentrates on the problem of the identity of religious groups as social organizations, their interaction with the state and social life at large, and their interaction with other intellectual resources when Christian values engage in the discourse on a particular issue. This mode of enquiry will also help us to see the continuity and evolution of the public sphere from a traditional to a contemporary China.

According to Xiaochao Wang's 王曉朝 analysis, the government as an influential power in the public domain in China penetrates into the religious sphere:

> Those with a public identity like the monarch and nobles are, of course, religious leaders or presiders of religious cults. Nation, politics, society, individual, morality, nature, religion, gods, and ghosts are all unified in this public domain—an area of political domination.[46] . . . This pattern of the "public" was a mode of political thinking as well as a norm of social behavior; it was a cosmic order as well as a moral spirit; it was autocratic monarchy as well as religious worship. Within these parameters, religion was brought into the field of public politics and became part of the

---

44 David Tracy, *The Analogical Imagination: Christian Theology and the Culture of Pluralism* (New York: Crossroad Publishing Company, 1981), 61.

45 Tracy, *The Analogical Imagination*, 31.

46 Xiaochao Wang, "Gongsi lingyu de huafen dui dangdai zhongguo de lilun yiyi" 公私領域的劃分對當代中國的理論意義 ["The Theoretical Significance of Division of Public-Private Areas for Contemporary Chinese Religion"], *Zhongguo zongjiao* 中國宗教 [*Religions in China*] no. 8–9 (2008): 33. My translation.

52

government framework. Religion was a kind of power or resource that could not be completely consigned to the private.[47]

The public nature of religion in China is under the control of the public political domain.

The concept of *public* in the Chinese tradition implies that portions of social life apart from the government category are very limited. Likewise, in today's mainland China, the development of social life is subject to the government's strong influence. With the changes in contemporary Chinese society, different interest groups have diversified social demands, and the issue concerning the social domain and its significance in China has been raised. The emergence of the social domain is mainly reflected in the growth of organizations that make up a civil society. Although there are different understandings of the concept of a civil society[48] and its manifestations, it is possible to discern the emergence and development of various kinds of organizations in contemporary China. The Chinese mass organizations cover many types of interests and commitments. Some are registered; some are not. Some are quasi-government organizations; others are grassroots organizations.[49]

The identity of these social organization groups is still a problem. In contemporary China, social spheres gradually shift from unification to differentiation: on the one hand, the life of a mass organization becomes more and more complicated and diversified; on the other hand, "its typical characteristics such as autonomy, voluntariness, and being

---

[47] Wang, "Gongsi lingyu de huafen dui dangdai zhongguo de lilun yiyi," 33. My translation.

[48] As there are different interpretations of the connotation of civil society, I refer mainly to the description by Keping Yu 俞可平, a Chinese scholar, and understand it as "relatively independent civil and public realm from political state, its foundation and main body are various non-governmental organizations," and its constituent elements include "a variety of non-government and non-business civil organizations, including civil rights organizations, various industry associations, private charitable organizations, community organizations, interest groups, colleague groups, mutual help organizations, various spontaneous combinations of interest groups and citizens." See Keping Yu, "Zhongguo gongmin shehui: gainian, fenlei, yu zhidu huanjing" 中國公民社會: 觀念、分類與制度環境 ["Civil Society in China: Concepts, Classification, and Institutional Environment"], in *Guojia yu shimin shehui: zhongguo shijiao* 國家與市民社會: 中國視角 [*State and Civil Society: A Chinese Perspective*], ed. Zhenglai Deng 鄧正來 (Shanghai: Gezhi chubanshe/ Shanghai renmin chubanshe 格致出版社 / 上海人民出版社, 2011), 37–38. My translation.

[49] Shaoguang Wang 王紹光 and Jianyu He 何建宇, "Zhongguo de shetuan geming: zhongguo ren de jieshe Bantu" 中國的社團革命: 中國人的結社版圖 ["The Revolution of Chinese Mass Organizations: A Map of Chinese Association Life"], in *Guojia yu shimin shehui*, ed. Deng, 185.

nongovernment do not stand out" because "civil society in China is typically government-dominated with an obvious duality of the government and the people."[50] The state remains skeptical of the function of various social groups: "The state is willing to allow the emergence of organizations engaged in social services and humanitarian and charitable work."[51] Yet the state still restricts those organizations likely to be hostile to the government. Against this background, key questions for the development of Chinese social organizations include: "Do they contribute to the consolidation of the prevalent community system as media or to the prosperity of civil society, which is more autonomous, more differentiated, and even more critical? Are they autonomous organizations that can determine their own programs and rely on their own resources or social organizations listening to the party and the government?"[52]

It can be said that the model of social life has been dominated by the state in contemporary China thus far. It is so even while the independence and identity of social organizations are particularly important. Zhenglai Deng and Yuejin Jing 景躍進 have conducted an analysis of how civil society is constructed in China. They concluded that "in addition to the acquisition of independent identity from the State, Chinese civil society strives for participation so as to facilitate positive interactive relations between itself and the State."[53] This independent identity and participation ensure autonomy and plural developments of social organizations and civil society. These issues are certainly reflected in religious groups (including various types of churches), as Fuk-Tsang Ying 邢福增 has noted: "The problems facing the patriotic religious associations (such as the Three-Self Patriotic Movement and the China Christian Council), the illegal religious organizations, and

[50] Keping Yu, "Zhongguo gongmin shehui: gainian, fenlei, yu zhidu huanjing," 58. My translation.

[51] Andrew Watson, "Civil Society in Transitional Countries", 46.

[52] Jude Howell 朱迪·豪威爾, "Zhongguo shehui bianyuan qunti de zuzhi hua yu gongmin shehui de fazhan" 中國社會邊緣群體的組織化與公民社會的發展 ["The Organization of Marginal Groups and the Development of Civil Society in China"], in *Gongmin shehui yu zhili zhuanxing: fazhan zhong guojia shijiao* 公民社會與治理轉型 [*Civil Society and Governance Transition: Perspectives from Developing Countries*], ed. Mingzhen Liu 劉明珍 (Beijing: Zhongyang bianyi chubanshe 中央編譯出版社, 2008), 146. My translation. Regarding the struggle between the growing nongovernmental public sphere and the governmental intervention, see William T. Rowe's case study in Hankow.

[53] Zhenglai Deng and Yuejing Jing, "Constructing Civil Society in China" 建構中國的市民社會 ["Jiangou Zhongguo de Shimin Shehui"], in *Guojia yu shehui*, ed. Deng, 18.

non-registered gathering points (such as the house church) rely on the extent as to how non-governmental organizations are given autonomy and space for activities by the Party and the State, namely, enjoying freedom of association."[54]

It is in the very nature of a public theology to be concerned with the church's public engagement. In the Chinese context, this involvement highlights an important dimension to a local expression of a public faith. The acquisition of any degree of church autonomy, the church's relationship with the state, and a wide range of issues related to social life have become important subjects in reference to the development of public theology. In 2012 the Chinese government issued a document entitled "A Proposal on Encouraging and Regulating Religious Circles Engaging in Charitable Activities." It declared, "At present, religious circles shall be supported in the following areas to carry out nonprofit activities: disaster relief, assistance to the disabled, elders, nurseries, kindergartens, poverty alleviation, donation for education, health service, environmental protection, construction of public facilities and other legitimate charitable activities."[55]

Engagement in charity work by churches and other religious groups has been widely recognized by Chinese society and the government as well. This recognition provides more opportunities for these groups to participate in social life: "Although Chinese religions have limited access to social affairs, in terms of the number of their followers and organizational structure, religious groups are the largest social organizations in China; [they] are bound to make a contribution to the construction of China's civil society while striving for their own rights and interests, services for the lower classes of society, and desires for participation in social activities."[56] In this way, religion's social practice

---

54 Fuk-Tsang Ying, "Minjian zuzhi zhengce yu zhongguo jidujiao" 民間組織政策 與中國基督教 ["Policy on Nongovernmental Organizations and Christianity in China"], *Er shi yi shiji* 二十一世紀 [*Twenty-First Century*], no. 114, (2009): 33. My translation.

55 See "Guanyu guli he guifan zongjiaojie congshi gongyi cishan huodong de yijian," 關於鼓勵和規範宗教界從事公益慈善活動的意見 ["A Proposal on Encouraging and Regulating Religious Circles Engaging in Charitable Activities"], The Central People's Government of the People's Republic of China, accessed January 24, 2022, https://tinyurl.com/2a73v22w. My translation.

56 Shining Gao 高師寧, "Dangdai zhongguo zongjiao san yi" 當代中國宗教三議 ["Three Issues in Contemporary Chinese Religions"], *Daofeng jidujiao wenhua pinglun* 道風基督教文化評論 [*Logos and Pneuma: Chinese Journal of Theology*], no. 36 (2012): 33–34. My translation. In the case of Christianity and civil society, see Haibo Huang, "Approaching Civil Society under Construction: Protestant Churches in China in 2010, Responsibility and Introspection," in Paulos Z.

will have a positive impact on the development of the different social spheres in China.

The way in which *public* is understood in the Chinese intellectual tradition presents the government as a strong public sector. The contrast can be made with the absence of a strong social life and the relative lack of autonomy for religious organizations. Not surprisingly, this state of affairs raises particular issues of public theology. The Christian groups in China demand autonomy and legal status on the one hand and have a growing motivation for public engagement on the other. At the same time, there are some fundamentalist theologies that rely on the principles of spirituality and salvation and tend to be against the public, or, in Ken-pa Chin's terms, "refuse publicity."[57]

Lap-yan Kung has further suggested there is a kind of "anti-public public theology" among Chinese churches. Originally, a public theology aimed to go beyond personal mystical experience by exploring the significance of religious ideas for the existential problems of being human, but this theological voice now serves as merely one among many voices present in the public discourse. It is evident that an "anti-public public theology" wants to dominate society with its religious ideas "because it understands the notion of public not as the platform for common communication as (Jürgen) Habermas suggests but as one to be governed by Christian values."[58] In such a view, this sort of theology is designed to protect church interests and maintain the social status quo. It is inclined to be concerned more with moral issues (such as homosexuality) while tending to be conservative on political issues. According to Lap-yan Kung's observation, this theology is common among many churches in Hong Kong and reflects the mainstream position regarding the church's participation in society. There is no doubt these theological tendencies bring certain constraints to the development of a Chinese Christian public theology. According to Lap-yan Kung's understanding, a public theology should include a communicative and critical nature: "Public theology strives to express Christian values and ideas in non-Christian

Huang, ed., *Yearbook of Chinese Theology 2015* (Leiden: Brill, 2015), 217–48. He suggests that "the primary way for Christianity to make a contribution to China and its harmonious society is to move towards the civil society that is under construction," 218.

57   Chin, "Zhongguo jidujiao gonggong shenxue wenxuan xilie zongxu," xvi. My translation.

58   Lap-yan Kung, "Jidujiao youpai de gonggong shenxue: yige pipanxing de yuedu" 基督教右派的公共神學—個批判性的閱讀 ["Public Theology of Christian Right: A Critical Reading"], in *Zongjiao youpai* 宗教右派 [*Religious Right*], eds. Lo Wing-sang 羅永生 and Lap-yan Kung 龔立人 (Hong Kong: Hong Kong Christian Institute 香港基督徒學會 and Dirty Press, 2010), 56. My translation.

languages by the principle of public reason. Its purpose is not merely to convince other participants but also to be willing to accept criticism and make self-amendments as well."[59]

For the development of public theology in the Chinese context, both the sociopolitical context and the theological constraints are the indispensable elements and issues to be reckoned with. Basically, the discussion surrounding a Chinese Christian public theology is not simply concerned with the situation of Christianity in the Chinese context. It is also concerned with the significance of the Christian engagement with the extensive nature of Chinese public life. Furthermore, the study of various dimensions of public life in areas such as politics, the economy, and culture has always been the focus of attention in Chinese academia. What this means is that this Christian inquiry is placed alongside voices from Confucianism and other Chinese traditional thought, Marxism, and other Western schools of thought like liberalism. A Chinese Christian public theology is necessarily obliged to be in dialogue with these schools of thought on the issues of public life. One example of such, Ken-pa Chin argues, is the way in which the New Left and Christian theology should have more explicit dialogues on Chinese modernity. According to Ken-pa Chin, "In the discourse of Chinese modernity, the New Left ignores Christianity; in this case, the New Left is quite similar to liberalism, though the former pays more attention to 'nationality' while the latter is more concerned with 'individualism.' Neither of them hold that religion is capable of providing intellectual resources for Chinese modernity."[60]

It is Ken-pa Chin's belief that "it is impossible for the formation of Chinese modernity without an element of Christianity."[61] As for specific

---

[59]   Kung, "Jidujiao youpai de gonggong shenxue: yige pipanxing de yuedu," 56. My translation.

[60]   Ken-pa Chin, "Hanyu shenxue yu xinzuopai de yinni duihua" 漢語神學與新左派的隱匿對話 ["The Hidden Dialogue between Sino-Christian Theology and the New Left"], *Daofeng jidujiao wenhua pinglun* 道風基督教文化評論 [*Logos and Pneuma: Chinese Journal of Theology*], no. 41 (2014): 36–37. My translation. In the Chinese context, the New Left, represented by Hui Wang, refers to the rationalizing understanding of modernity and employs postcolonial criticism, with some attention being given to the issue of social justice.

[61]   Chin, "Hanyu shenxue yu xinzuopai de yinni duihua," 30. Another Chinese scholar, Xilin You 尤西林, particularly points out that "any ethnic group or individual, even with no understanding of Christianity, shall inevitably receive a modern temperament through modernization and have mental relations with Christianity." See Xilin You, "Xiandaixing yu zhongguo dalu dangdai hanyu shenxue de sixiangshi genyuan" 現代性與中國大陸當代漢語神學的思想史根源 ["Modernity and the Origin of History of Thoughts of Contemporary

social problems (such as the problem of inequality), Christianity should respond to them and be in dialogue with the likes of Marxism. In this regard, Ken-pa Chin has referred to Y. T. Wu (Yaozong Wu, 1890–1979) 吳耀宗 as an example: "Y. T. Wu conducted in-depth reflections on Christianity and Marxism and conducted dialogue between them. He supported a set of Christian tasks as follows: to deal with the two evils that plague humankind, namely, international inequality and social inequality. China and the rest of the world are in such historical context. . . . For Y. T. Wu, the problem is how to face the future of Christianity and the reality of China simultaneously."[62]

Social injustice is still a problem Christianity encounters in the Chinese-speaking world today. It is a problem studied by other disciplines (such as ethics, political science, law, and sociology). The critical issue becomes how to integrate the intellectual resources of Christianity with the resources of these disciplines for the sake of an effective Christian participation in public discourse.

REFLECTIONS

In this chapter, I have examined three issues. The first was the Chinese traditional understanding of the public, the second dealt with the tradition of public theology in China, and the third explored the tensions that the individual words *public* and *theological* engender and how they may be reconciled to one another in the ways in which a public theology plays out in the Chinese context. This literary survey has highlighted the problems of a governmental-dominated public sphere, issues around the identity of social organizations, and the theological character and political entanglement of Christian engagement in public life. I believe the way in which we deal with these problems will contribute to the development of public theology in the Chinese context as well as beyond.

In the Chinese tradition, despite the emergence of a nongovernmental public sphere and its struggle with governmental intervention, the meaning of *the public* is primarily dominated by the government. There remains a lack of any strong sense of diverse social spheres. The government is expected to be responsible for public affairs, and social (including religious) organizations are under governmental watch. Within this governing structure, religious affairs are absorbed into the framework of political governance. In the case of Christianity, some churches remain

---

Sino-Christian Theology in Mainland China"], *Daofeng jidujiao wenhua pinglun* 道風基督教文化評論 [*Logos and Pneuma: Chinese Journal of Theology*], no. 41 (2014): 63. My translation.

[62] Chin, "Hanyu shenxue yu xinzuopai de yinni duihua," 47. My translation.

indifferent to public affairs, with too much attention being paid to individuality; some others become too involved in social and political matters without any obvious Christian motivation or principle, and yet others attempt to dominate the public discourse in terms of Christian values but without an adequate communicative and critical sensitivity. There lies within this typology some important issues that must be addressed if a plausible public theology is to be constructed in and for the Chinese context.

First, from the perspective of both the intellectual tradition and socio-political realities in China, the development of public spheres in China is closely related to and constrained by the government and political affairs. During the twentieth century, Christianity in China had a tradition of participating in social transformation, economic development, national revolution, and reconstruction of the country. In this sense, apart from social concerns, political issues were seen as unavoidable when Christianity was involved in the public life of the country. When social spheres are not open enough for the engagement of social organizations, these organizations, including religious ones, must seemingly encounter strong political resistance while struggling for their more autonomous identity and greater social space. Their involvement in political and social matters drives them back to their own religious/theological perspectives. It is probable that religious groups then bear too much political and social burden—and, as a consequence, they might not demonstrate their particular religious character in public life. At the same time, we may notice that among Chinese churches, there is a tendency of rejecting the public. There are nevertheless some Chinese Christians, including scholars, who understand faith's "publicity" in terms of maintaining the integrity of Christian faith and its moral position. They do so in a way that does not foster a Christian participation in public life at large. As to the problem of how Christianity may go public, Chinese churches have an obvious preference of serving vulnerable groups.

Second, the relevance of theology to public life is a balance between a uniqueness expressed within a local context and a broader universality. In this regard, public theology should not be seen as an optional extra to a proper and authentic theology. This understanding of public theology has at least two meanings: first, Christians, particularly theologians, have the dual and inseparable vocation of serving the church and engaging with culture; second, since public theology serves people both inside and outside the church, Christianity in China must acknowledge that it remains a religion of a minority in a multireligious and multicultural context. It is important, as well as challenging, to make its unique theological voice able to attain general relevance in the public domain. This demanding task requires that a theological expression made in public must be of a finely balanced communicative nature. The public statement derived from Christian theology should be justifiable and persuasive, advocating without the tendency to become overbearing and dominating. The Christian engagement in public affairs inevitably requires communication, negotiation, and cooperation with people of different cultural, disciplinary, and intellectual backgrounds. In this process of communication, if Christians only place an emphasis on the commonalities between Christianity and other religious and cultural perspectives, then the distinctive and unique Christian understanding and positions have not been properly presented. Even though the Christian perspective is different from other perspectives, it must be expressed in a way that the public can understand and respect what is being said. Only then can it participate in the construction of public policies by negotiating with other perspectives.

This chapter considers that public theology as a whole is relevant to the Chinese context. The "publicness" of a public theology demonstrates the fullness of faith and theology toward public life. Its theological character derives from the will of God toward humanity and the world. It expects the involvement of Christian convictions in the public debate. In this sense, it is public theology that transforms and transmits the Christian message to the world effectively and broadly in specific contexts. To reconsider the nature of church and theology in such a socially and politically transitional era in China, public theology is an option appropriate to both church and academia.

4

FROM "CHRISTIANITY IN CHINA" TO "CHINESE CHRISTIANITY"

A Public Theological Approach to the "Chineseness" of Christianity

As described in the last chapter, public theology in China tends to be politically entangled while retaining its theological character. This chapter further explores this characteristic in a case study about Chinese Christianity recently exemplified by the movement for "sinification of Christianity."

As a religion from outside the country, Christianity in China has been in a struggle with Chinese culture, society, and politics. This can be demonstrated in various forms of efforts taken toward localization (*Bentu hua* 本土化), indigenization (*Bense hua* 本色化), and contextualization (*Chujing hua* 處境化) and examples such as the "Three-Self Patriotic Movement" and "sinification" (*Zhongguo hua* 中國化), on the one hand, and the quest for the "evangelization of China" and "Christianization of culture" on the other hand. Christian scholarship in contemporary China attempts to write theology in Chinese with reference to Chinese culture and Chinese lifestyle through an ongoing movement of "Sino-Christian theology."

According to Peter Tze Ming Ng's observation, "It was a shift of focus from 'Christianity in China,' which centered on the work of Western missionaries, to 'Chinese Christianity,' which gave a higher priority to the role of Chinese Christians."[1] Regarding this shift, Ng particularly ascribes to Daniel Bays's *A New History of Christianity in China*, which turns to

---

[1]   Peter Tze Ming Ng, "Chinese Christianity: A 'Global-Local' Perspective," in *Handbook of Global Contemporary Christianity: Themes and Development in Culture, Politics, and Society*, ed. Stephen Hunt (Leiden: Brill, 2015), 154.

"Chinese Christians in the joint Sino-foreign endeavor to establish and nurture the faith on Chinese soil."[2] This paradigm shift weighs the role of Chinese Christians from a historical perspective. Of course, there are various interpretations of Chinese Christianity from different perspectives and concerns.

Recently, in 2018, the China Christian Council (CCC) and the Three-Self (self-governance, self-support, self-propaganda) Patriotic Movement of the Protestant Churches (TSPM) in China issued the document titled "Five-Year Planning Outline for Advancing the Sinification of Christianity (2018–2022)" (hereafter, "Outline"). It highlights the transformation in both faith and social practice from Christianity in China to Chinese Christianity rooted in Chinese culture, aiming at a "contextual theological acceptance" and an "adaption to socialist society." This chapter examines the challenges of this transformation for Chinese Christians and critically explores the meaning of Chinese Christianity. Therefore, this chapter starts with a historical review of Chinese Christianity in its various forms and then studies the problems of the "sinification of Christianity" associated with the "Outline." The historical review and contemporary problems lead us to understand Chinese Christianity in terms of public responsibility and theological engagement in Chinese culture and society, contrasted with the "adaption" model.

A Journey of Searching for Chinese Christianity

As we saw in chapter 1, there is an "anti-Christian tradition" in Chinese history; as Paul A. Cohen suggests, "It is a fact of singular note that, in the nineteenth century, the vast majority of the educated classes of China either passively or actively rejected Christianity. Passively, they did so by remaining coldly indifferent to Christianity's message; the percentage of officials and literati who embraced the foreign religion was infinitesimally small."[3] This results from his studies of the missionary movement of 1860–1870 in China. Not only during the nineteenth century but for much of Christianity's time in China, there has been widespread indifference or hostility to the religion from not just the educated classes but government officials and ordinary people as well. That explains to some degree why there have been various struggles with Christianity for many Chinese, culturally, socially, and politically by way of localization,

---

[2]   Daniel H. Bays, *A New History of Christianity in China* (Chichester: Wiley-Blackwell, 2012), 1.

[3]   Paul A. Cohen, *China and Christianity: The Missionary Movement and the Growth of Chinese Antiforeignism 1860–1870* (Cambridge, MA: Harvard University Press, 1963), 3.

indigenization, contextualization, and accommodation ("Christianity with Chinese characteristics").

Matteo Ricci (1552–1610) and the strategies of other Jesuit missionaries in China are important in the development of Christianity in China through their emphasis on principles such as "accommodation and adaption to Chinese culture" and "openness to and tolerance of Chinese moral values and some ritual practices."[4] Consequently, the "Chinese Rites Controversy" during the seventeenth and eighteenth centuries centered on the relationship between Chinese ritual practices such as ancestor worship and Catholic belief. Although some Jesuits saw them as compatible, Dominicans and Franciscans disagreed. The debate reflects the tension and accommodation between Christianity and Chinese culture and traditions. The controversy resulted in the "forbidding Christianity" (*Jinjiao* 禁教) and "missionary cases" (*Jiaoan* 教案) occurring in missionaries in the eighteenth to nineteenth centuries.

Since the 1800s, there have been several struggles among localization, indigenization, and anti-Christianity. A typical controversial event is the Taiping Rebellion (1851–1864). Even though some argue it deviated from genuine Christian faith, and others describe it as a quasi-religious movement, some studies describe it as a localization of Christianity in China. Carl S. Kilcourse reinterprets the Taiping Rebellion as "a highly original, localized version of the Christian faith" and suggests that "Taiping's transformation of Christianity was encouraged by terms and themes from the Chinese Christian literature."[5] He demonstrates "how Confucian principles contributed to the Taiping's localization of Christianity but also how Taiping recreated Confucian doctrine via the beliefs of the imported religion."[6] Bays also claims "the formal Taiping articles of faith to be Christian enough," and "in behavioral terms, the Taiping appeared more akin to Chinese folk or popular religion." In particular, its leader, Xiuquan Hong 洪秀全 (1814–1864) showed a "bizarre display of concern for making the Bible conform to traditional Confucian 'family values,' leading to his insistence on rewriting the Bible in several places."[7]

The quest for localization and indigenization has coexisted with anti-Christianity throughout the long history of Christianity in China. There was a continuous anti-Christianity sentiment from the 1860s through the 1920s. Cohen explains, "Because Christianity was viewed as

4   Bays, *A New History of Christianity in China*, 21–22.
5   Carl S. Kilcourse, *Taiping Theology: The Localization of Christianity in China, 1843–64* (New York: Palgrave Macmillan, 2016), 4.
6   Kilcourse, *Taiping Theology*, 6.
7   Bays, *A New History of Christianity in China*, 54.

an external force that aspired to revolutionize the entire spiritual foundations of Chinese culture, a force moreover which was transmitted by outsiders and which after 1860 enjoyed outside political-military backing, antiforeignism naturally became an ingredient of overriding importance in all opposition to it."[8] This antiforeignism evolved in the Boxer Rebellion (*Yihetuan yundong* 義和團運動, 1899–1901), with its dramatic opposition to Christian missionaries and imperialists as well. In the 1920s, the anti-Christian movement became associated with the idea of science and anti-religion, which grew from the May Fourth Movement in 1919, when many missionaries were attacked and churches, Christian schools, and hospitals were destroyed.

Meanwhile, we also see the tendency both by missionaries and Chinese Christians to accommodate Christianity within Chinese culture. In 1865 British Protestant missionary James Hudson Taylor (1832–1905) founded the China Inland Mission (*Zhonghua neidihui* 中華內地會), which attempted to build up a characteristic local church with Chinese elements. He gave high praise to Chinese culture during his evangelicalism; for example, he was able to preach in different local Chinese dialects.

Besides the efforts of missionaries to localize and contextualize Christianity in China, many Chinese Christians started to found indigenous Chinese churches in different forms beginning in the late nineteenth century, including the Church of Christ in China (*Zhonghua jidu jiaohui* 中華基督教會).[9] As Bays observes, "Despite the accusation of losing their culture, and the perhaps well-meaning foreign missionary intention that they adopt 'Christian civilization,' Chinese Christians on the whole remained thoroughly steeped in their own culture."[10] Another movement of indigenization was established between 1919 and 1927 in response to the anti-Christian movement. The movement aimed to help Chinese churches to become more independent from foreign missionaries, more cross-denominational, and more integrated with Chinese culture and society.[11] The principles of self-government, self-support, and

---

8   Cohen, *China and Christianity*, 60.

9   See Tiangang Li 李天剛, "Ershi shiji zhongguo jidujiao bensehua he chujinghua de taolun," 二十世紀中國基督教本色化和處境化的討論 ["Discussion on Indigenization and Contextualization of Christianity in 20th Century China"], Sina, accessed January 22, 2022, https://tinyurl.com/ym9wpfbf.

10   Bays, *A New History of Christianity in China*, 78.

11   See Jonathan Tien-en Chao 趙天恩, *Zhongguo jiaohui bensehua yundong 1919–1927: jidu jiaohui dui xiandai zhongguo fan jidujiao yundong de huiying* 中國教會本色化運動 1919–1927: 基督教會對現代中國反基督教運動的回應 [*The Chinese Indigenous Church Movement, 1919–1927: A Protestant Response to the*

self-propagation proposed by the movement of indigenization were later adopted by the National Committee of Three-Self Patriotic Movement of the Protestant Churches in China. This movement, formed in 1954, aimed to build up an independent Chinese church. To some degree, it is right that "to assert that Christianity can belong to China is tantamount to acknowledging its long sought-after independence from foreign control and influence."[12]

THE PROBLEM RAISED BY "SINIFICATION OF CHRISTIANITY"

The wresting between Christianity and China and the efforts to make Christianity more "Chinese" has continued in various forms and with different focuses throughout Chinese history. A persistent issue seems to be the question of why Christianity should be adapted for China. In recent years, there has been a demand for the "sinification of Christianity" as part of the "sinification of religion" advanced by the Chinese government and implemented by patriotic religious associations. The movement calls for Christian adaptation to the political and cultural traditions of contemporary China and conscious integration of Christian ideas into a Chinese context. According to the "Five-Year Planning Outline for Advancing the Sinification of Christianity" (2018–2022) proposed by the TSPM and China Christian Council, there exists the demand for transformation from Christianity in China to Chinese Christianity:

> To set up a church that holds up the union of Christ and conservatism; a church that is faithful to biblical truth, rooted in Chinese culture, and able to contextualize its theology; a church that boldly takes on social responsibility and lives as a testament to life; a church that can connect devotees everywhere and make a unique contribution to the global church, bringing about the transformation from "Christianity in China" to "Chinese Christianity." The sinification of Christianity is an important goal for churches, running in accordance with the three principles, and is a necessary path for adapting to socialist society.[13]

Furthermore, Christian adaptation to socialist society is demonstrated particularly in the case of "core socialist values" such as patriotism,

---

Anti-Christian Movements in Modern China] (New Taipei: Olive Press 橄欖出版有限公司, 2019).

12 Anthony E. Clark, "Introduction: 'China's Christianity' and the Ideal of a Universal Church," in *China's Christianity: From Missionary to Indigenous Church*, ed. Anthony E. Clark (Leiden: Brill, 2017), 1.

13 See "Five-Year Planning Outline for Advancing the Sinification of Christianity (2018–2022)," China Law Translate, accessed January 4, 2019, https://tinyurl.com/muvyaf6j.

harmony, fraternity, democracy, freedom, equality, justice, and the rule of law. The Outline says:

> Sinification is the sustaining direction for religions in China, meaning that religious doctrines are to be guided by the core socialist values, are to promote excellent Chinese traditions, and are to cultivate ideas such as unity, progress, peace, and tolerance; extracting content from the doctrines that are conducive to social harmony, contemporary progress, health, and civility while preserving fundamental beliefs, core religious doctrine, and ritual systems, sinification aims to extract and interpret doctrines in ways that meet the requirements of China's contemporary development and progress and fit with exceptional Chinese traditional culture. The sinification of Christianity means preserving fundamental religious beliefs in accordance with the Bible, inheriting the traditions of the Catholic Church and the Protestant Reformation, anchoring faith and social practice in Chinese culture, practicing the core socialist values, preaching the gospel, testifying for Christ, and running churches in this context.[14]

Accordingly, the Tenth National Chinese Christian Conference issued an "Initiative on Actively Promoting and Practicing Socialist Core Values," which highlights "patriotism and love of church" and Christian "contribution to a good society of freedom, equality, justice, and the rule of law."[15] It is also emphasized in the "Outline" that sinification is the expectation of the Chinese government. It is understandable that both the Chinese government and Christian communities endeavor to adapt Christianity into their own context, through localization, indigenization, and now sinification developed from the basic principle of accommodation of religion to a socialist society. This principle was established after the legal approval of normal religious activities and the corresponding revival of religion since the 1980s.

Some discussions on the sinification of Christianity have raised several concerns and problems. The "Outline" proposes to "pull out content of the Bible that is consistent with the core socialist values" and "include the core socialist values as an important part of the phase of preaching,"[16] Fuk-tsang Ying 邢福增 points out that there may exist certain tensions between core socialist values and religion. As some local churches under the TSPM/CCC have edited and used their own biblical texts in terms of

---

[14] "Five-Year Planning Outline for Advancing the Sinification of Christianity (2018–2022)."

[15] Anonymous, "Tenth National Chinese Christian Conference issued an Initiative on Actively Promoting and Practicing Socialist Core Values," *Chinese Theological Review* 29 (2019): 4–5.

[16] See "Five-Year Planning Outline for Advancing the Sinification of Christianity (2018–2022)."

the Christian adaption to socialist core values, Fuk-tsang Ying reminds us that we must be attentive to the authority of biblical hermeneutics.[17] In other words, there has been a long history of biblical hermeneutics, and it remains a problem how church workers and believers are compatible with those core values while respecting the biblical tradition.

Although the core values are an important part of theological reconstruction in China with the purpose of "contextual theological acceptance," this further raises another concern about the motivation of theological development or the contextualization of Christianity in China: whether it is derived from Christian communities themselves or forced by the government or other outside entity. As we see, the movement of sinification of religion was initiated by the government and followed by religious circles. One challenge here is that, as Aiming Wang 王艾明 reminds us, "If it simply starts with sentiments of nationalism, fosters the nationalization of Christian faith and tradition, refines faith and tradition in terms of national ideology, and particularly confines the ultimate faith in the real political positions, 'sinification of Christianity' will become a non-Christian Chinese religion."[18]

One controversial example of sinification is that the TSPM/CCC-affiliated magazine *Tianfeng* 天風 has used "Chinese" fashions to demonstrate biblical figures such as Jesus and Mary on its cover: Jesus wears Chinese clothes, and Mary looks to be an ancient Chinese woman. It is helpful to introduce Christian narrative in a way that is more familiar to the Chinese, but it must be done without altering that narrative when relating it to the Chinese experience.[19]

Seen from a historical perspective, the theological contextualization in the 1920s and 1930s in China was influenced to some degree by

---

[17] See "Jidujiao lianghui dui jidujiao zhongguohua wunian jihua: xuezhe: xu liuyi shengjing quanshiquan wenti" 基督教兩會推基督教中國化五年計劃 學者: 需留意聖經詮釋權問題 ["Scholars' Response to TSPM/CCC's Five-Year Planning Outline for Advancing the Sinification of Christianity: The Problem of the Authority of Biblical Hermeneutics"], *Shidai luntan* 時代論壇 [*Christian Times*], May 30, 2018, https://tinyurl.com/d73fvkej.

[18] Aiming Wang, *Tizhi jiaohui yu ziyou jiaohui* 體制教會與自由教會 [*Magisterial Church and Free Church*] (Hong Kong: Center for the Study of Religion and Chinese Society, Chung Chi College, The Chinese University of Hong Kong 香港 中文大學崇基學院宗教與中國社會研究中心, 2017), 309. My translation.

[19] Anonymous, "Zhongguohua yi rumo: rujia jingdian jieshi shengjing renwu quan huicheng zhongguo guren" 中國化已入魔: 儒家經典解釋聖經人物全繪成中 國古人 ["The Distorted Sinification: Interpreting the Bible by Confucian Classics and Describing Biblical Figures as Ancient Chinese"], Association for the Defense of Human Rights and Religious Freedom, accessed May 19, 2020, https://tinyurl.com/5n85wjt7.

the theology of social gospel, with reference to the religious, social, and political conditions in China in that period. Even though the Chinese Christian Movement of Rural Construction in the period tended to be less religious to some degree,[20] we must keep in mind that the social involvement of the period should be understood in the theological framework of social gospel, while Chinese Christians were well aware of the challenges due to circumstances in China such as the New Culture movement, the anti-Christian movement, and the great turbulence of the period. With a belief that "the purpose of religion is to transform society," one leading Chinese theologian, Leichuan Wu (1870–1944) 吳雷川, argued that the premise of theological contextualization in China is the church's engagement in Chinese social transformation.[21]

"Chineseness" of Christianity: Publicly Responsible and Theologically Engaged

Under the umbrella of "sinification of Christianity," the "Outline" underscores the idea of Chinese Christianity rooted in Chinese culture and adapted to socialist society. With an understanding of the historical quest for Chinese Christianity in different forms and an analysis of contemporary sinification of Christianity, this section further critically examines the problems arising from this quest for Chinese Christianity.

With regard to the contextualization of Christianity in China, Peter Tze Ming Ng gives an account about this necessity and the concrete contextual elements in China: "Chinese Christians were living in very different situations, and they had to work out a great variety of ways to contextualize Christian faith in their own situations. Besides, Chinese Christians had their own local issues: they had to work to affirm and be assured that 'Chinese Christianity' did belong to the Chinese people, not foreigners; they had to assume, by all means, their responsibility of working out their own 'Three-self'; and the issues of maintaining both 'the Chinese and Christian identities' and of seeking proper 'Church-state relations.'"[22]

These local cultural, social, and political situations and issues demand that Chinese Christians respond by searching for an appropriate strategy to accommodate, survive, and even influence society to some extent from Christian perspectives. To that end, I employ the idea of public theology to study the issue of Chinese Christianity, and I am concerned with two

---

[20] See chapter 3.
[21] See Tiangang Li, "Ershi shiji zhongguo jidujiao bensehua he chujinghua de taolun."
[22] Ng, "Chinese Christianity: A 'Global-Local' Perspective," 156–57.

issues about Christian public engagement in China: to simultaneously be publicly responsible and theologically engaged. The demand of Christian adaption to core socialist values and engagement in public welfare and philanthropy in service of society proposed by the "Outline" can, in my view, be understood as "publicly responsible," though with some limitations. To be publicly responsible presents a lot of challenges for Chinese Christians.

First, when Christians are called to engage in public issues, they should respond to the issues in a constructive and appropriate way. The values listed in the core socialist values are, in principle, "public values" such as democracy, equality, freedom, and justice. Even though they are advocated by the government, I believe they are common and widely recognized by Chinese people. As Aiming Wang sees it, the vision of sinification of Christianity attempts to "include Christian faith into the national order, connecting to the rationalized norms of public issues."[23] It is important for Chinese Christians to understand the meaning of those values—not only in the Christian sense but also in a general sense, along with their implications for a society like China. Without this public awareness among Chinese Christians, it would not make sense for them to accommodate and practice those values. In this regard, both the church and academia have a burden to cultivate this public awareness. Michael R. Wagenman explains Abraham Kuyper's idea of *church* in terms of its public responsibility: "It is the role of the gathered church to disciple Christian believers to be responsible and engaged citizens."[24] The church is to equip and train Christians so that "they can take the light of Christ and the word of God into the world as they pursue their callings and vocations."[25] For the academic circles, as I suggested in chapter 2, Chinese Christian scholarship has the responsibility to articulate the relevance and significance of Christian faith and theology to public issues.[26]

Second, this understanding leads us to another concern with Chinese Christianity. When Chinese Christians (including a certain number of Christian scholars) respond to and cultivate the core values in China, the public has reasons to expect they do so in a Christian way. When we recognize the necessity of any accommodation by or contextualization of Christianity in a particular context, it should be determined by core Christian faith and its ecumenical spirit. The well-known public

---

[23] Wang, *Tizhi jiaohui yu ziyou jiaohui*, 308.
[24] Michael R. Wagenman, *Engaging the World with Abraham Kuyper* (Bellingham: Lexham Press, 2019), 74.
[25] Wagenman, *Engaging the World with Abraham Kuyper*, 73.
[26] See chapter 2.

theologian Jürgen Moltmann urges, "The specific contribution of theology cannot be to reiterate secular options. Taking the categories of what is in correspondence and harmony with God and what is in contradiction to him, it has to set the common good in the light of the kingdom of God and his righteousness and justice. That is to say the contribution of theology must be a theological contribution."[27] Furthermore, "Christian theology's justification of these ethical values must be specifically Christian and will inescapably be so. But the values nevertheless acquire general relevance in the social ethos of a society."[28]

The values to be advocated by Christian circles should increase their public concern, yet they should have the capacity to offer their own reflections on and constructions of the values from Christian traditions and resources. This task demands Christians to be genuinely biblically based and theologically motivated during the adaption and contextualization, without simply endorsing the governmental slogan or reiterating secular positions. Chinese Christians should have a drive to provide their own biblical and theological understanding of such values as fraternity, freedom, equality, justice, and democracy, ideas listed in the core socialist values, which may challenge the secular discourse on those ideas, informing them from a different perspective.

One helpful clarification is the three levels of values defined by the government: values for the national level include democracy and harmony, the societal level includes freedom, equality, justice, and rule of law, and the citizen level includes patriotism, trust, and fraternity. In most circumstances, the concrete meaning of the values is ambiguous and allows space for interpretation. On this point, Chinese Christians bear the responsibility to expound the meaning of the concepts from a Christian understanding. For instance, with regard to the idea of justice, Christianity has its own spiritual and moral justification regarding the rights of poor people, marginalized people, those who are disabled, and so on.[29] Christianity also has strong resources to connect the idea of justice with love and even develop the idea of justice within Christian love,[30] which seems to be overlooked by the governmental strategy and even by general academic discourse. In this sense, Chinese Christians should search for

---

[27] Jürgen Moltmann, *God for a Secular Society*, 256.

[28] Moltmann, *God for a Secular Society*, 256–57.

[29] See Duncan B. Forrester, *Christian Justice and Public Policy* (Cambridge: Cambridge University Press, 1997), and Wolterstorff, *Justice: Rights and Wrongs*.

[30] See Reinhold Niebuhr, *Love and Justice: Selections from the Shorter Writings of Reinhold Niebuhr*, ed. D. B. Robertson (Louisville: Westminster John Knox Press, 1992 [c1957]), and Nicholas Wolterstorff, *Justice in Love* (Grand Rapids: Eerdmans, 2011).

their own biblical and theological reasons to engage with Chinese society, either in moral discourse or social practice. This allows them to constructively become involved in the public discourse from their particular Christian perspective, which would contribute to Chinese Christianity in a very active manner. The "theological contribution" of public theology, as Moltmann proposes, can be applied to the issue of Chinese Christianity.

Andrew F. Walls suggests, "Christian faith is repeatedly coming into creative interaction with new cultures, with different systems of thought and different patterns of tradition . . . its profoundest expressions are often local and vernacular."[31] Within this process of Christianity-culture encounters, Chinese Christianity is one such typical example. As Bays claims, "Chinese Christianity is already one of the, if not the single, most interesting and important examples of inculturation of the essential doctrines and rituals of 'world Christianity' into an originally non-Christian cultural setting."[32] Being both "unique" and "contextual," Chinese Christianity is meant to be theologically engaged and publicly responsible within Chinese culture and society, thus going far beyond the adaption model. In this way, it will contribute to a particular form of Chinese Christianity in the contemporary world.

---

[31] Andrew F. Walls, *The Cross-Cultural Process in Chrstian History: Studies in the Transmission and Appropriation of Faith* (Maryknoll: Orbis Books, 2002), 30.

[32] Bays, *A New History of Christianity in China*, 205.

5

SHAPING PUBLIC THEOLOGY IN CHINA, WITH REFERENCE TO CIVIL RELIGION AND POLITICAL THEOLOGY

As seen in previous chapters, it is important to note that religions in China, Christianity in particular, wrestle with politics. Religions must confront politics if they want to engage with wider public life, as political factors are often involved in public affairs. In contemporary China, various versions emerge with regard to the role of religion in politics and society (i.e., civil religion, political theology, and public theology). These versions pit Confucianism and Christianity against the background of religious diversity in China. They are concerned with issues such as public morality, social solidarity, political legitimacy, and state sovereignty.

Within this context, Christian public theology in China must encounter the following factors: Confucianism proposed as either political Confucianism or a civil religion and the influence of Carl Schmitt's political theology, which some Christian political theologians address.

Inspired by Max L. Stackhouse's distinction among civil religion, political theology, and public theology, this chapter examines the types of civil religion and political theology (in its broad sense) as having some shared characteristics with Christian public theology to see their commonality and divergence and how they may distinguish and enrich each other and to explore the development and challenge of Christian public theology in China.

According to Stackhouse, a basic distinction among civil religion, political theology, and public theology is that civil religion is "bottom up," political theology "top-down," and public theology "from the center out." He explains this in detail:

> Civil religion is, essentially, as Rousseau in one way and Durheim and
> their American followers (like Feuerbach in Germany) in other ways

73

argued, a projection by a civic order of its experiences and values onto the cosmic order for the sake of social solidarity. It is, so to speak, society worshiping the image of itself, from the bottom up. A political theology, in this respect like a public theology, claims that its origins are essentially divine, from the top down as it were, and not simply a human construction of those seeking power.[1]

Regarding public theology, he continues:

> They work their way through the convictions of the people and the policies of the multiple institutions of civil society, where the people live and work and play, that make up the primary public realm. Indeed, it holds that these convictional commitment-incarnate multiple centers in the lives of the public are, together, the most decisive core of civilizational life. With the proper cultivation and development, they are refined as they work their way not from the bottom up, nor from the top down, but from the center out.[2]

The direction of "from the center out" locates the wider "public" reach of public theology, not limited to political life nor simply serving social solidarity or political legitimacy. In this way, public theology "focuses less on any saving faith than the ordering faith that helps constitute civil, political, and social life from a theological point of view."[3] In its impact on wider public life, public theology is "understandable both to those within its own religious tradition and to those outside it."[4]

CONFUCIANISM AS "POLITICAL CONFUCIANISM" AND AS CIVIL RELIGION

Due to the particular role Confucianism plays in Chinese tradition and society, there is still increasing interest in Confucianism in contemporary China, politically and socially, from which two major forms arise, namely political confucianism and civil religion. Political Confucianism, as defined by Qing Jiang 蔣慶, arose due to deep concern both with political legitimacy in China being backed up by Confucianism and Confucian's revival against the background of the increasing Christian influence in contemporary China. He attempts to restore Confucianism as core values of Chinese civilization in the overall social and political order in China so as to construct political institutions with Chinese cultural characteristics.

---

[1]   Max L. Stackhouse, "Civil Religion, Political Theology and Public Theology: What's the Difference?" *Political Theology* 5, no. 3 (2004): 291.

[2]   Stackhouse, "Civil Religion, Political Theology and Public Theology," 291.

[3]   Steven M. Tipton, "Public Theology," in *The Encyclopedia of Political and Religion*, (editor in chief) Robert Wuthnow (Washington, DC: Congressional Quarterly, 1998), 624.

[4]   Breitenberg, Jr., "What Is Public Theology?," 4.

In his *Confucian Constitutional Order*, according to Daniel A. Bell's explanation, it is Qing Jiang's belief that "an official embrace of Confucianism can save China from its moral and political predicament,"[5] and "the constitution should be explicitly based on sacred Confucian values."[6] For Qing Jiang, Confucianism plays a role in reconstructing social morality, national spirit, and political order, including the constitution, and contributing to a moral foundation of modernization in China to overcome problems such as lack of faith, decline of morality and traditional culture, and nihilism.[7]

Qing Jiang's version of political Confucianism raises problems not only regarding the political and social role of Confucianism but also regarding political legitimacy, public morality, and faith in general in contemporary China. It has undergone some debate and criticism. Here I include the criticism of Joseph Chan's 陳祖為 moderate perfectionism, Albert Hung-yee Chen's 陳弘毅 appeal to Fuguan Xu's (1904–1982) 徐復觀 idea of democracy, Ming Chen's 陳明 proposal of civil religion, and, finally, Jiantao Ren's 任劍濤 concern with civil religion and institution.

What we can read from Qing Jiang's Confucian constitutionalism, as Chinese political philosopher Joseph Chan suggests, is a sort of "extreme perfectionism" that insists "the state should adopt a comprehensive doctrine of the good life as the basis of the state constitution, legislation, and policy."[8] This comprehensive version is problematic for Chan as it is pluralistic in terms of the view of the good life among Chinese people, and the position that the legitimacy of political authority in China should be grounded on Confucianism is not fair to many other Chinese.

Joseph Chan offers an alternative version, moderate perfectionism, which Confucian values can accommodate: "Moderate perfectionism suggests that Confucian values concerning the good life (e.g., Confucian views concerning family, wisdom, or virtuous character) and concerning the social and political order (e.g., trust and trustworthiness, fairness, harmony, support for the poor, mutual care) can be invoked in a piecemeal manner during the legislative process."[9]

---

5   Daniel A. Bell, introduction to *A Confucian Constitutional Order: How China's Ancient Past Can Shape Its Political Culture*, by Qing Jiang, ed. Daniel A. Bell, trans. Edmund Ryden (Princeton: Princeton University Press, 2013), 1.

6   Bell, "Introduction," 21.

7   See Qing Jiang, *Wangdao zhengzhi yu rujiao xianzheng: weilai zhongguo zhengzhi fazhan de ruxue sikao* 王道政治與儒教憲政: 未來中國憲政政治發展的儒學思考 [*Kingcraft Politics and Confucian Constitutionalism: Confucian Thinking on Political Development for Future China*] (Guizhou: Yangming jingshe 陽明精舍, 2010).

8   Joseph Chan, "On the Legitimacy of Confucian Constitutionalism," in *A Confucian Constitutional Order*, by Jiang, 101.

9   Chan, "On the Legitimacy of Confucian Constitutionalism," 109.

With regard to the moral and political order in China, in contrast to Qing Jiang's proposal that "any society must have a comprehensive, systematic, leading orthodoxy to direct its values for the betterment of human life and social order,"[10] Joseph Chan's version of moderate perfectionism accommodates Confucian values (virtue, human ethical relations, and the principle of benevolent politics) in political life in a liberal and civil way. Under certain circumstances, Confucian values, including benevolence, can be incorporated in the legislative or policy process in an accessible way, even though citizens do not necessarily embrace the comprehensive doctrine of Confucianism and the state does not aim for "ideological politics," "providing Confucianism with a hegemonic ruling position" (in Jiang's view).[11]

Chinese legal scholar Albert Hung-yee Chen criticizes Qing Jiang and Xiaogang Kang's 康曉光 ideal of political Confucianism. For Albert Hung-yee Chen, Qing Jiang's ideal concerns the "Confucianization" of both state and society in China: Confucianism as national ideology and the establishment of Confucian association, along with the revival of social Confucianism, attempting to spread Confucian education in the wider society. Although Qing Jiang criticizes liberal democracy, he does not totally reject the introduction of some elements from Western democratic traditions to Confucian governance, such as institutional and procedural protections, even though he does not support the merging of Confucian political philosophy and Western liberal democracy advocated by contemporary neo-Confucianism.[12]

In a similar way, Xiaoguang Kang argues that Western democracy cannot contribute to the solution of the major problems such as corruption, poverty, and social injustice in contemporary China.[13] Instead, Xiaoguang Kang insists that Confucianism and benevolent rule should form the basis of Chinese society, including a government consisting of Confucian scholars. Albert Hung-yee Chen points out that both Qing Jiang and Xiaoguang Kang do not support the principles of equality and political neutrality, which agree with liberal democracy.[14] Albert Hung-yee Chen then turns to another Chinese Confucian scholar, Fuguan Xu, to

---

[10] Jiang, *A Confucian Constitutional Order*, 163.

[11] Chan, "On the Legitimacy of Confucian Constitutionalism," 103.

[12] See Albert Hung-yee Chen, "Zhengzhi ruxue yu minzhu" 政治儒學與民主 ["Political Confucianism and Democracy"], *Fazhi yu shehui fazhan* 法制與社會發展 [*Law and Social Development*], no. 2 (2009): 5.

[13] See Xiaogang Kang, *Renzheng: zhongguo zhengzhi fazhan de disantiao daolu* 仁政: 中國政治發展的第三條道路 [*Benevolent Rule: The Third Way of Political Development in China*] (Singapore: Global Publishing 八方文化創作室, 2005).

[14] See Chen, "Zhengzhi ruxue yu minzhu," 7–8.

advocate the compatibility and integration of Confucianism and liberal democracy; in Fuguan Xu, freedom, equality, and human rights are advanced in modernized Confucian philosophy.[15] In Albert Hung-yee Chen's judgment, "Confucian scholars should support free space in civil society and the improvement regarding the constitutional and legal protection of human rights so that Confucianism, together with other types of religious faith, can flourish in civil society."[16]

Whereas Joseph Chan and Albert Hung-yee Chen's criticisms of political Confucianism rely on the liberal principles of pluralism and democracy, Qing Jiang's idea of political Confucianism has also been criticized from the perspective of civil religion, which encourages social capital in Confucianism and prevents it from being a state religion. Ming Chen is one important figure who proposes Confucianism as a civil religion.[17] Ming Chen's concern with the role of Confucianism in contemporary China is directed at the needs of the societal level, in which Confucianism enables moral consensus and contributes to cultivation of civility and social organisms. In his view, this perspective sees the cultural resources in Confucianism as shaping cultural identity. Furthermore, Ming Chen understands the publicity of civil religion and suggests that "China is a country where civil religion is fully developed" in terms of the sacred figures bestowing sublime meanings to national life, sacred sites, sacred rites, and faith in the Confucian narratives.[18] For Ming Chen, this public approach to civil religion in China allows an integration of civil society, Chinese nationality, and Confucianism. Hence, Confucianism can help with the formation of social consensus, the construction of Chinese nationality, and the construction of political ideas and institutions deriving from its sacred elements, even in a growing social differentiation.[19] In this way, Confucianism as a civil religion can pave a path to Confucian revival.

---

[15] Chen, "Zhengzhi ruxue yu minzhu," 9.

[16] Chen, "Zhengzhi ruxue yu minzhu," 11. My translation.

[17] Ming Chen's proposal of Confucianism as civil religion is inspired by the debate on civil religion in America initiated by Robert Bellah, among others. See Ming Chen, "Rujiao zhi gongmin zongjiao shuo" 儒教之公民宗教說 ["On Confucianism as Civil Religion"], in Ming Chen, *Wenhua ruxue: sibian yu lunbian* 文化儒學: 思辨與論辯 [*Cultural Confucianism: Speculative and Deliberative*] (Chengdu: Sichuan renmin chubanshe 四川人民出版社, 2009), 41–51.

[18] Ming Chen, "Rujiao zhi gongmin zongjiao shuo," 46–47.

[19] Ming Chen, "Rujiao yanjiu xin sikao: gongmin zongjiao yu zhonghua minzu yishi jiangou" 儒教研究新思考:公民宗教與中華民族意識建構 ["A Reconsideration of Confucianism Studies: Civil Religion and the Construction of Chinese National Consciousness"], in *Yu Dunkang xiansheng bashi shouchen jinian ji* 余敦康先生八十壽辰紀念集 [*A Tribute to Mr. Yu Dunkang*], ed. Ming Chen (Bejing: Shoudu shifan daxue chubanshe 首都師範大學出版社, 2009]), 241–50.

It seems to me that although Ming Chen promotes Confucianism in wider Chinese life, from civil life to political life, he recognizes the fact of social and values pluralism in contemporary China. Another Chinese political philosopher, Jiantao Ren, criticizes the ideology of Confucianism as a state religion, which refers to Qing Jiang's idea. Jiantao Ren is sympathetic with the idea of civil religion while he is concerned with its aspect of political institution. He calls for a structural accommodation in Confucianism to ensure its role in modern society: commitment to individual values; virtue norms and institutional constraints to state power; and competitive resources among Confucianism, Buddhism, and Taoism for political development in China.[20] For this purpose, the function of civil religion must work along with liberal democracy so as to avoid intolerance.[21] He proposes a sort of "liberal civil religion," which appeals to both the values of social habits and sound political institutions, and rejects the combination of Confucianism and state power, thus creating space for a variety of religions in political life.[22]

Both Ming Chen and Jiantao Ren see Confucianism functioning as a religion when they use the term *civil religion*. It is different from its use in the Western context, at least in America, where civil religion is taken not as a form of religion in the traditional sense but as "differentiated from the church" and "elaborated and well-institutionalized,"[23] "neither sectarian nor in any special sense Christian,"[24] which provides "an understanding of the American experience in light of ultimate and universal reality."[25] What inspires Confucianism as a civil religion from the discourse on civil religion in America is its focus on social capital, moral consensus, and religious dimensions in regard to political life as well.

THE RECEPTION AND PROBLEMS OF CARL SCHMITT'S POLITICAL THEOLOGY IN CHINA

The use of *political theology* in China is ambiguous, especially in the case of Carl Schmitt, who defines it in terms of a theory of state, as he claims

---

[20]   See Jiantao Ren, "Gongming zongjiao yu zhengzhi zhidu: zuowei gongmin zong-jiao de rujiao jiangou zhi zhidu tiaojian) 公民宗教與政治制度: 作為公民宗教的儒教建構之制度條件 ["Civil Religion and Political Institution: Constitutional Conditions of Construction of Confucianism as Civil Religion"], *Tianjin shehui kexue* 天津社會科學 [*Tianjin Social Sciences*], no. 4 (2013): 48.

[21]   Ren, "Gongming zongjiao yu zhengzhi zhidu," 48.

[22]   Ren, "Gongming zongjiao yu zhengzhi zhidu," 49.

[23]   Robert N. Bellah, "Civil Religion in America," *Daedalus* 96, no. 1 (1967): 1.

[24]   Bellah, "Civil Religion in America," 8.

[25]   Bellah, "Civil Religion in America," 18.

that "all significant concepts of the modern theory of the state are secular-ized theological concepts."[26] As Scott Paeth explains, "Schmitt's political theology was not, contrary to the name, a theological conception of the role of Christianity in the political realm. It was not theological in any sense,"[27] and "it was a purely political account of the nature of sovereignty in politics."[28] However, the issues deriving from Schmitt's studies can be seen as an important reference for developing Christian political theology in China. According to Ryan Martinez Mitchell's survey, there has been a history of reception of Schmitt in China since 1929: "Schmitt's views have broadened the scope of discourse on issues such as the Communist Party's role in governance, judicial constitutionalism, economic systems, and China's place in international order."[29] In his view, Schmitt has been a source of critical perspectives on liberal constitutional democracy in Chinese public discourse.

Departing from this historical review, Xie Libin and Haiga Patapan provide a more recent study about "Schmitt fever" in contemporary China. They examine Schmittian concepts such as friend-enemy, sover-eignty, and decisionism, which are used by three groups of scholars: the China Path, New Left, and liberal schools of thought. In doing this, they show the limitations of socialist and Marxist thought in contemporary debates: "The political use of Schmitt's philosophical concepts such as the friend-enemy distinction, decisionism, and absolute sovereignty as ideational tools or weapons in political struggles allows us to understand the nature of political struggles taking place in contemporary China."[30] According to their evaluation, a general picture of Schmitt studies in China is that "defense of the current government; nostalgia for a revolu-tionary past; the promise of liberal individualism, democracy, and pros-perity; and an abiding fear of increasing inequality and injustice that is the consequence of such liberalism are some of the profound concerns revealed from our examination of Schmitt fever."[31]

---

26   Carl Schmitt, *Political Theology: Four Chapters on the Concept of Sovereignty*, trans. George Schwab (Chicago: University of Chicago Press, 2005), 89.
27   Scott Paeth. "Jürgen Moltmann and the New Political Theology," in *T&T Clark Handbook of Political Theology*, ed. Rubén Rosario Rodríguez (London: T&T Clark, 2020), 211.
28   Paeth. "Jürgen Moltmann and the New Political Theology," 211–12.
29   Ryan Martinez Mitchell, "Chinese Receptions of Carl Schmitt Since 1929," *Penn State Journal of Law and International Affairs* 8, no. 1 (2020): 181.
30   Xie Libin and Haiga Patapan, "Schmitt Fever: The Use and Abuse of Carl Schmitt in Contemporary China," *International Journal of Constitutional Law* 18, no. 1 (2020): 145.
31   Xie and Patapan, "Schmitt Fever," 146.

Sebastian Veg also contends that the new statists and sovereignists among Chinese legal scholars and critics of liberalism have strong connections with Schmitt: "The critique of the judicialization of society, the need to reaffirm sovereignty as the supreme political principle, and the imperative to repoliticize governance under the aegis of the Party."[32]

The use of *Schmitt* with the terms *political* and *political theology* among Chinese intellectuals reflects the problems arising from Chinese politics and intellectuals' responses to them. Some of them expect that the political theory of Schmitt can be adopted to criticize liberalism and strengthen the authority of state sovereignty,[33] even "intending to offer the Communist Party ideological justifications for its policies."[34] Ben Xu 徐賁 believes that neither the concept of sovereignty nor the decision in exceptionalism by state sovereignty in Schmitt is appropriate to apply to the Chinese context.[35] As Xie Libin and Haiga Patapan indicate, other liberals in China who endorse a liberal democratic order also question "the relevance of Schmitt's insights for China."[36]

I will not go into further detail about these debates on the implications of Schmitt in China, but I think this brief introduction can provide a background of public discourse to think about Christian political theology, particularly with regard to the task of the church in the face of state ideology and power.

THE RISE AND PROBLEMS OF CHRISTIAN POLITICAL THEOLOGY IN CHINA

The implication of Christian political theology in the Chinese context is primarily its stance of the "church's social criticism," as we will see in Jürgen Moltmann's definition of *political theology*. There is a tension between "servant" and "prophet" regarding the role of the church in China. Xinping Zhuo 卓新平 points out:

> There are two basic attitudes toward society by the church: one is a critical attitude, called the "prophet" tradition, and the other is a "serving" attitude, called the "servant" tradition. In the context of Chinese

---

[32] Sebastian Veg, "The Rise of China's Statist Intellectuals: Law, Sovereignty, and Repoliticization," *China Journal* 82, no. 1 (2019): 45.

[33] See Ben Xu, "Zhongguo bu xuyao zheyang de 'zhengzhi' yu 'jieduanlun'-'shimite re' he guojia zhuyi" 中國不需要這樣的 "政治" 與 "決斷論"—"施密特熱"和國家主義 ["China Does Not Need 'Politics' and 'Decisionism' as Such: 'The Fervor of Schmitt' and Nationalism"], *Er shi yi shiji* 二十一世紀 [*Twenty-first Century*], no. 94 (2006): 31.

[34] Mitchell, "Chinese Receptions of Carl Schmitt Since 1929," 244.

[35] Ben Xu, "Zhongguo bu xuyao zheyang de 'zhengzhi' yu 'jieduanlun,'" 31–32.

[36] Xie Libin and Haiga Patapan, "Schmitt Fever," 141.

society and culture, in retrospect of actual impact of Christianity in modern China, Chinese church prefers the latter, namely, conducting social service in the spirit of "servant" and as "salt and light" in Chinese society. . . . If the church exalts its "prophet" role with criticism of society in terms of Christian faith, doubtlessly it will result in the opposite reactions—bringing about social tension instead of a positive response from society.[37]

The church, after all, is a specific institution. Out of its beliefs come a specific understanding of and concern with society. In the meantime, this kind of social participation helps the church to strengthen its self-consciousness. As Baoping Kan 闞保平, a Chinese churchman, pointed out, "If a church cannot provide a vision for society, in other words, it can no longer serve as a prophet in society, then it is no longer a church but a social organization at best. . . . Theology must be related with social issues and deal with social problems because the church preaches the gospel in the society. And as an 'entity in the aspect of sociology,' church is an integral part of society."[38]

Therefore, even in the theological thought of a Chinese institutionalized church, besides the dominant theological discourse ("servant church"), we can see the emergence of an "alternative theological discourse" ("prophet church"), which approves "social care, social participation, and even a possible critique of the current social and political situation" of Christianity and the church.[39] According to the sketch made by Francis Yip, this kind of alternative discourse mainly displays two aspects: "First, carrying forward the prophetic tradition. Alternative discourse believes that when facing the social problems brought by China's opening up and reform, the church must fulfill its social responsibilities, be light and salt, and play its role as a prophet, including participating in society and responding to as well as criticizing social problems." Second is "pointing out and criticizing China's existing social evils, as well as social

37 Xinping Zhuo, "Zhongguo jiaohuiyu zhongguo shehui" 中國教會與中國社會 ["Chinese Church and Chinese Society"], in *Jidu zongjiao yu dangdai shehui* 基督宗教與當代社會 [*Christianity and Contemporary Society*], eds. Xinping Zhuo and Joseph Sayer 薩耶爾 (Beijing: Zongjiao wenhua chubanshe 宗教文化出版社, 2003), 249. My translation.

38 Baoping Kan, "Xiandaihua dui jiaohui de tiaozhan," 現代化對教會的挑戰 ["The Challenge of Modernization to the Church"], *Jinling shenxue zhi* 金陵神學志 [*Jinling Theological Journal*], no. 2 (1994): 29. My translation.

39 Francis Ching-wah Yip 葉菁華, *Xun zhen qiu quan: zhongguo shenxue yu zhengjiao chujing chutan* 尋真求全: 中國神學的政教處境初探 ["Chinese Theology in State-Church Context: A Preliminary Study"] (Hong Kong: Christian Study Center on Chinese Religion and Culture 基督教中國宗教文化研究社, 1997), 147. My translation.

and political self-absolutization and idolization in an implied manner, and suggesting that the church has no fear of political power but that it hold on to the truth and fulfill its prophetic duty."[40] This discourse highlights the relevance of the church to society, especially the church's critical stewardship:

> Its prophetic-critical-dialectical theological orientation, on the one hand, does not adopt the theology of consecration, like the dominant theological discourse does, which affirms and embraces social and political reality; however, it endeavors to point out the cultural origins of political disasters, for example, the Cultural Revolution. It criticizes (and encourages the church to criticize) the current social issues in China (including corruption, economic inequality, materialism, etc.), and even questions the attitude of the institutionalized church toward the government. On the other hand, it neither adopts the popular discourse, which insists the irrelevance of faith to social and political reality, nor takes an evasive theological attitude, which believes that the church only needs to focus on "spiritual" affairs. Instead, it emphasizes social responsibility of the church to participate in society and act as prophet.[41]

As an important theological spokesperson of the Chinese church, Bishop K. H. Ting (Guangxun Ding, 1915–2012) 丁光訓 also fully affirmed social responsibility of the church. In the early 1980s, he emphasized that the patriotism of the Chinese institutionalized church "should not praise everything in the country blindly but should be worked out prophetically and critically."[42] Philip and Janice Wickeri also pointed out, "He [Guangxun Ding] emphasizes the centrality of ethics and political participation in theological thinking. He believes that love is the most important attribute of God. This makes it possible and necessary for Christians to fight for love and justice in society."[43] The emphases on ethics and the social participation in his theological thought are also fully reflected in his response to the idea of liberation theology.

Seen as a form of political theology, liberation theology shows concern for poor people. In his "Inspiration from Liberation Theology, Pierre Teilhard de Chardin's Theology and Process Theology," Guangxun Ding points out that liberation theology emphasizes practice and engaging the world: "Exposing social darkness, colonialism, and imperialism with a

---

[40]   Yip, *Xun zhen qiu quan*, 165. My translation.

[41]   Yip, *Xun zhen qiu quan*, 183. My translation.

[42]   See Yip, *Xun zhen qiu quan*, 142. My translation.

[43]   Philip and Janice Wickeri, "Yiwei dui pushi shenxue you tuchu gongxian de zhongguo shenxuejia" 一位對普世神學有突出貢獻的中國神學家 ["A Chinese Theologian Making Great Contributions to Ecumenical Theology"], *Jinling shenxue zhi* 金陵神學志 [*Jinling Theological Journal*], no. 1 (2002): 7. My translation.

lot of facts is enlightening. We Chinese Christians appreciate that Latin Americans who believe in liberation theology want to change the social system. Also, we find it is very helpful that liberation theology advocates that theology should have more dialogue with social sciences and less with philosophy. It is very enlightening for us Chinese Christians reading the Bible that liberation theology points out that God shows partiality to the rich and the poor."[44] However, "ending poverty cannot be ignored in reforming society. But we should not idealize or absolutize the poor."[45] Here, Guangxun Ding advocated that the transition from poverty to wealth is a necessary process and that poor people cannot always be the "motivating force of the revolution." It is particularly instructive in contemporary China, which bears many social problems, especially inequality problems, to bring social and political issues (such as reflection on social justice and concern with poverty) into the view of Chinese Christian thinking and thus shape some Christian understandings in the Chinese context, for example, the Christian basic positions on poverty; theological interpretation of the poor; and the duty of the church, government, civil society, the rich, and the poor in ending poverty.

Because the Chinese government always has reservations and suspicions about the church's social and political participation, the influence of this "alternative" discourse has many restraints. However, we cannot ignore the prophetic tradition and the criticism of social problems in the Chinese church. In this regard, the distinction between political theology and political religion is particularly inspirational for Chinese Christianity, especially the critical reflection on and the criticism of political religion (politics making use of religion, religion becoming a vassal of politics) by new political theology. For this purpose, Moltmann's ideas on political theology are relevant to further our thinking on the development of Christian political theology in China.

Moltmann proposes a new political theology that is critically distinguished from Schmitt's use of political theology. Moltmann's political theology is primarily concerned with the role of the church "in the face of political religion or state ideology."[46] It is in this regard that Moltmann demands the necessity of church criticism. In his view, Schmitt's idea of political theology "was limited to the doctrine of sovereignty": "He saw as the determining subjects of political sovereignty only governments, revolutionary and counter-revolutionary movements. But the goal of

---

[44] Guangxun Ding, *Dingguangxun wenji* 丁光訓文集 [*Collected Works of Guangxun Ding*] (Nanjing: Yilin chubanshe 譯林出版社, 1998), 194. My translation.

[45] Ding, *Dingguangxun wenji*, 195. My translation.

[46] Moltmann, *God for a Secular Society*, 39.

his political theology was to fit religion into the confines of politics."[47] On the contrary, Moltmann defines theology as being "ideologically and socially critical"[48]: "The aim of the new political theology is to strip the magic from political and civil religion and to subject to criticism the state ideologies which are supposed to create unity at the cost of liberty. In this way, it places itself in the history of the impact of Christianity on politics, which means the desacralization of the state, the relativization of forms of political order, and the democratization of political decisions."[49]

This idea challenges the concept of religion's subjection to politics and takes the church's distance from state ideology, while positively engaging political justice, to assure the common good of humanity and creation in general. It does not privilege religion in political life: "This must be critical toward political religion and religious politics and affirmative toward the specific, practical commitment of Christians to 'justice, peace and the integrity of creation.'"[50]

Paeth understands Schmitt's political theology as untheological in a strict sense: "A God concept does emerge from his conception of power, violence, and the nature of the state."[51] He further explains the distinction between Moltmann's definition of political theology and Schmitt's in two ways: "first by making his approach explicitly and confessionally theological, and second by disregarding the Schmittian arguments in favor of authoritarianism and separation of friend from enemy and instead embracing principles of democratic equality and universal human rights."[52]

Where Moltmann criticizes Schmitt in terms of a new political theology, we find the limits of the Chinese reception of Schmitt, or "Schmitt fever," in China, the real task of the Chinese church and Christians in the face of political power, and thus the "self-understanding" and "self-discovery" of the church, as Francis Schüssler Fiorenza claims.[53] For Fiorenza, the church has a responsibility to develop a political theology in its "political and social ministry,"[54] and in so doing, the church affirms its own identity: "Political theology as integral to the Church's mission also entails

---

47 Moltmann, *God for a Secular Society*, 44.
48 Moltmann, *God for a Secular Society*, 49.
49 Moltmann, *God for a Secular Society*, 44.
50 Moltmann, *God for a Secular Society*, 43.
51 Paeth, "Jürgen Moltmann and the New Political Theology," 212–13.
52 Paeth, "Jürgen Moltmann and the New Political Theology," 213.
53 Francis Schüssler Fiorenza, *Foundational Theology: Jesus and the Church* (New York: Crossroad, 1992), 227.
54 Fiorenza, *Foundational Theology*, 227.

a self-discovery."[55] This task demonstrates itself in both social charity and political concern with justice: "In such a situation, the churches as religious institutions should have the role not only of sanctioning mutual assistance or of encouraging charity and almsgiving but also of examining critically and of reflecting consistently upon how political decisions affect the demands of justice in relation to human lives and interaction."[56] When a church engages in society and politics in a critical and appropriate way, it demonstrates its own distinctiveness, being the church itself.

In addition to the alternative theological discourse among the institutionalized Chinese church, the critical voice of political theology tends to be more independent, outstanding, and stronger in academia and noninstitutionalized (nonregistered) churches (so-called house churches). As early as 1992, Renlian Wei 隗仁蓮, a Chinese scholar, noticed the distinction between "political theology and political religion" in an afterword of a translated version of Moltmann's "Political Theology of the Cross." Renlian Wei pointed out that political religion is the religion of nation and state serving their rulers, becoming a vassal of politics. However, political theology "tries to get rid of this state of obedience." It should "follow desacralization (not taking the state as a sacred thing), relativization (political decree is relative), and democratization (politics should serve the welfare of the people)."[57]

In a seminar on "Political Theology and Contemporary China: In Dialogue with Jürgen Moltmann" in Beijing in 2014, one Chinese political and legal scholar, Quanxi Gao 高全喜, agreed that Moltmann's political theology provides a new transcendent perspective for the Chinese, which tends to be peaceful, just, and friendly. Political theology proposed by Moltmann distinguishes itself from Schmitt's political theology as the latter focuses on friend-enemy difference and dictatorship. Quanxi Gao suggests that this new political theology causes certain burdens for the political, social, and legal spheres in China.[58] What we can learn from

---

[55] Fiorenza, *Foundational Theology*, 228.

[56] Fiorenza, *Foundational Theology*, 233.

[57] Renlian Wei, "Shizijia de zhengzhi shenxue yihouji" 《十字架的政治神學》譯後記 ["Comments on Political Theology of the Cross"], *Jinling shenxue zhi* 金陵神學志 [*Jinling Theological Journal*], no. 2 (1992): 46. My translation. See Yip, *Xun zhen qiu quan*, 156–57.

[58] Quanxi Gao, "Fayan" 發言 [Speech], in "Zhengzhi shenxue yu dangdai zhongguo: Moltamann Beijing gaoji zhuanjia duitanhui shilu (I)" 政治神學與當代中國: 莫爾特曼北京國際專家對談會實錄一 ["Political Theology and Contemporary China: In Dialogue with Jürgen Moltmann (I)"], *Jidujiao wenhua xuekan* 基督教文化學刊 [*Journal for the Study of Christian Culture*], no. 34 (2015): 38.

Moltmann is the significance of transcendental foundation of justice so as to achieve political and legal justice and liberal constitutionalism.[59]

On the other hand, most of the nonregistered churches in China take the position of evangelical theology. Those churches are characterized by "focusing on evangelism and saving the soul, and their indifference, alienation, and passiveness while facing political issues"—in other words, their political stance—is "apolitical."[60] However, there is a rising urban church group following Calvinist teachings that shows their engagement with public and political issues such as constitutionalism, human rights, and church-state relations. Jie Yu 余傑 from a Chinese nonregistered church has clearly proposed the concept of "Christian public intellectuals" and their social and cultural mission. Jie Yu considered that there are four aspects for Chinese intellectuals to demonstrate their publicity: (1) artistic work in culture and literature; (2) developing new values, ethics, and cultural systems in Chinese communities; (3) responsibility for pushing for religious legislation, completing legal registration, and attaining the status of legal entity; and (4) fighting actively for the rights of the missionary in public and participating in social services, such as education and charity.[61] Therefore, in the situation of Chinese politics, the "apolitical" stance of the nonregistered churches becomes "irony": their criticism about the government's management policy toward religious affairs, their questioning the "institutionalized church" (in particular, its dominant theological discourse), and their efforts and struggle in pursuit of legalization determine that they cannot stay away from the framework of politics.

It appears to me that the ideas of new political theology supported by alternative theological discourse occurred to institutionalized churches, a group of Chinese intellectuals, and nonregistered churches who tend to reject the use of Schmitt in defense of state sovereignty and ideology.

---

[59]   Gao, "Fayan," 39.

[60]   Fenggang Yang 楊鳳崗, "Cong poti dao jieti: souwang jiaohui shijian yu zhongguo zhengjiao guanxi chuyi" 從破題到解題:守望教會事件與中國政教關係芻議 ["Comments on Shouwang Church Events and Church-State Relationship in China"], *The Chinese University of Hong Kong Center for Christian Studies and Christian Study Center on Chinese Religion and Culture Newsletter* 香港中文大學基督教研究中心暨基督教中國宗教文化研究社, no. 13–14 (2011): 3.

[61]   See Jie Yu余杰, "Zhongguo jiating jiaohui de gongkaihua ji jidutu gonggong zhishifenzi qunti de chuxian," 中國家庭教會的公開化及基督徒公共知識分子群體的出現 ["The Publicization of House Churches in China and the Emergence of Public Christian Intellectuals"], *The Chinese University of Hong Kong, The Center for Christian Studies and Christian Study Center on Chinese Religion & Culture Newsletter* 香港中文大學研究中心暨基督教中國宗教文化研究社通訊, no. 6 (2009): 9–11.

They are not in the same line with the dominant theological discourse among the Chinese institutionalized church—that is, "the institutionalized church should support the Party and the state, gain the approval of the people, and stay in harmony with socialism. Its keynote is the affirmation of all people, of secular life, and of history."[62]

CHRISTIAN PUBLIC THEOLOGY IN CHINA

Even though there are different approaches to political Confucianism, Confucianism as a civil religion, and Christian political theology with a critically transcendental perspective on justice, it appears to me that these versions demonstrate their public concern with social morality or moral cultivation of citizens, social capital, and political order and institutions. A group of them sees the need for social solidarity and attempt to provide certain core values deriving from Confucianism. Considering the fact of religious diversity in China, we have to show respect to the contribution of other religions, as Jiantao Ren already acknowledges, while we recognize the particular role of Confucianism with regard to social and political order in China. In the case of Christianity, it is still a minority religion in China, and tensions exist between Christian beliefs and traditional Chinese thought. As Christianity is still marginalized in Chinese societal and political life, it is far from realistic to believe that Christianity is becoming a resource of civil religion in China, but it is worth exploring Christian values and dynamics in the modernization of China. According to Fenggang Yang, as Christianity can provide important resources in China, including the transformation of traditional Chinese culture, the ideal of civil religion in China is based on Confucianism and Christianity as well.[63]

These values and dynamics contain the moral significance implied in the increasing Christian organizations, such as cultivation of civility and participation in civil society, on the one hand, and rich Christian studies since the 1980s offering a variety of resources touching on public issues at large, on the other.[64] Those values and dynamics cannot be ignored as some versions of political Confucianism do and should play a role in the construction of social consensus and core values. This raises the relevance of Christian theology to public issues in China. On this point, we refer to the idea of public theology, broadly understood, to describe

---

[62] Yip, *Xun zhen qiu quan*, 163–64. My translation.

[63] See Fenggang Yang, "Confucianism as Civil Religion," in *Confucianism, A Habit of Heart*, eds. Phliip J. Ivanhoe and Sungmoon Kim (Albany: State University of New York Press, 2015), 25–46.

[64] See chapter 6.

Christian moral and spiritual engagement with the wide public life, in Moltmann's terms, "the public relevance of theology": "It gets involved in the public affairs of society."[65] More specifically, "As public theology, Christian theology is relatively independent of the church, for it too has political, cultural, economic, and ecological mandates, parallel to the mandate of the church."[66]

As a general observation, this discipline of a public theology has become progressively more familiar to many Chinese Christians and scholars; they are currently studying and putting it into practice. It has been observed that Christians are becoming more public in their concerns. Christian studies are being undertaken from interdisciplinary perspectives and with a public concern.[67] The topic of public theology has been receiving increasing attention and debate among academia and the church as well within the Chinese context.[68]

However, there are issues a Christian theological engagement must consider to enter a public space beyond its immediate personal and ecclesial setting. Even though the development of Christian public theology in China goes beyond political issues, it encounters the distinctive nature of state intervention in economic and social life that is bound to a state ideology and pervades the whole of public life and discourse.[69] On this point, I have suggested this idea earlier: that the government and political issues play an important role in perceiving Christianity in public life in China.[70]

In addition to the struggle with political factors, public theology in China is also conditioned by the background of religious diversity and further demonstrated in interdisciplinary character. Regarding Christian theological engagement with various public issues in China, although it

---

65   Moltmann, *God for a Secular Society*, 1.

66   Moltmann, *God for a Secular Society*, 252.

67   See Zhibin Xie 謝志斌, "Cong 'duoxueke yanjiu' dao 'keji zhenghe': hanyu jidujiao yanjiu de kua xueke tezhi de huigu yu qianzhan" 從'多學科研究'到'科際整合':漢語基督教研究的跨-學科特質的回顧與前瞻 ["From 'Multidisciplinary Studies to 'Interdisciplinary Studies: An Overview and Prospect for 'Across Disciplines' Character of Sino-Christian Studies"], *Daofeng jidujiao wenhua pinglun* 道風基督教文化評論 [*Logos and Pneuma: Chinese Journal of Theology*], no. 41 (2014): 103–26.

68   See Pan-chiu Lai and Zhibin Xie, "Guest Editorial," *International Journal of Public Theology* Special Issue: "Public Theology in the Chinese Context" 13, no. 4 (2017): 375–76. This special issue of the journal presents a series of theological responses to the emerging social, economic, ecological, and political issues in the Chinese context.

69   See Lai and Xie, "Guest Editorial," 376.

70   See chapter 3.

refers from time to time to the ecumenical resources of a public theology, Christians should demonstrate an awareness of their own religious heritage. In this public discursive act, Christian voices will be received against a religiously pluralistic background in the Chinese context, which differs from the multicultural societies found in the West. The task of a Chinese public theology is to be understandable both within and outside its own tradition. It must be true to its religious traditions, but a suitably informed and endowed theology may make an effort to find ways of integrating some insights from those Indigenous Chinese traditions. As Pan-chiu Lai claims, there is wisdom regarding public affairs from various religions and even atheism, which Christians should take seriously in the construction of public theology. In the context of religious diversity in China, Christians need an openness to these religions or nonreligions to enrich the discourse of public theology.[71] In this way, Christian churches and theologies present distinctive and constructive perspectives in responding to the emerging social, political, economic, and ecological issues. Not only the Chinese context of rapid economic-social-political change but also radical religious diversity (where Christianity remains a minority) constitutes a serious challenge to the development of public theology in China.[72]

This openness also situates the interdisciplinary character of Christian public theology in China. In this regard, the Institute of Sino-Christian Studies has held various programs to promote the integration of Christian studies with other disciplines such as philosophy, political science, law, and sociology on some common issues such as human dignity, human rights, social justice, and religion-state relationship.[73] These programs inform that the impact of interdisciplinary studies on Christian theology in the Chinese context is twofold. On the one hand, it is often necessary to include Christian resources in studying some big questions to work together with other disciplines. On the other hand, interdisciplinary studies demonstrate the essence of Christian theology itself. To participate in interdisciplinary studies effectively, Christian scholars are expected to

---

71 See Lai, *Gonggong guangchang shang de hanyu shenxue*, 334.
72 This paragraph is partly adapted from Lai and Xie, "Guest Editorial," 378–79.
73 Some outcomes of these programs are Zhibin Xie (guest editor), special issue on "Dignity, Morality and Rights: Interdisciplinary Studies," *Daofeng jidujiao wenhua pinglun*道風基督教文化評論 [*Logos and Pneuma: Chinese Journal of Theology*], no. 49A (2018); Joshua Mauldin and Zhibin Xie (guest editors, special issue on "Human Dignity, Religion, and Rights in Contemporary China," *Political Theology* 20, no. 5–6 (2019); and Zhibin Xie, Pauline Kollontai, and Sebastian Kim, eds., *Human Dignity, Human Rights, and Social Justice: A Chinese Interdisciplinary Dialogue with Global Perspective* (Singapore: Springer Singapore, 2020).

be sensitive to other disciplines, which examine issues (such as freedom and rights) in a different way from Christian perspectives, those issues becoming public issues at the same time. It thus demonstrates the relatedness of Christian studies to public life and its fundamental issues. Christian studies may take part in public discourse and show their theological relevance and distinctiveness. To some extent, Christian theology can be regarded as "reflecting on *all* things in relation to God."[74] And those things can be studied by other disciplines and "interpreted in nontheological terms"[75] as well. Thus, "today's interdisciplinary and multidisciplinary intellectual circumstances present Christian theologians with opportunities for a more collaborative manner of envisioning God, the world, and ourselves."[76] To that end, the development of pubic theology in China is demonstrated in its interdisciplinary character underlined by a particular Christian worldview.

The kind of public theology construed in the above way and developed mainly from academia demonstrates itself as dialogical, cooperative, and constructive as it encourages interreligious and interdisciplinary approaches concerning public issues. This public theology obviously distinguishes itself from public theology proposed by Chinese church circles. "An Outline of Christian Public Theology in China," presented by Zhiyong Wang 王志勇, a Chinese churchman, proposes the main elements of public theology, including abiding with the Bible, emphasizing politics and laws, advocating freedom and justice, and affirming transformation of society and culture.[77] His public theology—I would call it *confessing public theology*—does not create the space to strictly distinguish itself from political theology nor extend itself to wider society as it focuses too much on political matters and lacks motive to work along with other disciplines on the common issues.

CONCLUDING REMARKS

In contemporary China, the three versions of civil religion, public theology, and political theology have been the major resources to think about how religion (Christianity in particular) and theology relate to and

---

[74] Douglas F. Ottati, "A Collaborative Manner of Theological Reflection," in *Theology as Interdisciplinary Inquiry: Learning from the Natural and Human Sciences*, eds. Robin W. Lovin and Joshua Mauldin (Grand Rapids: Eerdmans, 2017), 136.

[75] Ottati, "A Collaborative Manner of Theological Reflection," 137.

[76] Ottati, "A Collaborative Manner of Theological Reflection," 136–37.

[77] Zhiyong Wang, "Zhongguo jidujiao gonggong shenxue gangyao" 中國基督教公共神學綱要 ["An Outline of Christian Public Theology in China"], Zhongguo gaigezong shenxue 中國改革宗神學 [*China Reformed Theology*], accessed January 30, 2022, https://tinyurl.com/37d6nfzs.

interact with Chinese society and politics. In a religiously diverse context in China, these three versions must recognize other religions' relevance and potential contributions to civil life and political life. What is common among them is that they wrestle with political affairs in distinctive yet probably overlapping ways.

Although the new political theology has an obligation to be critical both of political religion and of Schmitt's use in China, it may be sympathetic with the camp of Albert Hung-yee Chen's support of liberal democracy and Jiantao Ren's concern with the institutional aspect of civil religion in their criticism of political Confucianism. Furthermore, when Christian political theology is concerned with political justice, with criticism of political religion and religious politics, it must be aware of both political legitimacy and political order as concentrations of political Confucianism, on the one hand, and of the Christian worldview and wider public life that root Christian public theology, on the other. To fully understand the church's self-discovery of social and political ministry, as Fiorenza proposes, the public role of the church and Christians in civil and public life, from which public theology derives, is a good companion to political theology, which points to the church's political role beyond its work of social charity.

As Paeth rightly notes, "Moltmann has increasingly taken to referring to his political theology by the moniker of 'public theology.'"[78] For Moltmann, theology is essentially a function of the kingdom of God. "Kingdom-of-God theology is *public theology*, which participates in the *res publica* of society, and 'interferes' critically and prophetically, because it sees public affairs in the perspective of God's coming kingdom. . . . As *public theology*, Christian theology is relatively independent of the church, for it too has political, cultural, economic and ecological mandates, parallel to the mandate of the church."[79] Moltmann "insists that the political character of Christian theology remains an inescapable aspect of its identity"[80] in the face of political religion and religious politics, and he develops this further into a wider vision of kingdom-of-God theology as public theology. Ted Peters further strengthens this idea by stating that "the public theologian will begin with a normative political vision and draw middle axioms that could guide and direct the course of human social affairs."[81] For him, "a constructive political theology" should work within "a more comprehensive public theology with a commitment to

---

[78] Paeth, "Jürgen Moltmann and the New Political Theology," 222.

[79] Moltmann, *God for a Secular Society*, 252.

[80] Paeth, "Jürgen Moltmann and the New Political Theology," 222.

[81] Ted Peters, "Public Theology: Its Pastoral, Apologetic, Scientific, Political, and Prophetic Tasks," *International Journal of Public Theology* 12, no. 2 (2018): 169.

common good," both of which direct to "the dimension of civil order within human community."[82]

What inspires a Chinese political theology is that when Chinese churches and Christians have their own distinctive and independent responsibility toward political issues, they are invited to perceive their Christian holistic view of human beings and the world, in other words, public life in a general sense. Furthermore, Christian engagement with public issues such as cultural, economic, and ecological issues are inter-twined with political issues. Christian public engagement should be aware of its prophetic and critical mission; as John W. de Gruchy reminds us, "Prophetic witness always remains a necessity in public life."[83]

Engaging in public issues, Christians and others are also called to work together with other cultural and religious resources in China such as Confucianism, and the resources from other disciplines, such as philosophy, political science, law, and sociology to explore the just social, religious, and political structure constructively. In this sense, a Chinese public theology tends to be politically critical and publicly responsible indeed.

---

[82] Peters, "Public Theology," 170.
[83] John W. de Gruchy, "From Political to Public Theologies: The Role of Theology in Public Life in South Africa," in *Public Theology for the 21st Century: Essays in Honour of Duncan B. Forrester*, eds. William F. Storrar and Andrew R. Morton (London: T&T Clark, 2004), 59.

PART II

CONSTRUCTIVE APPROACH: CHRISTIANITY AND PUBLIC ISSUES IN CHINA

6

CHRISTIAN ETHICS AND PUBLIC
ISSUES IN CHINA

With Reflection on Christian Love

In part I, I have explored the methodology of Christian public theology in China, paying special attention to its background of religious diversity and presenting its characteristics as publicly responsible, theologically engaged, and politically critical. Moving from this methodological approach to public theology in China, in this part, I further study the public issues in China theologically and ethically to demonstrate Christian constructive engagement in public discourse in the Chinese context.

Christian ethics, including their public reach, represent one important component of Christian theological studies. Based on the content and achievements in this branch of study, it has become a rich part of Sino-Christian studies since the 1980s. Study of Sino-Christian ethics mainly focuses on two subjects: introducing basic Western Christian ethical thought and concepts related to it[1] and studying the relationship between Christian ethics and Chinese culture and social

---

[1] A lot of works in the field of Christian ethics from Western languages have been translated and published in Chinese, such as Petrus Abaelardus's *Ethic*, Reinhold Niebuhr's *An Interpretation of Christian Ethics* and *The Nature and Destiny of Man*, Dietrich Bonhoeffer's *Ethics*, and Karl-Herinz Peschke's *Christliche Ethik*, etc. There are numerous works on the theory of Christian ethics by Sino-Christian scholars, for example, Lap-yan Kung 龔立人, *Renji shehui de jianli: jidujiao shehui lunli* 人際社會的建立:基督教社會倫理 [*Building Up Interpersonal Society: Christian Social Ethics*] (Hong Kong: Hong Kong Christian Institute 香港基督徒學會, 1999); Kai-man Kwan 關啟文, *Jidujiao lunli yu ziyou shisu shehui* 基督教倫理與自由世俗社會 [*Christian Ethics and Liberal Secular Society*] (Hong Kong: Tiendao 天道書樓, 2007); and Shigong Liu 劉時工, *Ai yu zhengyi: nibuer jidujiao yanjiu* 愛與正義: 尼布爾基督教倫理思想研究 [*Love and Justice: A Study in*

95

context. This chapter investigates the important achievements of study in the latter area. Through this investigation, this chapter probes the methodological approach behind studies of Christian ethics in Sino-Christian theology. Within this overall goal, it particularly concerns itself with the public significance of Christian values within specific societal circumstances in China.

This chapter contains two large sections. The first examines the main content of studies of Sino-Christian ethics since the 1980s. It is further divided into two parts, the first of which studies and contrasts fundamental ethical concepts such as love and human nature with related ideas from traditional Chinese thought. The second part focuses on practice and specific social circumstances, including Christian perspectives on Chinese Christians' moral lives as well as public issues in areas such as ecology, economics, politics, global issues, and moral education on both the local and global scale.

The second section draws on the achievements of relevant Christian ethical scholarship. By referring to Chinese intellectual resources, Chinese people's life experiences, and current moral questions in society, it revisits questions related to Sino-Christian theology's context and seeks again to explain the possibility of reinterpreting some Christian doctrines, including love. This study uses real and contextual approaches of Christian ethical studies to operate within a Chinese cultural and social context. It also examines its specific and immediate conditions and develops discourse on Christian ethical thought.

CHRISTIAN ETHICS AND "ETHICALIZATION OF SINO-CHRISTIANITY"

Studies concerning Christianity's ethical perspectives and thought, as well as its relationship with Chinese culture and social circumstances, always attract obvious concern within Sino-Christian studies and can even be considered the crucial point in understanding the development of Christianity in China. Its importance becomes more and more obvious. Huilin Yang 楊慧林 points out, "The 'ethicalization' or 'moralization' of behavioral standards is from beginning to end the primary orientation of Sino-Christianity."[2] He uses the concept of

Reinhold Niebuhr's Christian Ethics] (Beijing: Zhongguo shehui kexue chubanshe 中國社會科學出版社, 2004).

2   Huilin Yang, "'Lunlihua'hanyu jidujiao yu jidujiao de lunli yiyi-jidujiiao lunli zai zhongguo wenhua yujing zhong de kenengxing jiqi nanti" "倫理化"的漢語基督教與基督教的倫理意義—基督教倫理在中國文化語境中的可能性及其難題 ["Ethicalization of Sino-Christianity and Ethical Significance of Christianity: The

"ethicalization of Sino-Christianity'" as a framework to overview the historical distinctive characteristics and current significance of development regarding Christianity in China. He also analyzes the challenges that this idea may encounter in a Chinese cultural context as well as the ethical resources Christianity provides as contributions to Sino-Christianity.

This characteristic, ethicalization of Chinese Christianity, is carried out in specific Christian doctrines such as Christology. Yongtao Chen 陳永濤, in "Ethical Christology: A Possible Direction of the Chinese Church's Theological Construction of Christology," tries to understand Christology within current Chinese conditions and expounds on the possibility of constructing an ethical or practical Chinese Christology. He points out that this kind of ethical Christology is practical, but it is not the rational type of Christology of Western tradition. He believes this kind of ethical Christology's significance lies in its demand that Christians not discuss Christ but imitate Christ and thus produce for Chinese society and the church innumerable noble Christians.[3] Moreover, Chinese Christianity's ethical orientation is embodied in its relationship with Chinese culture and specific cultural context and practices.

THEORY: CHRISTIAN ETHICS AND CHINESE CULTURE

The relevance of the intellectual resources accumulated by Sino-Christian studies to the Chinese context is mainly focused on examining the relationship among God, human nature, and the world, as well as its unique understanding of love as a moral law. These ideas have some differences with traditional Chinese thought, but dialogue and communication about them have already accumulated quite a few results and have even formed one key aspect of the content of Sino-Christian studies. In studies concerning the relationship between Christianity and Chinese culture, the relations between Christian ethics and Confucian ethics hold a prominent

---

Possibility and Difficulties of Christian Ethics in the Chinese Cultural Context"], *Jidujiao wenhua xuekan* 基督教文化學刊 [*Journal for the Study of Christian Culture*], no. 8 (2002): 265.

3   Yongtao Chen, "Lunli de jidulun: zhongguo jiaoshui shenxue sixiang jianshe zhong jidulun sikao de yige keneng de fangxiang" 倫理的基督論: 中國教會神學思想建設中基督論思考一個可能的方向 ["Ethical Christology: A Possible Direction of the Chinese Church's Theological Construction of Christology"], in *Xinyang zhijian de zhongyao xiangyu* 信仰之間的重要相遇 [*Faith Encounters: Religion and Cultural Exchanges between Asian and the West—Proceedings from an International Conference*], eds. Xinping Zhuo 卓新平, Judith Berling 伯玲, and Philip Wickeri 魏克利 (Beijing: Zongjiao wenhua chubanshe 宗教文化出版社, 2005], 165–96.

position. This has also become a crucial aspect of Sino-Christian ethical study.[4] In Dunhua Zhao 趙敦華's opinion, "Systematically comparing the similarities and differences of Christianity and Confucianism will at a minimum involve six levels: divine realities, absolute commandments, ethical motivation, moral responsibilities, hierarchy of virtues, and practical channels."[5] Below, I use the concepts of love and human nature to sort out the results of studies of Sino-Christian ethics.

1. The Concept of Love

Love holds a remarkable position within Christian belief and ethics. No other religion places love and God in the same position the way Christianity does: "Christianity is a religion of love, and Christian ethics is ethics of love."[6] Sino-Christian scholars have demonstrated deep interest in and concern for this concept.

Ping-cheung Lo 羅秉祥, in "Love and Imitation—A Dialogical and Hermeneutical Theological Ethics," tries to establish a kind of model for the study of the Christian concept of love from a Sino-Christian

---

[4]   Some representative works are as follows: Xiaofeng Liu 劉小楓, ed., *Dao yu yan: huaxia wenhua yu jidu wenhua xiangyu* "道"與"言":華夏文化與基督文化相遇 [*Logos and Word: Encounters between Chinese Culture and Christian Culture*] (Shanghai: Shanlian shudian 三聯書店, 1996); Guanghu He 何光滬 and Zhiwei Xu 許志偉, eds., *Ru shi dao yu jidujiao* 儒釋道與基督教 [*Confucianism, Buddhism, Taoism, and Christianity*] (Beijing: Shehui kexue wenxian chubanshe 社會科學文獻出版社, 2001); Mikka Ruokanen 羅明嘉 and Paulos Huang 黃保羅, eds., *Jidujiao yu zhongguo wenhua* 基督教與中國文化 [*Christianity and Chinese Culture*] (Beijing: Zhongguo shehui kexue chubanshe 中國社會科學出版社, 2004); Pan-chiu Lai 賴品超 and Peter K. H. Lee 李景雄, eds., *Ru ye duihua xin licheng* 儒耶對話新里程 [*A New Stage in Christian-Confucian Dialogue*] (Center for the Study of Religion and Chinese Society, Chung Chi College, The Chinese University of Hong Kong 香港中文大學崇基學院宗教與中國社會研究中心, 2001); and Pan-chiu Lai 賴品超, ed., *Jidu zongjiao yu rujia duituan shengming yu lunli* 基督宗教與儒家對談生命與倫理 [*Christian-Confucian Dialogue on Life and Ethics*] (Center for the Study of Religion and Chinese Society, Chung Chi College, The Chinese University of Hong Kong, 香港中文大學崇基學院宗教與中國社會研究中心, 2002).

[5]   Dunhua Zhao, "Jidujiao lunli yu rujia lunli de 'jiuhua' yu 'xinti'" 基督教倫理與儒家倫理的"舊話"與"新題" ["The Old and New Themes in Christian Ethics and Confucian Ethics"], *Jidujiao wenhua xuekan* 基督教文化學刊 [*Journal for the Study of Christian Culture*], no. 9 (2003): 289.

[6]   Ping-cheung Lo, "Ai yu xiaofa: duihua yu quanshixing de shenxue lunli xue" 愛與效法—對話與詮釋性的神學倫理學 ["Love and Imitation: A Dialogical and Hermeneutical Theological Ethics"], *Zhongguo shenxue yanjiuyuan qikan* 中國神學研究院期刊 [*Journal of China Theology Graduate School*], no. 35 (2003): 69. My translation.

perspective and to construct a paradigm of theological ethics distinct from descriptive Biblical ethics: "Theological ethics also must be dialogue-oriented and hermeneutical; in terms of methods, it should try to combine Christian moral vision and contemporary moral circumstances into a coherent point of view."[7] Thinking about specific Chinese moral circumstances, he tries to use neo-Confucianist thinker Zhu Xi 朱熹's study of benevolence (*ren* 仁) and Long Shu's (Nāgārjunabodhisattva) 龍樹 core idea of mercy within Mahayana Buddhism as examples, clarifying their similarities and differences with the Christian idea of love. This is a way of taking basic points within three kinds of religions and philosophies as the core of dialogue and interpretation of theological ethics. Furthermore, he also particularly points out, "At the same time, Christian theological ethics emphasizes that discontinuities exist between believers' love for other people and the ultimate reality's love for people, but these kinds of discontinuities do not exist in the ideas of benevolence and mercy as love."[8] From this, he questions the "Agape-Ren synthesis."[9]

Even more Sino-Christian scholars focus on a comparative study of Christianity's concept of love and traditional Chinese thought, especially the idea of compassion. Xinzhong Yao's 姚新中 monograph *Confucianism and Christianity—A Comparative Study of Jen and Agape* points out the difference between benevolence and agape, the Confucian tradition and the Christian tradition's respective core concepts and fundamental doctrines. Through a deep comparative analysis, the author arrives at an understanding of the similarities and differences of human benevolence and divine love—the discrepancies and unity between benevolence and agape along with their respective exclusive and inclusive characteristics. This kind of comparative study aims at revealing the deep layers of meaning concealed behind these two traditions and seeking out these two cultures' goals for human life and their ultimate values and deepest concerns.[10]

---

7   Lo, "Ai yu xiaofa," 68. My translation.

8   Lo, "Ai yu xiaofa," 68. My translation.

9   See also Ping-cheung Lo, "*Ren* as Fundamental Motif and the Promise and Problem of a Contextual Theology of an Agape-Ren Synthesis," in *Christianity and Chinese Culture: Proceedings of A Sino-Nordic Conference on Chinese Contextual Theology*, eds. Miikka Ruokanen and Paulos Huang (Grand Rapids: Eerdmans, 2010), 102–19.

10 Xinzhong Yao 姚新中, *Rujia yu jidujiao: ren yu ai de bijiao yanjiu* 儒家與基督教: 仁與愛的比較研究 [*Confucianism and Christianity: A Comparative Study of Jen and Agape*], trans. Yanxia Zhao 趙艷霞 (Beijing: Zhongguo shehui kexue chubanshe 中國社會科學出版社, 2002).

This type of comparison of specific ethical concepts can be implemented with respect to the thought of two related ancient thinkers. One example is Kin-ming Au's 歐建銘 "Love and *Ren*: A Comparative Study of Paul Tillich and Zhu Xi's Religious Ethical Principles." From an ontological perspective, a vertical perspective (directly addressing that which transcends the subject), and a horizontal perspective (relationships between people and the relationship of people to nature), he compares the two schools of thought, addressing the similarities and differences of the concepts of "love and *ren*." He believes "*ren* and love are both principles, and both propel us toward the reality of uniting the whole human race." However, "along with the differences between Confucianism's heaven and Christianity's God, Zhu Xi's benevolence takes humans to be the center, but Paul Tillich's love takes God to be the center."[11] Nonetheless, the important point is, "*Ren* and love both function as uniting forces."[12] Thus, through them, people can overcome humanity's isolated conditions.

2. The Question of Human Nature

The question of human nature is another important topic of communication and dialogue between Christian ethics and traditional Chinese thought and culture. Comparisons between Confucianism and Christianity have begun to develop in several aspects related to this issue: "From the outset, discussion of 'human nature' is the core of Chinese moral philosophy."[13] Yet Christianity's unique understanding of humanity is an outstanding focal point in its relations with other cultures: "Concerning Christianity in China and its areas that are not harmonious with the Confucianism that makes up mainstream Chinese culture, the center of every problem is the concept of humanity."[14] On this point, communication between the two includes the following aspects from contemporary Sino-Christian scholarship.

---

[11] Kin-ming Au, "Ai yu ren: bijiao tianlike yu zhuxi zongjiao lunli yuanze de yanjiu" 愛與仁: 比較田立克與朱熹宗教倫理原則的研究 [*Love and Ren: A Comparative Study of Paul Tillich and Zhu Xi's Religious Ethical Principles*], in *Jidu zongjiao yu rujia duitan shengming yu lunli*, ed. Lai, 191.

[12] Au, "Ai yu ren," 192.

[13] Milton Wai-yiu Wan 溫偉耀, "Xinxing zhi xue yu xinyue renxing lun" 心性之學與新約人性論 ["School of Mind and the Doctrine of Humanity in the New Testament"], in *Dao yu yan*, ed. Liu, 483.

[14] Delin Zhang 張德麟, "Rujia renguan yu jidujiao renguan zhi bijiao yanjiu" 儒家人觀與基督教人觀之比較研究 ["Comparative Study of the Confucian and Christian Concepts of Humanity"], in *Dao yu yan*, ed. Liu, 451.

2.1. Fundamental Understanding of Human Beings

Deli Zhang, in "Comparative Study of the Confucian and Christian Concepts of Humanity," points out that within the Confucian vision, people have a nature of principle (*yili zhixing* 義理之性) and a physical nature (*qizhi zhixing* 氣質之性); seen from a Christian perspective, the beliefs that humans were created in God's image yet are sinful combine to comprise a unique understanding of humanity. However, with respect to their understanding of the essential nature of humanity, the two have huge differences, even though one can discover some similar points.[15]

2.2. Comparison of Specific Doctrines

One example of this aspect is Confucianism's belief in the goodness of human nature compared to Christianity's concept of original sin. Dunhua Zhao points out, "Comparison between Confucianism's belief in human goodness and Christianity's doctrine of original sin is one focal point for the comparative study of Eastern and Western culture."[16] He proceeds to expound his views in three senses: the two are not logically contradictory; in theory, they can be complementary; and in practice, their effects can be similar. This sort of comparison can apply in other aspects of Confucian and Christian moral character, such as honesty and reverence.

2.3. Relationship

The category of *relationship* (*guanxi* 關係) also occupies an important position in traditional Confucian and Christian concepts of humanity. According to Zhiwei Xu's 許志偉 explanation, Western theology and philosophy (such as Thomas Aquinas's concept of "reality in relationship" and Martin Buber's category of "I-thou relationship") clarify the ontological meaning of relationship: "Humans' relational nature not only has ontological meaning, it also takes God's existence and will

---

[15] For other works on the comparison of humanity in Confucianism and Christianity, see Shi Yang 楊适 "Jidujiao yu zhongxi wenhua chuantong zhong de renxing guan" 基督教與中西文化傳統中的人性觀 ["Doctrine of Humanity in Christianity and Chinese-Western Cultural Traditions"], in *Ru ye duihua xin licheng*, eds. Lai and Lee, 175–93.

[16] Dunhua Zhao, "Xingshan yu yuanzui: zhongxi wenhua de yige qutong dian" 性善與原罪: 中西文化的一個趨同點 ["Human Goodness and Original Sin: A Point of Convergence between Eastern and Western Culture"], in *Jidu zongjiao yu zhongguo wenhua*, eds. Miikka Ruokanen and Paulos Huang, 3.

as its metaphysical foundation."[17] At the center of Confucian study of benevolence lies the relationships between people: "Confucianism's ideas of benevolence and compassion for people are not only regulations for interpersonal relationships or moral standards; benevolence is an embodiment of reciprocal relationships between people. Thus, interpersonal relationships hold a central position within the Confucian idea of humanity."[18] But the status of relationships in this tradition exactly conforms to the "relational" concept of humanity in the Bible: "The triune God also has a relational essence, so when God created humans in God's image, God also bestowed 'relationality' on God's image—in human beings' basic nature. This 'relationality' is also carried out in divine-human relationships."[19]

2.4. Similarities and Differences in Moral Practice

According to Delin Zhang's overview, Confucian moral practice demands "conscience" (*liangzhi* 良知) as original essence and sees "becoming sagelihood" (*chengsheng* 成聖) as its ultimate goal and as an endless process. On the other hand, in Christian moral practice, the initiative lies with God, and faith and practice are inseparably related: ethical action is analyzed from the standpoint of faith. Christian ethics builds on the concept of God, especially the concept of imitating God. Moreover, it is intimately related to the idea of the kingdom of God. This kind of moral practice is a dynamic process that continues without end. This type of comparison reveals that Christianity and Confucianism are equally certain of the necessity of moral practice and see it as a continuous process. Yet there exist large differences between the two concerning the methods of moral practice. The most significant is the difference in moral agency: Confucianism emphasizes inwardness, achieving original essence (that is, intuitive knowledge), whereas Christianity asserts that the initiative lies with God, and moral practice is a response to God's grace and actions.[20]

CHRISTIAN ETHICS AND SOCIAL CONTEXT

Even as Sino-Christian ethical studies began to develop foundational concepts of ethics and dialogue with Chinese thought and culture, they

---

17 See Zhiwei Xu, "Rujia yu jidujiao de renge guan zhong guanxi de zhongxin diwei," 儒家與基督教的人格觀中關係的中心地位 ["Relationship in Personality of Confucianism and Christianity"], in *Ru ye duihua xin licheng*, eds. Lai and Lee, 252.

18 Xu, "Rujia yu jidujiao de renge guan zhong guanxi de zhongxin diwei," 256.

19 Xu, "Rujia yu jidujiao de renge guan zhong guanxi de zhongxin diwei," 257.

20 See Zhang, "Rujia renguan yu jidujiao renguan zhi bijiao yanjiu," 474–76.

have also turned their horizons toward observing and investigating moral questions about specific social conditions. In my survey, this mainly includes three aspects: the moral life of Chinese Christians, Christian ethics and their public implications in societies in general, and Christian ethics in Chinese society in particular.

1. Theme One: The Moral Life of Chinese Christians

Content focusing on this topic is built on a foundation of empirical studies, basically involving three areas: Christians' family ethics, Christian work ethics, and the effect of Christian moral lives on social life. In "A Report: One Northern Coastal City's Christian Population's Family Ethics and Work Ethics," Jianbo Huang 黃劍波 and Fenggang Yang 楊鳳崗, through on-site investigation, study Chinese Christians' family ethics. These are mainly embodied in parent-children relationships, husband-wife relationships, and the like, and their work ethics such as the effect of the Christian concept of vocation on Christians' work: faithfulness, honesty, conscientiousness, courtesy, and other forms of moral character.[21] Zhijie Kang 康志傑 and Tao Xu 徐弢, in "Investigation of Contemporary Chinese Christians' Ethical Lives: Taking Christian Communities of Mopanshan in Northwestern Hubei as an Example," use "faith and ethics" as a framework to investigate the basic standards and unique characteristics of local Christians' ethical lives (such as filial piety, belief in conflict between good and evil, view of wealth, etc.) as reflected in economic relationships and family life. The essay even points out their influence on their local society, such as correcting long-running bad habits in secular life.[22]

Fenggang Yang and Xiangping Li 李向平 have written several articles professionally studying the issue of Christian ethics, particularly Protestant ethics in China.[23] In "Christian Ethics and the Chinese

---

[21] Jianbo Huang and Fenggang Yang, "Diaocha baogao: Beifang mou yanhai chengshi jidutu de jiating lunli he gongzuo lunli" 調查報告: 北方某沿海城市基督徒的家庭倫理和工作倫理 ["A Report: One Northern Coastal City's Christian Population's Family Ethics and Work Ethics"], *Jidujiao wenhua xuekan* 基督教文化學刊 [*Journal for the Study of Christian Culture*], no. 11 (2004): 326–54.

[22] Zhijie Kang and Tao Xu, "Dangdai zhongguo jidutu lunli shenghuo de kaocha—yi e xibei mopanshan jidutu shequ weili" 當代中國基督徒倫理生活的考察—以鄂西北磨盤山基督徒社區為例 ["Investigation of Contemporary Chinese Christians' Ethical Lives: Taking Christian Communities of Mopan Mountain in Northwest Hubei as an Example"], *Jidujiao sixiang pinglun* 基督教思想評論 [*Regent Review of Christian Thought*], no. 8 (2008): 295–307.

[23] Xiangping Li and Fenggang Yang, "Jidujiao lunli yu shehui xinren de guanxi jiangou—yi dangdai zhongguo de jidutu qiye weili" 基督教倫理與社會信任的關係建構—以當代中國的基督徒企業為例 ["Christian Ethics and the Chinese

Construction of Societal Trust: Contemporary Chinese Christian Enterprises as an Example," Xiangping Li and Fenggang Yang analyze the particular influence that Christian ethics has on Christian businessmen, especially as embodied in the formation of trust relationships in society (interpersonal trust and trust between organizations): "In constructing a kind of 'Christian workplace ethics' on the foundation of professional practice, they present a standard of action for the faith community."[24] In addition, employing Christians' ethical lives as a background, Xiangping Li explains and analyzes their social identity and identifying patterns of behavior in depth. Through this, he examines those religious citizens' rights, duties, and responsibilities as well as Chinese Christians' positions and functions in Chinese society. On this point, the identification of Christian ethics becomes an important channel for identifying Christianity's moral role and position in Chinese society.[25] Xiangping Li also examines the role of Christian institutions in the practice of Protestant ethics in Chinese business enterprises, which embodies the integration of Christian faith, rituals, and the management of corporations.[26] Furthermore, Fenggang Yang raises the issue of the possibility of "a hybrid Confucian-Protestant ethic" in the rise of a market economy in China.[27]

2. Theme Two: Christian Ethics and Social Public Issues

Sino-Christian studies, especially studies of Christian ethics' concern for societal conditions, are focused on and reflected in the following issues regarding ecology, economy, politics, and global ethics.

Construction of Societal Trust: Contemporary Chinese Christian Enterprises as an Example"], *Zhongguo minzu bao* 中國民族報 [*Chinese Nationalities Newspaper*], May 26, 2009, http://tinyurl.com/yckjjhrj.

    See also Xiangping Li, "Lunli shenfen rentong—zhongguo dandai jidujiaotu de lunli shenghuo" 倫理 身份 認同—中國當代基督教徒的倫理生活 ["Ethics, Identity, and Identification: Ethical Life among Contemporary Chinese Christians"], *Tian Feng* 天風 (*Heavenly Wind*), no. 7 (2007): 30–35, and no. 9 (2007): 26–33; Xiangping Li, "Xinjiao lunli jiqi zhongguo shijian moshi— yi jidutu qiye wei hexin" 新教倫理及其中國實踐模式—以基督徒企業為中心 ["Protestant Ethics and Its Model of Practice in China: Focusing on Christian Enterprises"], *Daofeng jidujiao wenhua pinglun* 道風基督教文化評論 [*Logos and Pneuma: Chinese Journal of Theology*], no. 29 (2008): 199–221; and Fenggang Yang, "Market Economy and the Revival of Religions," in *Chinese Religious Life*, eds. David A. Palmer, Glenn Shive, and Philip L. Wickeri (New York: Oxford University Press, 2011), 209–23.

24 Li and Yang, "Jidujiao lunli yu shehui xinren de guanxi jiangou."

25 See Li, "Lunli shenfen rentong—zhongguo dandai jidujiaotu de lunli shenghuo."

26 Li, "Xinjiao lunli jiqi zhongguo shijian moshi."

27 Yang, "Market Economy and the Revival of Religions."

2.1. Ecological Issues

"Ecological theology" has already appeared on Chinese Christian horizons and has even undergone more than a little introduction and study. The Institute of Sino-Christian Studies (Hong Kong) published *Logos and Pneuma: Chinese Journal of Theology* (no. 18, 2003), an issue that took "ecological theology" as a theological theme, introducing its fundamental concepts through the theology of certain leading theologians like Paul Tillich and Dietrich Bonhoeffer.

One model for Sino-Christian scholars integrating their own cultural traditions with the study of ecological questions is *Confucian-Christian Dialogue and Ecological Concern*, coauthored by Pan-chiu Lai 賴品超 and Hongxing Lin 林宏星.[28] They draw on ecological ethical concepts implicit in classical figures in Christianity and Confucian traditional thought, such as Christianity's Paul Tillich and John Cobb and Confucianism's Yangming Wang 王陽明 (1472–1529). They also touch on Christian-Confucian dialogue on ethical questions such as human nature and the categories of anthropocentrism and ecocentrism, learning from others' experiences (one article addressing this is "What Can Christianity Learn from Confucianism?").

2.2. Economic Life

The Institute of Sino-Christian Studies has done some work in the area of Christian ethics' concern for economic life, such as publishing the books *Catholic Economic Ethics* and *Economics and Ethics*.[29] These books touch on topics such as Christian economic ethical principles and standards, the Church in the economic domain, the Church and money, the Church and grace, and more. Renmin University of China's *Jidujiao wenhua xuekan* 基督教文化學刊 (*Journal for the Study of Christian Culture*) also published special issues entitled "Faith and Ethics" (no. 9, 2003) and "Choosing the Poor" (no. 16, 2006), which introduced and studied economic questions within Christianity's field of view. These texts include theological reflection on poverty by Sino-Christian scholars. They try to understand poverty (including their native country's circumstances) from the perspectives of the Bible, Christian theology, and ethics (such

---

[28] Pan-chiu Lai and Hongxing Lin, *Ru ye duihua yu shengtai guanhuai* 儒耶對話與生態關懷 ["Confucian-Christian Dialogue and Ecological Concern"] (Beijing: Zongjiao wenhua chubanshe 宗教文化出版社, 2006).

[29] Otto Schilling, *Catholic Economic Ethics*, trans. Renming Gu (Beijing: Renmin University of China Press 中國人民大學出版社, 2006), and Xiaochang Wang 王曉朝 and Daniel Yeung 楊熙楠, eds., *Jingji yu lunli* 經濟與倫理 [*Economics and Ethics*] (Guilin: Guangxi shifan daxue chubanshe 廣西師範大學出版社, 2006).

as the doctrines of the Trinity, creation, redemption, the Church, etc.) and discuss related Christian ethical thought on economic issues. *Jiandao xuekan* 建道學刊 (*Jiandao: A Journal of Bible and Theology*, published by Alliance Bible Seminary in Hong Kong) published a special issue on "The Poor and The Rich: Biblical and Theological Reflection" (no. 41, 2014), which provides biblical and theological insights on such issues as wealth, distribution of resources, giving, and poverty. Over the past few years, the topic of Christianity and economics has received gradually increasing interest among Chinese scholars, and related academic activities have taken place.[30]

2.3. Political Issues

Kai-man Kwan's 關啟文 "Christian Ethics and Secularist Ethics: A Critical Comparison" sketches Christian ethics' basic outline and explains human dignity, human rights, and democratic thought from a Christian ethical perspective.[31] Given that secular ethics will attempt a rebuttal of this, the author looks at the issues from multiple angles (such as the concept of human race as a large family, moral practice, social practice, and more), pointing out secularism's flaws and supporting Christian ethics' unique resources and contributions in these areas. Pan-chiu Lai examines some public and political issues in the Chinese context from the view of Christian theology such as a harmonious society and sustainable development, human rights, and patriotism.[32] Due to the specific social and cultural background, more than a few Christian scholars in Hong Kong actively participate in debates over pornography, the media, homosexuality, and other issues from a Christian perspective.

The relationship between Christianity and political issues has at the same time attracted the attention of scholars in mainland China. More than a few scholars have begun studies related to Christian theology and

---

[30] For example, a conference on "Christian Business Ethics and Management" was held by Sichuan University in 2008, and a conference on "Christianity and Economic Development" was held by Center for Christian Studies, Chinese Academy of Social Sciences in 2009.

[31] Kai-man Kwan, "Jidujiao lunli he shisu zhuyi lunli: yige pipanxing bijiao," 基督教倫理與世俗世俗主義倫理: 一個批判性比較 ["Christian Ethics and Secularist Ethics: A Critical Comparison"], *Jidujiiao wenhua xuekan* 基督教文化學刊 [*Journal for the Study of Christian Culture*], no. 7 (2002): 139–72. See Kai-man Kwan, "Shenxue nengwei renquan tigong jichu ma?" 神學能為人權提供基礎嗎? ["Can Theology Provide a Foundation for Human Rights?"], *Journal of China Graduate School of Theology* [中國神學研究院期刊], no. 43 (2007): 205–28.

[32] See Pan-chiu Lai, *Guangchang shang de hanyu shenxue*.

ethics and their relationship to the Western world's constitutional government, democracy, human rights, foreign policy, and other issues. Within these studies, there is no lack of introduction to and thought about issues from specific Christian theological traditions.[33]

2.4. Global Ethic

During the 1990s, the issue of a global ethic attracted extensive interest and discussion within the field of international religious studies. It began to be widely valued within the Chinese academic world (including scholars in Christian studies) and was promptly introduced into Chinese academia.[34] Chinese academics felt deeply that many problems that the human race faces (such as violence, terrorism, and polarization) are related to global ethic, and they took full note of the importance and urgency of pursuing a global ethic. Several Christian scholars eagerly participated in related academic discussion, working hard to unearth the relationship between traditional Chinese ethics and global ethic. This included participating in two international academic discussion forums conducted by Chinese academic circles entitled "Chinese Traditional Ethics and Global Ethic" in 1997 and 2001 under the auspices of the Institute for the Study of Christian Culture (Renmin University of China) and the Institute of Sino-Christian Studies (Hong Kong). These forums thoroughly discussed the main content of the Parliament of the World's

---

[33]   For example, Naisheng Cheng 程乃胜, *Jidujiao wenhua yu jindai xifang xianzheng linian* 基督教文化與近代西方憲政理念 [*Christian Culture and Ideas of Modern Western Constitutional Government*] (Beijing: Falü chubanshe 法律出版社, 2007); Jiasheng Zhang 張佳生, "Jidujiao lunli yu xifang shijie de xingqi" 基督教倫理與西方世界的興起 ["Christian Ethics and the Rise of the Western World"], *Journal of Nanhua University (Social Sciences Edition)* 1 (2008), 21–23, 64; Aiguo Xu 徐愛國, "Tansuo renquan de jidujiao shenxue jichu" 探索人權的基督教神學基礎 ["Exploring Christian Theological Foundations for Human Rights"], *Tongji daxue xuebao (shehui kexue ban)* 同濟大學學報 (社會科學版) [*Journal of Tongji University (Social Sciences Edition)*], no. 2 (2008): 48–57; Cheng Ji 冀誠, "Lun mengyue shenxue dui meiguo xianfa de yingxiang" 論盟約神學對美國憲法的影響 ["The Impact of Covenant Theology on the American Constitution"], *Journal of China Graduate School of Theology* 中國神學研究院期刊], no. 45 (2008), 149–64.

[34]   See Hans Küng and Karl-Josef Kuschel, eds., *Quanqiu lunli: shijie zongjiao yihui xuanyan* 全球倫理: 世界宗教議會宣言 ["A Global Ethic: The Declaration of the Parliament of the World Religions"], trans. Guanghu He 何光滬 (Chengdu: Sichuan renmin chubanshe 四川人民出版社, 1997), and Hans Küng, *Shijie lunli gouxiang* 世界倫理構想 [*World Ethic*], trans. Yi Zhou 周藝, (Beijing: Sanlian shudian 三聯書店, 2002). Hans Küng himself was also invited to participate in various academic programs in China these past years (like in Peking University, 2009).

Religions' 1993 *Declaration Towards a Global Ethic* and strove to advance discussion of the relationship between ethics-related resources from the Asian/Chinese context and a global ethic, focusing on the contribution of the idea of family.[35] In the second discussion forum, it was proposed that they compile documents about Chinese traditional ethics that would be beneficial for building a global ethic and organize them based on *A Global Ethic*'s "two basic principles" and "four irrevocable directives" and proceed to study and expound them.[36]

3. Theme Three: Reflection on Christian Ethics and Chinese Society—Historical and Modern

Generally, reflections on Christian ethics and Chinese society involve additional investigation into historical or modern aspects. Qingxiang Guo's 郭清香 *Comparative Study of Christian and Confucian Ethics— Confucian and Christian Ethical Thought's Conflict and Harmony in the Republic of China Period* comes from a historical perspective and uses comparative methods to study the relationship between Christian ethics and traditional Chinese ethical thought as well as their meaning within the rapid changes occurring in Chinese society.[37] She investigates these two sorts of ethics' rapid changes and manifestations of their conflict and harmony with respect to people's relationship to

---

[35] About the relationship of Chinese traditional ethics and world ethic (global ethic), see Litian Fang 方立天, "Fojiao zhexue yu shijie lunli gouxiang" 佛教哲學與世界倫理構想 ["Buddhist Philosophy and Global Ethic"], *Jidujiao wenhua xuekan* 基督教文化學刊 [*Journal for the Study of Christian Culture*], no. 6 (2001): 274–79; Xianglong Zhang 張祥龍, "Quanqiu lunli ruhe tixian 'jiating' yu 'xiaodao' de genben diwei" 全球倫理如何體現"家庭"與"孝道"的根本地位 ["The Place of Family and Filial Piety in a Global Ethic"], *Jidujiao wenhua xuekan* 基督教文化學刊 [*Journal for the Study of Christian Culture*], no. 6 (2001): 319–23; Albert Hung-yee Chen 陳弘毅, "Zhongguo jiating zhexue dui shijie lunli de keneng gongxian" 中國家庭哲學對世界倫理的可能貢獻 ["Chinese Philosophy of Family and Its Potential Contribution to a Global Ethic"], *Jidujiao wenhua xuekan* 基督教文化學刊 [*Journal for the Study of Christian Culture*], no. 6 (2001): 324–33.

[36] About the introduction of world ethic (or global ethic) in China, see Hans Küng 孔漢思, "Shijie lunli zai zhongguo de fazhan shi" 世界倫理在中國的發展史 ["A History of Development of World Ethic in China"], in Hans Küng, *Shijie lunli shouce* 世界倫理手冊 [*A Handbook of World Ethic*], trans. Jianhua Deng 鄧建華 and Heng Liao 廖恆 (Beijing: Sanlian shudian 三聯書店, 2012), 1–5.

[37] Qingxiang Guo, *Ye ru lunli bijiao yanjiu—minguo shiqi jidujiao lunli sixiang de chongtu yu ronghe* 耶儒倫理比較研究—民國時期基督教與儒教倫理思想的衝突與融合 [*Comparative Study of Christian and Confucian Ethics—Confucian and Christian Ethical Thought's Conflict and Harmony in the Republic of China Period*] (Beijing: Zhongguo shehui kexue chubanshe 中國社會科學出版社, 2007).

ultimate reality, the relationship between the individual and society, the relationship between saving the country and saving the world, the construction of social ideals, and the relationship between nationalism and universalism. She tries to prove that Christian and Confucian ethical thought developed through methods of integrating nationalism and universalism.

In reality, the meaning of Christianity's ethical resources for Chinese society is still being uncovered. In particular, the influence of its moral force has been reflected on many levels. In "Religion's Burden in the Contemporary Chinese Ethical Order," Xiaofeng Liu 劉小楓 particularly emphasizes the important role of religious ethics in Chinese moral education.[38] Weifan Wang 汪維藩, in "Christian Ethics and Contemporary Spiritual Reconstruction," claims that in a developing economy, at the same time as pursuing wealth, contemporary people urgently need spiritual reconstruction. As a spiritually revealed religious ethic, Christian ethics, in appealing to justice and rights and in the process of awakening conscience, demonstrates its necessity.[39] To understand Christian ethics' influence on Chinese society's transformation, one cannot abandon exposition and analysis of specific Christian theological doctrines (especially concerning ethical thought) such as love, covenant, calling, vocation, responsibility, and so forth. One must even connect these doctrines to life in Chinese society. Milton Wai-yiu Wan particularly articulates the meaning of Christianity's spirit of "sacrificial and suffering love" for Chinese society.[40] Shining Gao 高師寧 also points out that Christianity's influence on Chinese society in the area of moral values is obvious in some respects, such as when it rejects or supports traditional values and expresses its influence through fairly noble moral values.[41]

[38] Xiaofeng Liu, "Zhongguo dangdai lunli zhixu zhong de zongjiao fudan" 中國當代倫理秩序中的宗教負擔 ["Religion's Burden in the Contemporary Chinese Ethical Order"], *Er shi yi shiji* 二十一世紀 [*Twenty-first Century*], no. 30 (1995): 15–23.

[39] Weifan Wang, "Jidujiao lunli yu dangdai jingshen chongjian" 基督教倫理與當代精神重建 ["Christian Ethics and Contemporary Spiritual Reconstruction"], *Jinling shenxue zhi* 金陵神學志 [*Jinling Theological Journal*], no. 1 (2008): 61–91, and no. 2 (2008): 26–52.

[40] See Milton Wai-yiu Wan, *Shengming de zhuanhua yu chaoba: wode jidu zongjiao hanyu shenxue sikao* 生命的轉化與超拔: 我的基督宗教漢語神學思考 [*The Transformation and Transcendence of Life: My Thoughts on Sino-Christian Theology*] (Beijing: Zongjiao wenhua chubanshe 宗教文化出版社, 2009), 64–93.

[41] Shining Gao, "Cong shizheng yanjiu kan jidujiao yu dangdai zhongguo shehui" 從實證研究看基督教與當代中國社會 ["Christianity and Contemporary Chinese Society from Empirical Studies"], *Zhejiang xuekan* 浙江學刊 [*Zhejiang Academic Journal*], no. 4 (2006): 61.

THE MEANING AND PROBLEMS OF SINO-CHRISTIAN ETHICAL STUDIES: WITH A REFLECTION ON CHRISTIAN LOVE

I must admit this outline of the principal achievements in Sino-Christian ethical studies is not complete. There should be some more topics of study that are beyond the scope of this investigation. Aside from explaining Sino-Christian scholars' introduction and study of typical Christian ethical thought (including relevant theologians' ethical thought) when they engage in studies of Christian ethics, my other intention is obvious: to try to bring out distinctive contextual traits of Sino-Christian ethical studies related to its circumstances through examining the results of these studies. In addition to culture, there is always a social setting, which in China's case is embodied in the following: dialogue and communication between Christian ethical thought and traditional Chinese thought (concerning specific doctrines such as love, human nature, and specific issues like ecology and the question of a global ethic), investigation of the moral life of Chinese Christians, deep concern for public social issues, and reflection on Christian ethics and Chinese society. The explanation of these distinctive traits of Sino-Christian theology within the framework of general Christian theology has outstanding significance.

Veli-Matti Kärkkäinen points out, "Christian theology has always been contextual. What makes talk about contextual theologies relevant today is the extent to which theologians *acknowledge* theologies to be contextually shaped, if not determined."[42] Hans Frei once brought up five approaches to enter theological study, of which, aside from completely ignoring circumstances and seeing Christian tradition as the only way (Karl Barth), the other approaches relate culture to Christianity (Paul Tillich), try to make Christianity understood by the surrounding culture (conservative evangelicals), or explain Christianity based on a specific philosophy or worldview (process theology).[43] All of these recognize the importance of contexts to the study of theology. Chinese scholar Simon Shui-Man Kwan 關瑞文 displays the same concern for theology's context: "When theologians discover how Christianity responds to current context, they have finally begun to truly know God."[44] Theological study's dependence on context is self-evident.

---

[42] Veli-Matti Kärkkäinen, *The Doctrine of God: A Global Introduction* (Grand Rapids: Baker Academic, 2004), 199.

[43] See Hans Frei, *Types of Christian Theology* (New Haven: Yale University Press, 1992), and Kärkkäinen analyis in *The Doctrine of God*, 200.

[44] Simon Shui-Man Kwan, "Shenxue yu shehui jian de hudong: yi guangyi de chujing shenxue weili" 神學與社會間的互動: 以廣義的處境神學為例 ["Interaction between Theology and Society: The Case of Contextual Theology in the Broad Sense"], in *Zonjiao yu shehui juese chongtan* 宗教與社會角色重探 [*The*

According to Peter Phan's understanding, resources for Asian theology, in addition to the Bible and tradition, should refer to specifically Asian resources, including Asian people's stories about joy and suffering, hope and despair, love and hatred, freedom and repression, Asian religion and philosophy's sacred texts and ethical and spiritual practices, monastic traditions (religious ceremonies and ascetic practices) and social participation, and Asian culture as a whole (including mythology, folklore, poetry, stories, art, etc.).[45] Overall, "the Asian context can be described as a blend of a profound religiosity (which is perhaps Asia's greatest wealth) and an overwhelming poverty."[46] Different Asian societies have different conditions and circumstances, but in many places (including China), their own profound cultural and religious conditions cannot help but enter and influence the expression of their Christian theological thought. As a result, "everywhere in Asia, Christian theology dialogues with and is shaped by encounters with other living religions."[47]

China's rich religious and philosophical traditions, cultural resources, and unique social conditions are similarly important to the development of Sino-Christian theology. Even though different voices and understandings exist, Sino-Christian studies from the start advocated emphasizing integration of different regions' Chinese-speaking communities' life experiences and cultural circumstances. It has made clear the importance of these experiences and circumstances for expounding Sino-Christian theology. Sino-Christian theology and traditional Chinese culture, Chinese theology's potential influence on Chinese society, and similar topics have been considered and have been channeled into a major component of Sino-Christian theological studies.[48]

Based on the achievements of Sino-Christian studies over the past thirty years, the study of Christian ethics' content and orientation is one of the most outstanding areas in which Chinese theology connects to its own culture and social contexts. In this chapter, I do not intend to ignore

Social Role of Religion Reexamined], ed. Peter T. M. Ng 吳梓明 (Center for the Study of Religion and Chinese Society, Chung Chi College, The Chinese University of Hong Kong 香港中文大學崇基學院宗教與中國社會研究中心, 2002), 135.

[45] See Kärkkäinen, *The Doctrine of God*, 281.

[46] Aloysius Pieris, "Western Christianity and Asian Buddhism," *Dialogue*, no. 7 (1980): 61–62.

[47] Kärkkäinen, *The Doctrine of God*, 281.

[48] See Guanghu He 何光滬, "Hanyu shenxue de fangfa yu jinlu" 漢語神學的方法與進 ["Methodology and Approach of Sino-Christian Theology"], in *Hanyu shenxue chuyi* 漢語神學芻 [*Preliminary Studies on Sino-Christian Theology*], ed. Daniel Yeung 楊熙楠 (Hong Kong: Institute of Sino-Christian Studies 漢語基督教文化研究所, 2000), 39–53.

Jesus's related moral teachings that make up the heart of Christian ethics as well as study of Christian ethics' foundational thought and traditional systems. Yet what attracts our attention is Christian ethics serving as a practical orientation, especially in distinct branches of theology, where communication and connection with specific conditions seem especially outstanding and necessary. Under this premise, I am considering what our unique culture and social conditions can provide for Christian ethics within Sino-Christian theology: ethical resources related to Chinese cultural traditions, Chinese Christians' moral life and practice, and Chinese society's moral issues are not only conditions that Christian ethical studies must touch upon but are also meaningful in bringing about a special study place for Sino-Christian ethics. Moreover, they can provide some specific topics as we think deeply about and elucidate some doctrines in Christian ethics. Perhaps, on some occasions, what we need for moving forward in understanding related theological concepts is, to some extent, contextually explained ethics.

Taking the Christian ethical concept of love as an example, after Ping-cheung Lo confirms that divine love and *ren* are Christianity and Confucianism's basic subjects, respectively, he raises the question, "Can we do a Chinese contextual theology of *agape* that involves only a cultural synthesis not a religious synthesis?"[49]: To avoid religious synthesis, he acknowledges that the contextual theology should admit "the uniqueness of each religion and the structural differences among them."[50] On this point, Huilin Yang is equally enlightening: "The important resources that Christian ethics can provide will never again be a kind of 'bottom line ethics' but will be the ultimate explanation of the ideal of value. Thus, Sino-Christianity's 'ethicalization' must turn toward Christianity's own ethical meaning."[51] From this perspective, after pointing out Sino-Christian studies' contextual characteristics, the next step should be to answer questions connected to construction of Chinese theological concepts.

We have seen many achievements in Sino-Christian ethical studies, which include exploring the relationship between Christianity and Chinese traditions (whether dealing with specific doctrine or particular social issues) and investigating Christianity's influence on the moral plane. The goal of simultaneously connecting to contexts (whether it uses resources from traditional thought or current moral practice), while both

---

49 Lo, "*Ren* as Fundamental Motif and the Promise and Problem of a Contextual Theology of an Agape-Ren Synthesis," 118–19.

50 This point is based on the author's analysis of Anders Nygren's ideas. See Lo, "*Ren* as Fundamental Motif," 119.

51 Yang, "'Lunlihua'hanyu jidujiao yu jidujiao de lunli yiyi-jidujiiao lunli zai zhongguo wenhua yujing zhong de kenengxing jiqi nanti," 273.

respecting Christian theology and ethics' own fundamental traditions and trying to enrich and develop their content, and also trying to give new elucidation to some doctrines (such as human nature, love, justice, covenant, vocation, etc.) poses a great challenge for Sino-Christian studies. Yet this challenge could provide even more room for thought for the next in-depth study in terms of methods and related issues. The next chapter will continue this line to further examine this challenge to see the role and limits of Christian love in constructing social justice in the Chinese context.

7

THE DYNAMIC BETWEEN LOVE AND JUSTICE

A Confucian-Christian Dialogue in the Chinese Context

The topic of love and justice has been an outstanding issue in the area of public theology. The relationship between love and justice (with both terms used in a broad sense) has been a common issue in many cultures and societies and has been studied from philosophical, religious, political, legal, and sociological perspectives. In this regard, Reinhold Niebuhr is an important American Christian ethicist who proposes the dynamic relationship derived from his Christian realism, pointing to the possibility of transforming justice by love while acknowledging the distance between the two.[1] The problem of love and justice raised by Niebuhr has burdens, not only for American Christianity but also for other contexts where Christian love and other forms of love are concerned, deserving reconsideration either from a theological perspective or particular contextual perspectives. This chapter re-examines the dynamic between love and justice in the Chinese context, introducing a Confucian alternative to the Western theology of justice (in the version of the "Chinese theology of justice" of Yushun Huang 黃玉順) and to the Confucian capacity to avoid conflict between love and justice (in terms of the "Confucian love with distinction" of Yong Huang 黃勇). With reference to the concepts of love—both Confucian *ren* 仁(benevolence) and Christian *agape*—and the problem of social justice in contemporary China, this chapter presents the contributions and constraints of both concepts of love, demanding just institutions while revealing human limitations in the Chinese context.

---

[1] See chapter 2.

THE PROBLEM OF LOVE AND JUSTICE: REINHOLD NIEBUHR
AND NICHOLAS WOLTERSTORFF

For Niebuhr, the issue of love and justice is one of the key themes in his Christian ethics. In recognition of an imperfect world and the reality of sin and evil, Niebuhr emphasizes that the perfect love (*agape*) exemplified by Jesus is a kind of ideal and absoluteness of spirituality and morality. Indeed, as moral ideals, sacrificial love and forgiving love are the essence of Christian ethics and can only serve as the "highest virtue." Christian love may be realized in such conditions as intimate relationships and religious communities but not in complex social relationships. In other words, "'pure love' cannot be a possible foundation for an adequate social ethic because of man's sin, which an adequate ethic must take into account."[2] This reflects Niebuhr's distinction between religious ethics and rational (social) ethics: "A rational ethic aims at justice, and a religious ethic makes love the ideal."[3] For Niebuhr, the distinction between love and justice also demonstrates the distinction of individual and society, as he claims: "From the perspective of society the highest moral idea is justice. From the perspective of the individual the highest ideal is unselfishness."[4]

Based on these understandings, Niebuhr brings his vision of wider society in terms of justice: "The ordinary affairs of the community, the structure of politics and economics, must be governed by the spirit of justice and by specific and detailed definitions of rights and duties."[5] Just institutions locate different persons' and groups' needs, interests, and potential conflicts from within. Gary Dorrien provides a careful analysis of the development of Niebuhr's understanding of love and justice: "In the 1930s, Niebuhr equated justice with equality, or an equal balance of power, and he blasted everyone who tried to get a social ethic out of Jesus. Always he admonished that Jesus was no help with problems of proximate means and ends, necessary violence, and calculated consequences."[6] Later on, Niebuhr gradually recognized the problem of "dichotomizing between love and justice" and tended to underline the "social relevance"

---

[2]   D. B. Robertson, introduction to Niebuhr, *Love and Justice: Selections from the Shorter Writings*, 12.

[3]   Reinhold Niebuhr, *Moral Man and Immoral Society: A Study in Ethics and Politics* (Eugene: Wipf & Stock, 1998), 57.

[4]   Niebuhr, *Moral Man and Immoral Society*, 257.

[5]   Niebuhr, *Love and Justice*, 25.

[6]   Gary Dorrien, introduction to *The Children of Light and the Children of Darkness*, by Reinhold Niebuhr (Chicago: University of Chicago, 2011), xxii.

of the love ethic: "Love is not merely the content of an impossible ethical ideal. It is the motive force of the struggle for justice."[7]

It is now clear that Niebuhr's approach to the problem of love and justice moves further from the distinction to its internal relevance, that is, how the law of love is essential to the spirit of justice: "In so far as justice admits the claims of the self, it is something less than love. Yet it cannot exist without love and remain justice. For without the 'grace' of love, justice always degenerates into something less than justice."[8] He even expects that justice work toward the relative realization of love in the world: "Yet the law of love is involved in all approximations of justice, not only as the source of the norms of justice, but as an ultimate perspective by which their limitations are discovered."[9] This is how Niebuhr regards love as an "impossible possibility": impossible in its immediate implications in concrete complex social and political conditions, possible in its ultimate and guiding principles.

In Paul Ramsey's words, Niebuhr's basic understanding of love and justice shows their dynamic relationship: "While establishing the transcendence of love, he also seeks to point out the relevance of the transcendent as 'both the ground and the fulfilment of existence,' as 'a basis of even the most minimal social standards.'"[10] Robin W. Lovin describes it in this way: "Love draws our understanding of what justice requires in a more and more inclusive and generous direction, rather than allowing us to settle into a mutually disinterested, minimalist definition of justice."[11] John C. Bennett also emphasizes this by saying that "justice must always be thought of in dynamic terms, and that love can always raise justice to new heights. There is an indeterminateness about the possibilities of transforming justice by love. Love makes our consciences more sensitive to the needs of others, especially to the needs of those who have been neglected or exploited,"[12] yet "love never takes the place of justice even under the best possible human conditions."[13] The dynamic between love and justice points to the source, limitation,

---

[7]   Dorrien, introduction to *The Children of Light and the Children of Darkness*, xxii.

[8]   Niebuhr, *Love and Justice*, 28.

[9]   Reinhold Niebuhr, *An Interpretation of Christian Ethics* (New York: Meridian, 1958), 128.

[10]   Paul Ramsey, "Love and Law," in *Reinhold Niebuhr: His Religious, Social, and Political Thought*, eds. Charles W. Kegley and Robert W. Bretall (New York: Macmillan, 1956), 94.

[11]   Lovin, *Reinhold Niebuhr and Christian Realism*, 199.

[12]   John C. Bennett, "Reinhold Niebuhr's Social Ethics," in *Reinhold Niebuhr: His Religious, Social, and Political Thought*, eds. Kegley and Bretall, 59.

[13]   Bennett, "Reinhold Niebuhr's Social Ethics," 60.

and fulfillment of justice in terms of love while sharply recognizing the distance between the two.

Therefore, for Niebuhr, in general human and social conditions, in the face of cruel and conflicting social realities, Christian love is a kind of ultimate possibility but is not possible in reality: "It stood as a corrective over all of our efforts, but it could never fully be the operative principle in political affairs."[14] In Nicholas Wolterstorff's understanding, for Niebuhr, "What's called for in cases of conflict is justice, not agapic love."[15] The full realization of love is only possible under nonconflict conditions: "Justice is relevant where the self-interest of different parties is in conflict; it consists of the just resolution of those conflicts."[16] In principle, Niebuhr emphasizes the "conceptual incompatibility" between love and justice.

Distinguished from Reinhold Niebuhr, Wolterstorff attempts to develop the idea of "love incorporating justice" by suggesting that even in nonconflictual situations, it does not mean that justice is irrelevant. Justice in times of conflict does not represent the whole of justice: "I may treat you justly even though there is no conflict between two of us and even though neither of us has wronged the other. I may treat you justly in a situation of 'frictionless harmony.' I do so if I treat you in such a way as befits your worth."[17] For Wolterstorff, respect for the other's worth and just treatment of the other demonstrate love itself without conflicting with the law of love nor restraining or complementing the law of love. He says, "Treating the neighbor justly is not viewed as incompatible with loving the neighbor, nor is it viewed as an alternative to loving him. Treating the neighbor justly is an example of loving him, a way of loving him. Love is not justice-indifferent benevolence."[18] In this sense, even in nonconflicting situations, human beings should learn respect for the other and just treatment toward the other. It is justice generated by love, which distinguishes itself from Niebuhr's position of the incompatibility of love and justice.

Niebuhr and Wolterstorff have a distinctive understanding of love and justice, that is, there is only a relative distance between them on the one hand, and justice in love with the demand of justice in a harmonious situation on the other. I, however, consider there to be a central problem, that is, the dynamic relationship between love and justice. The main issues include: How is it possible for Christian love to engage social justice? Does love only serve an ideal and one kind of corrective power for justice? Or

---

14 Stanley Hauerwas and D. Stephen Long, foreword to *Basic Christian Ethics*, by Paul Ramsey (Louisville: Westminster/John Knox Press, 1993), xv.

15 Wolterstorff, *Justice in Love*, 66.

16 Wolterstorff, *Justice in Love*, 67.

17 Wolterstorff, *Justice in Love*, 90.

18 Wolterstorff, *Justice in Love*, 83.

how far can it be applied and embodied in complex social, economic, and political issues? In contemporary Western scholarship, against the background of pursuing an independent idea of political justice from diverse comprehensive doctrines (including religious love) advanced by political philosopher John Rawls, there are even more additional resources to develop and articulate the implications of Christian love in political and legal issues.[19] Inspired by the approach to justice in the Christian perspectives of Reinhold Niebuhr among theologians, political philosophers, and legal scholars, in the following sections, I shall locate this problem in the Chinese context and bring the perspectives of Confucianism and the related disciplines of the social sciences into dialogue to explore the possibilities and limitations of love in its implications for justice in a broader cultural context (without being limited by the idea of Christian love but the idea of love in a broad sense, including Confucian *ren*) beyond the West.

AN ENGAGEMENT WITH NIEBUHR AND WOLTERSTORFF'S PROBLEM: CONFUCIAN PERSPECTIVE OF LOVE AND JUSTICE

Indeed, there are rich resources in China to develop the understanding of Confucian values, including *ren*, and their engagement and contribution to social and political life. As I see it, there are several major versions of Chinese theories deriving from Confucianism that attempt to substitute Western-style political order, including norms and institutions of justice: Yushun Huang's version of the "Chinese theory of justice," Yong Huang's attempt to avoid the conflict between love and justice in terms of Confucian resources, and Qingping Liu 劉清平 and Qiyong Guo's 郭齊勇 debate on the problem of filial love and legal justice. These reflect Confucian moral and political culture, including Confucian *ren* and its possible relevance to justice.

Chinese philosopher Yushun Huang proposes a Chinese theory of justice expounded by the idea of benevolence in Confucianism. His proposal derives from his motive for theoretical interpretation of justice in terms of Chinese culture, especially Confucianism, while he recognizes "the need to re-establish social norms and institutions in both China and

---

19   See Jeffrie G. Murphy, "Christian Love and Criminal Punishment," in *Christianity and Law: An Introduction*, eds. John Witte Jr. and Frank S. Alexander (Cambridge: Cambridge University Press, 2008), 219–35; Timothy Jackson, *Political Agape: Christian Love and Liberal Democracy* (Grand Rapids: Eerdmans, 2015); Robert F. Cochran Jr. and Zachary R. Calo, eds., *Agape, Justice, and Law: How Might Christian Love Shape Law?* (Cambridge: Cambridge University Press, 2017).

the World."[20] He attempts to construct a universal general theory of justice through the engagement of the Chinese perspective, which has been ignored by modern academia and can be contrasted with the Western theory of justice. In his *Voice from the East: The Chinese Theory of Justice*, he raises his main concern: "In what way does the spirit of benevolence/humanness (*ren* 仁) lay a foundation for the principle of justice (*yi* 义)?"[21] He formulates the fundamental structure of this Chinese theory of justice as: benevolence/humanness→ interests→ intuitive knowledge→ the principle of justice→ reason→ rites/proprieties (norms/justice) music/harmony.[22]

The Confucian idea of benevolence is ordered from love of self, love of relatives, love of people, and love of things from which different people derive benefits. Conflicts occur when pursuing benefits, and consequently, it demands just institutions and principles to deal with conflicts. Here, the Chinese idea of justice is mainly concerned with the problem of benefits. Thus, the harmony of the institutions/norms ("rites") is achieved: "In the construction of the framework of '*ren*' 仁(benevolence/humaneness)—*yi*义 (justice/righteousness)—*li* 礼 (rites/proprieties), it is *yi*义 that plays the role of a bridge connecting benevolence/humanness and rites/proprieties."[23]

It is the idea of benevolence that invokes the emergence and resolution of conflicts of interest, which leans toward justice. As Yushun Huang states, "The Chinese Theory of Justice concerns itself with the question of interests, namely, the conflicts of interests that arise from 'graded love.' Nevertheless, the 'humanness of equal treatment for all' ensures the solution of the problem; in other words, it ensures the respect for the private interests of others and the public interests of a community."[24] Yushun Huang also recognizes that in Confucianism, the principles of justice (i.e., the principles of properness and fitness) express the sense of justice, which is "an intuitive wisdom or the 'Good Knowledge' that is acquired from the present life."[25]

---

[20] Yushun Huang, *Voice from the East: The Chinese Theory of Justice*, trans. Pingping Hou and Keyou Wang (Reading: Paths International, 2016), 1.

[21] Huang, *Voice from the East*, 8.

[22] Huang, *Voice from the East*, 45–46.

[23] Huang, *Voice from the East*, 7.

[24] Huang, *Voice from the East*, 46.

[25] Huang, *Voice from the East*, 46. Erin Cline studies the sense of justice in Confucius, which contrasts to that in Rawls. Even though there are differences between those two accounts of a sense of justice, both contribute "to a larger account of a well-ordered and stable society in Rawls and a harmonious and humane society in the Analects." See Erin Cline, *Confucius, Rawls, and the Sense of Justice* (New York: Fordham University Press, 2012), 24.

For Yushun Huang, the Western theory of justice too often excludes the sentiment of benevolence for the issues of justice. Probably at this point, he has not read Wolterstorff. Rather than going deeper into Yushun Huang's argument about Confucian ideas of benevolence and its implications for justice, I find a contrast between his "Chinese theory of justice" and Wolterstorff's idea of "loving justice." Wolterstorff's idea of Christian love is distinctive from the Confucian idea of benevolence, and they have their own understanding of justice. For Yushun Huang, benevolence ("graded love") serves as both the cause of conflict of benefits and the source of achievement of justice, and the final goal of his theory is "harmony." In my interview with Wolterstorff, he cites Yushun Huang as believing "just institutions and principles deal with conflict": "As I understand this Chinese philosopher, it appears to me that he, in effect, eliminates justice."[26] But for Wolterstorff, "nonconflictual" justice, to treat the other person justly and to seek one's good, is an important part of justice as a whole. Despite their differences, it seems to me that both Yushun Huang and Wolterstorff point to the moral significance of love in different religious and cultural traditions for understanding the problem of justice.

Obviously, Yushun Huang appeals to Confucian "graded love" in pursing his idea of justice. Similar ideas are presented by Wing-tsit Chan, who understands that the Confucian concept of *jen* (*ren*) is "essentially social, active, and dynamic." Two of its attributes are its "universalness" and "distinction." As he writes, "This love is universal in nature, but there must be distinctions, that is, an order or gradation in application, beginning with the love of parents."[27]

In this regard, Yong Huang further elucidates the idea of Confucian love with "distinction" and examines both the ideas of Confucian *ren* and Christian love and their relevance to justice. His understanding of Confucian love with distinction is that "we should love different people and things in ways that are appropriate to them, i.e., in ways that have taken into consideration the uniqueness of the objects of love"[28]—that is, "to love the same people and things in the same way and love different people and things in different ways."[29]

---

[26] Zhibin Xie (interviewer), "World-Formative Christianity: Wonder and Grief, Love and Justice: A Chinese Conversation with Nicholas Wolterstorff" (see appendix 1).

[27] Wing-tsit Chan, "The Evolution of the Confucian Concept Jen," *Philosophy East and West* 4, no. 4 (1955), 319.

[28] Yong Huang, "Confucian Love and Global Ethics: How the Cheng Brothers Would Help Respond to Christian Criticisms," *Asian Philosophy* 15, no. 1 (2005): 40.

[29] Huang, "Confucian Love and Global Ethics," 41.

Yong Huang strongly believes that "Confucian love is therefore not a love for the sake of love. It is a love to lead to some particular social consequences."[30] Contrasted with Yushun Huang's approach to justice starting from the idea of "graded love," Yong Huang's interpretation of Confucian love has its own advantage and can avoid the conflict between love and justice in that this kind of appropriate love can make it clear between different people and different ways of love, which certainly have social consequences, while learning "about their unique ideas, ideals, customs, and ways of behaviors" from people with different cultural and religious traditions.[31] In this sense, this kind of Confucian love is consistent with the conception of justice, except for the sense of justice as "to each the same thing."[32] He concludes, "It is perhaps precisely because of this that Confucian love with distinction can help us avoid the potential conflict between love and justice in Christianity."[33]

In this case, Yong Huang quotes Niebuhr to show the conflict between Christian love and social justice, particularly referring to Niebuhr's idea of the distance of the pure religious ideal with the problem of social justice.[34] We have already seen the dynamic relationship between Christian love and justice raised by Niebuhr beyond the conflict model, in which love relativizes, criticizes, and elevates social justice. Wolterstorff even proposes the compatibility of love and justice. It seems to me that both Niebuhr and Wolterstorff tend to provide an indispensable basis and guiding principles for the construction of justice in terms of Christian love, even though they are concerned with the implications of love in different circumstances, either conflictual or nonconflictual.

Nevertheless, we still find that some Confucian scholars struggle with the implications of Confucian love in social and political issues. There has been a debate between Qingping Liu and Qiyong Guo, who are concerned if filial love and kinship in Confucianism are the cause of corruption and legal injustice. Qingping Liu understands that "it is not humane love for all humans but filial love for parents that forms the ultimate value of Confucianism."[35] He argues that as Confucianism concentrates on the supremacy of kinship over human beings' social relationships and other

---

30   Huang, "Confucian Love and Global Ethics," 40.
31   Huang, "Confucian Love and Global Ethics," 50.
32   Huang, "Confucian Love and Global Ethics," 41. Yong Huang clarifies here, "Confucian love with distinction thus advocates equal consideration but not identical treatment" (54 fn).
33   Huang, "Confucian Love and Global Ethics," 41.
34   See Huang, "Confucian Love and Global Ethics," 39–40.
35   Qingping Liu, "On the Possibility of Universal Love for All Humans: A Comparative Study of Confucian and Christian Ethics," *Asian Philosophy* 25, no. 3 (2015): 230.

norms, even in conflictual circumstances, it should account for the emergence of corruption and illegal actions. Consequently, filial love may be given priority at the cost of the requirements of legal justice and benevolent politics; Confucianism does not propose the principles to resolve the conflict between kinship and social norms.[36] Qingping Liu points out, "In the Lunyu [Analects] and the Mengzi [Mencius], the two most authoritative Confucian classics, Kongzi [Confucius] and Mengzi never advise people to sacrifice filial piety for humane love in cases of conflict; rather, they always encourage people to give up humane love and choose kinship love without exception."[37]

Qiyong Guo does not agree with Qingping Liu's interpretation, whereas Qiyong Guo puts Confucian principles of kinship and criminal justice into their particular contexts. Qiyong Guo proposes that political and economic institutions are rightly located in terms of kinship in Mencius's age, and even today there is something more fundamental, such as daily life ethics, individual morality, and the ultimate way of heaven, than law and punishment.[38] A general observation is that contemporary Confucian scholars have a strong concern with the problem of justice deriving from Confucian virtues such as love, either embracing them too closely or criticizing their affinity. The problem arises regarding how far Confucian love bears on social justice in China and how we should distinguish both.

A QUEST FOR SOCIAL JUSTICE IN CHINA: INSTITUTIONAL APPROACH, CONFUCIAN *REN*, AND CHRISTIAN LOVE

Up to now, we have seen some scholars, such as Yushun Huang, Yong Huang, Qingping Liu, and Qiyong Guo, approach in their own ways the issues of political order and justice from a Confucian perspective, the idea of Confucian *ren* in particular. In contemporary China, the issue of justice—social justice, in particular—does not remain as an abstract concept; it is an emerging practical issue and receives wide attention and study from social scientists.

The issue of social justice in China today has increasingly become an outstanding moral, social, and political problem. The issue of social

---

[36] See Qingping Liu, "Meide haishi fubai? Xi mengzi zhong youguan shun de liangge anli" 美德還是腐敗? 析孟子中有關舜的兩個案例 ["Virtues or Corruption? An Analysis of Two Cases on Shun in Mencius"], *Zhexue yanjiu* 哲學研究 [*Philosophical Research*], no. 2 (2002): 43–47.

[37] Liu, "On the Possibility of Universal Love for All Humans," 231.

[38] Qiyong Guo, "Yetan 'zi wei fu yin' yu mengzi lun shun: jian yu liu qingping xiansheng shangque" 也談 "子為父隱" 與孟子論舜: 兼與劉清平先生商榷 ["Father and Son Screening Each Other" and Mencius on Shun: A Debate with Qingping Liu"], *Zhexue yanjiu* 哲學研究 [*Philosophical Research*], no. 10 (2002): 27–30.

justice has called special attention to the areas of education, employment, public health, social welfare, the protection of marginalized groups, gender equality, and so on. Some relevant studies from the perspectives of philosophy, political science, law, economics, and sociology have addressed a great deal on institutional and distributive arrangements, economic factors, and the rule of law from such principles as rights, duty, interests, just distribution, and equal opportunities. In general, regarding the problem of social justice, the subject of institutions has been extensively emphasized either by the government or academia. As Chinese legal scholar Zhiping Liang 梁志平 points out, "Social justice is always related to institutions. The realization of social justice ought to rely on the establishment and improvement of institutions as the absence of social justice emerges from the institution."[39] The call for institutional settings to achieve social justice finally appeals to political reform and the transformation of national governance, including constitutionalism.[40] It is obvious that both the values of social justice and fraternity (love, in general) are regarded as core values in contemporary China, and yet there is a lack of understanding of and attention to the internal relationship between those two concepts. However, diverse sources on the concept of love found in the rich traditions such as Confucianism and Christianity show the internal relationship between love and justice.

In this pursuit of social justice in China, the principle of equality is an important factor, and its implications for social justice are emphasized either in the theoretical studies of social justice or the practical investigation of social justice, including the equilibrium of equality, fairness, and effectiveness. The importance of equality in social justice in China is demonstrated by a sociological study. Through field work, Chinese sociologist Jing Zhang 張靜 points out that "the principles of equilibrium/ equality/need, investment/benefits, institutional equality, and procedural openness are the primary just values recognized by Chinese people."[41] For Jing Zhang, this understanding of social justice is common in many other societies in the world.

---

[39]   Zhiping Liang, "Daoyan" 導言 [Introduction], in *Zhuanxingqi de shehui gongzheng: wenti yu qianjing* 轉型期的社會公正:問題與前景 [*Social Justice in a Transitional Period: Problem and Prospect*], ed. Zhiping Liang (Beijing: Sanlian shudian 三聯書店, 2010), 5. My translation.

[40]   Liang, "Daoyan," 11.

[41]   Jing Zhang, "Qianyan" 前言 [Preface] in *Zhuanxing zhongguo shehui gongzhengguan yanjiu* 轉型中國社會公正觀研究 [*A Study in Viewpoints of Social Justice in Transitional China*], ed. Jing Zhang (Beijing: Zhongguo renmin daxue chubanshe 中國人民大學出版社, 2008), 8. My translation.

In a similar tone, Chinese philosopher Huaihong He 何懷宏 offers his framework for justice in China by emphasizing the equal significance of basic values, such as equal freedom and civil rights, and institutional elements, such as democracy, constitutionalism, and the rule of law, together with the spirit of charity with respect to labors and care for vulnerable and marginalized people. For He, this ideal of justice in China can be derived from the values of equality of personality and sympathy (*ceyin zhixin* 惻隱之心) in Chinese tradition.[42] Both institutional and moral aspects should be simultaneously taken into account in the pursuit of justice in China; here, the attention to and care for the social lower class and those who are vulnerable, inspired by Chinese tradition, contribute relevance to the ideal of justice.[43]

From the above review of Chinese discourse on love and justice, we may find that while the Chinese philosophers seek Confucian moral implications for the problem of social and political order (social justice, in particular), they might not be attentive enough to the concrete and practical problem of social justice in contemporary China. Although many social scientists, as well as legal and political philosophers, are exploring the problem of social justice in China, it seems that many of them do not attach much importance to the relevance and contribution of moral values, such as love, except for Huaihong He. On this point, what both Niebuhr and Wolterstorff raise and inspire in us is the dynamic between love and justice,[44] despite their differences. While I recognize that they bring Christian perspectives into the discussion on public issues such as social justice, I bear a burden to invoke the use of distinctive Confucian resources in its relation to social justice in engaging public discourse in China. To further explore the problem of social justice in China, I will refer to the comparison between Confucian *ren* and Christian love (*agape*) and see how both of them may supplement each other involving the pursuit of social justice in the Chinese context.

In chapter 6, we see that there is rich scholarship on the conceptual comparison between Confucian *ren* and Christian agape, such as

---

[42] Huaihong He, "Zhengyi zai zhongguo: lishi yu xianshi de—yige chubu de silu" 正義在中國: 歷史與現實的——個初步的思路 ["Justice in China: Historical and Contemporary—A Preliminary Approach"], *Gonggong xingzheng pinglun* 公共行政評論 [*Public Administration Review*], no. 1 (2011): 13.

[43] Huaihong He proposes this idea without giving detailed arguments.

[44] Even though Niebuhr and Wolterstorff point to the form of Christian love and its relevance to justice, I think it is still helpful to consider other forms of love, such as Confucian *ren*, and their relationship to the problem of justice as different kinds of love have something in common and have a drive for solving social issues to some degree.

the distinctions between inclusiveness and exclusiveness, and between God-centered and humanity-centered. This comparison can illuminate certain implications for their relevance to justice, particularly the debate on Confucian love with distinction.[45] Despite Yushun Huang's resolution of conflicts of interest deriving from the idea of benevolence, and Yong Hong's efforts to reconcile Confucian love and justice through his exposition of Confucian love with distinction, one cannot easily ignore the question about filiality as one aspect in Confucian love discussed earlier by Qingping Liu and Qiyong Guo, which distinguishes itself from Christian love when considering issues of justice, pointing to conflicts of interest and equality in particular.

As Namsoon Kang rightly points out, "The term *hsiao* (filiality or filial piety) presents one of the most basic social and religious concepts of Confucian society."[46] In Confucianism, the pursuit of steady social order attained by an individual's conformity to social norms "overrides the affirmation of the conflict between personal interests and the attention to social equality."[47] This difficulty in confronting conflicts of interest and social equality deriving from filiality and other social norms in Confucianism for the most part remains a critical problem. This problem leaves space for Christian engagement. Kang further suggests the need for the transformation of the Confucian idea of family with "a Christian principle of the renunciation of patriarchal value and the male-centered structure of family" and a theological and spiritual relativization of the traditional family as a biological or sociological unit[48]: "The theological principle of family . . . puts all other relationships in the service of a community that exists for the purpose of enabling and enhancing each person's relationship to God."[49] This way of understanding family leads to a fresh definition of love and justice from the perspective of the will of God: "Christians can therefore define family in terms of God-relation and

---

[45] Xinzhong Yao observes that the distance between Confucian *ren* and Christian love results in the different understanding of social justice, and both search for a kind of harmony between the transcendental ideal (*ren/jen* or agape) and the social idea (*yi* or justice). See Xinzhong Yao, *Confucianism and Christianity: A Comparative Study of Jen and Agape* (Brighton: Sussex Academic, 1996).

[46] Namsoon Kang, *Diasporic Feminist Theology: Asia and Theopolitical Imagination* (Minneapolis: Fortress Press, 2014), 302.

[47] Desheng Zhang 張德勝, *Rujia lunli yu shehui zhixu: shehuixue de quanshi* 儒家倫理與社會秩序:社會學的詮釋 [*Confucian Ethics and Social Order: A Social Interpretation*] (Shanghai: Shanghai renmin chubanshe 上海人民出版社, 2008), 111. My translation. About Confucian ideas of family and social order, also see chapter 9.

[48] Kang, *Diasporic Feminist Theology*, 305.

[49] Kang, *Diasporic Feminist Theology*, 305.

doing the will of God—the deeds of justice and love, grounded in Jesus's teaching."[50] This principle transcends the hierarchical family structure that has its own solution and difficulties regarding conflicts of interest and finally social justice: "A 'love ethic of equal regard' grounds this Christian family and places its value on mutuality, self-sacrifice, and individual fulfillment."[51] Even though Kang does not clearly make a distinctive use of love and justice, it appears to me that Kang would agree with Niebuhr that Christian love, with respect to God's commandments and beyond traditional biological family bonds, should make a difference to the meaning of justice (the principle of equality in particular), which distinguishes itself from Confucian familism and its social implications.

CHRISTIAN LOVE AND SOCIAL JUSTICE IN CHINA: THE POSSIBILITIES AND LIMITS

Although we recognize the particular implication of Christian love for social justice, we must discern the constraints upon this implication in the Chinese context.

1. The Ideal and Limitation of Love in the Chinese Context

As Niebuhr understands, the spirit of sacrifice, unselfishness, and forgiveness originated in Christian love has broad implications for Christian communities. In Chinese society, it is observed that a large number of Christians practice well the moral norms (including Christian love) in their personal life, family, church community, civil life, and professional life. Yet as Niebuhr suggests, "the full force of religious faith will never be available for the building of a just society . . . but does not conquer society."[52] Despite this, we cannot deny that the idea of love initiated by religious believers and communities can enhance individual moral life as well as bestow healthy components to intimate social relationships and even give a guide to resolve conflict and inequality in society. Even though Niebuhr insists that with respect to conflict realities in social, political, and economic life, religious ideals (such as love) and power cannot be applied directly to construct social justice, he thinks that if the ideal of justice is penetrated by the ideal of love, it will not become a purely political idea. As he claims, "Every genuine passion for social justice will always contain a religious element within it. Religion will always leaven the idea of justice with the ideal of love. It will prevent the idea of justice,

---

50 Kang, *Diasporic Feminist Theology*, 306.
51 Kang, *Diasporic Feminist Theology*, 306–7.
52 Niebuhr, *Moral Man and Immoral Society*, 81.

which is political-ethical ideal, from becoming a purely political one, with the ethical element washed out."[53] This point can be relevant in the Chinese context.

Within Chinese society, in its pursuit of social justice in various areas, considerations are given to the relationship of rights and duties, institutional arrangement, and rational measures on various issues. In these circumstances, it will make some differences if we have an eye on the moral ideal deriving from the religious and ethical system in order that the idea of justice does not collapse into pure political idea, without the direction of moral sensitivity and without recognizing the relative limitation of institutions and justice. It is a certain moral power that directs, criticizes, corrects, and then leads to perfect justice.

This support of moral ideal and conscience, according to Niebuhr, is rooted in religious communities. However, in contemporary China, Christian faith and practice and the formation of Christian communities face certain constraints and challenges. Culturally, Christians are still a minority among the practice of a variety of religions in China.[54] Politically, with regard to Christianity in China, there is a general structure of both churches registered with the government, under the umbrella of the China Christian Council and the Three-Self Patriotic Movement, and churches without government registration in terms of church governance. It is often the latter (even some cases of the former) that encounter pressures, closing churches, and demolishing of church buildings.[55] The expression of Christian love (like forgiveness) experiences limitations under these cultural and political conditions. It will be a far and hard process for maintaining this moral ideal in supporting and directing social justice from a long-term perspective.

2. Compatibility of Love and Justice in the Chinese Context

By way of contrast, Wolterstorff's account of compatibility of love and justice, which means justice as an expression of love in nonconflicting situations, respect for human worth, and just treatment of the other, may have certain implications in the Chinese context. It seems that the ideal of "justice in love" in Wolterstorff's version is consistent with Chinese church leader Guangxun Ding's understanding. Starting from the idea of "cosmic love of Christ," he insists on the compatibility of love and justice: "Justice, fairness—those are not the opposite of love; rather, they are entailed in love; when we practice love beyond one small scale and when

---

[53]   Niebuhr, *Moral Man and Immoral Society*, 80–81.
[54]   See chapter 1.
[55]   For more details in this respect, see chapter 10.

we distribute love to the masses rationally, love attains its form of justice and fairness."[56]

Justice ought to be indispensable in society; furthermore, to bind love and justice together even in harmonious situations is indeed an action of love. This understanding gives us a more general picture of what justice really is. In contemporary China, greater concern with social justice arises only when some unjust issues (such as corruption, rich-poor gap, unequal competition in economics, unequal treatment in education, and ecological problems) take place. It is supposed in Chinese society that the needs and circumstances of others should be taken into account in certain political considerations, along with the distribution of resources and opportunities such as education, employment, and medical care. This consideration would help minimize the opportunities of inequality and of harm to some special groups, particularly vulnerable and marginalized ones, who deserve equal regard when political power is operated and certain laws and public policies are exercised toward the resolution of these social problems. It is a basic requirement for a just institution.

Here, I would suggest that any social and political arrangements be guided by the principles of justice, supported by the spirit of certain religious and moral ideas such as love, in its concern with the moral worth of fellow human beings in various situations. Marginalized groups deserve constant respect and care in the moral sense, which affects the issue of whether they may be treated justly or not. I believe if this aspect is introduced into the process of governmental policy, it will contribute to the absence of "pure just legal institutions," which might contain some risks, such as discrimination and inequality. From this point of view, when we take into account the moral status of the vulnerable and marginalized groups, it is our hope that charity, love, and justice will not separate from each other toward a caring and just society. As Robert Goodin urges, we should "make duties of justice, morally binding considerations relating to the particular vulnerability of one person to another—also give rise to far more extensive duties of charity or humanity. The effect of that is to put duties like charity or humanity morally on a par with those of justice and to say that (depending on the circumstances) charity can be every bit as compelling as justice, narrowly construed."[57] In my view, this approach stands along the line of "compatibility between love and justice" proposed by Wolterstorff and Guangxun Ding as well.

---

[56]   Guangxun Ding, *Ding guangxun wenji* 丁光訓文集 [*Collected Works of Guangxun Ding*] (Nanjing: Yilin chubanshe 譯林出版社, 1997), 214. My translation.

[57]   Robert E. Goodin, *Protecting the Vulnerable: A Reanalysis of Our Social Responsibility* (Chicago: University of Chicago Press, 1985), 26–27.

A Critical Evaluation: The Distinction and Interrelation of Love and Justice in the Chinese Context

As Lauretta Conklin Frederking suggests, "Social justice is also a place where religions can come together and must come together to sort out agreements and disagreements."[58] Especially for Christianity, its tradition gets involved in the understanding of love, and justice bears the burden of these matters. Christian theologians "speak from a community of faith, which includes worldwide a multitude of the victims of injustice and oppression, whose cry is part of the theologian's task to articulate. They claim to have insights into the nature and the demands of justice which are true and are sometimes recognized as such in a broader arena than the church."[59]

Initiated by the discourse on love and justice from Christian perspectives (in the cases of Niebuhr and Wolterstorff), I have outlined Confucian perspectives (in the cases of Yushun Huang, Yong Huang, Qingping Liu, and Qiyong Gu), Confucian discourse on social and political order, and philosophical, sociological, and political discourse regarding the problem of social justice in contemporary China. A crucial theme arising within their discussions is: To what degree does love give impact to justice? It seems to me that for the most part, they agree that love acts as the spirit of justice even though its manners of impact are different. The various love traditions, either in Confucianism or Christianity (and probably in other cultural and religious traditions), despite their divergence and even differences among the interpretations in a specific tradition, have the common impetus to move beyond an intimate relationship and to provide a certain burden for social and political relationships. The various love-justice interrelations in different traditions may learn from each other.

As I see it, discourse on Confucian resources on social and political issues, including social justice, basically agrees with the relevance to Confucian moral values, such as benevolence, humanness, sympathy, and equality of personality, to those issues to some degree, either directly or indirectly. Whereas Qing Jiang concentrates on the Confucian constitutional order in a comprehensive way, Joseph Chan attempts to accommodate Confucian values in political life in a civil way rather than to

---

58 Lauretta Conklin Frederking, *Reconstructing Social Justice* (New York: Routledge, 2014), 97.

59 Duncan B. Forrester, *Forrester on Christian Ethics and Practical Theology: Collected Writings on Christianity, India, and the Social Order* (Farnham: Ashgate, 2010), 252.

embrace Confucianism comprehensively.[60] Although Yushun Huang develops a Chinese theory of justice rooted in benevolence to achieve the goal of harmony, Yong Huang makes an effort to expound Confucian love with distinction to make it compatible with the conception of justice so as to avoid the conflict between love and justice from a Christian perspective, as he interprets it. Whereas Qingping Liu ascribes social and legal injustice to Confucian filial love with its limitations, Qiyong Guo affirms the significance of Confucian virtues for social and political life. Huaihong He also supports Chinese moral values, alongside some basic institutions, in the construction of justice in China.

The dynamic of love and justice informed by Niebuhr suggests that social justice, including the principle of equality, is not complete without love, while concrete just political and economic arrangements cannot be simply replaced by pure love or its direct implications. In pursuit of social justice in China, the issue of equality has been commonly raised by many philosophers, legal scholars, and social scientists, either in general discussions or in practical problems. Some of them refer to political philosopher John Rawls for the principle of equality.[61] There have been a lot of institutional efforts to overcome the inequality problem in various areas. However, there is always something beyond the institutional aspect with regard to the problem of equality. Niebuhr himself points to Christian love as the root and motive of the principle of equality. This is what Confucianism resources, other resources in various disciplines, and practical efforts can learn from Niebuhr with regard to love and justice on the issue of equality, observing Confucian contributions and limitations in this regard and taking into account Christian engagement in the matter of equality rooted in the spirit of love with an orientation toward justice. Political and legal scholar Jeremy Waldron also reminds us what we can learn from John Locke is his assumption of a Christian foundation for equality: "Equality cannot do its work unless it is accepted among those whom it consecrates as equals. Locke believed this general acceptance was impossible apart from the principle's foundation in religious teaching."[62]

---

[60] Seen from chapter 5.

[61] For example, Joseph Chan also refers to Rawls for his understanding of a comprehensive doctrine and political discussion when he responds to Qing Jiang's version of Confucian constitutionalism. See Joseph Chan, "On the Legitimacy of Confucian Constitutionalism," in Jiang, *A Confucian Constitutional Order*, 99–112. Rawls is also quoted frequently by authors from various disciplines in Liang, ed., *Zhuanxingqi de shehui gongzheng*.

[62] Jeremy Waldron, *God, Locke, and Equality: Christian Foundations in Locke's Political Thought* (Cambridge: Cambridge University Press, 2002), 243.

Although acknowledging Christian love's engagement with the principles of social justice as a motive, a corrective power, or an end, we are to recognize human limitations in pursuing social justice, as Robin Lovin reminds us: "Where Rawls characterizes the searches for truth and justice as the most important achievements of thought and action, Niebuhr sees both quests as also revealing characteristic human limitations."[63] The limitations suggest a religiously moral involvement (with the idea of love) that motivates, corrects, and elevates social justice without confining justice as a purely political concept. For Niebuhr, Christian love works for this purpose; for many Confucian scholars, Confucian *ren* has applications for social justice in its distinctive ways.

Niebuhr reasons, though, that the dynamic of love and justice, which is to distinguish and yet to interrelate both, underlines the pure and absolute form of Christian love as the ultimate possibility only. For Yong Huang, his interpretation of Confucian love with distinction is even "more difficult to practice . . . than Christian love (which, of course, does not mean that it is easy to practice Christian love at all) since one has to determine in each case which love is appropriate based on one's empirical knowledge of the particular object of love."[64] It remains a problem how this kind of Confucian love distinguishes itself from social justice while it also has potential to be consistent with social justice (as Yong Huang argues). An additional point is to consider the influence of filial love in Confucianism on familial and social structures in China and the possibilities and difficulties in confronting conflicts of interest and social inequality in pursuing social justice in this context. What is inspiring here is that the Christian version of love and justice developed by Niebuhr and Wolterstorff should engage the concrete familial, social, and political order when it comes to the issues of social justice in a particular context.

When Niebuhr claims that "American Christianity tends to be irrelevant to the problems of justice because it persists in presenting the law of love as a simple solution for every communal problem,"[65] my own concerns with love (in both Confucian and Christian senses) and social justice in the Chinese context are the following. Although some attempt to relate and even integrate Confucian values to social and political issues, including social justice, too closely, they may not be aware of the relatively independent political and social inquiry into justice. While some are confronted with the issues of social justice in practice, such as inequality, and approach them from philosophical, political, and

---

63   Lovin, *Reinhold Niebuhr and Christian Realism*, 191.

64   Huang, "Confucian Love and Global Ethics," 41.

65   Niebuhr, *Love and Justice*, 25.

sociological perspectives, they may not be attentive enough to the religious ethical contribution, such as the ideal of love, to create a just society. Yet the relevance of love to social justice cannot be simply interpreted from any defined version of that relationship in the Chinese context. We probably need a kind of Niebuhrian religious passion for an ideal conferred on justice in order to direct, guarantee, and correct the principles and practice of justice; we also need to go further to put into effect the idea of the compatibility of love and justice. The ideal and implication of love, in its specific moral resources, will enrich and advance the view of social justice in the Chinese context. Wherever love confines itself, justice deserves its role. Wherever love demands, justice finds its limits and elevation. At this point, the dynamic of love and justice is relevant to and challenging in the Chinese context.

8

HUMAN RIGHTS IN CHINA

A Social-Constructive Theological Approach

The discussion of the dynamic demonstrates resources concerning the moral and spiritual aspect of justice. With focus on the issue of human rights as the core of justice, this chapter deepens this dynamic approach to human rights with references to Confucian and Christian resources again and with a focus on the morality problem (human aspect) of human rights.

Discussing human dignity and human rights in China in a universal language is challenging as, in the Chinese context, human rights are more often connected with the privileges of economic well-being (including escape from poverty),[1] with "state-authorized channels to enhance national unity and prosperity"[2] in an authoritarianism state,[3] with social order and stability,[4] and with the moral integrity of citizens and its relevance to the problem of human dignity.[5] As I see it, debates over human rights in the Chinese context center on the controversy between the

---

[1]   Claude E. Welch, Jr., and Sergio Brian Cruz Egoávil, "China's Rising Power: Economic Growth vs. Freedom Deficit," *Journal of Human Rights* 10, no. 3 (2011): 290–310.

[2]   Elizabeth J. Perry, "Chinese Conceptions of 'Rights': From Mencius to Mao and Now," *Perspectives on Politics* 6, no. 1 (2008): 46.

[3]   Eva Pils, *Human Rights in China: A Social Practice in the Shadows of Authoritarianism* (Cambridge: Polity Press, 2018).

[4]   Sarah Biddulph, *The Stability Imperative: Human Rights and Law in China* (Vancouver: UBC Press, 2015).

[5]   Perry Keller, "The Protection of Human Dignity under Chinese Law," in *The Cambridge Handbook of Human Dignity*, eds. Marcus Düwell, Jens Braarvig, Roger Brownsword, and Dietmar Mieth (Cambridge: Cambridge University Press, 2014), 414–21.

Western understanding of human rights and a distinctively Chinese conception of human rights. As Stephen Angle argues, "Chinese concepts of rights over the years have differed in important ways from many Western conceptions of rights . . . it has a coherent history and is made up of Chinese concepts and concerns . . . China has a rich and distinctive rights discourse."[6] In confronting the controversy, it is important to take stock of the local nuance of human rights in China and to explore the implications for how the West perceives human rights.

The model of "human rights as social construction" proposed by Benjamin Gregg rejects theological and metaphysical constructions of human rights, which are often the basis of universalistic conceptions of human rights. The conception I seek to advance is a political and "this-worldly" construction, which "takes human nature as biologically understood and eschews supernatural explanations, whether theological or metaphysical"[7] and tends to be "less culturally exclusive than are religious faiths."[8] In his critical exchange with Andrew Koppelman,[9] Gregg emphasizes "social construction's capacity to coexist with a wide range of competing comprehensive doctrines," and contends that "it can cooperate with persons of faith who share the goal of advancing human rights."[10]

Morton Winston highlights this ideal by emphasizing the justification of human rights as a "pragmatic, conditional one" instead of basing upon "religious doctrines, metaphysical postulates, or speculative philosophical conceptions of human nature."[11] In particular, human rights are socially constructed with response to "historically experienced oppression"[12] and "through political struggle."[13] For him, this approach "has a better chance of becoming the basis of a cosmopolitan consensus on human rights because one can accept it without carrying a lot of philosophical, religious,

---

6   Stephen Angle, *Human Rights and Chinese Thought: A Cross-Cultural Inquiry* (Cambridge: Cambridge University Press, 2002), 206–7, 250–51.

7   Benjamin Gregg, *Human Rights as Social Construction* (New York: Cambridge University Press, 2012), 185.

8   Gregg, *Human Rights as Social Construction*, 17.

9   Andrew Koppelman affirms that Benjamin Gregg "oscillates between two concepts of this project: an abstemious, neo-Rawlsian political liberalism, and a comprehensive view that rejects religious and metaphysical claims." See Andrew Koppelman and Benjamin Gregg, "Critical Exchange on Human Rights as Social Construction," *Contemporary Political Theory*, no. 13 (2014): 380.

10   Koppelman and Gregg, "Critical Exchange on Human Rights as Social Construction," 384.

11   Morton Winston, "Human Rights as Moral Rebellion and Social Construction," *Journal of Human Rights* 6, no. 3 (2007), 280.

12   Winston, "Human Rights as Moral Rebellion and Social Construction," 286.

13   Winston, "Human Rights as Moral Rebellion and Social Construction," 293.

or cultural baggage."[14] In this sense, a social construction model of human rights tends to be "'metaphysically lighter' than religiously based theories of rights or traditional natural law theory."[15]

In its struggle with the implications of philosophical and religious ideas, the social construction of human rights heavily relies on local cultural expression and political experiences. In this chapter, I adopt this "social construction" model of human rights to expound the problem of human rights in China in its cultural and social settings, examining the challenges from within, and exploring how Christian theology in its local (Chinese) expression can be brought to bear on this debate. Even though the social construction position attempts to eschew theological and metaphysical foundations, my goal is to show that even when a social construction model is applied to human rights in China, the metaphysical and theological aspects of human rights continue to enrich the discussion, particularly by underscoring the "human aspect of human rights."[16] In other words, I wish to test its philosophical and theological applicability given the social construction of human rights in the Chinese context.

HUMAN RIGHTS AS A SOCIAL CONSTRUCTION IN CHINA

In recent years, China has launched two "Five-year Human Rights Action Plans" (2012–2015, and 2016–2020) and signed various UN human rights treaties such as the "International Covenant on Economic, Social and Cultural Rights" and the "International Convention on the Elimination of All Forms of Racial Discrimination," among others. There also exists in China a sound human rights protection system.[17] In some ways, it seems that China tends to respect and adhere to international human rights treaties. However, for the most part, the Chinese government continues to struggle with the concept of human rights itself, emphasizing its historical and cultural setting to propose a "China model" of human rights. It has been reported from time to time that there are constraints on human rights practices in China.[18]

---

[14] Winston, "Human Rights as Moral Rebellion and Social Construction," 296.

[15] Winston, "Human Rights as Moral Rebellion and Social Construction," 300.

[16] I take the "human aspect of human rights" among "the fundamentals of human rights" that academics and religious leaders should address, as John Witte, Jr. advocates. See Zhibin Xie (interviewer), "Freedom and Order: Christianity, Human Rights, and Culture: A Chinese Conversation with John Witte Jr." (see appendix 3).

[17] See Pinghua Sun, *Human Rights Protection System in China* (Berlin: Springer-Verlag, 2014).

[18] See Pils, *Human Rights in China*, 57.

Chinese participation in human rights discourse has often begun with the assumption that Confucianism is central to the Chinese understanding of human rights and even that Confucianism provides moral resources that can contribute to international understandings of human rights, even beyond the realm of China. The question of whether Confucianism is compatible with the notion of human rights is a perplexing philosophical inquiry. At a practical level, a question remains regarding the extent to which Confucian ideas permeate the Chinese understanding and practice of human rights in the contemporary context. As Marina Svensson suggests, "Human rights debate in China . . . has generally been motivated by political concerns and concrete human rights violations, so that human rights writings, as a consequence, have a tendency to be very political and polemical in character."[19]

About the idea of human rights and its meaning in China, Eva Pils has raised this point: "There are many ideas resonating with that of rights as a particular conception of justice in China's long moral tradition; but the contemporary Chinese *words* for 'rights' and 'human rights' were only coined in the second half of the nineteenth century."[20] Although Svensson tends to emphasize contemporary political concerns and debate over the influence of historical traditions, it remains true that political concerns and practices are inevitably interwoven with certain moral and philosophical ideas. It thus remains important to explore the potential contribution of Confucian concepts to the discourse of human rights.

A proposal for the compatibility of Confucianism and human rights in light of Confucius and Mencius put forward by Joseph Chan concentrates on the question: Under what conditions would Confucianism accept human rights? Chan contends that Confucianism can accept an instrumental approach to human rights that protects the human being's fundamental interests but cannot support human rights as an expression of human dignity or worth. As Chan puts it, "Confucians want to give human rights only a fall-back instrumental role, rather than construing them as an abstract ideal that expresses human dignity."[21]

Other scholars discussing the relationship of Confucianism and human rights have focused on such issues as the Confucian emphasis on social and communitarian values, the dignity of the self and person,

---

[19]   Marina Svensson, *Debating Human Rights in China* (Lanham: Rowan & Littlefield, 2002), 5.

[20]   Pils, *Human Rights in China*, 52.

[21]   Joseph C. W. Chan, "Confucianism and Human Rights," in *Religion and Human Rights: An Introduction*, eds. John Witte Jr. and M. Christian Green (Oxford: Oxford University Press, 2012), 97.

civility, humane concern, and mutual respect.[22] Louis Henkin, for example, notes that "the values reflected in the commitment to human dignity, in the idea of human rights, and in the particular rights set forth in the Universal Declaration, do not appear to be foreign to the values of Confucianism as presented in this volume."[23] Sumner B. Twiss also supports the contribution of Confucianism to the discourse on civil-political liberties and human rights: "I see no reason why Confucian moral and political thought could not make further contributions—for example, strengthening a moral communitarian receptive understanding of civil-political liberties as empowerments aimed at community involvement and flourishing, strengthening the thesis about the interdependence and indivisibility of the three generations of human rights; advancing the cause of those developmental-collective human rights particularly with matters of peace, harmony and ecological responsibility."[24]

Pinghua Sun, a Chinese scholar, has further argued that the Confucian contribution to human rights centers on the concepts of *ren* (humanness) 仁, people's dignity, grand harmony, and the priority of morality to self-interests.[25] Nevertheless, other scholars continue to emphasize the noncompatibility of Confucianism and human rights.

Although Robert Weatherley depicts Confucianism as evincing a "distinctive lack of a rights tradition" (including a conception of moral equality),[26] he recommends that "the West might pay closer attention to China's historical and cultural traditions before condemning its human rights policy out of hand."[27] Such an appeal to China's historical and cultural tradition does not necessarily amount to the rejection of universal values regarding human rights. Instead, to conceive of human rights in the Chinese context involves exploring how the Chinese actually understand human rights from within their own cultural traditions and life experiences. This includes, especially, examining how Confucian assumptions permeate this understanding.

My goal here is not to engage deeply in the debate over the relationship between Confucianism and human rights. My purpose in introducing this

---

22 See Wm. Theodore de Bary and Tu Wei-ming, eds., *Confucianism and Human Rights* (New York: Columbia University Press, 1998).

23 Henkin, "Confucianism, Human Rights, and 'Cultural Relativism,'" in *Confucianism and Human Rights*, eds. de Bary and Tu, 310.

24 Sumner B. Twiss, "A Constructive Framework for Discussing Confucianism and Human Rights," in *Confucianism and Human Rights*, eds. de Bary and Tu, 46.

25 See Sun, *Human Rights Protection System in China*.

26 Robert Weatherley, *The Discourse of Human Rights in China: Historical and Ideological Perspectives* (New York: St. Martin's Press, 1999), 38.

27 Weatherley, *The Discourse of Human Rights in China*, 12.

debate is instead to raise the broader question of how cultural resources distinctive to China relate to international conceptions of human rights. Beyond this, it is also important to recognize that the contemporary Chinese government tends to invoke Confucianism as a tenet for the future of the Chinese state and Chinese culture.

In retrospect, Confucian beliefs influenced the idea of universal human rights during the formation of the Universal Declaration of Human Rights. In 1947 and 1948, P. C. Chang 張彭春 (Pengchun Zhang, 1892–1957) served as the Chinese delegate to the Commission on Human Rights of the United Nations. In this capacity, his emphasis on the interconnection of human rights with duties and responsibilities made a mark on "the more individualistic rights documents of countries in the Anglo-American sphere."[28] According to Frédéric Krumbein, Chang's contribution to universal human rights discourse emphasized "the goodness of human beings; their possibility of personal development; and their capacity for displaying sympathy for others. . . . It strikes a good balance between social and economic rights and civil and political rights, between rights and duties, and between education and personal development and law and punishment as the means to realize human rights."[29]

Chang's understanding of human rights was deeply rooted in Chinese thought and, in particular, Confucianism. As one writer explains, "P. C. Chang argued successfully for the inclusion of the basic Confucian ideal of benevolence, and 'conscience' was added as a fundamental basis of human rights."[30]

In addition to the Confucian tradition, socialist ideas have influenced the Chinese understanding of human rights. Discourse on human rights in contemporary China, as Robert Weatherley explains, bears the imprint of "the ideology of the Marxist State," such as the "class nature" of rights, the law of the party-state in relation to rights, the superiority of collective interests, a harmony of interests, the priority of welfare rights, and the primacy of citizens' duties.[31] To a large degree, the human rights discourse in socialist China is based on authoritarian conceptions of sovereignty and the national interest, alongside conceptions of national unity and prosperity. State sovereignty and security are seen to override individual

[28] Jun Zhao. "China and the Uneasy Case for Universal Human Rights," *Human Rights Quarterly* 37, no. 1 (2015): 35.
[29] Frédéric Krumbein, "P. C. Chang—The Chinese Father of Human Rights," *Journal of Human Rights* 14, no. 3 (2015), 349.
[30] Craig Williams, "International Human Rights and Confucianism," *Asia-Pacific Journal on Human Rights and the Law* 7, no. 1 (2006), 48.
[31] See Weatherley, *The Discourse of Human Rights in China*, 90–100.

rights, causing suspicion of human rights practices in the name of maintaining social stability.[32]

The Chinese discourse on human rights has emphasized the tension between individual rights and collective interests. The problem is highlighted by the influence of both Confucianism and Marxism (in its Chinese version). As one scholar puts it, "In China, the effects of Confucian collectivism, promoted by imperial bureaucrats and modern socialist philosophy, have combined to reject the primacy of individual rights in favor of the interests of the Party and the State."[33] Andrew J. Nathan supports this idea, noting the subordination of individual interests to the higher interests of the party, class, and nation:[34] "In short, the Confucian understanding of the empirical and ethical relationship between the individual and society continues to inform Chinese political thought in this century—the factual opposition that properly understood the individual's interest are inseparable from those of society, and the ethical injunction to place the interests of society first."[35] Generally speaking, Confucianism and Marxism combine in the contemporary Chinese worldview to emphasize the collective interest over the rights of the individual.

In addition to focusing on the collective interest, the Chinese understanding and practice of human rights tend to give priority to economic growth, and to security and stability, over civil and political liberties. This priority undermines the idea of individual human rights and thus the basic Western conception of human rights. As Louis Henkin suggests, "In the Chinese tradition, the individual was not central, and no conception of individual rights existed in the sense known to the United States. . . . In traditional China, the idea was not individual liberty or equality but order and harmony, not individual independence but selfless and cooperation, not the freedom of individual conscience but conformity to orthodox truth."[36]

While there are good reasons to value the Confucian emphasis on humaneness, conscience, mutual respect, and duties that concern human

---

[32] See Plis, *Human Rights in China*, 31.

[33] David E. Christensen, "Breaking the Deadlock: Toward a Socialist-Confucianist Concept of Human Rights for China," *Michigan Journal of International Law* 13, no. 2 (1992), 471.

[34] Andrew J. Nathan, "Sources of Chinese Rights Thinking," in *Human Rights in Contemporary China*, eds. R. Randle Edwards, Louis Henkin, and Andrew J. Nathan (New York: Columbia University Press, 1986), 141.

[35] Nathan, "Sources of Chinese Rights Thinking," 143.

[36] Louis Henkin, "The Human Rights Idea in China," in *Human Rights in Contemporary China*, eds. Edwards, et al., 21.

well-being, the question remains whether the Confucian worldview can maintain an integral conception of the human person, which supports the idea and institution of human rights. This remains a problem for the practice and implementation of human rights in China.

Although it is difficult to precisely measure the ongoing impact of Marxist ideology on contemporary Chinese politics and society, there is no doubt that Marxism provides intellectual resources to understand the problem of human rights practice in China. The discussion of the influence of both Confucianism and Marxism can be helpfully placed within the framework of human rights as a social construction in the Chinese context, with its focus on how historical and cultural resources affect concrete problems of human rights practice. This examination, with reference to Confucianism and socialist discourses on human rights, leads to the crucial problems regarding the human rights discourse in China (i.e., the conception of the individual person and thus individual rights, on the one hand, and the communal aspects of human rights, on the other).

CHRISTIAN ENGAGEMENT WITH HUMAN RIGHTS IN CHINA

Although the Chinese government remains skeptical of universal conceptions of human rights, a vigorous engagement with human rights has been undertaken by Christians in the Chinese context, in the form of human rights defense and in theological appraisals of Chinese cultural resources such as Confucianism, in relation to human rights.[37] In this section, I present and examine how Christians (and especially Christian lawyers) participate in human rights defense and citizens' rights movements, reflecting theologically on human rights conceptions in an effort to construct a Chinese theological understanding of human rights. Here I continue with the social construction approach to human rights in its local practice. Yet I take a further step to explore how theological elements contribute to human rights discourse in China, and in particular with regard to the "human problem."

As David E. Christensen observes, "The solution lies in finding a source of human rights in society itself. . . . If dignity and rights are society-based, and thus subject to historical forces, then there must be a place for them in socialist society."[38] As we have seen, in a country like China, human rights debates center on political considerations and human rights practice. Besides the controversy about the idea of human rights itself, it is important to examine how human rights practice, in the name of human

---

[37] See Pan-chiu Lai. "Human Rights and Christian-Confucian Dialogue," *Studies in Interreligious Dialogue* 23, no. 2 (2013): 133–49.

[38] Christensen, "Breaking the Deadlock," 513.

rights defense (*weiquan* 維權), shapes the understanding of human rights in China. Here I concentrate on human rights practice and defense on the part of Christians in China.

According to Fuk-tsang Ying's 邢福增 description, one quarter of lawyers in the rights defense movement in contemporary China are Christians. This percentage far surpasses the percentage of Christians in the population of China as a whole. They are called the Group of Christian Lawyers for Rights Defense in China. These Christian lawyers dare to speak out and defend the rights of Christians and ordinary people, including believers of other religions. In public statements, these lawyers express their Christian faith, not least through their actions of rights defense. Their theology tends to focus on human sinfulness, whereas their courage and persistence in the face of great pressure and danger are based on their faith and belief in the values of democracy and freedom. For them, rights defense aims not only for a better political and social order but also for the moral integrity of human beings. They even pray for the people whose actions violate human conscience and thus for the moral restoration of these people who attack human rights.[39] This movement of Christian lawyers bears far-reaching significance for the future of human rights in China. Understanding the role of human rights in China today requires understanding the Christian beliefs expressed by this group of Christian lawyers.

Christian beliefs can be further demonstrated in some other Christian social activism. In *Christian Social Activism and Rule of Law in Chinese Societies*, Chris White and Fenggang Yang lay out Chinese Christian activism in its various historical aspects from the founding of the Republic of China, the campaign for religious freedom in the constitution in the new republic, Christians in the democratization of Taiwan, and Christian activism in Hong Kong to Chinese Christian activism in the People's Republic of China.[40] It is worth noting that Chinese Christian activism through the century has relied on certain theological ideas such as human nature, the God-human relationship, love, peace, and repentance, to some degree, in the advocacy for

---

[39] Fuk-tsang Ying, "Zhongguo weiquan yundong yu zhongguo de jidujiao xinyang" 中國維權運動與中國的基督教信仰 ["Rights Defense Movement and Christian Faith in China"], *The Chinese University of Hong Kong, The Center for Christian Center and Christian Study Center on Chinese Religion and Culture Newsletter* 香港中文大學基督教研究中心暨基督教中國宗教文化研究社通訊, no. 21 (2014): 1–7.

[40] Chris White and Fenggang Yang, "A Historical Overview of Chinese Christian Activism: Institutional Change toward Democracy," in *Christian Social Activism and Rule of Law in Chinese Societies*, eds. White and Yang, 1–30.

religious freedom, religious equality, and democracy:[41] "The diverse ways Chinese Christians have participated in social or political movements over the decades suggest there is something about the faith of these individuals that motivates such activism."[42] However, those theological elements deserves further examination for their implications on human rights advocacy. In addition to the rights defense movement among Christian lawyers and other social activism, there are some cases of Christian communities defending the interests of the church in their public resistance to governmental actions toward churches.[43] It could be seen as a courageous defense of religious human rights and church autonomy in the face of state power.[44]

In this Christian social activism, Christians involve the issues of citizenship and civil society in their own ways. In his book *Christianity and Civil Society in China*, Mark Chuanhang Shan proposes that Christianity promotes citizenship rights in China today primarily through "invisible and unstructured church communities" in their struggle for the right to religious freedom.[45] Christianity's ethical culture, focused, in his view, on love and justice, contributes to the emergence of a kind of "quasi-political culture." Shan contends that "the growth of Christianity of China has already become a crucial element in advancing citizenship rights and the development of a civil society in China."[46] In an analysis of Shouwang Church's (Beijing) outdoor worship as a form of protest,[47] Hao Yuan 袁浩 suggests that the church as a new type of urban church in China further indicates Christianity's potential contribution to the strengthening of civil society confronting with state power. Hao Yuan sees the church's civil

---

[41] Particularly see Yan Liu's discussions on the concepts of human nature and God-human relationship. Yan Liu, "Christian Faith Confessions in the Chinese Jiating Church Context: The Discourse of Sovereignty and the Political Order," in *Christian Social Activism and Rule of Law in Chinese Societies*, eds. White and Yang, 297–99. "*Jiating* church" means "nonregistered church."

[42] White and Yang, "A Historical Overview of Chinese Christian Activism: Institutional Change toward Democracy," 22.

[43] See more details in chapter 10.

[44] Regarding the significance of social movements for human rights, Stammers claims, "Ideas and practices in respect of human rights have been socially constructed in the context of social movement challenges to extant relations and structures of power." See Neil Stammers, "Social Movements and the Social Construction of Human Rights," *Human Rights Quarterly*, no. 21 (1999): 981.

[45] Mark Chuanhang Shan, *Christianity and Civil Society in China: Christian Ethics Is Transforming Citizenship Rights and Church-State Relations in China through Invisible and Unstructured Church Communities*, accessed January 30, 2022, https://tinyurl.com/2p94vvkx.

[46] Shan, *Christianity and Civil Society in China*.

[47] See a more detailed analysis about this event in chapter 10.

disobedience as "often intertwined with the awaking of citizen identity and sense of rights."[48] In their seeking identity as both Christians and Chinese citizens, Christians in China invariably encounter the power of the state and perform their social responsibility in various instances, which in turn has advanced civil participation, community formation, and civil and religious rights.[49]

Along with the implications of Christian practice for the development of civil and political rights in China, a more basic question is about the theological roots of Christian practice, which is particularly raised by the rights defense movement among lawyers in China. This can be referred to as the "human problem," including such questions as moral integrity of human beings, human sinfulness, and human suffering. Here, the issue connects to broader theological discussions of what it means to be human and its relevance to the idea of human rights in Chinese Christian scholarship.[50] Jürgen Moltmann is an important figure in these discussions as he associates "fundamental human rights" with a conception of what it means "to be truly human." The problem of human rights and the related topic of human dignity thus center on the idea that individuals "are human and should be human."[51] Moltmann's main concern is the ideological challenge to human rights and human dignity, which is "identified narrowly with only a few dimensions of human life or with a limited number of human rights,"[52] in the form of either "individual's rights in a market society" or social rights assumed by the state. In responding to this challenge, he argues for the indivisibility of human dignity and thus for the totality of human rights from a Christian theological perspective. He therefore rejects a "narrow, ideological definition

48 Hao Yuan, "Zhongguo jidujiao yu bufucong de chuantong: yi wang mingdao, tanghe jiaohui yu shouwang jiaohui weili" 中國基督教與不服從的傳統: 以王明道、唐河教會與守望教會為例 ["Chinese Christianity and Its Tradition of Disobedience: Wang Mingdao, Tanghe Church, and Shouwang Church as Examples"], *Daofeng jidujiao wenhua pinglun* 基督教文化評論 [*Logos and Pneuma: Chinese Journal of Theology*], no. 44 (2016): 119–20. My translation.

49 See Zhibin Xie, "Between Individuality and Publicness: Christianity in Urban China Since the 1980s," in *World Christianity, Urbanization, and Identity*, eds. Moses Biney, Kenneth Ngwa, and Raimundo Barreto (Minneapolis: Fortress Press, 2021), 252.

50 See, for example, *Daofeng jidujiao wenhua pinglun* 基督教文化評論 [*Logos and Pneuma: Chinese Journal of Theology*] (49A, 2018) published a special issue on "Zunyan, daode yu quanli: kuaxueke yanjiu" 尊嚴、道德與權利:跨學科研究 ["Dignity, Morality, and Rights: Interdisciplinary Studies"].

51 Jürgen Moltmann, *On Human Dignity: Political Theology and Ethics*, trans. M. Douglas Meeks (London: SCM Press, 1984), 10.

52 D. Douglas Meeks, introduction to *On Human Dignity*, by Moltmann, x.

of human dignity as reducible to any specific rights or political-economic arrangements."[53]

We find a similar idea in the work of theologian Stanley Grenz, who emphasizes the significance of the idea of the "image of God" for understanding the human person: "Through much of Christian history, the link made in scripture between humans and the divine image has served as the foundation for the task of constructing a Christian conception of the human person or the self."[54] For Moltmann, the human being as created in the image of God marks the human future, a human destiny yet to be realized. This understanding is grounded in humanity, understood in terms of how the image of God reshapes our understanding of human communities, including human community with nonhuman creation. This is brought to bear on the meaning of human rights: "The human rights to life, freedom, community, and self-determination mirror God's right to the human being because the human being is destined to the human being because the human being is destined to be God's image in all conditions and relationships of life."[55]

Human beings as the image of God embody the fullness of human life in all life's relationships: economic, social, political, and personal. In this sense, "the right of God to all human beings"[56] is expressed in the human person's various relationships and rights, assuring human fullness and true humanness before God: "There is no priority of individual rights over social rights, no priority of social rights over individual rights."[57] This totality of human rights is established to affirm the wholeness of human beings.

On this account, human destiny before God and the right of God vis-à-vis human beings are key to an understanding of human dignity and human rights. According to Moltmann, "By fundamental human rights we mean those rights and duties which belong essentially to what it means to be truly human, because without their being fully acknowledged and exercised human beings cannot fulfil their original destiny of having being created in the image of God."[58]

Theological contributions to human rights thus focus on "the grounding of the fundamental human rights upon God's right to human

---

[53]   Meeks, introduction to *On Human Dignity*, x.
[54]   Stanley J. Grenz, *The Social God and the Relational Self: A Trinitarian Theology of the Imago Dei* (Louisville: Westminster John Knox Press, 2001), 183.
[55]   Moltmann, *On Human Dignity*, 17.
[56]   Moltmann, *On Human Dignity*, 17.
[57]   Moltmann, *On Human Dignity*, 25.
[58]   Moltmann, *On Human Dignity*, 23

beings."[59] As Moltmann suggests, the "image of God, as destiny, points to God's indivisible claim upon beings and therefore to their inalienable dignity."[60] The claims of the indivisible right of God to the human being, the irreducible dignity of the human being, and the indivisible totality of human rights are central to what it means to be truly human. Regarding Christian understanding of humanity and its implications for human rights, in my interview with legal scholar John Witte Jr., he states it in this way: "The Christian tradition built a number of its basic teachings of human rights on fundamental ideas of the image of God, which vests each person with inherent dignity; on the fundamental ideas that we are prophets, priests, and kings with natural rights to speak, worship, and rule."[61]

In a similar way, the Christian ethicist William Schweiker affirms the significance of being truly human in public life: "To be human is to be constantly engaged in the task of world-making culture, creation."[62] In my view, this creativity involves a commitment to human rights. Schweiker proposes the idea of "integrity of life before God," which expresses "the proper relation among natural, social and reflexive goods" and entails that we should "in all actions and relations respect and enhance the integrity of life."[63] These actions and relations contain what human beings, created in the image of God, need in terms of natural, social, economic, and political relations and, furthermore, the rights implied in these relations. To acknowledge these relations and rights for the existence of human beings is to promote the realization of being truly human.

Moltmann's claim that individuals "are human and should be human," and other discussions of human beings from a Christian perspective, relate to our concern with the problem of human rights in China in terms of the ideological challenge to the integrity of human life and the irreducibility of human rights. These theological approaches to what it means to be human, defined in terms of true humanness and the integrity of life, both inform and are informed by fundamental human rights. They also underscore the indivisibility of individual rights and social rights, which secure basic human needs while affirming human communities. As a scholar writing on human rights in the Chinese context, I find this theological idea helpful in articulating and understanding human rights in China.

---

59   Moltmann, *On Human Dignity*, 15.
60   Moltmann, *On Human Dignity*, 23.
61   Xie, "Freedom and Order: Christianity, Human Rights, and Culture."
62   William Schweiker, *Theological Ethics and Global Dynamics: In the Time of Many Worlds* (Malden: Blackwell Publishing, 2004), xiii.
63   Schweiker. *Theological Ethics and Global Dynamics*, xiv.

SOCIAL AND THEOLOGICAL CONCEPTIONS
OF HUMAN RIGHTS IN CHINA

This chapter focuses on human beings as the key to understanding human rights in China in its dialogue with universal perspectives. The issue itself is raised from the Chinese social and cultural settings with regard to the idea of human rights and their practice, including Christian engagement in human rights and theological reflection on human rights. As David N. Stamos writes, "If human rights are the rights that one has by virtue of being human (and this is the consensus concept), then we cannot sidestep or ignore what 'being human' means."[64] But this understanding of what the human being is tends to vary by culture. Regarding the difference between the Asiatic and biblical understandings of the human being, for example, Moltmann notes that "whereas all Asiatic and African religions understand human beings as part of nature, the biblical traditions introduced into the world the understandings of the individual human being as a person."[65]

It is not easy to provide a singular picture of the Chinese understanding of the human being. Even if we focus entirely on Confucianism, the tradition is incredibly complex and varied. Nonetheless, some preliminary conclusions can be ventured. On the one hand, many will point to the Confucian contribution to human rights discourse through its concepts of benevolence, conscience, goodness of human beings, personal development, sympathy for others, mutual respect, civility, and balance between rights and duties. On the other hand, we have also explored the questions raised about the cultural tradition and social practice of human rights in China: the absence of a sense of moral equality, questions about the origin of human dignity and worth, and the primacy of communal rights over individual rights, or the primary of welfare rights over civil and political rights. These challenges are not easily solved.

In an essay called "Do You Want to Be a Human Being?" the Chinese philosopher Haiguang Yin discusses the relevance of human rights in light of what it means to be truly human. He contends, "Fundamental human rights are the essential conditions for being a human. Fundamental human rights are the innate rights of every individual; we should enjoy them fully

---

[64] David N. Stamos, *The Myth of Universal Human Rights: Its Origin, History, and Explanation, along with a More Humane Way* (Boulder: Paradigim, 2013), 33.

[65] Jürgen Moltmann, "Christianity and the Revaluation of the Values of Modernity and of the Western World," in *A Passion for God's Reign: Theology, Christian Learning, and the Christian Self*, by Jürgen Moltmann, Nicholas Wolterstorff, and Ellen T. Charry, ed. Miroslav Volf (Grand Rapids: Eerdmans, 1998), 28.

and develop them. . . . If our fundamental human rights are jeopardized or violated, it is our humanity (*zuoren*) which is being violated. If our due fundamental human rights are not fully respected, then our humanity is compromised. If we are completely derived of our human rights, then our humanity is at an end."[66] In other words, "being a human" is defined by the enjoyment of fundamental human rights. Insofar as these rights are violated, our basic humanity is violated. As P. C. Chang put the point in another context, "Stress should be laid upon the human aspect of human rights."[67]

"The human aspect of human rights" becomes a central problem when discussing human rights, whether in a Chinese context or elsewhere. However, it is not altogether clear how the understanding of being human in the Chinese context might develop into an understanding of human rights, even less a commitment to human rights. As one scholar notes, there is a difference between "a language of benevolence" and "a language of rights," and in the Chinese context, "injunctions to benevolent actions by no means necessarily refer to possessions that we today call 'rights,' whether conventional or natural."[68] What this might mean, therefore, is that commitment to "welfare rights" understood as "welfare benefits" is not a commitment to human rights in its full sense.

According to the Chinese social construction of human rights, either in its Confucian or socialist version (or in their mixture), the status of the human being and the integrity of human life remains an outstanding problem. Although I do not dismiss Confucian contributions to the idea of human rights in various ways, neither do I overlook the reality of how this tradition is reformulated in the socialist emphasis on certain dimensions regarding human rights practice in China. To some degree, I acknowledge the Confucian contribution to the idea of human well-being. But I am also aware of the socialist emphasis on national unity, social order, and stability over the civil and political rights of individuals. This framework tends not to demonstrate sufficient emphasis on individual rights, which are overridden in the name of any collective interests. The Chinese tradition has a rich cultural understanding of the human being, but the problem remains regarding how traditional resources can support human rights practice and institutional protection.

---

[66] Haiguang Yin, "Do You Want to Be a Human Being? (1958)," in *The Chinese Human Rights Reader: Documents and Commentary 1900–2000*, eds. Stephen C. Angle and Marian Svensson (New York: Routledge, 2015), 522–23.

[67] P. C. Chang, "Chinese Statements during Deliberations on the UDHR (1948)," in *The Chinese Human Rights Reader*, eds. Angle and Svensson, 481.

[68] See Stamos, *The Myth of Universal Human Rights*, 111.

What are the implications of focusing human rights debates in China on the question of what it means to be truly human? Although moral resources from the Confucian tradition can help us answer this question in a way distinctive to the Chinese context, we should also take into account the implication of Christian practice and theological approaches to human rights, including the practice and theological work of Chinese Christians and theologians. Christian theological involvement in human rights struggles is based on an understanding of the human being's relationship to God. Christian theological accounts of human beings and human rights emphasize the Christian idea of the human person created in the image of God, seen as the basis of true humanness and the integrity of life. This conception is grounded in an understanding, for Christians, of the indivisible right of God in all action and relations. The debate over the distinctively Chinese contribution to human rights debates must not ignore the role of Chinese Christian engagement in human rights struggles nor the theological ideas emerging from and grounding these very struggles. These ideas can contribute to the issue of how to ground conceptions of dignity and rights across cultural contexts and national boundaries. As we have seen, the significance of the human person is found in the midst of the struggle between individual rights and collective interests and at the intersection of welfare rights and civil rights. Whatever Chinese people understand the nature of human being and such ideas as goodness, virtue, duties, and harmony to be, a theological account of humanity and human dignity in particular can be introduced into Chinese discourse on human being and human rights. As Nicholas Wolterstorff claims, "Rights are grounded in dignity and worth."[69]

CONCLUDING REMARKS

This chapter examines the problem of human rights in China by deploying a social construction model, which rejects "a single formulation"[70] and takes into account its local cultural resources and social and political practices. The issue of the human aspect of human rights arises from these discussions in China, and therefore I introduce Christian theological appraisals of the human person to show the implications of humanness and human dignity for the human rights discourse in the Chinese context. I refer to this position as the social-theological construction of human rights in China, by which I point to a dual

---

[69]   Xie, "World-Formative Christianity: Wonder and Grief, Love and Justice."

[70]   John Witte says, "Human rights should not be reduced to a single formulation." See interview in appendix 3.

movement that shows respect to distinctive cultural conditions on the one hand, while on the other hand taking account of the fundamental human aspect of human rights in reference to basic theological understandings of God in relation to the human person. This theological anthropology helps reorientate questions of human rights in China, attentive to the Christian engagement both in practical and theological aspects working in the Chinese context.

9

THE STRUCTURAL PROBLEM OF RELIGIOUS FREEDOM IN CHINA

Toward a Confucian-Christian Synthesis

THE PROBLEM DEFINED

In the last chapter, I attempted to construct an understanding of human rights in China involving China's own cultural, social, and political conditions while particularly introducing theological contribution to the issue concerned. This social-constructive theological approach to human rights is further demonstrated in the case of religious freedom in this chapter.

In his "A Research Agenda on Religious Freedom in China," Fenggang Yang lays out three aspects of religious freedom to be understood in China: conception, regulation, and civil society.[1] This general understanding may suggest scholarly study in these areas from philosophical, political, legal, and sociological perspectives, among others. Some studies focus on legal regulations on religious practice as evidence of the Chinese government's perspective on religion and its intervention in religious affairs.[2] Political science perspectives on religion-state relationship examine religion and social harmony, governmental support to religion,

---

[1] Fenggang Yang, "A Research Agenda on Religious Freedom in China," *Review of Faith and International Affairs* 11, no. 2 (2013): 6–17.

[2] See, for example, Zhang Qianfan and Zhu Yingping, "Religious Freedom and Its Legal Restrictions in China," *Brigham Young University Law Review*, no. 3 (2011): 783–818, and Hong Qu, "Religious Policy in the People's Republic of China: An Alternative Perspective," *Journal of Contemporary China* 20, no. 70 (2011): 443–48.

and other such questions in the context of China.[3] Sociologists of religion are concerned with such issues as the religious market and religious communities' social involvement.[4] One major concern of these studies is how the Chinese government regulates religious activities and influences the development of religious groups.

As I see it, the state plays a critical role in determining the space of religious practice and social impact in China. Still, some may suggest that "religious freedom is not merely a nice thing tolerated by the state," as "religious communities are historically and ontologically prior to the modern state, and their autonomy deserves protection from over-reaching political authorities."[5] When reviewing the church-state issues in China and comparing it with the principle of church-state separation, Christopher Marsh and Zhifeng Zhong mention, "Under a system of church-state separation, the success and failure of religious organizations is in the hands of the people, not the state," and "the state's role is simply that of providing a system of religious liberty while also ensuring the public welfare."[6] An undeniable fact in China is that religious believers and communities have always wrestled with the state in their basic attempt to survive: "In such a highly centralized political country as China, religion has had little chance to become independent of the state."[7]

The current Chinese government's treatment of religion tends to be pragmatic. It neither encourages religion nor attempts to eliminate it, but it requires religion to cooperate with the government under the principle of "accommodation of religion to socialist society," particularly underlying religious contribution to the government's expectation

---

[3] See, for example, Lap-Yan Kung, "The Emergence of Exchange Politics in China and its Implications for Church-State Relations," *Religion, State, and Society* 38, no. 1 (2010): 9–28; Christopher Marsh and Zhifeng Zhong, "Chinese Views on Church and State," *Journal of Church and State* 52, no. 1 (2010): 34–49.

[4] See, for example, Fenggang Yang, "Religion in China under Communism: A Shortage Economy Explanation," *Journal of Church and State* 52, no. 1 (2009): 3–33; Fuk-tsang Ying, Hao Yuan, and Siu-lun Lau, "Striving to Build Civic Communities: Four Types of Protestant Churches in Beijing," *Review of Religion and Chinese Society* 1, no. 1 (2014): 78–103; Zhidong Hao, Shun Hing Chan, et al., "Catholicism and Its Civil Engagement: Case Studies of the Catholic Church in Hong Kong, Macau, Taipei, and Shanghai," *Review of Religion and Chinese Society* 1, no. 1 (2014): 48–77.

[5] Allen D. Hertzke, "Introduction: Advancing the First Freedom in the Twenty-First Century," in *The Future of Religious Freedom: Global Challenges*, ed. Allen D. Hertzke (Oxford: Oxford University Press, 2013), 6–7.

[6] Marsh and Zhong, "Chinese Views on Church and State," 42.

[7] Yao and Zhao, *Chinese Religion*, 128.

of social harmony. The state's tolerance of religion extends to certain officially recognized religions and their normal activities within the structure of state-sanctioned religious organizations. In principle, the state makes constraints on political appeals by religious believers while managing religious affairs to ensure religious contribution to national well-being rather than placing emphasis on how to guarantee the freedom of the individual to choose their own faith and concrete practice.

I have to place great emphasis on the role of the state when thinking about the scope of free religious practice, growing religious interaction with government, and religious dynamics in Chinese society today. The focus of this chapter is to give a structural analysis of the relationship among the state, religious communities, and other social institutions in an authoritarian state like China with the state's strict restrictions,[8] yet also with religious revival, many religious believers, growing religious dynamics, and the cry for more autonomy. For this purpose, in this chapter, I explore the structural problem of religious freedom in China—namely the relationship of the state and social institutions (including religious ones)—from religious and ethical perspectives. I attempt to integrate Confucian ideas of the state and association (including religious) with a Christian social theory of the state and social institutions to work out a proper philosophical and theological interpretation on the structural problem of religious freedom (the role of the state in particular) in China, with respect to traditional Chinese cultural and religious resources, political order, and the current religious situation.

There have been some comparative studies between Confucianism and Christianity regarding the ideas of God, worldview, human nature, and some practical issues such as ecological ethics. Yet there is not much work on the dialogue on social and political theory between the two. Here, I attempt to work in this vein to develop and integrate both sources addressing religious freedom in China. The Confucian and Christian resources used in this study derive from my research into the following concerns: (1) Confucian tradition regarding the space between state and family, (2) the problem of justification for religious autonomy, and (3) state authority toward religious exercise. I will try to show some complementary points between the two regarding the problem of religious freedom in China.

---

8   See Brian J. Grim and Roger Finke, *The Price of Freedom Denied: Religious Persecution and Conflict in the Twenty-First Century* (Cambridge: Cambridge University Press, 2011), 120–59.

CONFUCIAN IDEAS OF THE FAMILY, STATE, AND ASSOCIATION

Even though it is hard to give an exact measure of how much Confucian ideas influence political structure (including political arrangement of religious affairs) in communist China, I agree with Daniel A. Bell's position regarding Confucianism's far-reaching influence in East Asian Societies. Bell states, "Rather than condemn any deviations from liberal goals, anybody who wants to engage with East Asian societies in respectful ways must understand the Confucian ethical thinking that inform social and political practices in that region."[9]

In the first place, Confucianism "takes as its theoretical and practical basis the natural order of things in human society: the family, neighbor, kinship, clan, state and world."[10] This order focuses on moral cultivation at all levels of society. Personal moral cultivation beginning with family life extends to the community and then to rulers of the state, which requires certain institutions such as "community schools, community compacts, local temples, theater groups, clan associations, guilds, festivals, and a variety of ritual-centered activities."[11]

Under this framework, "Confucianism in many ways modelled its understanding of the state on its understanding of the family. In Confucianism, the ruler is unambiguously represented as the parent of the people, which reinforces an organic view of society as an enormous quasi family with the ruler as its paterfamilias."[12] The traditional Confucian state is expected to exercise parental function, and the government has the power in controlling all social affairs, including religious ones. Under this overall governing strategy, religions have to wrestle with the state at many occasions. Of course, state authority and its goal to rule have roots in the moral and spiritual cultivation of the human person and their conformity to social norms, which serves to maintain a certain social order. As Desheng Zhang says, "Confucianism employs the ideal of value consensus, which focuses on the subjection of

---

9   Daniel A. Bell, "Preface," in *Confucian Political Ethics*, ed. Daniel A. Bell (Princeton: Princeton University Press, 2008), xi.
10 Tu Wei-ming, "Embodying the Universe: A Note on Confucian Self-Realization," in *Self as Person in Asian Theory and Practice*, ed. Roger T. Ames, with Wimal Dissanayake and Thomas P. Kasulis (Albany: State University of New York Press, 1994), 181.
11 Richard Madsen, "Confucian Conceptions of Civil Society," in *Confucian Political Ethics*, ed. Bell, 9.
12 Peter Nosco, "Confucian Perspectives on Civil Society and Government," in *Confucian Political Ethics*, ed. Bell, 25.

individual to social norms. If each person obeys the norms, order will be developed accordingly."[13]

The basic purpose of social order, which is attained by an individual's conformity to social norms, is stability and harmony. The ideals of social norms, stable social order, and personal conformity to society enforced by Confucianism are bound together by the principle of the priority of totality. As Desheng Zhang states, "Confucianism always sees things from the totalistic perspective, viewing individuals as inseparable parts of society. This view results in the structural flaw of considering society solely without taking individual interest into account."[14] Indeed, Confucianism concentrates the significance of personal moral cultivation as the means of serving social norms and order, which contributes to "value consensus" and the totality perspective and compels us to think through various problems caused by modern society.[15] From a sociological perspective immersed in Confucianism, "traditional Chinese society is large-community-centered society and these communities restrain individual potentials and personal development. This rules out the space of the development of individual potentials and personality and even reduces the space of autonomy of smaller communities."[16]

We may see that due to an emphasis on the totality, it is hard to find sufficient resources in Confucianism that support the development of small communities or organizations. Two points should be noted here regarding the Confucian ideas of state and society. One is its focus on a stable society with a common moral basis. The other is the absence of an independent status of voluntary associations; all voluntary associations benefit from the state, and yet the state has no necessity to form any voluntary or communal associations, which remain always subject to the state's control.

According to C. K. Yang's interpretation, the state's dominance over social organizations constrains the development of religious and other groups: "When voluntary religion was developed, it faced a

13 See Zhang, *Rujia lunli yu shehui zhixu*, 181. My translation.
14 Zhang, *Rujia lunyu yu shehui zhixu*, 180. My translation.
15 See Zhang, *Rujia lunyu yu shehui zhixu*, 180–81.
16 Hui Qin秦暉, "Cong gongtongti benwei dao shimin shehui: chuantong zhongguo jiqi xiandaihua zairenshi" 從共同體本位到市民社會: 傳統中國及其現代化再認識 ["From Communities to Civil Society: A Reconsideration of Traditional China and Its Modernization"], in *Guojia yu shimin shehui*, ed. Deng, 277. Here, large communities specify nation, while small organizations contain kinship associations, villages, diocese, and professional associations. My translation.

well-entrenched political institution that had long assumed a controlling position over religious matters."[17] Another factor that contributes to the limited independence of organized religious organizations (with separate functions and structure) is the diffused character of classic religion in China: "The classic religion in its actual operation was largely diffused into the social institutions, and thus it was not independent institutional religion competing against other religions."[18]

Two other Chinese thinkers account for the absence of organizations in Chinese tradition. Chinese philosopher Shuming Liang (1893–1988) 梁漱溟 gives his famous account on his understanding of Chinese social structure compared to the Western structure: "Chinese tradition concentrates on familial life surrounding certain ethical values; in the West, organizations based on professionals, locality, and religious beliefs, etc., depart from familial structure."[19] In his view, Christianity contributes much to the formation of associations with their scope beyond family chains and relations (in Chinese tradition, *guanxi*), in that the extending objects of religious beliefs bring about the expansion of social institutions.

Here, according to Shuming Liang, lies the sharp contrast between organizational life and familial life: "The difficulty of co-existence of organizational life and familial life demonstrates the absence of associational life in China. Developing from familial life, it is questionable not only to build up a country but also to construct a real large local autonomous institution."[20] It is observed that it does not leave much space for the formation of autonomous associations in Chinese tradition. Norman Stockman explains Shuming Liang's positions about Chinese perception

---

[17] Yang, *Religion in Chinese Society*, 211–12.

[18] Yang, *Religion in Chinese Society*, 216. C. K. Yang further describes diffused religion as follows: "Diffused religion is conceived as a religion having its theology, cultus, and personnel so intimately diffused into one or more secular social institutions that they become a part of the concepts, rituals, and structure of the latter, thus having no significant independent existence" (Yang, *Religion in Chinese Society*, 294–95). "Diffused religion, on the other hand, may be less apparent as a separate factor, but it may be very important as an undergirding force for secular institutions and the general social order as a whole" (Yang, *Religion in Chinese Society*, 295). In Chinese society, the different forms of diffused religion are ancestor worship, the worship of community deities, and the ethicopolitical cults. See Yang, *Religion in Chinese Society*, 295.

[19] See Shuming Liang, "Zhongguo wenhua yaoyi," 中國文化要義 ["The Essence of Chinese Culture"], *in Liang Shuming Quanji 3* 梁漱溟全集三 [*Collected Works of Liang Shuming, Vol. 3*] (Jinan: Shandong renmin chubanshe 山東人民出版社, 1990), 72. My translation.

[20] Liang, "Zhongguo wenhua yaoyi," 78. My translation.

of organization in the following: "On the one hand, he claimed, China had only a weakly developed concept of the individual self, of individual rights, individual self-development and individual freedom from interference by others. On the other hand, he argued that China had only a weakly developed notion of group, the organization, and of society as a whole, that might enable mobilization for the pursuit of collective societal goals. What is central to Chinese society is the quality of human relationships."[21]

Fei Xiaotong (1910–2005) 費孝通, a Chinese sociologist, shares similar ideas with Shuming Liang on Chinese social structure regarding the association problem. He contrasts Chinese "differential mode of association" (*chaxu geju*) with "Western organizational mode of association": "In the pattern of Chinese organization, our social relationships spread out gradually, form individual to individual, resulting in an accumulation of personal connections. These social relationships from a network composed of each individual's personal connections."[22] In Western society, "personal relationships depend a common structure. People attach themselves to a preexisting structure and then, through that structure, form personal relationships,"[23] where organizational life has a central place in one's life: "Individuals form organizations. Each organization has its own boundaries, which clearly define those people who are members and those who are not."[24] In contrast, "Chinese social patterns, unlike Western ones, lack organization that transcends individual personal relationships."[25] In China social relationships (starting from kinship) are concentric and self-centered: "It is like the circles that appear on the surface of a lake when a rock is thrown into it. Everyone stands at the center of the circles produced by his or her own social influence. Everyone's circles are interrelated. One touches different circles at different times and places."[26] In this sense, "Confucius's difficulty is that, with a loosely organized rural society such as China's, it was not easy to find an all-encompassing ethical concept."[27]

---

[21] Norman Stockman, *Understanding Chinese Society* (Cambridge: Polity Press, 2000), 72–73.

[22] Fei Xiaotong, *From the Soil, the Foundations of Chinese Society: A Translation of Fei Xiaotong's Xiangtu Zhongguo*, trans. Hsiang t'u Chung-kuo, with an Introduction and Epilogue by Gary G. Hamilton and Wang Zheng (Berkeley: University of California Press, 1992), 79.

[23] Fei, *From the Soil*, 71.

[24] Fei, *From the Soil*, 61–62.

[25] Fei, *From the Soil*, 76.

[26] Fei, *From the Soil*, 62–63.

[27] Fei, *From the Soil*, 75.

In their "Introduction" to Fei Xiaotong's text in English, Gray G. Hamilton and Wang Zheng explain, "With this mode of association, the society is composed not of discrete organizations but of overlapping networks of people linked together through differentially categorized social relationship."[28] These networks have four key features: being discontinuous (not in single systematic way), being defined in terms of a dyadic social tie, being without explicit boundaries, and having situation-specific morality.[29] These explain that the Chinese differential mode of association is an egocentric system of social networks rather than a group-orientated association: "This is a society in which considerations of order, not law, predominate; and in this context, order means—to paraphrase the *Xiaojing (The Classic on Filial Piety)*—that each person must uphold the moral obligations of his or her networks ties."[30] Within this network structure, one's obligations to family and kinship has a priority over more distant people in one's network. Besides the priority of obligations to family and kinship networks, there exists control of the family and social network of relationships, "in the patriarchal control of the family, in the elder's control of villages, and in the notable's control of other kinds of associational networks."[31] Therefore, "as Fei describes them, Chinese political institutions work in the way his metaphor about the spreading ripples of water would suggest: from the inside out. Institutions of control in families and lineages are more important for establishing social order than are those in locales, which are in turn more important than those in more distant government locations. Ties of kinship and locale create core sets of ego-centric networks, which individuals can manipulate and expand to take advantage of economic and other kinds of opportunities."[32]

Both Shuming Liang and Fei Xiaotong attempt to develop the Confucian logic of social relationships, the relationships among persons, family, social life, and the state. In general, China has traditionally had great interest in stable and totalistic social order supported by certain social norms and moral cultivation at different levels of people, as well as concentration on familial life surrounding certain ethical values, thus resulting in the weak development of organizational life beyond family and kinship relationships, concentric circles, and an egocentric system of social networks rather than group-orientated association, control of networks of relationships, and even the state's control of religious and

---

28   Gary G. Hamilton and Wang Zheng, introduction to *From the Soil*, by Fei, 20.

29   Hamilton and Wang, introduction to *From the Soil*, 20–24.

30   Hamilton and Wang, introduction to *From the Soil*, 24.

31   Hamilton and Wang, introduction to *From the Soil*, 29.

32   Hamilton and Wang, introduction to *From the Soil*, 30.

other organizations. All these understandings of Chinese social structure are connected to the idea of Confucianism in different ways.

In communist China, as C. K. Yang describes, "while certain politically neutral religious beliefs can theoretically continue to have a measure of independent existence in the mind of the believer, the religious organization must structurally become a part of the Communist sociopolitical organizational system and accept strict control from the Communist authorities. For the Communists, the religious organizations, like any other social groups, constitute an integral part of society and its system of political authority, and there can be no organizational separation of religion and the state."[33] Religious organizations again serve as one chain in the state's holistic administrative work toward various social groups: "Through these government agencies, religious activities and organizations are controlled and directed so that they function as part of the Communist sociopolitical order."[34] Due to the communist atheist ideology, more suspicion of religious belief and practice has developed, which has led to further control over certain religious communities. As Qianfan Zhang and Yingping Zhu point out, "In recent years the religious associations in China have increasingly become quasi-state organizations, with their independence continually declining."[35] In this sense, "all religious associations are explicitly subordinate to the administrative organs."[36] C. K. Yang also highlights the persistent problem of religious autonomy in China: "Organizational autonomy of religious bodies in the Western sense never existed under the traditional government, and certainly does not under the contemporary Communist rule."[37] The autonomy problem of religious organizations under state authority stands as a good example for the common problem of social organizations in contemporary China.

Today, the Chinese government and society have to face new religious realities that have developed since the 1980s: there have emerged more dynamic religious communities in terms of their interactions with state and society, such as the ongoing unregistered church movement; religious negotiation with government and even resistance to state control for the

---

33 Yang, *Religion in Chinese Society*, 393.
34 Yang, *Religion in Chinese Society*, 394. *Governmental agencies* mean the State Bureau of Religious Affairs, the Religious Affairs Department in the provincial and municipal governments, and various patriotic religious organizations at national and local levels such as the China Christian Council/Three-Self Patriotic Movement, Catholic Patriotic Association, etc.
35 Zhang and Zhu, "Religious Freedom and Its Legal Restrictions in China," 814.
36 Zhang and Zhu, "Religious Freedom and Its Legal Restrictions in China," 815.
37 Yang, *Religion in Chinese Society*, 393.

rights, interests, and organizational autonomy of religious communities; and increasing religious engagement in social and political life in China, while social and collective expression of religion is subject to administrative management by the state.[38] The consistent pattern of religion-state relationship is being challenged, and the reality calls for a reconsideration of the role of the state and the identity of religious organizations as well in China.

Both Shuming Liang and Fei Xiaotong specify the relevance of Christianity to Western social organizational structure, yet they do not deeply examine its theological foundations. They are concerned with the relationships among persons, family, social life, and the state, which require deeper elaboration. Questions remain about social organizations (seen from the perspective of religious groups in particular) and their relationship with the state, in which we may see more clearly the characteristic and weakness of Confucianism. For this purpose, I attempt to develop the idea of the state and social institutions from Christian social theory in terms of the Reformed principle of sphere sovereignty and the Catholic social doctrine of subsidiarity to see how they may work together in contributing to a remodeling of the state with particular attention to religious practice in China. The reasons for turning to Christian social theory are basically theoretical considerations due to its different approach to the state and social institutions from the Confucian approach.[39] Meanwhile, I acknowledge that some unregistered churches are emerging in China that practice the Calvinist tradition and strive for new church-state interactions, while some Christian lawyers are getting more actively involved in some human rights matters. There are also cases of Catholic churches (both official and underground ones) that seek "religious freedom and resist government control" for the sake of church autonomy: "Pro-government groups that support the government are weak in the dioceses, whereas groups advocating stances of negotiation and opposition are strong."[40] To some degree, we may expect some theological practice among Chinese churches to exert certain impacts regarding their relationship to the state and society as well.

---

[38] See Fenggang Yang, *Religion in China: Survival and Revival under Communist Rule* (New York: Oxford University Press, 2012).

[39] I realize that some other ideologies such as Marxism impact the state-society structure in China. My study in this chapter is limited to two resources: Confucianism and Christianity's approach to this structure and their differences and possible synthesis, even though I take into account the existing communist ideology to some degree to develop my thinking.

[40] Shun-Hing Chan, "Civil Society and the Role of Catholic Church in Contemporary China," in *Christianity in Contemporary China: Socio-Cultural Perspectives*, ed. Francis K. G. Lim (London: Routledge, 2013), 134.

CHRISTIAN PERSPECTIVES ON THE STATE
AND SOCIAL INSTITUTIONS

Christianity presents its characteristic perspectives on the state and its relationship to various social institutions, including religious ones. Both the Reformed principle of sphere sovereignty and the Catholic social doctrine of "subsidiarity" propose the idea of social pluralism either at the horizontal or vertical level.[41]

The doctrine of subsidiarity is primarily concerned with the relationship between the state and lesser communities in endorsing "a divinely ordered hierarchy of qualitatively different communities" (plurality of communities) and supporting the principle of nonabsorption of lesser communities by greater ones (i.e., the maintenance of communities' separate identity and independent value). According to Jonathan Chaplin, the state may perform enabling, intervening, and substituting activities toward lesser communities to support their flourishing and the common good of society: "The state has a duty to offer lesser communities such help as is needed in order for the latter to realize their distinctive ends."[42]

Patrick McKinley Brennan believes there is both a negative and positive sense in the principle of subsidiarity: negatively, "it is a principle of non-absorption of lower societies by higher societies, above all by the state," and positively, "subsidiarity is also the principle that when aid is given to a particular society, including the state, it be for the purpose of encouraging and strengthening that society; correlatively, flourishing societies contribute to the flourishing of the great societies of which they are so many irreducible parts."[43] The principle of subsidiarity endorses certain functions of the state toward various communities while confirming their independent identity.

On the Protestant side, the principle of sphere sovereignty suggests that God alone possesses ultimate sovereignty, and is the origin of all earthly sovereignties, without "mediating earthly sovereignty from which

---

[41] In my interview with James W. Skillen, he mentioned that the two major traditions of Christian thought about the diversified structure of modern societies were the Roman Catholic tradition of social teaching and the Protestant Kuyperian tradition. See appendix 2.

[42] Jonathan Chaplin, "Subsidiarity and Sphere Sovereignty: Catholic and Reformed Conceptions of the Role of the State," in *Things Old and New: Catholic Social Teaching Revisited*, eds. Francis P. McHugh and Samuel M. Natale (Lanham: University Press of America, 1993), 182.

[43] Patrick McKinley Brennan, "Subsidiarity in the Tradition of Catholic Social Doctrine, " in *Global Perspectives on Subsidiarity*, eds. Michelle Evans and Augusto Zimmermann (Dordrecht: Springer), 35.

others are derivative,"[44] and our lives are divided into separate spheres, each with its own sovereignty. The principle has been significantly developed by John Calvin, Abraham Kuyper, Herman Dooyeweerd, and others. The development of this principle has attended to the relationship between all social institutions, each of which should work out its characteristic function without interfering in one another's functional exercise. As for Kuyper, he affirms the independent character of social spheres: "In a Calvinistic sense we understand hereby, that the family, the business, science, art, and so forth are all social spheres, which do not owe their existence to the state, and do not derive the law of their life from the superiority of the state, but obey a high authority within their own bosom; an authority which rules, by the grace of God, just as the sovereignty of the State does."[45]

In other words, the sovereignty of state must be in line with that of other social spheres and not be deducible from the family or other spheres nor applied to other spheres: "Even the spheres of politics and society have their law-structures imposed upon them by God. These law spheres are therefore sovereign within themselves, but God is sovereign over all of them as they are coordinated together. The law-spheres cooperate but cannot be reduced to one another; each has an element of uniqueness, given it by God."[46] As James W. Skillen sees it, from God as the creator of all things, we can understand "how to do justice to both individual responsibilities and the diverse institutions and associations of society at the same time."[47]

In this framework, the state as "the sphere of spheres" is not allowed to intrude upon the laws of other spheres: "In this independent character a special higher authority is of necessity involved and this highest authority we intentionally call—*sovereignty in the individual social spheres*, in order that it may be sharply and decidedly expressed that these different developments of social life have *nothing above themselves but God*, and the State cannot intrude here, and has nothing to command in their domain."[48] Yet, standing alongside other spheres, the state as the unique public authority involves the task of balancing and protecting the diverse social spheres, while state intervention may take place in such circumstances as the

---

[44] See David T. Koyzis, "Introductory Essay: Political Theory in the Calvinist Tradition," in *Political Philosophy—Selected Essays*, by Herman Dooyeweerd (Grand Rapids: Paideia Press, 2012), 4.

[45] Kuyper, *Lectures on Calvinism*, 90.

[46] Anonymous, "Concerning Abraham Kuyper," in *Sacred Theology*, by Abraham Kuyper (Lafayette: Sovereign Grace, 2001), 10.

[47] Xie, "Sovereignty of God: Church, State, and Society."

[48] Kuyper, *Lectures on Calvinism*, 91.

conflict of spheres, the abuse of power on individuals by other members of the sphere, and so forth.

In affirming the diversity of social life, Dooyeweerd developed this principle in terms of the "creation's ontic structure" into differentiation of institutions and relationships, particularly in a way of modal analysis. For him, that diversity has creationally normative meaning; that is, "created reality displays a great variety of aspects or models of being in the temporal order."[49] Each of God's diverse creations is bound by its own laws. Therefore, "sphere sovereignty points us to God as the author of all diversity and unity and meaning in life. . . . Social diversity is always connected with creational unity from a Christian point of view. . . . Sphere sovereignty is simply a shorthand phase to express the idea that a diversity of creational arenas call for human obedience to God as part of humanity's unified service to the Creator."[50] The institutions and relationship ought to be developed in terms of their being created, and this kind of development recognizes the function of the existing reality (including social reality) as a creature with its determined features on the one hand, and embodies human beings' obedience and service to God in the created order on the other.

Deriving from this creational principle of unity and diversity, Dooyeweerd's peculiar contribution to the development of the idea of sphere sovereignty lies in his interpretation of the modal structure of reality, the complex nature of the typical "identity structures" (or individuality structures) of social reality: "Each exiting thing, including every social entity, reveals a distinct qualifying aspect while functioning in all the modal dimensions of the creation. For example, a family is 'qualified' differently than a state or a business enterprise. A family exists normatively as a community of kinship love. A state, on the other hand, is qualified by a guiding juridical norm."[51] Again, family and state should be distinguished from each other, each law of which cannot be applied or extended to the other: "Each is qualified by a different modal 'leading function' which is constitutive of its peculiar identity and purpose. Thus, when the 'whole' institution or organization is analyzed with regard to

---

49 Herman Dooyeweerd, "Roots of Western Culture," in *Political Order and the Plural Structure of Society*, eds. James W. Skillen and Rockne M. McCarthy (Atlanta: Scholar Press, 1991), 278.

50 James W. Skillen and Rockne M. McCarthy, "Sphere Sovereignty, Creation Order, and Public Justice: An Evaluation," in *Political Order and the Plural Structure of Society*, eds. Skillen and McCarthy, 403.

51 Skillen and McCarthy, "Sphere Sovereignty, Creation Order, and Public Justice," 404.

its sphere of responsibility (or sphere of sovereignty), it displays a typical character (a distinguishable 'identity structure')."[52]

Dooyeweerd's interpretation of sphere sovereignty has implications for the distinction "between the 'whole/part' relationship and 'sphere sovereignty,'" regarding the role of the state in particular: "This allows for a better understanding of how the state can, thorough public law, integrate into a community of public justice all other institutions and societal relationships without thereby reducing them to 'parts' of a single whole."[53] This principle supports social diversity without being absorbed into political entity while recognizing the "public-legal integrating functions of the state." For Chaplin,

> The state is not responsible for the *internal* legal domain of a social structure; it may not impose compulsory dieting on persons or families, or set prices for private industries. It lacks the competence to fulfill such internal responsibilities and is empowered only to establish legally the external, public conditions in which these can be adequately pursued.... The state is to create a network of just interrelationships between the various social structures and persons within its territory. Not only is the state to refrain from violating the sphere sovereignty for other spheres, but it is to prevent any other structure from violating such sphere sovereignty.[54]

For Kuyper and Dooyeweerd, the principle of sphere sovereignty informs the basic relationship among individuals, social institutions and organizations, and the state, involving issues such as individual capacity and responsibility, identity and structure of institutions, and the integrating function of the state under God's ordinances. It affirms the relatively independent character and diversity of social spheres of life while encouraging personal vocational responsibility in developing these spheres: "Sphere sovereignty provided Kuyper with a conceptual tool for Christian action in society in its various aspects. God has created all things, and Christians were called to develop each 'sphere' in accordance to its own God-given ordering and potential."[55] This principle also serves as an idea to define

---

52   Skillen and McCarthy, "Sphere Sovereignty, Creation Order, and Public Justice," 404.

53   Skillen and McCarthy, "Sphere Sovereignty, Creation Order, and Public Justice," 407.

54   Jonathan Chaplin, *Herman Dooyeweerd: Christian Philosopher of State and Civil Society* (Notre Dame: University of Notre Dame Press, 2011), 225.

55   Timothy I. McConnel, "Common Grace or the Antithesis? Towards a Consistent Understanding of Kuyper's 'Sphere Sovereignty,'" in *On Kuyper: A Collection of Readings on the Life, Work and Legacy of Abraham Kuyper*, eds. Steve Bishop and John H. Kok (Sioux Center: Dordt College Press, 2013), 315.

the state's authority.[56] More specifically, "government must recognize and do justice to both individuals and the diverse non-government associations and institutions of society."[57]

Both Christian principles of subsidiarity and sphere sovereignty of the state and social institutions support the plural structure of society by seeking to strengthen intermediate associations and balancing diverse associations.[58] They attempt to overcome the flaws and dangers of individualistic or collectivist deduction of social structure. Although both principles have different angles on the state and social institutions, both support the plural structure of society and reject the absolutism of the state or the individual by seeking to strengthen intermediate associations and balancing diverse associations through "solidarity."[59]

Regarding the state function, recent studies show the commonality between these two principles[60] and point to a synthesis of them by suggesting a Christian social vision of empowerment and the state's occasional and exceptional intervention within the different spheres of society when the authority of that sphere is abused.[61] Chaplin suggests that the acknowledged diverse communities must be enabled by the state to pursue their own particular purposes, and state intervention happens when the common good is deficient or distorted (for the doctrine of subsidiarity).[62] Under some circumstances, the state must "coerce all citizens to bear personal and financial burdens for the maintenance of the natural unity of the state" (Kuyper's position).[63]

These positions are implied for religious communities and their relationship with the state, especially in the case of church autonomy.[64] For

---

56   See Gordon J. Spykman, "Sphere Sovereignty in Calvin and the Calvinist Tradition," in *Exploring the Heritage of John Calvin*, ed. David E. Holwerda (Grand Rapids: Baker, 1976), 163–208.
57   Xie, "Sovereignty of God: Church, State, and Society."
58   See Kent A. Van Til, "Subsidiarity and Sphere-Sovereignty: A Match Made in . . . ," *Theological Studies* 69, no. 3 (2008): 610–36.
59   See Van Til, "Subsidiarity and Sphere-Sovereignty."
60   Patrick McKinley Brennan proposes compatibility between two principles in his "The Relationship Between Sphere Sovereignty and Subsidiarity," in *Global Perspectives on Subsidiarity*, eds. Evans and Zimmermann, 49–63.
61   David H. Mcilroy, "Subsidiarity and Sphere Sovereignty: Christian Reflections on the Size, Shape and Scope of Government," *Journal of Church and State* 45, no. 4 (2003): 739–63.
62   See Chaplin, "Subsidiarity and Sphere Sovereignty," 185, 191.
63   Chaplin, "Subsidiarity and Sphere Sovereignty," 196–97.
64   See Johan D. Van Der Vyver, *Leuven Lectures on Religious Institutions, Religious Communities and Rights* (Leuven: Uitgeverij Peeters, 2004), especially its "Second Lecture: The Doctrine of Sphere Sovereignty."

Chaplin, church-state relationship is a "central implication of sphere
sovereignty, as we saw, that all social structures receive their authority
directly from God. It is also true that the church possesses penal (though
not physically coercive) sanctions (e.g., excommunication), though these
must be governed by the faith of the church, not by political principles."[65]
The state must respect and protect the sphere sovereignty of the church.
Here, church autonomy stands: "The unity of the church cannot be based
upon any external political criterion but only upon the internal criterion
deriving from its qualifying functions of faith."[66]

REFLECTION: A POSSIBLE SYNTHESIS, AND HOW MUCH RELIGIOUS FREEDOM IS GRANTED IN CHINA?

In this case study into the structural problem of religious freedom, I
examine the role of the state in China in its interaction with society and
religion and recognize the resources of Confucian understanding of
family, state, and social association. Meanwhile, I suggest that the shape
of the modern state in China should take into account the fact of rising
social groups, including the dynamic of religious communities and religious perception of state and society. In my case, I introduce Christian
social theory of the state and social institutions in dialogue with and
further integration with Confucian resources in reshaping the role of the
state encountering the demand of growing social life and religious life
in particular. As Karrie J. Koesel claims, "In authoritarian regimes, religious communities tend to represent the most diverse and robust forms of
associational life outside the state."[67] I also suppose that no other groups
have such a strong and deep concern and struggle with their own rights
and autonomy as do religious groups, which demand that the state create
space for them.

To this end, this chapter is a search for some complementary points
between Confucian resources and Christian social thought as an outlet to
reconsider the structural problem of religious freedom in China, which
recognizes their significant difference. It seems to me the role of the state
serves as a bridge concept for this study. On the one hand, the Confucian
paternalistic perspective concentrates on a common moral basis and state
control as necessary for the good of the whole nation. The relationships
between the person, family, other voluntary associations and the state
are regarded as concentric circles; thus, these associations, including

---

65   Chaplin, *Herman Dooyeweerd*, 247.
66   Chaplin, *Herman Dooyeweerd*, 248.
67   Karrie J. Koesel, *Religion and Authoritarianism: Cooperation, Conflict, and the Consequences* (Cambridge: Cambridge University Press, 2014), 3.

religious groups have never gained their own independent status while being immersed into the whole sociopolitical order in traditional and present communist China. On the other hand, Christian social theory acknowledges one kind of specific "order" (laws structure) within creation in different social entities and "solidarity" for common humanity in different social entities, social institutions at both horizontal and vertical levels. It distinguishes the authority of the state from that of other spheres, including family. My concern here is how the Christian ideas of the state and social institutions may contribute to China's remodeling the role of the state while the state's power and intervention will still be regulated, limited, and effective, yet social institutions, including religious groups, will practice their relatively independent tasks.

The relationship of religion and state has developed in the forms of subordination, cooperation, negotiation, and resistance among various religious groups in China. Yet the state is far stronger in terms of power when compared to religion, and by no means will the state lose its dominant position. On this point, rather than exploring such ideals as freedom of conscience and individual choice, I hesitate and yet have to ask the more limited and modest question: How much freedom may religion receive from the state in China? It seems to me that real freedom is granted only with a certain cost, either through some kind of compromise or through a struggle for the sake of religious autonomy.

The autonomy of religious and other social organizations can be reinforced by its distinction from "whole/part" relationship expounded by Dooyeweerd. If various social institutions (including religious ones) exist as parts of a whole for the whole purpose, they will lose their independent status and their autonomous development together with individuals' different responsibilities in these institutions. In confronting the distinctive and characteristic function of social institutions, it is not allowable to overstate the function of "the whole." On this point, the state, as public authority and through its public-integrating function, can protect and promote the plural social structure.

Today, many are concerned with the limited freedom given to religious worship in China from the perspectives of religion-state relationship, religious policy, and even the rule of law. We must acknowledge constraints on religious practice, the problem of autonomy of religious organizations in China in particular. However, besides the traditional religion-state framework still effective in contemporary China, we must take seriously the following aspects of reality: the constitutional protection of normal religious activities, religious revival and growth since the 1980s, the wide impact of religion on Chinese life, the positive influence of religious moral teachings such as benevolence and tolerance, and religious contributions to the cultivation of good citizens in a community. The Chinese government has officially affirmed a positive side of promoting economic, social, and cultural development by religious groups, especially religious philanthropy concerning medical service, educational support, environmental protection, and poverty alleviation. Here, it is essential to normatively affirm the differentiation of social spheres (such as agriculture, industry, business, transportation, arts, media, education, etc.), which has taken place in contemporary Chinese society and may tend to deepen in the future. In these emerging spheres, religion, through its various works, is expected to get more engagement, promote its influence, and develop more organically in a pluralistic-orientated Chinese society. Furthermore, religious groups, along with their social participation in different spheres, constitute an important component of China's emerging "civil society," which, in spite of the restrictions imposed by the state, manages to create a greater social space. The space of religious autonomy depends on its interaction with the state and society as well.

In contemporary China, both the state's regulation of religious affairs and recognition of positive religious resources (moral force, in particular) in society, from my point of view, will lead to one kind of collaborative relationship between religion and state, within which I am more concerned with religious public engagement in Chinese society. Under general guidelines from the state authority on religion's social participation, there is a certain social and public space for religious believers and groups to become actively rather than passively involved. They may creatively explore specific issues in various social spheres and develop strategies accordingly. It is also the responsibility of religious circles to work together with the authorities and other groups (religious and otherwise) to find a consensus concerning the common good of the whole society deriving from their unique religious insights while not simply compromising the core interests defined by the state. Under these circumstances, we may expect the Chinese government to take into account new problems arising from religion's social engagement and open more public space for religious groups through dialogue with them.[68] This proposal emphasizes social and public space for religious engagement as well as

---

[68] As Karrie J. Koesel states, in China, "top-down policies were instrumental in lifting the lid on religion and creating greater space for religious actives." See Koesel, *Religion and Authoritarianism*, 160. Through comparatively studying the religion-state relationships in China and Russia, Koesel proposes the space of one kind of cooperation relationship rather than one of domination or resistance between religion and the authoritarian state. Whereas Koesel's study is a political approach, my concern with the religion-state-society problem in China is philosophical and theological.

religious contribution to social development, which is operated under the state's guiding framework of religious activities. It demands the state's constructive role in regulating social institutions while acknowledging their diverse existence and the interaction among them, along with its affirmation of religion as a societal force and its willingness to become more open and allow more space for religious engagement.[69] It aims to expand the role of religion in the social and wider public realm. In this way, it is my hope to strengthen religious practice in the public dimension and to transform the traditional subordination of religion to political dominance through promoting religious vitality in public life and religious interactions with the state so as to foster religious freedom in China.

---

[69]   A theological account of the state's constructive role toward religion and society can be found in Chaplin, *Herman Dooyeweerd: Christian Philosopher of State and Civil Society.*

10

CHURCH'S ENCOUNTERS WITH STATE IN CHINA

Case Studies and Theological Appraisal

Bearing in mind the role of the state in religious affairs in the Chinese context as laid out in chapter 9, this chapter moves further to provide a theological interpretation of the stance of Chinese churches toward the state seen from the perspective of three cases in contemporary China. This chapter also echoes chapter 9 in advancing religious freedom constructively through the perspective of ecclesiology developed from the Chinese context. This chapter presents how contemporary Chinese churches (both registered and nonregistered) view their relationship with the state and how their theological views are reflected in their Christian practice toward the state.

In recent years, important issues have been raised by various Protestant groups in regard to the church-state relationship in China. Consider, for example, the Three-Self Church's accommodation with the government in principle alongside its disobedience to the state in the case of the demolition of church buildings and crosses in the Zhejiang Province. Another example is the opposition to the recent movement toward the sinification of Christianity, opposition to which is voiced in a document titled "Reaffirming Our Stance on the House Churches (95 Theses)" (hereafter, "95 Theses"), issued by the Chengdu Early Rain Reformed Church (Qiuyu zhifu jiaohui) 秋雨之福教會 in 2015. Finally, consider Beijing Shouwang Church's 守望教會 reaction to governmental restraints and its position regarding outdoor worship, as well as the unregistered church's acts of public disobedience in opposition to various public policies in China.

The interaction between Chinese churches and the government, whether in harmony or in conflict, requires deeper theological understanding. Questions that must be explored include: How do contemporary Chinese churches (both registered and nonregistered) view their relationship to the state? How are their theological views reflected in their Christian practice toward the state? Does the church have the responsibility to resist state pressure or to exercise political loyalty? What is the state's authority in regard to the church? What are the limits of this authority from the Christian perspective? Finally, what theology is needed as the foundation for a proper understanding of church and state in China? Many today are concerned with the problem of religious freedom in China. In the case of Christianity, the church's view of the nature of the state and its relationship to the church is itself central to this debate about religious freedom.

As seen in the last chapter, there are a great deal of scholarly works on the religion-state questions in China, but fewer scholars have examined this question from a theological and normative perspective. Among those theological considerations, Siu Chan Lee highlights "a balance between differentiation and coordination" regarding church-state relations in the contemporary Chinese context.[1] Christie Chui-Shan Chow examines religious convictions in the social protest undertaken by Seventh-Day Adventists in Zhejiang Province; she looks at "how these religious protesters *theologized* their collective actions" and examines the "*theological frames* they used to sustain their struggle."[2] Chloë Starr suggests that the church-state relationship has been a central issue in modern Chinese theology. She writes, "The relation of church to state, and the locus and nature of authority, has been one of the central issues of modern Chinese theology, inspiring a spectrum of writings and responses from extreme separatism to the programmatic adaption of theology to Socialism."[3]

In this chapter, I theologically examine the encounters of churches with the state, ranging from acquiescence to increasing resistance among registered and nonregistered churches, deploying these examples as sources for an integrated theological account of the church-state relationship in China. Against the background of the active role of the state in religious affairs, I examine various Protestant churches' encounters with the state and relate these approaches to their theological backgrounds.

---

[1] For example, Siu Chan Lee, "Toward a Theology of Church-State Relations in Contemporary Chinese Context," *Studies in World Christianity* 11, no. 2 (2005): 251–69.

[2] Christie Chui-shan Chow, "Demolition and Defiance: The Stone Ground Church Dispute (2012) in East China," *Journal of World Christianity* 6, no. 2 (2016): 254.

[3] Chloë Starr, *Chinese Theology*, 279.

Based on these theological understandings, I suggest what kind of theology is useful for the Chinese church-state structure overall, with particular attention to the role of the state and the nature of the church, including its resistance activities. Although the focus of this chapter is on Christianity, I think it also applies to other faiths in China as well and bears certain implications for the religion-state relationship in China in a broader sense.

THE CHURCH'S ENCOUNTERS WITH THE STATE IN CHINA: THREE CASE STUDIES

The state's treatment of religious groups elicits a variety of responses from Christian groups in China and raises theological issues regarding the nature of the church in relation to the state and society. A distinct principle of religion-state separation is here affirmed from the governmental perspective, in the sense that religion is not allowed to interfere in the administrative, judicial, and educational departments of society. The revised version of Religious Affairs Regulations released by the State Council in September 2017 covers management of the affairs of religious groups, religious schools, religious venues, religious professionals, religious activities, religious assets, and legal responsibility while strengthening rules regarding religious venues as well as the financing of religious groups and missions.[4] It remains a question whether the new regulations allow religious groups more power to manage themselves or actually impede their ability to do so.[5]

The revised Religious Affairs Regulations have been criticized by religious scholars, Christian pastors, and lawyers, who are concerned about clarifying several concepts raised by the regulations, such as the definitions of *religion* and *faith* in judicial practice and the meaning of "normal" religious practice, which leads to a legal distinction between

---

[4]   "Religious Affairs Regulations 2017," China Law Translate, accessed January 6, 2020, https://tinyurl.com/3crcd6wj.

[5]   Fuk-tsang Ying suggests that the authority of the Department of Religious Affairs at different levels is reinforced by the new regulations. See Fuk-tsang Ying, "Chuangxin zongjiao guanli? Haishi qianghua zongjiao kongzhi? Ping Zongjiao shiwu tiaoli caoan (songshen gao)" [創新宗教管理? 還是強化宗教控制? 蘋《宗教事務條例草案》 (送審稿)] ["Initiating Management of Religious Affairs or Enforcing Control of Religious Affairs? Comments on the New Religious Affairs Regulations (Draft Revisions)]," Pushi shehui kexue wang 普世社會科學網 [Pushi Institute for Social Science], accessed January 4, 2020, https://tinyurl.com/3nedj24n. Also see Mini Lau, "China's Religious Groups Brace for Tighter Scrutiny Closer to Home," *South Morning Post*, September 8, 2017, https://tinyurl.com/4uks2mpp.

normal and abnormal religious activities. The criticism centers on the concept of religious freedom itself: Does freedom of religious belief include freedom of religious practice?[6] Does freedom of religious belief include collective worship, setting up religious venues, use of religious symbols, publication of religious books, and the propagation of religious faith in terms of free religious practice? Does freedom of religious belief include freedom for parents to instruct their children in the teachings of their religious faith or choose a religious education for them? Finally, what is the relationship of religious freedom to other basic freedoms?[7] Clarifying these deep questions regarding the meaning of religious freedom requires reflecting theologically on the religion-state relationship in the Chinese context. This goes beyond simply criticizing governmental constraints on existing religious activities. Take Christianity as an example; besides this reflection on official regulations, there are several cases regarding the church's encounter with the state's authority in both registered and nonregistered Christian communities that offer examples of both resistance and dialogue.[8] In the midst of these struggles, we find evidence of the value of a variety of theological responses on the part of the churches.

1. Registered Churches Movement

Since the early 1950s in socialist China, there has been an indigenous Christian movement organized under the auspices of the TSPM in China; after 1980, this has also been under the banner of the CCC. This official form of Christianity emphasizes the adaption of Chinese theological reflection to the context of socialist China. A key figure in these developments was Guangxun Ding. Central theological concepts included the "Cosmic Christ" and "ethical Christianity." According to Guangxun Ding, the Cosmic Christ underscores Christ's dominion and care throughout

---

6   The term *freedom of religious belief* is used in the revised regulations and in Article 36 of the Chinese Constitution: "Citizens enjoy freedom of religious belief . . . The state protects normal religious activities." Yet the meanings of both *freedom of religious belief* and *normal religious activities* are ambiguous.

7   "A Proposal for Explaining Articles 36 and 89 of the Constitution," accessed January 6, 2020, https://tinyurl.com/ycy56vse. Although this document serves as a reaction to the revised regulations (draft for public feedback) released earlier in September 2016, and there are some modifications in the final version of the new regulations released in September 2017, the final version is actually more restrictive than the draft concerning various aspects of religious affairs.

8   The cases and positions used here are not exhaustive, and they do not represent the church groups as a whole in China today, but the theological ideas underlying their understanding of church-state relations provide distinctive resources to study this topic.

the whole cosmos, a universal dominion characterized by love.[9] On this basis, he argues for the compatibility of atheism and the Cosmic Christ. He writes:

> Can we square the existence of atheism with the cosmic role of Christ? I think we can, as such as we can square the existence of many other things in the world with his cosmic role. In the first place, we have good reason to be grateful if we realize how much any denial of God, just the use of the term atheism, helps bring up the question of God, and that is an evangelistic service in any society which has little to suggest the idea of God. Then, atheists are not all of a piece. . . . Atheistic humanism can be our ally as it can help greatly to salvage authentic faith. . . . From our point of view, in the human pilgrimage towards the Kingdom of God, we need not absolutize the opposition between theists and atheists.[10]

According to Fuk-tsang Ying (Fuzeng Xing), "The development from the 'Cosmic Christ' to 'ethical Christianity' reveals the structure of Ding Guangxun's theology, and how it deals with and resolves the contradiction between faith and unbelief. In summary, the contradiction between faith and unbelief is lessened on the basis of 'love.'"[11] In this way, the theological and organizational adaption to the reality of socialist society has included elements of patriotism and support for various policies of the country.[12] Guangxuan Ding's conception of the Cosmic Christ may be criticized for weakening the church's ability to challenge the governing authority in China. Edmond Tang has noted that Guangxuan Ding's ecclesiology had developed over time. Tang writes, "The cosmic dimension is not only used to extend the domain of Christ beyond the church to include the 'non-church' values and allies in society and thus set the context for Christian discernment and action: more important, the cosmic dimension became the principal hermeneutical key to penetrate the mystery of God."[13]

Nonetheless, the development of a theology of the Cosmic Christ exemplifies Chinese attempts to grapple theologically with the state. The cosmic dimension of God was also explored by church leaders such as T. C. Chao and Y. T. Wu. For these figures, "the concept of the

---

[9]   See Guangxun Ding, *Ai shi yongbu zhixi:ding guangxun* wenji 愛是永不止息: 丁 光訓文集 [*Love Never Ends: Papers by K. H. Ting*], ed. Janice Wickeri (Nanjing: Yilin chubanshe 譯林出版社, 2000), 412.

[10]   Ding, *Ai shi yongbu zhixi*, 413–14.

[11]   See Fuzeng Xing, "Church-State Relations in Contemporary China and the Development of Protestant Christianity," *China Study Journal* 18, no. 3 (2003): 36.

[12]   Xing, "Church-State Relations in Contemporary China," 38–39.

[13]   Edmond Tang, "The Cosmic Christ—The Search for a Chinese Theology," *Studies in World Christianity* 1, no. 2 (1995): 140.

Cosmic Christ serves as correction of false dichotomies prevalent in the Chinese church and opens a way to collaboration with non-believing communist."[14] As one component of his contextual theology, "whereby Christians in China could best exemplify a God of love,"[15] the idea of the Cosmic Christ enables Guangxun Ding to support collaboration with the Communist Party as it "balanced his dual roles before the communist state and the Christian church."[16] In this way, Guangxun Ding's idea of God's love can be reconciled with the reality of socialist China. As Starr explains, "The Three-Self Movement, Ding notes, is often represented in the West as a sign that the church had yielded to Communist pressure, whereas in reality it 'represents God's act of great mercy in giving Christians a new chance in China'; Liberation and the new Socialism were not 'God's punishment or judgment, but an act of God, showing God's love for China.'"[17]

This official form of Christianity in contemporary China emphasizes state authority and the church's conformity to society. In principle, this official movement demands the Chinese church's identification with and unwavering loyalty to Chinese political and social institutions, completely avoiding any social criticism. As Fenggang Yang explains, "While the party-state insists that religious believers must accommodate to social and political reality, many religious leaders like to emphasize the importance of mutual accommodation between the CCP [Chinese Communist Party] and religious believers."[18] The registered church and its leaders are expected to support this accommodation policy. Nevertheless, there are cases in which registered churches have resisted governmental interference in church practice.[19] Thousands of Christians protested and engaged in conflict with the police during the demolition of church buildings and crosses in the Zhejiang Province between 2014 and 2016. Among the protestors were a number of registered church leaders.[20] Their

---

[14] Tang, "The Cosmic Christ," 137.

[15] See also Alexander Chow, *Theosis, Sino-Christian Theology and the Second Chinese Enlightenment: Heaven and Humanity in Unity* (New York: Palgrave Macmillan, 2013), 90.

[16] Chow, *Theosis, Sino-Christian Theology and the Second Chinese Enlightenment*, 109.

[17] Starr, *Chinese Theology*, 199.

[18] Fenggang Yang, "From Cooperation to Resistance," 83.

[19] See more details in this regard in Carsten Vala, "Protestant Resistance and Activism in China's Official Churches," in *Handbook of Protestant and Resistance in China*, ed. Teresa Wright (Northampton: Edward Elgar, 2019), 316–30.

[20] The Zhejiang Christian Council issued an open letter against the campaign of cross removal in July 2015. See "Zhejiang jidujiao xiehui tianzhujiao lianghui shouci gongkai shengming yaoqiu tingchai shizijia" 浙江基督教協會、天主教

disobedience may have originated in their genuine Christian faith in response to the needs of thousands of suffering Christians.

Fuk-tsang Ying summarizes various statements regarding church officials' reactions to this campaign: "(1) Forced cross demolitions are acts that violate the constitution and the law. (2) The principle of separation of church and state, as well as respecting and obeying the government as a principle of biblical truth, is insisted upon; however, if the government refuses to obey God's will, as indicated in the Bible, then churches must be faithful to God. (3) Churches will respond to forced demolitions through nonviolent civil disobedience, will never compromise, and will refuse to take down their own crosses with determination."[21]

Christie Chui-Shan Chow contributes to this an analysis of the "religious dimension of social protest."[22] For example, one elder "drew on the Old Testament to rationalize his calling to defend the church against any hostility" by "imaging himself as a God-chosen watch-man."[23] In reality, church leaders face enormous pressure to coop-erate with the Communist Party, and some have agreed to voluntarily remove the cross from their building so that the entire building would not be demolished and they would not lose their jobs due to govern-mental pressure on their employers. In the latter case, church leaders sometimes suggest that the church has faced persecution throughout its history, and so the best thing to do is to pray. After all, compared to thirty years ago, they now have many more church buildings for worship.[24] Here we find certain pragmatic considerations that deserve theological investigation.

2. Chengdu Early Rain Reformed Church

A more theologically informed statement regarding unregistered churches' views of the state in China is found in the document "95 Theses,"

兩會首次公開聲明要求停拆十字架 ["Zhejiang Christian Church Council and Associations of Catholic Church Publicly Declare the First Time to Stop Cross Removal"], *Jidu shibao* 基督時報 [*Gospel Herald*], July 15, 2015, https://tinyurl.com/2p8ht7nm.

21 See Fuk-tsang Ying, "The Politics of Cross Demolition: A Religio-Political Anal-ysis of the 'Three Rectifications and One Demolition' Campaign in Zhejiang Province," *Review of Religion and Chinese Society* 5, no. 1 (2018): 35.

22 Chow, "Demolition and Defiance," 272.

23 Chow, "Demolition and Defiance," 270.

24 See Ian Johnson, "Decapitated Churches in China's Christian Heartland," *New York Times*, May 21, 2016, https://tinyurl.com/3uj65j2f.

issued by the Chengdu Early Rain Reformed Church in 2015.[25] Appealing primarily to the doctrine of the sovereignty of God, biblical authority, and the two kingdoms doctrine, this statement takes positions on the authority and limitations of government, as well as on ecclesiology, based on the tradition of Reformed theology. It supports the principle of "religion-state independence" (*zhengjiao fenli* 政教分立) and opposes the official structure of the China Christian Council as well as the sinification of Christianity, in which Christian faith departs from its Catholic tradition in its subjection to political obligations. The document insists that local Christian groups register with the Department of Civil Affairs to obtain their legal status. Beyond this, Christian groups (referred to as the "unregistered churches") should show proper respect to governmental authority as the "sword" while practicing nonviolent resistance, when necessary, in defense of Christian freedom of conscience and church autonomy.[26] Relying on the Reformed ideas of ecclesiology and government, the document calls for a change of policy regarding the regulation of religious groups in China.

Starr highlights theological elements embodied in the "95 Theses": "a Calvinist political community under the lordship of Christ, with both state and church accountable to God; the church as a restored community; a neo-Calvinist belief in the limited role of government and civil protection for religious freedom; a Lutheran call to take up a (metaphorical) sword when the state transgresses into the spiritual realm."[27] But this statement leaves little room for the church to negotiate its relationship to the state. "The 95 Theses document arrogates to the church the right to define relations to the state, based on a biblical view and on a particular reading of theological history, leaving little room for dialogue."[28]

As I see it, the "95 Theses" agrees with the basic teaching of Calvinism on church and state, as summarized by H. Henry Meeter: "The state is to have authority with respect to the church only insofar as it concerns matters *circa sacra*, not *in sacra*, which means that the state shall have authority with regard to the externalities of the church, its buildings and

---

25 See "Women dui jiating jiaohui lichang de chongshen" 我們對家庭教會立場 的重申 (95條) ["Reaffirming Our Stance on the House Churches (95 Theses)"], Shengming wang 生命網 [CCLiFe], accessed December 19, 2019, https://tinyurl.com/2p8ya2ff.

26 As one example of resistance in practice, the Early Rain Reformed Church appealed in court when the local Bureau of Religious Affairs intervened in church activities and exercised a forced investigation in 2008.

27 Chloë Starr, "Wang Yi and the 95 Theses of the Chinese Reformed Church," *Religions* 7, no. 12 (2016), https://tinyurl.com/3cwkdbp9.

28 Starr, "Wang Yi and the 95 Theses of the Chinese Reformed Church."

other properties, and afford it the same protection under the law as any organization in society within the confines of the country."[29]

Furthermore, to a degree, the document also supports the two-kingdoms doctrine in its understanding of the church-state relationship. As David Fergusson explains, in addition to the traditional understanding of the two kingdoms doctrine (traced back to Martin Luther) focused on the "spiritual independence of the church" and the separation of the temporal and the spiritual realms, the doctrine develops "so as to maintain a strong interest in the political activity of the Christian and the more positive role of the state."[30] With this understanding, the state thus acts as an "instrument of divine agency," embodied in a "just ruler" who "has a duty to maintain the security and well-being of the church" and "maintain the case of true religion and to this extent to preserve the ideal of a Christian society."[31] The two kingdoms doctrine thus underscores both the distinct authorities of the church and the state as well as their mutual interaction and cooperation.

As the "95 Theses" employs both the Calvinist teaching and the two kingdoms doctrine to expound its understanding of church-state relations,[32] it would be valuable to examine further the relationship between the two. David VanDrunen provides a helpful analysis in this regard, noting that "Calvin's two kingdoms doctrine was fundamental and foundational for the early Reformed tradition's articulation of the distinction between and relationship of church and state."[33] He affirms the role assigned to the civil magistrate in protecting and cultivating true religion. Furthermore, VanDrunen offers an insightful study of the implications of the two kingdoms doctrine for Chinese Reformed Christianity, especially in regard to the priority of the church; the church's jurisdiction over its own government and discipline; the legitimacy of civil authority; the church's independence from nations, cultures, and political agendas; proclamation based on the word of God alone; and

---

[29]   Meeter, *The Basic Ideas of Calvinism*, 135.

[30]   David Fergusson, *Church, State, and Civil Society* (Cambridge: Cambridge University Press, 2004), 39.

[31]   Fergusson, *Church, State, and Civil Society*, 36–37, 38–39.

[32]   According to Yan Liu, "Many Chinese jiating churches today clearly distinguish the church as a spiritual kingdom and the state as a secular one." See Yan Liu, "Christian Faith Confessions in the Chinese Jiating Church Context: The Discourse of Sovereignty and the Political Order," in *Christian Social Activism and Rule of Law in Chinese Societies*, eds. Chris White and Fenggang Yang (Bethlehem: Lehigh University Press, 2021), 300.

[33]   David VanDrunen, "The Two Kingdoms Doctrine and the Relationship of Church and State in the Early Reformed Tradition," *Journal of Church and State* 49, no. 4 (2007): 744.

blessing China's future without redeeming it.[34] His primary concern is the nature of church authority and its distinction from political authority.[35] The two kingdoms doctrine remains relevant for providing a theological account of the church-state relationship in China, underscoring the distinctive character of church and state in their relationship to religious practice.

3. Beijing Shouwang Church

A more moderate encounter between an unregistered church and the governmental authority is exemplified by Beijing Shouwang Church. Shouwang Church attempted to register with the government as a legitimate religious group, but it failed. It also faced governmental interference in indoor worship spaces. As a result, Shouwang Church moved to outdoor worship beginning in 2009. This strategy resonates with the church's ecclesiology, which emphasizes the image of the "city on a hill." This vision portrays the church as a faith community whose identity and witness motivate its pursuit of registration with the government and outdoor worship as a form of protest. Outdoor worship originates in the radical conflict between the ideal of ecclesiology and the political realities of China. Yet Shouwang's persistence in outdoor worship aims at supporting worship as a basic requirement of Christian life; it is for religious purpose above all. Although Shouwang supports the principle of church-state separation and resists calls to join the official TSPM structure, it insists that the church should engage in dialogue and collaborate with the government in discussions about the unregistered churches and the government.[36] For Shouwang, the church's interaction with the government is a social witness and is the responsibility of the faith community, grounded in the hope of improving the religion-state relationship in China so as to benefit

---

[34] See David VanDrunen, "Two Kingdoms in China: Reformed Ecclesiology and Social Ethics," in *China's Reforming Churches: Mission, Polity, and Ministry in the Next Christendom*, ed. Bruce P. Baugus (Grand Rapids: Reformation Heritage Books, 2014), 199–222.

[35] Another theological treatment of the separation of church and state, as well as church autonomy, can be expounded in the doctrine of sphere sovereignty; see Robert Joseph Renaud and Lael Daniel Weinberger, "Sphere of Sovereignty: Church Autonomy Doctrine and Theological Heritage of the Separation of Church and State," *Northern Kentucky Law Review* 35, no. 1 (2008): 67–102.

[36] See Yi Sun 孫毅, "Women weihe bu jiaru 'sanzi'aiguohui" 我們為何不加入"三自"愛國會? ["Why Are We Reluctant to Join the Three-Self Patriotic Movement?"], Pushi shehui kexue wang 普世社會科學網 [Pushi Institute for Social Science], accessed January 6, 2020, https://tinyurl.com/mv3azta6.

society as a whole.[37] Shouwang's creeds highlight its understanding of ecclesiology by focusing on certain themes: Christ as head of church, separation of church-state, respect for governmental authority derived from God and based on the principle of conscience, and church auton-omy.[38] This ecclesiology leads to Shouwang's outdoor worship as a form of protest, characterized by its public nature and its peaceful worship, as Hao Yuan argues.[39]

Besides generally resisting the TSPM structure (in which worship and evangelism are only allowed within the approved locations), unregistered churches present several cases of civil disobedience. Their disobedience extends from church institutional structures to broader social action, such as homeschooling children, organizing unregistered Christian schools as alternatives to atheist education, refusing to wear red scarves and sing red songs or otherwise take part in nationalistic education, publicly renouncing Communist Party membership, speaking up against social injustice, and defending human rights (especially among Christian lawyers). For these Christians, conversion leads to an ideological shift and a clash with public policies, grounded in theological convictions, including that Christians serve only one Lord; Christ alone is the head of the Church; children should be brought up according to God's commands and standards as laid down in scripture; nationalism and pledging loyalty to a political party through quasi-religious rituals are forms of idolatry; and God calls Christians to defend the weak and oppressed.[40] According to Li Ma and Jin Li, "Being a member of an unregistered church itself means challenging the unwritten law of 'no assembly' in this country. And being an evangelizing believer makes one even more culpable, for he or she becomes an active diffuser of an alternative ideology. So the

---

[37] A detailed analysis of the ecclesiology of Shouwang can be found in Yi Le 以勒, "Shouwang huwai juhui de beihou: zhongguo jiating jiaohui dui jiaohuilun de fansi" 守望戶外聚會的背後: 中國家庭教會對教會論的反思 ["Behind Shouwang's Outdoor Worship: A Reflection on Ecclesiology by House Church in China"], Beijing shouwang jiaohui 北京守望教會 [Beijing Shouwang Church], accessed December 19, 2019, https://tinyurl.com/2p8hpmb3.

[38] See "Jidujiao Beijing shouwang jiaohui xinyue" 基督教北京守望教會信約 ["Creeds of Beijing Shouwang Christian Church"], Beijing shouwang jiaohui 北京守望教會 [Beijing Shouwang Church], accessed December 19, 2019, https://tinyurl.com/2p8pn5ka.

[39] Hao Yuan, "Zhongguo jidujiao yu bufucong de chuantong: yi wang mingdao, tanghe jiaohui yu shouwang jiaohui weili," 114.

[40] See Li Ma and Jin Li, "Remaking the Civil Space: The Rise of Unregistered Protes-tantism and Civil Engagement in Urban China," in *Christianity in Chinese Public Life: Religion, Society, and the Rule of Law*, eds. Joel A. Carpenter and Kevin R. den Dulk (New York: Palgrave Macmillan, 2014), 11–28.

Protestant faith with its core concern to spread the message poses a boundary-breaking action against government prohibitions."[41] Obviously, unregistered churches represent a strikingly different conception of the church-state relationship from that found in the official church structure and ideology.

Protestant groups' dealings with the state in contemporary China are complex and varied. As Fenggang Yang has observed, "Many urban house churches have also adopted avoidance as a resistance strategy. However, since 2000, more and more Christians in the urban house churches have adopted a positive way of resistance—challenging the authorities using the existing law."[42] In addition, "more and more Christians have taken up challenging authorities through legal means. Active resistance has grown in the 21st century and is likely to grow further in the coming years."[43] As we have seen, this ongoing resistance found in various church groups has theological roots. The next section further examines this theological background.

A Critical Posture: Theological Accounts of Church and State in China

In the cases examined above, we see the theological struggle with the state taking place across different churches, both registered and nonregistered. These debates center on the role of state, state action toward the church, ecclesiology, church autonomy, and Christian identity. Protestant encounters with the Chinese government today include elements of acquiescence, collaboration, and resistance. The responses illustrate various yet overlapping theological appraisals of the church and the government, including governmental policy toward religious practice and other social activities by religious groups. The core issue underlying the theology of the church-state relationship in China is whether to accommodate or resist political realities. This reflects alternative postures toward the state already found in the New Testament. As Walter E. Pilgrim suggests, "The New Testament has two contrasting positions towards the state: the attitude of subordination found in Paul and related texts, and the call to resistance in Revelation."[44]

---

41 Ma and Li, "Remaking the Civil Space," 22.
42 Fenggang Yang, "From Cooperation to Resistance," 86.
43 Yang, "From Cooperation to Resistance," 89.
44 Walter E. Pilgrim, "God and/or Caesar," in *God and Country? Diverse Perspectives on Christianity and Patriotism*, eds. Michael G. Long and Tracy Wenger Sadd (New York: Palgrave Macmillan, 2007), 23.

The church, under the auspices of the TSPM and CCC, relies on the doctrine of the Cosmic Christ as one theological account to harmonize the relationship between Christians and unbelievers (including communists). This results in the church's accommodation of the state.[45] Yet there remain opportunities for resistance in accommodation and accommodation in resistance.[46] Although the registered church struggles between accommodation and resistance, some unregistered churches appeal to the two kingdoms doctrine to define the respective authority of church and state, church autonomy, and the proper role of the state in regard to the church. From the perspective of those unregistered churches, church autonomy is undermined by being associated with the TSPM and CCC.

The early doctrine of two kingdoms emphasizes the state's divine agency and just rulership, assuming the magistrate bears duties to God and to a Christian society. The situation is different when we are talking about an officially atheist state like China. Some churches reject all collaboration with the state, while others attempt dialogue and collaboration with the government regarding certain church interests and rights. Political struggle and criticism on the part of the Chinese church are grounded in the belief in Christ as head of the Church as the foundation of civil disobedience.

It is necessary to further understand Christ as head of the Church and at once as the Lord over the various areas of life, including the state and society. As the Calvinist Abraham Kuyper claims:

> We can only conclude that there is a twofold kingship, that both proceed directly from the Triune God, and that they run parallel to each other. On the one hand, here is the kingship of the world that proceeds directly from God and calls governmental authority here on earth into being. On the other hand, there is the kingship of Christ that is not from here—not from the world and reigning elsewhere—but that reigns here and proceeds just as directly from God. Government authority has been ordained by God. Alongside it, "all authority in heaven and on earth" has been given to Jesus as King of God's kingdom.[47]

---

45 Of course, there are some other theological and political reasons accounting for the church's accommodation of the state and society in China.

46 Zhidong Hao and Yan Liu, "Mutual Accommodation in the Church-State Relationship in China? A Case Study of the Sanjiang Church Demolition in Zhejiang," *Review of Religion and Chinese Society* 5, no. 1 (2018): 26–42.

47 Abraham Kuyper, *Pro Rege: Living under Christ the King* (Vol. 1), ed. John H. Kok with Nelson D. Kloosterman and trans. Albert Gootjes (Bellingham: Lexham Press, 2016), 104.

In this sense, "Christ's kingship extends over all things, extends to every part of human life, also in society."[48] This belief enables many Chinese Christians' courageous confrontation with the government in various circumstances and their public practice of their Christian faith, as shown in their social and political positions and their civil disobedience. How they see God as the divine origin of government and as the kingship over the world determines their view of the governmental role in religious affairs and their social actions as well.

As developed by the Reformation thinkers, both church and state have their own God-centered origin and unity. As William Muller suggests regarding the ideas by both Martin Luther and John Calvin, "The church and state are both subject to the sovereign rule of God. The authority of both spheres inheres in the will and purpose of the living God."[49] Thomas Sanders describes church and state as "unified by the sovereignty of God and the loyal submission of the believer to both."[50] The sovereignty of God in church and state supports the Chinese Christian worldview of church and its relations with state and society and encourages both their respectful and critical view of political authority, as we see in Fergusson's statement: "There is one loyalty to God and therefore to the community under God's rule. By divine grace, secular forces, institutions and rulers may fulfil the will of God and therefore be worthy of support and respect. But acknowledgement of this possibility arises from an undivided loyalty to one end alone."[51]

According to Thomas Strieter, there are three critical stances the church may take toward the state: "(1) The critical-constructive stance is appropriate when the powers that be are attempts to achieve justice. (2) The critical-transformative stance when authority errs but can be realistically moved to salutary change. (3) The critically-resistive stance when the powers are responsible for demonic injustice or idolatry and refuse to be responsible to change."[52] These critical stances rely on two basic assumptions: the state serving the common good and the necessity of a critical posture toward all political authorities. The critical-constructive, transformative, and resistive positions can be integrated in

---

[48] Abraham Kuyper, *Pro Rege Living under Christ the King* (Vol. 2), ed. John H. Kok with Nelson D. Kloosterman and trans. Albert Gootjes (Bellingham: Lexham Press, 2017), 6.

[49] William A. Muller, *Church and State in Luther and Calvin: A Comparative Study* (Garden City: Anchor Books, 1965), 127.

[50] Thomas G. Sanders, *Protestant Concepts of Church and State: Historical Backgrounds and Approaches for the Future* (New York: Anchor Books, 1965), 31.

[51] Fergusson, *Church, State, and Civil Society*, 22.

[52] See Pilgrim, "God and/or Caesar," 47.

the church's attitude toward the state, even if unifying various churches' different perceptions of the state is no easy task. I would suggest that the experiences of the churches in China point to a possible mixed use of these stances.

It is actually not all that clear what the authority of the Chinese government is toward religious affairs. Although the Chinese government claims to grant basic freedom to religious practice and to serve the well-being of the common people, it poses certain constraints on religious groups regarding registration and organizational structure, and from time to time, it intervenes in church affairs (e.g., removal of the crosses in the churches) and makes demands regarding the content of religion (e.g., the sinification of Christianity). This critical stance of the church demands that political authority in all its attitudes and actions toward religious beliefs and practice should work toward justice with regard to the protection of church interests, Christian integrity, and the church-state collaboration.

Two aspects should be highlighted regarding the critical stance of the church toward the state in China. On the one hand, although Chinese churches maintain a critical posture toward political authority, it is crucial for them to show their responsibility and wisdom in political and civil life as citizens for the greater justice in Chinese society, whether in constructive, transformative, or resistive ways, particularly concerning both the limited role of government in church affairs and church autonomy itself. As James W. Skillen urges, "Christians . . . should see life in the political community as one of the arenas in which they have been called to serve in organized ways as stewards of justice and reconciliation for the sake of all their civic neighbors. Active citizenship orientated justice for all should be understood as an integral part of the Christian way life."[53] On the other hand, the critical posture underscores the enduring problem of religious freedom in China, centered on the meaning of religion-state separation.

There are several different labels for the pattern of the religion-state relationship in China. The Chinese government officially supports "separation of religion and state" (*zhengjiao fenli* 政教分離), in the sense that religious groups are not allowed to interfere with governmental affairs. This separation is not meant to suggest that the state may not interfere in religious activities. The "95 Theses" understands the Chinese government as supporting the "unification of religion and state" (*zhengjiao heyi* 政教合一), which is taken to mean that religious affairs come under the umbrella of internal governmental affairs. Others portray the

---

[53] James W. Skillen, *The Good of Politics: A Biblical, Historical, and Contemporary Introduction* (Grand Rapids: Baker Academic, 2014), 144.

religion-state relationship in terms of the "subordination of religion to the state" (*zhengzhu jiaocong* 政主教從).[54] The "95 Theses" understands the religion-state relationship in terms of the independence of each sphere. This principle stresses governmental authority over the social order and the public interest but not over religious beliefs or ecclesiastical authorities regarding worship and evangelism. It also highlights the church's spiritual authority while stopping short of any outright resistance of the existing secular authority and without seeking administrative privileges to influence society. Still, it upholds the church's right to lawful resistance insofar as the civil rights of church members are infringed upon by the government or other institutions. Among these different understandings of the religion-state relationship, it is crucial to contextualize definitions of both state authority and religious identity in the conditions of China. Both the state and religious groups possess particular interests, yet both are also concerned with the well-being of society as a whole.

Although the TSPM and CCC claim certain political and cultural obligations toward the state, they still demonstrate adherence to the Bible, based on the long-standing traditions of the Catholic Church and the Protestant Reformation.[55] Some unregistered churches, such as the Early Rain Reformed Church and Shouwang Church, emphasize both Christ as the head of the Church and source of the Great Commission and the hidden idea of the sovereignty of God in church, state, and the wider world. Both the Early Rain Reformed Church and Shouwang Church also reject patriotic religious organizations. The "95 Theses" states that the TSPM and the CCC are a "false church" rather than the true church of Christ. The "Theses" also states that the sinification of Christianity amounts to a rejection of Jesus Christ and of traditional Christian teaching. The Shouwang Church rejects the TSPM for similar reasons, seeing it as a government organization and not as the authentic church. These positions can be understood under the key idea of Christ's kingship over the church and the world at large.

Concluding Remarks

Against the background of the role of state in religious affairs in the Chinese context, this chapter provides a theological interpretation of a critical and realistic posture of the Chinese churches toward the state.

---

[54] See Xinping Zhuo 卓新平, "*Quanqiuhua*" *zongjiao yu dangdai zhongguo* "全球化" 宗教與當代中國 [*"Global" Religions and Contemporary China*] (Beijing: Shehui kexue wenxian chubanshe 社會科學文獻出版社, 2008].

[55] See "Five-Year Planning Outline for Advancing the Sinification of Christianity (2018–2022)."

As many call for greater religious freedom in China, this demands a careful examination of various models of religion-state relations, which requires theological justification. Based on studies of several cases of the church's encounter with the state and the theological themes behind that encounter, it can be observed that various theological ideas that influence their attitudes and actions toward the state are forming among Christians; in turn, those ideas expressed either in Christian communities or in their political and social engagement may be introduced to reform and reshape the government's attitude and actions toward the church. Those theological ideas can have a strong influence on remodeling the religion-state relationship in China to some degree if we can theologically (in a wider sense) understand the traditional and contemporary realities of religion-state relations in China and the church's different encounters with the state in the forms of accommodation, criticism, and resistance.

The core question is how to redefine the meaning of religion-state separation, where the government's concern differs from that of the unregistered churches, even though both use the same label. The Chinese government tends to supervise religious groups and activities so as to ensure social stability and cohesion, whereas the unregistered churches employ the idea of religion-state dualism. For these churches, separation implies that religious practice must have no official connection to the government. The type of theology for the Chinese church-state structure must take into account a Christian worldview, the reality of the state, and new church realities in contemporary China. These include such factors as high numbers of conversions to Christianity and increasing demand for the church's autonomy and freedom from governmental intervention and political obligations. Although courageous disobedience has taken place among both the registered and unregistered churches, the Chinese government's tendency is to control all social affairs, including religious activities. From the perspective of Chinese state leadership, it is the government's responsibility to guide, support, use, and restrict religious activities. Under a wider administrative network, "religious attachment to the state is part of an overall ruling strategy."[56] This structure places strong obligations on unregistered churches in particular for dialogue and collaboration with the government in working out an appropriate church-state relationship (as seen in the case of the Shouwang Church), even while resisting the official church structure. This structure also creates space for the officially approved church to reflect on its ecclesiology and its political obligations, particularly when the government does not adequately take into account the needs of religious adherents and communities.

---

56   Yao and Zhao, *Chinese Religion*, 128.

The theology of the Chinese church-state structure is sympathetic to the ideas of dualism and separation, which highlight the respective authority and limitations of church and state.[57] This framework can support some collaboration with the government on the part of church, regarding this activity as part of the church's witness as a faith community and its public responsibility as a social institution.

This study is suggestive and not meant to be comprehensive. My core concern is the theological framework found in both implicit and explicit forms in the Chinese church-state structure. There is a growing demand for Christian identification with Chinese culture, politics, and society (as seen in the "sinification of religion" movement). There is increasing Christian activity in China, not only in terms of the vast number of religious believers but also in terms of Christian confrontation with the state and engagement in social life, including theological engagement. While the church-state structure in China continues to depend largely on a top-down policy, efforts being made by Christians and others on the ground are important. These realities should be considered in any discussion of the church-state relationship in China, and this relationship requires a theological framework in which to take place.

This chapter has sought to shed light on the differing theological views undergirding debates over church and state in China today. It proposes a critical theology of the Chinese church-state structure, which emphasizes dialogue with the government and highlights the respective authority of both the church and the state, grounded in a thorough understanding of ecclesiology.

---

[57]   According to Thomas G. Sanders, "Dualism finds expression in Protestantism in the notion of the two kingdoms and the emphasis on religious liberty and separation of church and state as theological concepts . . . Religious freedom and separation of church and state, on the other hand, grew from the protests of minority groups against restrictions on their religious activity or against the privileges of an established church." See Sanders, *Protestant Concepts of Church and State*, 8.

CONCLUSION

Moral Triumph—Christianity in Public Life in China

In this book, I have attempted to use the tool of public theology in its methodological and constructive approaches to understand and shape the public face of Christianity in China, highlighting its moral implications. It is my desire that this project has the potential to play a part in a paradigm shift regarding the role of Christianity in China. Many struggle with the cultural conflict between Christianity and traditional Chinese culture; others strive for the accommodation between Christianity and concrete Chinese circumstances, including various social charity works; and still others advocate for Christian social activism, including its role in democratization in the Chinese context. These faces of Christianity in China do not fully account for its public face.

Religions in China face a complex social and cultural life while they wrestle with politics. They must recognize the fact of diverse religions and interact with them in Chinese life; they also have to pursue an impact on wider social life when their political participation is constrained, provided their religious doctrines encourage. To some degree, this encounter with other religions and political life lies in their own theological interpretation of culture and politics. Religions from outside China, including Christianity, weigh a lot on their cultural encounter with different religions in China while they have had to learn how to accept and deal with political authority in differing periods of Chinese history. Christianity has increasingly grown out of its theological engagement and construction of political and public life among the circles of academia and church in China, such as in mainland China and in Hong Kong. Indeed, this deserves an examination of the theological transformation from a missionary and anti-intellectual focus to active response to social and political life in China.

Considering the nature of Christianity itself in modern society, the moral concern with public life in public theology, and the cultural, theological, and social factors in China, we have good reasons to focus on the moral accomplishments of Christianity regarding its public face in China. On the one hand, it drives Christianity to be morally responsible for public life. On the other hand, even when Christians participate in social and political matters, including social justice and human rights, they must articulate their adequate theological and moral groundings; these groundings identify the problems of those public issues and engage the public discourse in terms of particular Christian contributions. They do this in a way that is critically transformative, constructive, or resistive for public life, being really both "public" and "theological" and being critically responsible to shape the public face of Christianity in China as a whole. To this end, Christian theology and ethics should engage with concrete religious, social, and political realities, which various disciplines involve—I call this position a social-theological construction of public life in the Chinese Context. Furthermore, this "moral triumph" for the public face of Christianity also creates much space for Chinese Christian scholarship or others concerning the role and development of Christianity in China to expound Christian public responsibility in the face of religious diversity and the church-society-state structure in China. In this sense, it is promising that a typical Chinese public theology is taking place.

APPENDICES

Reformed Public Theology and Christianity in China: A Chinese Engagement with North American Christian Public Intellectuals

INTERVIEW PROJECT DESCRIPTION

In August 2019, I traveled to the United States and conducted interviews with Nicholas Wolterstorff, James W. Skillen, and John Witte Jr. in different locations. All three of them have, to some degree, been influenced by Reformed public theological tradition represented by Abraham Kuyper (1837–1920) in their own intellectual journeys across different disciplines, including Christian philosophy, political philosophy, and law. They all admire Kuyper's vision for Christian public responsibility in abundant ways such as for flourishing culture, passion for justice, plural social structure, and religious and political pluralism. These interviews cover the themes of Kuyper's public theology, love and justice, church, society and state, freedom and order, human rights, and culture both in the West and China. In these interviews, Chinese Christianity, Confucianism, and the social and political circumstances in contemporary China are brought into dialogue with these scholars. These conversations demonstrate how the resources of Reformed public theology, derived from Kuyper, shape public life in the West, particularly in the United States, and bear certain implications in the Chinese context as well. This interview project was supported by the Institute of Sino-Christian Studies (Hong Kong) and was designed to commemorate the hundredth anniversary of Kuyper's death.

APPENDIX 1
WORLD-FORMATIVE CHRISTIANITY: WONDER AND GRIEF, LOVE AND JUSTICE

An Interview with Nicholas Wolterstorff

Interviewee: Nicholas Wolterstorff (hereafter "Wolterstorff")

Interviewer: Zhibin Xie (hereafter "Q")

Interview date: August 13, 2019

Interview location: Grand Rapids, Michigan

BIOGRAPHY OF NICHOLAS WOLTERSTORFF

Nicholas Wolterstorff is Noah Porter Professor Emeritus of philosophical theology at Yale University and Senior Research Fellow at the Institute for Advanced Studies in Culture at the University of Virginia. He graduated from Calvin College in 1953 and received his PhD in philosophy from Harvard University in 1956. He taught philosophy at Calvin College from 1959 to 1989 and then joined the faculty of Yale Divinity School, with adjunct appointments in the Yale philosophy department and religious studies department. He retired at the end of 2001. During leaves of absence, he has taught at the Free University of Amsterdam, Princeton University, and University of Notre Dame.

He has been President of the American Philosophical Association (Central Division) and President of the Society of Christian Philosophers. He is a fellow of the American Academy of Arts and Sciences. Among the named lecture series he has given are the Wilde Lectures at Oxford, the Gifford Lectures at St. Andrews, the Taylor Lectures at Yale, and the Stone Lectures at Princeton Theological Seminary. He is the author of thirty books, including *Art in Action* (Eerdmans, 1980), *Lament for a Son* (Eerdmans, 1987), *Justice: Rights and Wrongs* (Princeton, 2008), *Justice in Love* (Eerdmans, 2011), *Understanding Liberal Democracy* (Oxford, 2012),

The God We Worship (Eerdmans, 2015), *Art Rethought* (Oxford, 2015), *Acting Liturgically* (Oxford, 2018), *In This World of Wonders: Memoir of a Life in Learning* (Eerdmans, 2019), and *Religion in the University* (Yale, 2019).

Kuyper, *Shalom*, and "World-Formative" Christianity

Q: As a Christian philosopher and theologian, you are the recipient of the Abraham Kuyper Prize for Excellence in Reformed Theology and Public Life by Princeton Theological Seminary. You graduated from Calvin College, which has a Dutch Reformed background. You have a long relationship with the Free University of Amsterdam, which Kuyper founded: in 1981 you delivered the Kuyper Lectures at the university; in 1985 you were appointed as a part-time professor there; and in 2007, you received an honorary doctorate from the university. In many places, you have mentioned the influence of Kuyper, such as in your new book published in 2019, *In This World of Wonders*, in which you highlight that "this 'Kuyperian' version of the Reformed tradition that I imbibed in college has remained mine throughout my life."[1] How do you appraise the enduring impact of Kuyper and the Kuyperian tradition in your intellectual endeavors in various fields?

Wolterstorff: You know I grew up in a very small farming village in the state of Minnesota, the extreme southwest corner. My parents and grandparents had immigrated from the Netherlands, and my grandfather was a farmer, but he didn't really like farming. What he much preferred doing was reading theology. He read Dutch theology as much as he had time for. He talked about Kuyper. But I don't recall when I was growing up that he explained anything about Kuyper; he just mentioned Kuyper and talked about him. My first real acquaintance with Kuyper came when I was a student at Calvin College, beginning in 1949. It was there that I was introduced to the thought of Kuyper. So what inspired me about his thought? I suppose a number of things. The most basic thing, I think, was that in Kuyper, you get the conviction that Christians should be engaged in the world and a vision of how they should be engaged. They should not just try to fly off, talk about heaven and the afterlife and so forth.

Kuyper's perspective was that the Christian should engage with other people, with other citizens in the institutions and practices of American society, Chinese society, Dutch society—politics, economics, university education—participate along with others. But it was also Kuyper's view that we human beings have different worldviews; there's not some neutral

---

[1]   Nicholas Wolterstorff, *In This World of Wonders: Memoir of a Life in Learning* (Grand Rapids: Eerdmans, 2019), 56–57.

worldview. Christians have a distinct worldview, secularists and naturalists do, Jewish people do. And it was Kuyper's view that each of us, as we engage in politics or economics or art, should give expression to our worldview—our views of justice, what's good and bad, right and wrong, and so forth.

So it was that picture of not trying to avoid the world, not trying to avoid politics, art, and so forth—which is the attitude of many fundamentalist Americans—but to engage in art, philosophy, politics, and economics and to do so as a Christian, that inspired me. That was the most basic thing that I learned from Kuyper: to engage with our fellow citizens in the practices of society, not in some neutral way but in a distinctly Christian way.

That's what inspired me in college. Study philosophy, talk to other philosophers, go to philosophy conventions, but be a Christian philosopher, not try to be some sort of neutral philosopher. That's what especially inspired me about Kuyper. But there were other things as well, for example, his idea of sphere sovereignty. It was Kuyper's view that in a well-functioning society, human beings get together to form institutions—schools, labor unions, churches, and so forth—and that each of these has its own authority structure, not given to it by the state but created by the institution itself.

What this implied for Kuyper is that we should not ask the state to do everything but that the state should instead regulate the activities of these institutions, which have their own distinct authority in the sphere of education, in the sphere of politics, in the sphere of economics, and so forth. That's another facet of what inspired me in Kuyper.

Q: In your career, how has Kuyper initiated and inspired your Christian thinking in various spheres such as theology, liturgy, philosophy, education, art, and politics from the issues of beauty to justice and so on? In all these fields, you have made outstanding achievements. You say that "it is tied together by shalom." At this point in time, how is Kuyper's Christian worldview relevant?

Wolterstorff: The idea of shalom did not come from Kuyper. In the Reformed tradition, as I knew it, there wasn't much talk about shalom. Kuyper didn't talk about it, Bavinck didn't, Calvin doesn't. It was reading the Old Testament one day that the idea of shalom suddenly jumped out at me.

So yes, as I see it, what unifies these various interests of mine—philosophy, liturgy, art, politics, and so forth—is the Hebrew biblical concept of shalom. The word has usually been translated in English Bibles as *peace*.

But I think that's a poor translation. I think the best into English is *flourishing*. I did not find the idea of shalom in Kuyper. I am not aware that he ever talked about it. But for me, that's what holds things together. In our many activities in all these different areas, we work and struggle for the shalom, the flourishing, of the city. Art contributes to flourishing, economic activity does, or can—it doesn't always—politics can, medicine, law, and so forth. So you are right; for me the unifying idea is shalom. My interest is in education, in politics, in art, in liturgy, and so forth. These interests hang together. They are not just separate parts of my life.

Q: You have proposed the ideals of "world-formative Christianity" and "a socially progressive version of the Reformed tradition." How does this vision play a central role in your thinking about our world, particularly this world with injustice and grief, as well as about various social institutions?

Wolterstorff: In one of my early books, *Until Justice and Peace Embrace,* I contrasted two understandings of Christianity. One of them I called "world-avertive" Christianity. (The word *avertive* here means "avoidance.") A lot of fundamentalist Christians think that one should live a pure moral life and not get involved in politics, art, etc., any more than necessary. We're just pilgrims here, on the way to heaven. So you don't engage with art, you warn your children against philosophy, and so forth.

The other understanding of Christianity, which I called "world-formative" Christianity, is that we are called to contribute, each in our own way, to shaping this world, to shaping art, philosophy, economics, and so forth. The Calvinist tradition is very much this second sort of Christianity, world-formative. This was certainly Abraham Kuyper's view. As Christians, we are to seek to contribute to the formation of our social world, to its art, to its philosophy, to its politics, etc.

Two very different versions of Christianity. In "world-avertive Christianity," you avoid the world as much as possible—stay away from philosophy, stay away from art, and so forth. You still have to make a living. You find some job that pays you enough to live. In "world-formative Christianity," you contribute to forming society and its institutions. To me, it seems to me clear that scripture teaches the second, teaches us not to avoid but to contribute to shaping this world of ours, God's world.

For me, a central part of world-formative Christianity has been working for justice. In my thinking about justice, I was profoundly influenced by my contact with people of color in South Africa and by my contact with Palestinians; I talk about this in some of my books.

The world is full of injustice. We as Christians are called to participate, each in our own way, in the struggle for justice—to participate in what scripture makes clear is God's love of justice and God's call for justice. A crucial part of world-formative Christianity is participating in the struggle for justice in South Africa, in the Middle East, in American cities, in China, etc.

Another aspect of working for shalom is dealing with grief, of which the world is, of course, full. It's my view that we who are Christians should seek to own our grief, not disown it. Many Americans, when a child dies or a mother or father, try to forget about it, put it behind them, get on with things. That seems to me all wrong. To grieve over the death of a child is to honor the child and to honor one's love for the child. To fail or refuse to grieve is an act of dishonoring.

We own our grief, not disown it, make it part of who we are, get to the point where one can say, "I am someone whose son was killed in a mountain-climbing accident." But I have come to think that we are called to do more even than own our grief. We are called, if at all possible, to bring forth from this evil a good of some sort: become more sensitive to the grief of other people, perhaps to write about grief and how to deal with it. I put it like this: We are called to own our grief redemptively.

Those, as I see it, are two fundamental components of world-formative Christianity: to struggle against injustice and to seek to own one's grief, rather than disown it, and to do so redemptively. The goal of world-formative Christianity is the flourishing of oneself and one's fellow human beings. And these are certainly components of flourishing.

Let me also bring politics into the picture here. Governments are decisive in promoting or inhibiting shalom. If one seeks shalom, one has to be engaged, in one way or another, in politics. Political action is a crucial component of world-formative Christianity.

This seems obvious. But it's probably something I learned from Kuyper. Kuyper's way of thinking was strongly opposed to individualism. Recall his doctrine of sphere sovereignty, for example; what the doctrine emphasizes is the authority of social institutions: economic institutions, political institutions, educational institutions, and so forth. Kuyper's picture of society is a very much institutional picture. The flourishing of individuals depends on the flourishing of institutions. I'm fond of a verse in the Old Testament book of Jeremiah 29:7. Jeremiah is speaking to his fellow Jewish captives in Babylon. He says to them, "Seek the shalom of the city, for in its shalom you shall find your shalom." Their shalom depends on the shalom of the community: its institutions, its practices, etc.

Love, Justice, and Human Rights

Q: In another interview in *Christian Century*, you said, "It was hearing the voices and seeing the faces of the wronged that evoked in me a passion for justice."[2] You proposed the notion of "justice in love" (loving justice), departing from Anders Nygren and Reinhold Niebuhr in terms of love-justice relationship by stressing the implications of "love your neighbors as yourself."[3] In *Justice: Rights and Wrongs*, you argue that natural human rights are grounded in God's love for "each and every human being equally and permanently."[4] How do both your experience of injustice and your sense of Christian love work together toward your pursuit of human rights and justice?

Wolterstorff: I was awakened to the call for justice by my experience of attending a conference in South Africa in 1975, hearing the people of color express their pain at apartheid and hearing them issue a call for justice. The same thing happened in 1978 when I attended a conference of Palestinians. They spoke of the pain of the Israeli occupation, and they, too, issued a call for justice. It was those two very vivid experiences that alerted me to the importance of justice. If somebody had asked me before these experiences, "Do you think justice is important?" I probably would have said, "Yes, of course." But I was not energized. It was those two experiences that energized me to start thinking and writing about justice and to become active.

Those two experiences also alerted me to the prominence of justice in scripture. I'm sure that if I'd been asked, before these two experiences, whether scripture talks about justice, I would have said yes. But now the passages jumped out in a way that they hadn't before. Then the issue that confronted me was, how is justice related to love? Because scripture also teaches about love. The question of the relation between justice and love cannot be avoided. And what I saw when reading the literature is that, in the Western tradition, justice and love are often pitted against each other. The Swedish Lutheran bishop Anders Nygren, who published his famous *Agape and Eros* between the two world wars, says that justice in the Old Testament is replaced by love in the New Testament. The American theologian Reinhold Niebuhr did not agree with that. What he said is that justice is for conflict situations, and love is for situations in which there is no conflict. In most situations in this world of ours, there obviously is conflict. In most situations, we have to live by justice rather than love.

---

2   "An Interview with Nicholas Wolterstorff: Rights and Wrongs," *Christian Century* (March 25, 1998), 28.

3   See Wolterstorff, *Justice in Love*.

4   See Wolterstorff, *Justice: Rights and Wrongs*, 260.

Love can be prominent in small family situations, in classrooms, etc. But when it comes to politics, forget love and go for justice.

Pitting love and justice against each other like this felt intuitively wrong to me. So I said, "I have to read scripture closely, to see whether love and justice are described as being in opposition to each other." Jesus says that the essence of the law (Torah) is loving God above all and your neighbor as yourself. It turns out that, for both of these, Jesus was not just summarizing the law but quoting from the Old Testament. And when we look at the passage in Leviticus containing the second love commandment, what we find is a long list of examples of love, among them, treating your neighbor justly.

I came to the conclusion that the biblical understanding of love embraces justice; doing justice is an example of love. Love sometimes goes beyond justice, doing things that justice doesn't require. But it never falls short of justice. Justice is incorporated within love. When I call my book *Justice in Love*, I mean justice within love, not justice against love. Not love instead of justice but love that incorporates treating your neighbor justly.

Q: It seems to me that your own interpretation of justice developed from your own experience and from your understanding of the relation between love and justice. It's different from both Anders Nygren and Reinhold Niebuhr. It's my understanding that you also distinguish your interpretation of justice from that of secular philosophers like John Rawls. My question is: How does your own biblical and theological interpretation of justice distinguish your view from that of other political philosophers?

Wolterstorff: Let me speak of the Western tradition; I don't know about the Chinese. Going back into antiquity, there are two ways of thinking of justice in the Western tradition. One comes from Aristotle. Justice is fairness or equity in the distribution of goods and evils, benefits, and burdens. John Rawls was in the Aristotelian tradition. His principles of justice are principles for the fair distribution of benefits and burdens. The other traditional way of thinking about justice that comes to us from antiquity begins with the Roman lawyer Ulpian of the fourth century CE. Ulpian says that justice consists of rendering to each what is their due, their right. His Latin word for what I am translating as "due" or "right" was *ius*.

I think Ulpian's way of thinking about justice is the better way. Not all kinds of injustice consist of inequitable distribution of benefits and burdens. If I spy on someone, read their diaries and letters, hack into their email, but never tell them or anybody else about it, if the only thing I do is sit at home and read over the letters and diaries that I've stolen and the emails that I have hacked, then there is no inequitable distribution of benefits and burdens involved; nonetheless, I have wronged you, treated you unjustly.

I'm attracted to the Ulpian tradition: justice consists of rendering to each person what is their due or right; I think justice is grounded in rights. And then I go on to develop a theory of rights, arguing that we have to explain how it is that even human beings who are sunk into dementia, who are not capable of functioning as persons, have the right to be treated in certain ways.

I argue that to explain how it is that even such human beings have rights, we have to appeal to God, to God's love for each and every human being who bears the image of God. I think secularists can give a plausible account of the rights of well-functioning human beings; most secularists ground rights in the capacity for rational agency. But they cannot give an account of the rights of human beings who are severely mentally disabled. Such human beings no longer have a capacity for rational agency. That's my argument. I think only a theistic account can explain why even the human being who has sunk deep into dementia has a right to be treated in certain ways—the right, for example, not to be shot and have their corpse be tossed into a dumpster.

Let me add a historical point here. The notion has been spread abroad that the idea of natural rights began with the secular Enlightenment in the European eighteenth century. We now know that that's just false. The church lawyers of the twelfth century were using the idea of natural rights. The idea of natural rights grows out of the seedbed of Christianity. The Calvinist and Lutheran reformers made abundant use of the idea.

A question I've asked is this: If, in the seventeenth century, the Lutheran and Calvinist theologians and political philosophers were making abundant use of the idea of natural rights, why did Christians forget this part of their history? How did the idea arise that it was the secular Enlightenment philosophers who devised the idea? I've never gotten a satisfactory answer to this question from my historian friends. They say they don't know why this forgetfulness occurred.

Chinese Theory of Justice and Cross-Cultural Ideas of Justice

Q: For me, the topic of love and justice has been a universal issue in different contexts. In Chinese culture, there are also rich resources for developing the understanding of love and justice. A Chinese philosopher, Yushun Huang, has proposed a Chinese theory of justice, which is expounded by benevolence from Confucianism, from which the institutions/norms ("rites") and thus harmony is achieved. The basic structure of this Chinese theory of justice is: benevolence—benefits—conscience—justice—rational—harmony. For Huang, the Western theory of justice too often excludes the sentiment of benevolence from the issues of justice.[5] Would you please give some comments on his ideas on Confucian benevolence and justice?

Wolterstorff: Here's how I see it. You report him as saying that for justice, we need just institutions and principles to deal with conflict. When I hear that, I think immediately of Niebuhr. That's exactly what he said: justice is necessary when conflicts arise. As I understand this Chinese philosopher, it appears to me that he, in effect, eliminates justice. Here's what I mean. Benevolence consists of seeking the good of the other person. Sometimes, if I don't seek a certain good of the other person, I treat them unjustly, I wrong them. But in other cases, if I don't seek a certain good of the other person, I don't wrong them, don't treat them unjustly. If I don't give you the art hanging on my walls, then I deprive you of a good, but I don't wrong you, I don't treat you unjustly. I think the most basic question that has to be faced by a theory of justice is this: Why is it that sometimes, when we don't extend a certain good to somebody else, we are not treating them unjustly, whereas other times, when we don't extend a certain good to somebody else, we do treat them unjustly?

Why is it that extending some sorts of goods to you are required for treating you justly and others are optional? I sometimes give a whimsical example. There's a wonderful Rembrandt painting in the Rijksmuseum in Amsterdam, "The Jewish Bride." I think it would be wonderful if the museum would say, "Wolterstorff, we'd like to give you this painting to hang on your wall." It would be a wonderful thing in my life if they would do that. But they haven't. And I'm not wronged.

So as I understand the Chinese philosopher that you refer to, he hasn't faced what I regard as the fundamental question: Why is it that some goods are required by justice and others are optional? My view is this: I think rights are grounded in dignity and worth. You have a right to my extending some good to you just in case, if I didn't, I would not be treating you with due respect for your worth, your dignity. Rights are what respect for worth, for dignity, requires.

Here's an example. In the American system of schooling—I don't know about the Chinese—if a student writes a really good paper in one

---

[5]   See Huang, *Voice from the East*. Also see chapter 7.

of my philosophy courses, they have a right to an A because they have acquired the worth of doing excellent work. If I don't give them an A, I am wronging them, not treating them in a way that they have a right to be treated, not treating them in a way that befits the worth they have acquired of writing a top-notch paper.

Treating somebody justly always consists of dispensing some good to them. But a theory of justice has to face the question: Why are some good ways of treating people required of us for justice, and why are some other ways nice but not required?

In the nineteenth century, the southern slave owners often said that their slaves were happy. I think usually they were not happy, but maybe sometimes they were. Sometimes the slaves seem to have internalized the slaveholders' views about them, namely, that they were inferior human beings and didn't have the same worth as white people. Perhaps some of the slaves were happy. But the fact that they were happy didn't make their treatment just. It was still unjust. It may be that some Black people in South Africa were happy under apartheid. I think very few were happy, but maybe some of them were. But that didn't make apartheid just. Happiness is not enough for justice. Even happy people can be treated unjustly. Perhaps they don't recognize that they are being treated unjustly; perhaps they have learned to put up with their treatment. But that doesn't make it just. The African Americans in the US South in the nineteenth century had dignity. It may be the some of them believed what the slaveowners said about them and believed that they didn't have much dignity. But whether they believed they had dignity or not, they did have dignity.

Q: I want to add something more to this question. In Chinese society today, there is also a general call for benevolence or friendship and justice, which is among the list of socialist core values. In reality, we see cases of seeking justice from time to time in various social and legal practices. Some Christians in China are also struggling for issues of social justice in terms of church-state relations, constitutionalism, and human rights, etc. As you state "a passion for justice," how do you observe that Confucianism, Christianity, and other similar resources, as well as social witness, can work together to promote a just and loving society in China?

Wolterstorff: I don't know enough about China and Chinese tradition to answer you. You and your fellow Chinese Christians have to answer the question. But I would say two things to my fellow Christians in China. Be aware of the call for justice in the Christian scripture, and be aware of the fact that, in Christian scripture, love and justice are harmonious—not pitted against each other. And be aware also of the rich resources in the Christian tradition for understanding justice.

Then, second, as you engage in your daily life with people who are not Christians, have a conversation with them about justice and dignity and rights: Are there resources in Confucianism or Daoism, or some other part of the Chinese tradition, for the recognition of human dignity and rights? If there are any difficulties, then do your best to persuade your fellows that each and every human being does have dignity, a dignity that calls to be recognized. You will succeed for some; you will fail for others. That's how it goes.

We have the same problem in the West. As I was saying earlier: when it comes to people who are severely impaired mentally, old people with dementia, children who were born severely mentally impaired, secular perspectives do not, so far as I can see, have the resources for recognizing the dignity of such people. Is it the same case in China? I in my society and you in yours do our best to persuade people that all human beings do have dignity and therefore have the right to be treated in a way that befits their dignity.

Q: Furthermore, with regard to the theme of justice between Confucianism and Western theory (say, political theory), in addition to the Christian tradition discussed above, there is a publication entitled *Confucius, Rawls, and the Sense of Justice* by the Western scholar Erin Cline. This book argues that the central concerns of the Confucian *Analects* and Rawls's work intersect in their emphasis on the importance of developing a sense of justice—despite the absence of a term for *justice* in the *Analects*—and that, despite critical differences between their accounts of a sense of justice, this intersection contributes to "a well-ordered and stable society in Rawls and a harmonious and humane society in the *Analects*."[6] As a long-term advocator of and expert in justice, how do you evaluate the sense, concept, and theory of justice developed in different cultures and societies for a common world? In other words, do the cross-cultural ideas of justice have any implications from your point of view?

Wolterstorff: I cannot speak to whether or not there is a cross-cultural sense of justice. To find out, one would have to look carefully at China, at Africa, etc. I don't know. But to go back to Rawls. I mentioned that in the West, we have two ways of understanding justice that go back into the ancient world. One begins with Aristotle: justice consists of the fair or equitable distribution of benefits and burdens, goods and harms. The

---

6   Cline, *Confucius, Rawls, and the Sense of Justice*, 24.

other begins with Ulpian: justice consists of rendering to each person what is their right or due.

What the scholar you mention has found, apparently, is that in the *Analects,* there is some indication of the idea of the fair distribution of benefits and burdens. That's the Rawls idea. But given my understanding of justice, the interesting question for me is not whether one can find in the *Analects* the notion of a fair distribution. For me, the interesting question is whether one can find, in the *Analects* or somewhere else in the Chinese tradition, the idea of rendering to each their due or right and the idea of the dignity of the human being.

If I were doing cross-cultural studies, I would want to ask, To what extent do societies in general have an idea of fair distributions? That's the Aristotelian question. But I would also want to ask: To what extent do societies in general have the idea of treating someone in accord with their due or right? That's the Ulpian question. And I would want to ask: To what extent do societies in general societies have an idea of human dignity? That's the Jewish-Christian question.

A striking feature, as you know, of the United Nations documents on rights is that they are all dignity documents. They are rights grounded in human dignity.

Kuyper and Christian Scholarship: China and the West

Q: In your book *Religion in the University,* published in 2019, you argue that religious orientations and voices have a home in the modern university against the background of freedom of expression and intellectual diversity. You remind us that a scholarly ethic would guard us against becoming "specialists without spirit and sensualists without heart" (Max Weber's words).[7] In a similar tone, in his *Scholarship: Two Convocation Addresses on University Life,*[8] Abraham Kuyper shares his view of the divine purpose of scholarship for human culture. Kuyper uses "sovereign" and "organic" to define the spheres of life, and I think it is applied to scholarly life and university too.

In China there has been increasing interest and rich scholarship in Christian studies (the scholars are often not Christian) since the 1980s from biblical, theological, philosophical, historical, cultural, political, sociological, and anthropological perspectives. There is also growing

---

[7]   See Nicholas Wolterstorff, *Religion in the University* (New Haven: Yale University Press, 2019).

[8]   See Abraham Kuyper, *Scholarship: Two Convocation Addresses on University Life* (Grand Rapids: Christian's Library Press, 2014).

suspicion about Christian studies in universities and academia, being afraid of Christian studies' relevance to missionary work. I myself have been struggling about the role and spirit of religious scholarship (Christian scholarship in particular) in such a university setting as in China, where Christian studies and religious studies in general are still attempting their relatively independent status. Would you please share something more about this issue of Christian scholarship in university?

Wolterstorff: The main point Kuyper wished to make about the relation between religion and scholarship was that scholarship does not consist of some neutral report of facts but that one's scholarship is shaped, in various ways, by one's worldview, whether that worldview be religious or secular, and that different scholars have different worldviews. Though I don't mention Kuyper's name in that new book of mine, *Religion in the University*, the essence of the position I develop there is this Kuyperian view about religion and scholarship.

Now to the question you raise. As you describe it, the situation in China concerning Christian scholarship is similar in one way to the situation in my country and different in another way. As I understand you, there is openness to Christian scholarship in some places in China and hostility in other places. The same is true in the United States. My own university, Yale, is very open to Christian scholarship. But there are other universities, especially state universities, that are, so I am told, quite hostile to it.

The source of the hostility in your country and mine is quite different, however. You indicate that the source of the hostility in China is, typically, that Christian scholars are suspected of being missionaries. The source of the hostility in the United States, and in the West more generally, is not that but, rather, that religion in general is irrational, and for that reason has no place in the university. The idea behind this charge of irrationality is almost always that, for one's religion to be rational, one has to hold one's religious beliefs on the basis of arguments, whereas most religious people do not hold their religious beliefs on the basis of arguments but on faith.

In the third chapter of my book, I address directly this charge that religion is irrational. I do so by tracing some of the extraordinary developments concerning the epistemology of religious belief that have taken place in philosophy of religion over the past forty or fifty years. Philosophers of religion have pointed out that many of the ordinary beliefs of all of us are not held on the basis of arguments—when I believe I have a toothache, for example, I don't do so on the basis of an argument. And they have then gone on to argue, in detail, that there is nothing about religious beliefs in general that makes it necessary to hold them on the basis of arguments for them to be rational. It is my impression that almost all philosophers—whether religious or secular—who have followed this discussion agree with this conclusion. There is no basis for the claim that religious beliefs, in general, are irrational.

You indicate that you would like me to say something in general about the issue of Christian scholarship in the university. I think there's not much that can be said in general. We each have to address the situation as we find it in our country. You in China have to address the charge that Christian scholars are related to missionaries; we in the West have had to address the charge that religion is irrational.

Praise and Lament

Q: Let's move to the final question, a kind of summary of our conversation. You have shared about "a life of wonder and grief" and that "grief led me to see God and the world differently." As you may know, there have been marvelous cultural, economic, and social achievements in China throughout its history that continue today, while, at the same time, I still see some struggles for social justice among many Chinese. Would you please share something more about these matters (i.e., wonder, grief, justice, the world, and God) with a Chinese audience from your own understanding of Chinese culture, politics, and society (i.e., is there a difference between these ideas in the West and the East)?

Wolterstorff: It's not easy to summarize. I am deeply grateful for the life God has granted me. I have not had to live through serious social turmoil. I have never experienced warfare firsthand, never served in the military. I have lived through a golden age in American history—a golden age for white men, not a golden age for African-Americans or for women.

Two things have dramatically changed the trajectory of my life. One was the confrontation, in 1975 and 1978, with the injustice being done to people of color in South Africa and to the Palestinians in the Middle East. It was because of those experiences that the cause of justice became important for me in a way in which it had not been before.

The other thing that changed the trajectory of my life, as you know, was the death, in 1983, of our son Eric in a mountain-climbing accident. Early on, I| decided that I would not do what many Americans do, and other people in the West, namely, try to put it behind me, act as if it never happened, thereby dishonoring both my son and my love for my son. I would make it part of who I was, part of my identity: I am someone whose son was killed in a mountain-climbing accident. I would own my grief, own it redemptively.

It was especially my experience of grief that led me to understand God differently. It's not so easy for me to put the difference into words. I have never tried to explain why God allowed Eric to die. A lot of philosophers have tried to explain natural evils. I do not. I do not try to explain the evil of Eric's early death. I do not *want* to try to explain it. I live with it. God has become more mysterious for me. Also more awesome but more mysterious. Looking back, I thought I more or less understood God, more or less had God figured out. My grief has led me recognize that God is beyond my understanding, a mystery. That's the best I can do by way of putting the change into words.

And lament has become a part of my life, especially the psalms of lament. I don't think I paid much attention to the psalms of lament before. Now they are an important part of my life. Praise and lament live side by side.

APPENDIX 2
SOVEREIGNTY OF GOD: CHURCH, STATE, AND SOCIETY

An Interview with James W. Skillen

Interviewee: James W. Skillen (hereafter "Skillen")
Interviewer: Zhibin Xie (hereafter "Q")
Interview date: August 11, 2019
Interview location: Birmingham, Alabama

BIOGRAPHY OF JAMES W. SKILLEN

James W. Skillen received his BA at Wheaton College (1966), BD at Westminster Theological Seminary (1969), and PhD at Duke University (1974). From 1969 to 1970, he studied philosophy at the Free University of Amsterdam (VU). After teaching political science and philosophy at three colleges, he became the director and then president of the Center for Public Justice in Washington, DC, from 1981 until his retirement in 2009. He continues to write, speak, and mentor young people.

His publications include *The Good of Politics: A Biblical, Historical, and Contemporary Introduction* (Baker Academic, 2014); *Prospects and Ambiguities of Globalization,* editor and contributor (Lexington Books, 2009); *With or Against the World? America's Role among the Nations* (Rowman & Littlefield, 2005); and "International Politics in an Era of Kaleidoscopic Change and Uncertainty," *Philosophia Reformata* 80/1 (2015). His latest book is *God's Sabbath with Creation: Vocations Fulfilled, the Glory Unveiled* (Wipf & Stock, 2019).

Kuyper, Intellectual Life, and the Center for Public Justice

Q: As a Christian political philosopher, you are the recipient of the Abraham Kuyper Prize for Excellence in Reformed Theology and Public

Life awarded by Princeton Theological Seminary. You studied at the Free University of Amsterdam, which Kuyper founded. Your doctoral dissertation focused on the work of Herman Dooyeweerd in the Kuyperian tradition, and you have several publications related to Kuyper, such as *Political Order and the Plural Structure of Society* and a new book published this year, *God's Sabbath with Creation*. How do you appraise the enduring impact of Kuyper and the Kuyperian neo-Calvinist tradition in your intellectual endeavors in your (Christian) political thinking?

Skillen: The influence of Kuyper came almost at the beginning of my intellectual venture. It was when I began undergraduate study in the United States at Wheaton College that I first engaged in serious study. I grew up in a Christian family, but I knew nothing about the Dutch and the Kuyper tradition. I also knew almost nothing about China. In fact, I knew relatively little about the social, political, and economic structure of the United States, given my family's background. But the thing I was struggling with at the time I was in college was the degree to which the claims of Christianity, which I took seriously, related to all of life. In the tradition in which I grew up, the Christian faith was largely a personal and church matter and didn't necessarily have to do with other areas of life.

That didn't quite make sense to me. I was struggling with that question because of the claims that are in the Bible and so forth. For me, it had to do very much with who I am, what I'm going to do, whether I'm going be a Christian or not. But I got hold of Kuyper's Stone Lectures—lectures on Calvinism—which he gave at Princeton in 1898. Those lectures had a great impact on me primarily because Kuyper was talking about all areas of life—about politics and the sciences, about art and economics. That was the very thing I wanted to know about from a Christian point of view.

Many years later, I met Max Stackhouse, who was teaching at Princeton Seminary, and he told me that after all his study of social ethics in the Christian tradition, he saw that the only two major traditions of Christian thought that had something significant to say about the diversified structure of modern societies were the Roman Catholic tradition of social teaching and the Protestant Kuyperian tradition.

In any case, as an undergraduate, I became very interested in Kuyper, whose writings helped me to answer some of the questions I had about being a Christian in all areas of human social life. At that point, I set my heart on going to study at the Free University of Amsterdam (now the VU University) that Kuyper founded. I studied there for a year, learned enough Dutch to be able to read and work with it. Afterward, at Duke, I wrote my doctoral thesis on the development of Calvinist political theory in the Netherlands.

After the Duke years, I taught at the undergraduate level for almost ten years, yet during those years I was becoming involved with a group of people who wanted to do something political. That led eventually to the founding of the Center for Public Justice, for which I became the first executive director. At the Center, we worked on issues of politics and government in relation to the most basic questions of political life—about justice, public well-being, fairness in the distribution of public services, and so forth.

Q: As the director and the president of the Center for Public Justice (CPJ) for about three decades, how are Kuyper's ideas relevant to the CPJ's exercise in fostering the idea of public justice? At this point, what is the purpose of the related Kuyper Lecture program at the center?

Skillen: Well, actually, it's not so much that Kuyper gave me ideas that I wanted to apply. It was more that in reading Kuyper and then Herman Dooyeweerd, the legal and political philosopher that followed in Kuyper's line, I gained a point of view, a standpoint, from which to look critically at American politics and government. From Kuyper and those he influenced, I learned to ask important questions about the way society is structured, particularly about the relation of government to other institutions and organizations of society. It helped me gain some perspective on American society and politics that I had given much thought to before. I could also see how Kuyper's pluralist approach to complex societies is relevant not only for the Netherlands and the United States but also for other countries, including China.

The structure and processes of American political life have been shaped very much by John Locke, the English philosopher. That is what we generally refer to as the liberal tradition. That tradition of thought and practice begins with the assumption that the first and primary sovereign of political life is the single person—the autonomous individual. As those individuals mix their labors with the world around them and acquire goods and property, they soon realize that they need an umpire who will protect their lives and properties, so they agree to give up a bit of their sovereignty through a social contract and deposit it in a limited government. From that point of view, the government doesn't govern a political community from the beginning. It doesn't have an office of responsibility in what today we would call a polity, a political community, a *res publica* (public thing)—a "republic." Government's obligation from a liberal point of view is to protect the lives and properties of individual persons and enhance their freedom and autonomy. That is why almost all Americans think in terms of individual freedom and how the government can either protect or endanger that freedom or autonomy.

213

People who are most conservative, called *libertarians*, want the least government possible. They want government to do nothing more than provide police and military protection. Every other social concern should be handled by individuals alone or by individual contracting with one another to achieve common interests.

The fact is, however, that there is much more to human social life than the liberal tradition can understand. Families and schools, business enterprises and scientific laboratories, art galleries and publishing companies are different in character and purpose from one another and from the public political community. And their identities and functions cannot be reduced to mere contracts among individuals. It is this diverse character of human social life that Kuyper illuminated through his actions and thinking.

What takes shape as a school has a different identity than a family, and the school has a different identity than a business enterprise. This raises the big question: What constitutes a good school? What does a business enterprise exist for? Those are questions that can't be answered just by asking individuals what kind of freedom they want. You have to get inside the work of schools and look at what they actually do, how they educate students. Similar questions have to be asked about what distinguishes the particular work of a business enterprise from other organizations and institutions. In order to answer these questions about a complex, diversified society, we need a different kind of perspective and framework of evaluation to provide answers to those questions.

The primary way of thinking about complex societies that contrasts with liberal thinking is some form of socialism. The starting point in this case is with the entire human community rather than with individuals. The concern is first of all with the ideal of a society in which everybody is treated as part of a common bond that they all share. From that point of view, individual freedom is not first in importance. Individual freedom is important only insofar as it contributes to the communal enterprise, the total social good.

What Kuyper saw was that it is a mistake to try to order a society on the basis of either individualist or collectivist thinking. Humans are social creatures, but their social character is always diverse, not monosocial. And individuals bear real responsibility for themselves as well as for others. In every association and organization, each person should bear some responsibility. Individualism is a misleading ideology. No child is born by itself. It doesn't create itself. It doesn't feed itself. It doesn't raise itself. It is dependent upon a family and diverse social relations and institutions. Human beings have different kinds of responsibility all at the same time, and they don't all coalesce into a single collective. Collectivism as a political ideology is equally as misleading as individualism. What holds a society together is neither individual autonomy nor a totalistic collective.

Kuyper argued that you have to recognize the importance of individuals and their responsibilities, but it is a mistake to imagine that individuals are autonomous and the creators of society by means of contracts. He would also say that you need to recognize the very great importance of governments, nations, large organizations, but none of them, not even the state, can serve as the single, comprehensive, omnicompetent authority over all and in all.

So if neither of those ideologies is correct, then from Kuyper's point of view, we need to see all of our responsibilities in a diversified society as dependent on a higher authority beyond them all. That higher authority for Kuyper is the creator of all things, the God who creates us and all things for a wide range of responsibilities. And we can then begin to understand how to do justice to both individual responsibilities and the diverse institutions and associations of society at the same time.

The perspective we have developed at the Center for Public Justice is what we call *principled pluralism*. The character of political communities is that they are to provide a public-legal order in which, as *a matter of principle*, government must recognize and do justice to both individuals and the diverse nongovernment associations and institutions of society. Government should not be empowered to have total jurisdiction within every association and institution. The major challenge for government in a society is to see that every person and every organization is given its due, is treated justly for what it is. The wider social order does not belong to the political community, but a just society can only flourish if it has a public-legal order in which the law protects its right to exist and supports the public commons. How, then, should government act to do justice to agriculture, to the education of citizens, to the environment, to families, to business institutions, and so forth? How should each political community under its government be related to other political communities and governments? Kuyper did not give, and could not have given, answers to all those questions. But Americans and people in every other political community must ask these questions if we are to help build just societies and just relations among nations throughout the world.

I would say Kuyper's influence on me as an American was to expose the inner limits and problems of individualist ideology and the kind of social order Americans have fostered. China has a much different culture.

It has a different history. It has different kinds of successes and problems in governing a very large and complex social order. Yet Chinese people are human beings just like humans throughout the world. They have families and friendships, schools and the arts, universities and major corporations, churches and other religious institutions, trade and commerce. It seems to me that the same questions challenge China and the United States as they did the Netherlands when Kuyper was living. That's why I believe Kuyper is relevant for all of us today.

As for the Center for Public Justice, the comments I just made can serve as a pretty good introduction. What we have tried to do at the Center is to develop a kind of civic educational think tank that focuses on encouraging citizens to take there civic responsibility more seriously and with greater understanding of the "plural structure" of society, which calls for government to act in tune with "principled pluralism." And insofar as we have been able to develop public policy proposals from that point of view, the Center for Public Justice tries to introduce them to legislative and executive officials in Congress and other governing agencies. Americans need to understand that politics and citizenship are not first of all about individuals getting what they want. Rather, it should be about fulfilling our obligations as citizens for the healthy development of the political community in which everyone deserves fair treatment. We want to carry out civic education in a way that has an impact on the way citizens as well as governments act.

Now Kuyper was very much a dedicated Christian. I am also a Christian. For that reason, many people in America and other developed countries misunderstand Kuyper's and my intensions. They think that we want to influence government in order to gain privileges or special benefits for Christians. But that is not the case and should not be the aim of Christians who are obligated to love their neighbors as themselves. Kuyper led a movement, and those of us at the Center for Public Justice want to follow him in demonstrating that citizens can and should be motivated to help shape a political community that upholds justice and equal treatment for all, with no special privileges for Christians, or for rich people, or for white people, or for those of any other race, religion, or social status.

Kuyper in his day did not do much theorizing about all of these matters. He was an organizer, and he worked tirelessly to help organize Christians to play a constructive role in the Netherlands and beyond. He founded a university, the Vrije Universiteit (Free University) of Amsterdam—now the VU University. He organized the first major mass political party in Europe, a Christian-democratic party that called itself the Anti-revolutionary Party, to indicate that they wanted to be reformers of the political system, not revolutionaries as in the French Revolution. He helped to organize a national businessmen's association. He helped organize a school reform movement that was able (after about thirty years of effort) to convince Parliament to recognize the freedom of parents to choose different schools without discrimination for religious or other reasons, all of them with equal legal protection and funding. He also edited a daily newspaper for many years and wrote editorials, some of which came in a long series that were later organized into his many books.

The important lectures Kuyper gave in the United States in 1898, for example, were the Stone Lecture at Princeton Theological Seminary. At the Center for Public Justice in the 1990s, we decided we would start an annual Kuyper Lecture and invite some notable political leaders or authorities on particular public issues to give the lecture. The point was to introduce those in the audience to someone who had inspired us and to introduce our principled pluralist vision and approach to the responsibility of government and of civic engagement.

Kuyper's influence is still growing beyond the Netherlands and around the world. He had done his work one hundred years before us, showed a bit of a tradition that we share, believing that God created all humans in the divine image and that government ought to give equal treatment to everyone within US borders. Furthermore, Kuyper had a rather worldwide view of life, not a narrow nationalist preoccupation. I was, and still am, very much concerned that work in the political arena must, in our day, give more attention to the many issues of international justice and how justice on a global scale can be promoted.

I am very concerned today about the degree to which nations, including the United States, are moving in a nationalistic direction and away from cooperation in international organizations. Part of the reason, of course, is that international institutions and economic globalization are not succeeding in improving social, political, and economic life for all countries. But failures of governance require better governance not an escape from it. Therefore, especially from a Christian point of view, it seems to me that hardened nationalism, even civil-religious nationalism, is a serious danger. The world is very complex and increasingly interdependent on countless fronts. If we shape the world in ways that pit every nation against the other, then we are headed for disaster and likely greater local and regional warfare.

Sphere Sovereignty: Family, Society, and State—The West and China

Q: I'm quite impressed by your personal encounter with Kuyper, especially his Stone Lectures. In the earlier stage of your academic life, you were influenced by Kuyper's idea that Christianity relates, as you say, to the rest of life and the whole society. You also said something about how Kuyper's idea about God's sovereignty in the different fields of life and the idea of social diversity. The next question will be about this idea and its dialogue with the similar issues in the Chinese context.

As I see it, the Kuyperian vision of "sphere sovereignty" serves as a key idea to construct state, church, and society.[1] In particular, a family is essentially different from a state or a business enterprise. This plural structure of society creates intermediate associations and balances diverse associations. By contrast, in the Confucian tradition in China, the state is modeled after the family and thus the notion of autonomous organizations (including religious groups) is weakly developed.[2]

While I and probably many Chinese people are struggling to ascertain the appropriate relationship among family, society (social institutions), and state, would you please share your thoughts about this dilemma from your Calvinistic as well as more general political perspectives?

Skillen: That is a very good set of questions. This has to do with all of the West. From the time that Christianity came into the Roman Empire, it had to come to grips with it as the all-embracing authority of European, Mediterranean world. The Roman emperor was the one who connected earth and heaven, the one who represented God on earth and therefore established the religion or religions of the realm. There were some parallels between that Roman order and the imperial order in Chinese history. The son of heaven, who received the mandate of heaven to govern the people as a father of the family, as you indicated in your questions, was the one who connected earth and heaven.

Over time, as Christianity expanded in the Roman Empire, it was established by the emperor Constantine as the primary religion of the realm. In Western Europe, however, the struggle for supreme authority between the emperor and the pope (Roman church bishop) led to recognition of the pope as supreme in moral authority who delegated the sword of earthly power to the rulers in different parts of the realm. The church would not govern society directly, but it should be the one that recognized and blessed those who would govern. So instead of the Roman emperor determining right religion, the pope would choose and bless right government. Meanwhile, in the eastern region of Europe, the church (Eastern Orthodox) held on to the model of ancient Rome and subordinated itself to the superior authority of the emperor. That is basically the heritage of Russia in contrast to the western regions of Europe.

---

1   See Skillen and McCarthy, eds., *Political Order and the Plural Structure of Society.*
2   See chapter 9.

Now that's too brief a summary, but up into the nineteenth century in Western Europe and North America, those were the two models that were fought over both before and after the breakdown of Christendom. From about the late 1500s onward, nations such as Britain and France became independently governed, and a key question had to be answered: Should the church be subordinate to the government, or should governments be subordinate to the moral authority of the Roman Catholic Church, even if not to its canon law? Until the twentieth century, the Catholic Church insisted that governments ought to acknowledge the church's moral authority. Protestant countries insisted on the independence of their governments, and some of the new nation-states established churches. Kuyper argued that neither the church nor the state, neither pope nor emperor, should be acknowledged as the highest sovereign; only God is sovereign over all.

Now what does that say about human responsibilities on earth? Well, among other things, church and state are not the only institutions of human responsibility on earth. There are others, and Kuyper's argument is that sphere sovereignty should be the rule. We ought to reject the aim of identifying the chief sovereign on earth, whether an institution or the sovereign people. Only God is the chief sovereign and the delegator of limited sovereignty to human responsibility in a variety of institutions. That's the idea that a number of human institutions should exercise limited sovereignty, each in its own sphere.

Kuyper argues that in the family, for example, there is a distinct kind of responsibility—a limited sovereignty, you might say, of parents over their children. It is not political or ecclesiastical sphere sovereignty but familial sovereignty. What Kuyper did, then, was to pluralize sovereignty on earth. Or better said, Kuyper urged everyone to recognize the true diversity of human responsibilities on earth and to affirm government's responsibility to establish principled pluralism under public-legal protection. Because Kuyper was primarily contending against every kind of omnicompetent authority or total sovereignty of either state or church, he used the expression *sphere sovereignty* (sovereignty in its own sphere) to point to the diversification of sovereignty among human responsibilities and to oppose any human claim to supreme sovereignty over all.

I, and a number of others who have learned from Kuyper, prefer to use a different expression when speaking of Kuyper's idea of sphere sovereignty. My preference is to speak of *diversified spheres of responsibility*. In social analysis, the first question we should ask is: Who has responsibility for what? Before we can talk about who is chiefly responsible in a social sphere, we need to ask: What kind of responsibility is it? Then we can ask: Who is best qualified to give leadership in that arena of responsibility? If we only emphasize a family sphere of sovereignty, for example, we will tend to focus on the parents as the chief authority. A particular sphere of human responsibility bears limited responsibility under God. The bigger question we need to ask is: What is the meaning and purpose of each different sphere of responsibility?

Kuyper starts that chapter by quoting Aristotle and agreeing that humans are social creatures. That is certainly a direct confrontation with the liberal tradition in the United States. That is to say, individuals are not sovereign as isolated individuals. Rather, they are social by nature and bear different kinds of responsibility. But then Kuyper seems to contradict his idea of sphere sovereignty when he argues that if humans had not sinned against God, the social order would not have begun to break down, and society would have developed in a harmonious, organic way as one big *family*. This is very much like the Confucian idea of the nation as a family writ large, with the emperor as the father of the people.

Kuyper's argument is that humans would not have the kind of governments we have today if humans had no sinned against God. So whereas Aristotle and Plato thought of the political community as an individual writ large, and the individual as the microimage of the polis, Confucius and Kuyper had an idea of the nation and perhaps even the entire world as a family writ large. Kuyper then argues that because of human God intervened to establish government to restrain sin and protect individuals and various human institutions from interfering in the limited sphere of sovereignty that properly belongs to each one. Government of states does not exhibit the original familial harmony of created life. Rather, governments exist to keep society from disintegrating even further. Governments function more like a machine built to maintain order. That is something quite different from a natural organic community.

Unlike liberal individualists, however, Kuyper did have a strong sense of a national *commons* as shared public space and institutions. The Dutch nation in Kuyper's day did not merely restrain public crime and punishment criminals; it promoted the health and well-being of the commons. Promoting the good included building roads and parks, water and sewage systems, education and communication networks. Yet for Kuyper, the commons did not absorb into (or under) itself all other human responsibilities in families and churches, in the sciences and the arts. When Kuyper talked about political life, we immediately see where his idea of sphere sovereignty comes in. He had already rejected the idea that the church or the state should hold ultimate sovereignty over society. He had, in fact, already recognized that apart from sin, society would not unfold like one all-embracing family because families represent only one of many different spheres of human responsibility. What Kuyper was trying to sort out sorting out is that we should not confuse two different social entities. We shouldn't treat the political order like a family. A political order is not a business any more than it is a family.

If I understand it correctly, there is still a significant influence in China from the Confucian tradition, yet China is as complex and differentiated a society as any country in Europe or North America. China appears to be taking on more and more of the complex economic characteristics of capitalism, banking, trade, investment, and more. Yet to some degree, China continues to hang on to the ancient idea of a harmonious nation understood as an undifferentiated family whole. Although I know far too little about China, it seems to me that the leaders of the society, the economy, and the government could benefit from some of Kuyper's thinking.

So how will China deal with the diversity of institutions and human relations that do not have their origin in the state? Governments do not create families. Governments do not create scientific or artistic creativity. They do not create scholarship. Where do all these things come from, and how do they work together without being overtaken by one of them? Whether or not you want to bring God into this discussion the way Kuyper did, the people of China as of every other country on earth still must ask the questions of social diversity and differentiation and the question of the locus and limits of sovereignty. What makes for a healthy and just relationship among all these institutions, including government and personal responsibility?

Q: For me, as a Chinese, it's quite illuminating to understand the difference between the state and the family due to interruption by sin. There is a continuity between Confucian understanding of human nature and the idea of society as a big family. On the other hand, we have seen the weak development of social institutions in traditional China. Yet as I see it, and many other observers as well, there is the rise of society (civil society) together with individualism in China since the 1980s (the opening and reform era); Chinese scholars suggest the idea of the emergence of a "social" sector.[3] Society has gradually grown beyond the ability of the state to govern well. However, civil society in China is typically state-led.[4]

During this process, many Chinese people (the youth in particular) tend to be individualistic—: searching for a diversity of values; seeking

---

[3] See Gao, "'Gongmin shehui' gainian yu zhongguo xianshi", 30.
[4] See chapter 2.

individual freedom, independence, and happiness; and striving for individual rights—all of which lead to detachment from social relationships such as the family, kinship, and communities. However, individuals are often regarded as the means to serve the greater goals of society and the state in the Chinese context; individuals are confined within the framework of society and state, as the collective often exists to resist individualization.

One leading Chinese sociologist even suggests that the government, market, and society are the three main mechanisms on the road to modernization in China. Moreover, in the current stage, the relationship between the government and society demands more innovation or transformation than the relationship between the government and the market as we see the relative weakness of social forces and social governance.[5]

At this point, do you think the Kuyperian vision of sphere sovereignty is relevant and helpful as you support the view that it attempts to overcome the flaws and dangers from an individualistic or collectivist deduction of social structure? What insights would you offer about the complexity of the individual, society, and state in China? Does the context in China challenge your thinking in this regard?

Skillen: What you have just described is precisely the situation Kuyper faced in nineteenth-century Europe and that every developed country faces today. How can a government govern well as the society grows in diversity—diverse spheres of society and diverse opinions about society and human nature? The more a government tries to maintain harmony by forceful restraints and uniform behavior by trying to control everything, it will most likely undermine the diversity that makes human society ever more meaningful. The more government tries to force national unity, the greater the individualist reaction will be. And the greater the move toward individualism, the weaker the common bond of citizens will be.

In China, it appears that you are facing the problems that come from too great an attempt by government to control social relations even as the economy differentiates. In the United States, we face the problems of too much individualism. That is why I think Kuyper's work is so valuable to consider. It was not that he invented the idea of diversity

---

5   See Qiang Li 李強, "Cong shehuixue jiaodu kan xiandaihua de zhongguo daolu" 從社會學角度看現代化的中國道路 ["The China Path of Modernization from a Sociological Perspective"], *Shehuixue yanjiu* 社會學研究 [*Sociological Studies*], no. 6 (2017): 18–26.

and pluralism. He was simply recognizing the many differences among institutions and organizations to carry out human responsibilities. And his argument was that if the government of a society is to do justice to that diversity, it must establish laws that uphold pluralism in many arenas. He argued that a nation or political community has to have a degree of unity in order to function. But that national unity has to be a public-legal unity of a limited type. That kind of unity must, by its very nature, make room for nonpolitical, nonpublic-legal types of community to function freely in their own spheres of responsibility. And within those many different spheres, there needs to be room and public protection for people to develop in different ways, with different points of view. Once people realize that they have protection to exercise their diverse responsibilities freely, they will find greater agreement on their national, public-legal bond that makes pluralism possible. They will recognize the importance of a government that can protect the public commons and uphold health and safety standards, the rules for banking and trade, and so forth without trying to act as the superior authority over everything people do inside their families, schools, religious communities, business enterprises, publications, scientific laboratories, and so forth. Government can then focus on its highly important sphere of public-legal responsibility for the common good of all.

Dooyeweerd, a legal theorist who followed in the Kuyperian tradition, made a very important distinction between sphere sovereignty (different spheres of human responsibility) and what he called the whole-part relationship. Let me illustrate. If you ask, "What are the parts of a family?" we would say, "Parents and children and what they share in common." If we ask, "What are the parts of a politically organized nation or state?" we would say, "Departments of government, the courts, police forces, public utilities such as water and sewage systems, traffic laws, the banking system, and so forth." But you see, families, business enterprises, religious bodies, schools, and art galleries are not parts of the state. They are different spheres of responsibility, each with its own parts. Of course, all of those diverse social spheres are interrelated, and in order for government to do justice to them in the exercise of its public-legal responsibility, it will need to identify and recognize the independence of other spheres of society and protect them from doing harm to one another and to the public commons. Government will, indeed, need to establish the laws of civil and criminal justice.

We can talk about the importance of harmony and unity of the whole political order. But these other institutions aren't parts of the state. A family should not be thought of as a department of state. A business enterprise is not a department of state. That brings us back to the sphere sovereignty question.

The responsibility people have as citizens in the state or political community entails the obligation to participate lawfully in it and to seek justice. At the same time, people are always more than citizens. You and I are parents, scholars, consumers, friends, members of international organizations, and much more. Those are not public-legal responsibilities.

Of course, there are important dimensions of a harmonious public order that touch on every other sphere of human responsibility, but those have to do with how the public-legal order governs the interrelationships and interdependence of all social relationships in the public sphere. That is different, however, from governments trying to rule inside other spheres as if it is the ultimate family authority, scholarly authority, and authority over friendships.

What we have in the United States today is neither an authoritarian government nor a completely individualist society. We have a society of many different kinds of relatively independent social institutions and relationships. But in the US, we also have many public laws that intrude on the internal responsibilities of families, schools, businesses, and nongovernment associations. And we have some public officials who want to gain greater authoritarian control over society. We need a better balance of the kind Kuyper was working for and that I have been working for through the Center for Public Justice.

My impression from outside China is that for several decades, the leadership of China has been realizing that it may be losing its moral authority in Chinese society. That may be one reason why the leaders have tried to bring back greater regard for Confucius. They realize that if there isn't some moral glue in China that allows the people to feel they are part of the Chinese "family," the leaders will have no lasting authority. My sense is that if the leaders in any specific society do not do justice to people who want to exercise responsibility in different spheres of life, then the leaders will not be able to produce unity and harmony by using sheer force and intimidation.

Secularization: Church, Society, and State

Q: We have already talked about family and individualism in society and the state. You actually mention the relationship between church and state. Now I want to move to this question, which I think this is of the same importance in the West as in China. You emphasize that the West has developed the idea that neither the pope or church nor the emperor or state should have the ultimate sovereignty over society, the idea to which Kuyper himself made such a significant contribution. Regarding the interactions of church, state, and society, Kuyper claims the moral impact to the state and society by church without "confessional bonds" or "authoritarian control."[6] I believe there are certain implications of Kuyper's statement in the Chinese context regarding the church-state-society structure. As a foreign observer, would you please share your ideas on this topic about the nature of church, state, and society and its implications in the Chinese context?

Skillen: It is true that Christianity spread out most widely from Western Europe, but don't forget that there was, from its earliest history, the Eastern branch of Christianity that continues to have its greatest expression in Russian nationalism, nurtured in the Russian Orthodox Church. Furthermore, Marxism is a secularizing derivative of both Eastern and Western Christianity, and China absorbed and adapted a great deal of the Russian tradition, in which the church is subordinate to the emperor/ Czar/communist leadership. Whether in the West or the East, Christianity has not always been oriented to loving service outside the dominance of the state in which it is practiced. Even in Western Protestantism, many of the states that emerged from the collapse of medieval Christendom established a Protestant church—in Britain, the Netherlands, and the Scandinavian countries.

It was primarily in the United State that the practice of the disestablishment of a church was advanced, yet white, European Protestants in America used a great deal of government's power to impose Christian cultural practices on families, schools, and government. Still today in the US, the same structural features established by Protestants in the nineteenth century control our political practices. The big change that has taken place is that that now the majority culture is secularized and driven by an American civil-religious nationalism, which is not, in my mind, compatible with Christianity in its biblically grounded sense.

Part of what has attracted me to Kuyper is that he is the major Western figure to advance a two-dimensional interpretation of *secularization* that best describes what he was trying to do. Kuyper argued that one meaning of secularization (let's call it *secularization 1*) is that the state (the political community) should not establish by public law in its jurisdiction one or more religions and discriminate against all the others. The reason is that the basis of inclusion for a political community is citizenship not the religious beliefs of some of those citizens. In other words, a just state is not

---

6   Kuyper, "Common Grace," 197. See my "Introduction."

a confessional community but a public-legal community of citizens. The way to do justice to all citizens is to treat their religious beliefs impartially under public law. None should be favored or disfavored. Disestablishment of the church, then, means to de-ecclesiasticize the political order. That is the positive way to understand secularization.

The second way Kuyper thought about secularization (let's call it *secularization 2*) was in a negative way. This is what most people mean when they use the word. In this sense, it means that religious conviction and practice should be excluded from the public realm outside of religious organizations such as churches, synagogues, and mosques. Kuyper rejected this as a form of discrimination where a secular ideology takes the place of religious beliefs; a state-imposed practice of excluding religious belief becomes displacing religious belief. What should be protected by public law, Kuyper argued, is the freedom of all people to live in every sphere of earthly responsibility in keeping with their deepest convictions and beliefs about the meaning of life, about what human beings are, about how they believe they should live their lives.

Christians are not alone in believing that they have been called to serve God in all spheres of life, that their faith, their religion, is not merely *a way of worship* in private but *a way of life*. Therefore, the state's disestablishment of religion is one of the ways to protect the right of citizens to live in all spheres of responsibility according to their deepest convictions and not to be discriminated against by the state's imposition of a particular religion or ideology. This also means that secularism itself should not be established by the state. In many respects, secularism is now established in the United States by law. Most jurists and politicians believe that "religion" is a private matter and should be kept out of so-called "secular" life. But that kind of secularist imposition is the equivalent of establishing a religion.

For Kuyper, then, the community of Christian faith should be free to exercise their responsibilities in all spheres of life, just as every other group of people, without discrimination and without any particular public-legal privileges. In some cases, Christians, like others, will want to develop specifically Christian schools, and nonprofit organizations, and publishing companies. In other instances, they will want to engage in businesses, political parties, scientific projects, and music organizations in which they will offer their views and make their contributions alongside others in the same organizations. People of different faiths, including believers in secularism, may want to develop those responsibilities and organizations in different ways, and they should be free to do so, but the organizations are not, and should not be, qualified as either confessional or anticonfessional by government. The government should not act in ways that try to force such institutions to be secularized or to be confessional in a particular way. In Kuyper's view, Christians should be free to act on the basis of their conviction that Jesus Christ is lord of all of life, recognizing that Jesus told his disciples that "all authority in heaven and on earth has been given to me." But that very confession led Kuyper to believe that as long as God allows the sun and rain to fall on the just and unjust alike—on all people without discrimination—then the political communities and governments on earth should establish laws that do what God in Christ is now doing, namely, treating all citizens equitably and fairly without discrimination against some citizens because of their faith. Borrowing from Kuyper, I think Chinese Christians can exercise their citizenship by seeking to approve and encourage what is just and good for everyone in society. They should be ready to work for reform of unjust laws and government administration. Christians should not think that they must either stand entirely against the government or stand totally with it regardless of what the government does.

Early in the history of Christianity in the Roman Empire, Christians had no rights of citizenship, but they cared for the sick and the poor and showed high regard for women. They even made room for lepers who were shunned by others. That display of love and service to their neighbors had a huge impact on society and Christianity spread quickly and widely. I hope that helps to explain Kuyper's two views of secularization. Disestablishment of the church is good. The forced secularization of public life with the intention of keeping religion out of public life is not good or just. Yes, Kuyper was saying, we need to recognize the difference between church and state. They are two different types of institution. The church is a confessional community. When its members gather to worship the Lord, they are a confessional institution. The church is not a community of citizens in general. And yet church members are also citizens in their political communities and should serve God directly as citizens in working for a more just political community. Similarly, farmers don't serve God via the church institution. They serve God directly in their farming. Families don't serve God only by being part of the church institution. They serve God directly in the way they live as families. Therefore, Kuyper wasn't a secularist; he did not believe in disconnecting society from God. He just saw the relation between the whole of human life and God in a different way.

Kuyper also used another distinction that may help to clarify the matter. He spoke of the Christian community of faith in its fullness as an *organic* reality. He spoke of the organized church of which Christians are a part for worship, sacraments, and educational training as an *institution*.

The people of God in Christ are bound together in an *organic bond* that encompassed all of their responsibilities. By contrast, the church *institution* organizes the community of Christian faith for worship, celebration of the sacraments, rest, and instruction in the word of God. Today in most of the world, day church institutions are recognized as one kind of institution among many, but it is a mistake to think of the Christian bond with Christ as operative only (or primarily) on Sunday. I told my children when they were young that we should not say that we are *going to church* Sunday morning. Instead, we should say that the *church—the people of God in Christ—is gathering together for worship and fellowship* Sunday morning in a building designed for that purpose.

It appears to me that in United States and China the largest communal bond identified by the people in each country is their nation—the American nation, the Chinese nation. Within that bond, churches are perceived as one of many organizations in the nation. I would argue, along with Kuyper, that Christians should understand matters differently. They should see the worldwide "organic" community of Christ's disciples as the most encompassing communal bond of life. From that viewpoint they should then see every organization, institution, and community, including their "nation," as a sphere of human responsibility subordinated to God in which to serve God and their neighbors.

Calvinism, Confucianism, and Politics

Q: Our previous discussions have been concerned with Christianity and society in China and in the West, America in particular. Now I want to move to a particular theological trend and its interaction with Chinese society and politics. As you may know, there has been a growing "Chinese Calvinism" among Christians in China over the past few years. They believe the significance of Christian cultural legacy for Western political liberalism, which China should take seriously. They also insist that Confucianism and Calvinism have the capacity to complement each other.[7] Public intellectuals in contemporary China, including Christian public intellectuals, are shaped by a Confucian tradition of the intellectual "managing the world" (*jingshi* 經世). The Confucian ideal of "inward sageliness" (*neisheng* 內聖) and "outward kingliness" (*waiwang* 外王) prioritizes the cultivation of oneself—intellectually, morally, and spiritually—as a penultimate goal to cultivating the broader world. Would you please comment about this sort of "Christian political liberalism" in China from your own perspective?

---

[7]   See Chow, *Chinese Public Theology*, 124–29.

Skillen: I think some of the things I've already said would apply in any part of the world. It seems to me that it's always possible for people of any conviction to learn from Christians and for Christians to learn from them. As far as I know, Confucians and the writers of the Old and New Testament did not have interacting influence in ancient times. But if you can find something valuable anywhere if you look for it, because everyone who lives in God's creation has to touch and deal with what it means to be God's creature. So you know, good farming techniques may be found somewhere in the world where Christians have never farmed. The same can be said for good educational techniques, good business practices, and much more.

However, what are the criteria or standards for judging what is good and bad in each case? Given what I know about Confucianism, certain human relationships such as spouses in marriage and parents and children in the family are key to understanding what is right and just in all human relations, including that of government and citizens in the political community. If children learn how to honor their parents, then children will learn a great deal about how to honor and respect other people, such as their school teachers, government officials, and others.

As I've also indicated, however, to the extent that Confucianism has helped breed the idea of the nation as one big family, if that means Confucianism leads to obedience without limits to government authorities, then that can lead to injustice. Likewise, to the extent that Western liberal individualism leads to disrespect for almost any authority, including government, grave injustice can follow from that as well. One of the things that is most constructive from the neo-Calvinist tradition of Kuyper is the way his view of society leads to a very high level of respect for people who exercise authority in various spheres of society while also, at the same time, emphasizing the limits of any human authority to its sphere of responsibility. If we start with the assumption that humans are not God and that no human authority should have unlimited jurisdiction over the whole of life, then we can encourage one another to respect every office of authority in every sphere of life while also acting to hold it accountable to those responsibilities. But from Kuyper's point of view, we should all take very seriously every kind of human responsibility as part of our recognition of God's supreme authority over us.

If I were to say this in another way, using the word *jingshi* you mentioned, I would say that humans do indeed have responsibility to manage the world, but no single person or institution can or should try to manage the whole world. There are different kinds of management—family management, business management, media management, government management, and many more. Different kinds of wisdom—"sageliness"—are required for each kind of responsibility. We are back to the idea of sphere sovereignty or sphere responsibility. The difficulty in China may be imagining that the political leaders should have ultimate management responsibility for the whole of society. The problem with political liberalism in the West is to imagine that each individual is an independent sovereign and that when they agree on ways to cooperate through contracts they write, then they need not show respect for any human association that does not respect individual autonomy. I would argue, along with Kuyper, that many human institutions and organized responsibilities deserve respect from every other sphere of responsibility and also that there are many human relationships and institutions that are not created through contracts among individuals. Neither individuals nor a national government creates marriage, or the family, or agriculture, or political community.

Another point to emphasize here is that the same human beings bear different kinds of responsibility at the same time. I am part of the sphere of family responsibility, and the spheres of civic responsibility, educational responsibility, consumer responsibility, and friendship responsibility. Those types of responsibility do not exist in isolation, unrelated to all others. They all exhibit the capabilities and responsibilities of the same human beings. If we think in those terms, we will not fall into the trap of imagining that one sphere of responsibility exhausts the totality of human authority and responsibility. If you are a citizen of China as I am of the United States, we must always recognize that each of us is more than a citizen. Citizenship does not exhaust our human identity. I would argue, with Kuyper, that recognizing our total human identity as "the image of God" allows us to recognize two things. First, that our ultimate and life-encompassing responsibility is to God. Second, that since God gave us many different capabilities and responsibilities, each of them needs to be properly honored and exercised as part of our responsibility to God and to one another.

In general, these matters are related directly to our discussion of a diversified society with different spheres of responsibility. From a Christian point of view, humans bear different kinds of responsibility for which they need to have agency. That word *agency* really means people must be free and accountable in the exercise of their responsibilities. That basic insight is relevant to any cultural situation in any country. The questions that follow are about how to properly distinguish the types of responsibility, including the specific responsibility of governments for upholding public justice in a state.

Western liberalism has overemphasized the agency of individuals, particularly when it wants to absolutize individual autonomy. Yes, individual persons need to be able to act in every arena of their responsibility. At the same time, individuals are members of different kinds of institutions and associations that define the responsibilities of those who exercise them. Neither individuals nor institutions are autonomous and sovereign. All play a role in the manifold creation order, subject to the Creator. On the other side, the emphasis on collectivism can also be exaggerated in a way that overlooks or tramples on the responsibility of both the individual and the diversity of associations and institutions. In contrast to belief in the autonomous sovereignty of the individuals, the collectivist tendency locates autonomous sovereignty in the collective. That collective is typically identified as a social, national, or imperial totality. Neither individualist nor collectivist designs can ever succeed entirely because of the resistance of human nature with its diverse spheres of responsibility and inherent need for agency. That is why I believe both the United States and China can learn something from Kuyper's insights. American individualism hinders the agency of institutions and organizations, including the proper governing of its republic. Perhaps Chinese collectivism hinders the agency of individuals and nonpolitical, nongovernmental associations and institutions.

There are perfectly legitimate ways in which public law should set limits to the actions of individuals and nongovernment organizations. Businesses should not pollute air and water; parents must not abuse their children; nonprofit organizations, including churches, should not train their members to use violence against their neighbors. All of those public-legal limitations belong to the agency of government with responsibility to uphold the common good—the common political community. That is quite different, however, from government acting in ways that undermine the agency of business managers and workers in the business, or take away the responsibility of parents for their children, or overrule the agency of nonprofit organizations engaged in constructive social and communication responsibilities. The core principle behind the development of constitutional government has been to stipulate the basic boundaries and limits of government in and for a society. A constitution is supposed to function as the law to which even government officials are subject.

Vocation: Christianity as a Way of Life

Q: Let's move on to the last question, a kind of summary of our conversation today. We have talked about your academic career and some special topics related to Kuyper's thoughts such as sphere sovereignty, diversity of social institutions and responsibilities, church-state relations, and Christian political thoughts, related to both the Western and Chinese contexts. As Bruce Wearne suggests, you have made a "persistent pursuit of a renewed Christian contribution that challenges a political culture that has turned away from the Lord God."[8] In this regard, you have highlighted the ideas of "principled pluralism," "good of politics," "common grace," and human "vocations" by saying that "Christian faith calls for serving God in the exercise of all our responsibilities," and "the created cosmos has been destined to reveal the glory of God."[9] Would you please offer your thoughts about these matters for a Chinese audience—Christians in particular—from your own understanding of Chinese culture, politics, and society, i.e., is there a difference between these ideas in the West and the East?

Skillen: My latest book, *God's Sabbath with Creation*, was in development for fifty years. It reflects the attempt to understand what it means to live as a Christian in the world today. There are certain things about the biblical basis of Christianity that cannot be slighted, or one will be talking about another view of life. God is the creator of all things for a cosmic purpose to reveal the divine glory. Humans are central to that revelatory purpose because they are created in the very image of God and called to govern and develop the world as servants of God and neighbors. Every human vocation is important in the relation of humans to God, both for now and for eternity. Doing justice to neighbors and other creatures is fundamental to that way of life. To the extent that we turn away from God and our neighbors in selfish and degrading ways, we dishonor God and ourselves. Those are the actions that the Bible describes as sinful disobedience to God in failing to exercise our vocations in keeping with the two great love commands: to love God with all our heart and mind and to love our neighbors as ourselves. And yet the biblical story continues to affirm that God so loves the world, and particularly human creatures, that God has opened a way through covenants with Israel and the nations in Jesus Christ to reconcile all things, including sinful human beings, for the fulfillment of the divine purposes. The climactic fulfillment will be revealed in God's seventh-day Sabbath with creation.

Part of what makes the biblical story so unusual is that it can't be read as simply an ancient story or a novel, with the reader standing outside of it. Instead, the biblical texts unfold as a living drama that includes all human generations, including us today. The story—the drama—requires that we read it from the inside, which means participating in its drama. Everyone has been created in the image of God; everyone exhibits

---

8   Bruce Wearne, *Public Justice for All: An Annotated Bibliography of the Works of James W. Skillen 1967–2006* (unpublished manuscript, 2007), 10, accessed July 5, 2019, http://allofliferedeemed.co.uk/Wearne/JWSBibliogFull2008.pdf.

9   James W. Skillen, *God's Sabbath with Creation* (Eugene: Wipf & Stock, 2019), x.

sinful disobedience; and God's covenantal mercies, coming to fulfill-ment in Jesus Christ, call us to repent of evil ways to serve God and our neighbors in every sphere of life. To live in the biblical drama demands extreme humility. The Christian way of life is not something Christians have created or own, and sadly Christians do not always exhibit extreme humility.

Having said that much, what I would say to a Chinese audience is pretty much the same thing I would say to any audience in the world. As human beings, we have developed many different languages and cultures, and most of us now live in distinguishable states or political communities. We have developed family life, languages, education, music, science, liter-ature, agriculture, industry, and politics in different ways. The diversity is amazing, dazzling, and at its best is beautiful. From a biblical point of view, all of that presents a living exhibition of what it means to be crea-tures made in the image of God.

At the same time, if we look around the same world of peoples and nations, we are participants in some of the most egregious degradations imaginable—degradations of fellow human beings, of the global envi-ronment, and of every responsibility humans exercise. Millions of our fellow human beings go hungry; many are dying at the hands of thieves, as a result of racial hatred or ideological and religious fanaticism. From a biblical point of view, none of that is legitimate; none of it leaves us free of guilt. None of it is an expression of life's beautiful diversity but rather an exhibition of the drama of death.

Finally, throughout the world, there are countless exhibits of repen-tance, of turning from evil to genuine service and love of neighbors, of constructive efforts to educate and encourage neighbors to nurture healthy families, to provide better education, and to develop talents of music, engineering, and statecraft. That way of life ought to be shining brightly from every Christian community in the world, though all too often it does not. By God's grace, many of those virtuous deeds are exhibited by people who do not belong to Christian communities. The biblical story attributes all repentance, all good deeds and practices to God's grace—what Kuyper calls *common grace*—whether or not everyone recognizes it. Here again is where extreme humility is called for, especially from Christians. Biblically speaking, Christians do not possess and cannot deliver repentance from sin and restoration of just and loving lives in every sphere of life. Only God can do that.

What all of this means for both Christians and non-Christians in China will have to be worked out in the cultural and political context of China. It is clear that in many parts of the world, other religions and deeply rooted ideologies stand opposed to a Christian way of life and often to Christians. For Christians, this requires a deep commitment to their calling in Jesus Christ to serve and love their neighbors, both friends and enemies, in every sphere of life, by seeking justice for everyone and bearing witness to the God who is not under their control but who is above all humans and all gods and ideologies. Followers of Jesus Christ are called to leave final judgment in God's hands, to endure hardship and persecution, to give themselves up in service to neighbors and to the One who gives life from death. Christianity is not only a distinctive way of worship; it is a comprehensive way of life, a way to live in all arenas of the life for which God created us.

Q: Thanks so much. In this way, we can conceive all humanity from the vision of God's creation: how human beings participate in God's work in this world and give glory to God in our work, especially in political life, with our responsibilities. That leads us to a deeper understanding of the wider framework of our responsibility. In this sense, I think we should have a better translation of *responsibility* in Chinese. I look forward to having further conversations on these crucial issues.

APPENDIX 3
FREEDOM AND ORDER: CHRISTIANITY, HUMAN RIGHTS, AND CULTURE

An Interview with John Witte Jr.

Interviewee: John Witte Jr. (hereafter "Witte")

Interviewer: Zhibin Xie (hereafter "Q")

Interview date: August 9, 2019

Interview venue: Center for the Study of Law and Religion, Emory University, Atlanta, Georgia

BIOGRAPHY OF JOHN WITTE JR.

John Witte Jr.—JD (Harvard), Dr. Theol. h.c. (Heidelberg)—is Robert W. Woodruff University Professor, McDonald Distinguished Professor, and director of the Center for the Study of Law and Religion at Emory University. A leading specialist in legal history, human rights, religious freedom, marriage and family law, and law and religion, he has published three hundred articles, seventeen journal symposia, and forty books.

His recent book titles include *The Reformation of Rights* (Cambridge University Press, 2007), *Christianity and Law* (Cambridge University Press, 2008), *The Sins of the Fathers* (Cambridge University Press, 2009), *Christianity and Human Rights* (Cambridge University Press, 2010), *Religion and Human Rights* (Oxford University Press, 2012), *From Sacrament to Contract* (Westminster John Knox Press, 2nd ed., 2012), *Christianity and Family Law* (Cambridge University Press, 2017), *Church, State, and Family* (Cambridge University Press, 2019), *The Blessings of Liberty* (Cambridge University Press, 2021), *Faith, Freedom, and Family* (Mohr Siebeck, 2021), and *Religion and the American Constitutional Experiment* (Oxford University Press, 5th ed., 2022).

Professor Witte's writings have appeared in fifteen languages, and he has delivered more than three hundred and fifty public lectures throughout the world, including, recently, the Franke Lecture at Yale, the Jefferson Lectures at Berkeley, the Pennington Lecture at Heidelberg, the Cunningham Lectures at Edinburgh, the McDonald Lectures at Oxford, and the Gifford Lecture at Aberdeen.

Kuyper and Intellectual Life

Q: As a legal expert working in the field of law and religion, you are the recipient of the Abraham Kuyper Prize for Excellence in Reformed Theology and Public Life from Princeton Theological Seminary. You graduated from Calvin College, which has a Dutch Reformed background. Some of your publications relate to the Kuyperian tradition, and you turn to Kuyper's thinking in the concluding chapter of your book *The Reformation of Rights: Law, Religion, and Human Rights in Early Modern Calvinism*. How do you appraise the enduring impact of Kuyper and the Kuyperian tradition in your intellectual endeavors?

Witte: Thank you for your interest in Abraham Kuyper, who was one of the great Christian figures in the nineteenth century and early twentieth century. It's a fitting time, in 2020, on the centennial of his death, to remember his work and to take stock of the contribution he made to Western legal, political, and social thought and to consider the implications of that thought for the broader global conversation emerging today about the good life, the good society, just politics and laws, and other strong social support structures.

Kuyper has high standing in the broader Protestant world today, akin to what his contemporary, Pope Leo XIII, has in the Catholic world. Kuyper and Leo XIII were transformative figures in the later nineteenth century who reconstructed the earlier teachings of John Calvin and Thomas Aquinas, respectively, into powerful new Protestant and Catholic teachings for church, state, and society. They provide us with an interesting focus for ecumenical conversation and for Western and global conversations.

It was an honor for me to be part of the centennial of Abraham Kuyper Stone Lectures in 1998 at Princeton Theological Seminary. In 1898, Kuyper came to the United States and powerfully laid out his basic worldview—featuring sphere sovereignty, covenant politics, the role of religious reasoning in public and private life, the idea of the Christian vocation in all walks of life, the need to live faithfully with the Bible, and the tradition as captured in confession, creed, and catechism. That centennial conference on his 1898 Stone Lectures was an occasion for scholars from a number of different fields to come together and reflect on Kuyper's insights in the context of the late nineteenth century and to analyze and debate whether these insights still edify and endure in our day. I was asked to reflect on Kuyper's work on religious freedom and human rights, a topic that resonated with my own upbringing in the Kuyperian tradition.

I grew up in a Dutch Reformed home in Ontario, Canada. My parents were Dutch immigrants who came to Canada in 1953. I was schooled in Calvinist primary and secondary schools; learned the Heidelberg Catechism, as Kuyper had encouraged; and was taught many of the basic ideas that were part of Kuyper's vision. I went to Calvin College to study with some great Christian scholars of this tradition: Evan Runner, Uko Zylstra, Arie Leegwater, Nicholas Wolterstorff, George Marsden, and others who worked congenially within the Kuyperian tradition, even if they went well beyond Kuyper in setting out their own thought.

So Kuyperianism was part of my formative years as a youth and young college student and continued into my studies in law school as well. Now, some forty years later, Kuyperian thinking remains an important orientation for me. It provides a set of intellectual habits and methodological instincts—particularly the basic respect for scripture, tradition, reason, and experience; the emphasis on social pluralism and sphere sovereignty and the wariness of political, ecclesiastical, or any other kind of monism or monopoly in social organization and authority structuring; the appetite for covenant thinking; and the insistence that everyone operates with a basic worldview, a basic set of founding beliefs, values, or metaphors, even if they remain mostly implicit.

But that said, Kuyperianism tends to be increasingly a background orientation for me rather than a central part of what I'm about. I am not a philosopher, political theorist, ethicist, or theologian, though I dabble in those fields. I am a lawyer and legal scholar, focused on the history of law and religion.

As a historian, I work on some of the same figures and texts that Kuyper worked on, though I often interpret them differently than did Kuyper or his main legal protégé, Herman Dooyeweerd. I work closely with some of the same materials from the Protestant tradition in the sixteenth century forward that Kuyper found important and congenial. In recent years, I have worked intensely on contested issues of faith, freedom, and family, all of which Kuyper touched on in his writings too. But I'm interested in those topics largely as a historian, trying to retrieve and reconstruct the wisdom of the Protestant and broader Christian traditions on fundamental questions of law, politics, and society. I am not, as Kuyper was, a theologian or philosopher trying to extend the Kuyperian worldview to new areas of life nor a politician seeking to hammer out political platforms. I admire deeply Kuyper and others who do that kind of work; it's just not my vocation.

I also draw more eclectically than Kuyper—and many Kuyperians—from a variety of sources within and beyond the West. I draw widely from Patristic, medieval Catholic, Protestant, and Enlightenment liberal traditions alike. I am keenly interested in dialogue across religious traditions. In the Center for the Study of Law and Religion at Emory University, which I have directed for the past thirty-five years, we have rich conversations between and among Christians, Jews, and Muslims, and sometimes Eastern religions on fundamental legal, political, and social questions, and I find those deeply refreshing and engaging. In every instance, Kuyperian instincts remain part of who I am, but I cannot pretend to be advancing a Kuyperian project or agenda.

Kuyper's Vision in the American Context of Liberty and Pluralism

Q: Your article "The Biography and Biology of Liberty,"[1] published in 2000, summarizes Kuyper's appraisal of American principles of religious liberty and religious pluralism, ecclesiastical liberty and confessional pluralism, associational liberty and social pluralism, and political liberty and political pluralism. After twenty years, would you share something more about the implications of Kuyper's theological, social, and political vision in reflecting the American experiment in ordered liberty and ordered pluralism?

Witte: Kuyper reflected—as a European, a Dutchman, and a Protestant Christian—on what he saw in late nineteenth-century America and on the extent to which he thought American culture was consistent or inconsistent with the broader Calvinist vision that had inspired the original New England Puritans and their European forebears.

As you know from his *Lectures on Calvinism*, Kuyper often praised American culture and constitutional order as he saw it at the end of the nineteenth century. And he sometimes contrasted, wistfully, the American experiment with Dutch and broader European experience after the French Revolution and Napoleon had conquered and destroyed so much of what was considered sound, settled, and even sacred in the Western tradition.

First, Kuyper was particularly impressed with America's robust protection of religious freedom, freedom of conscience, and freedom of religious exercise and the country's healthy regard for religious and social pluralism. He lauded the American principle of the presumptive equality

---

[1]　See John Witte Jr., "The Biography and Biology of Liberty", 243–62.

of all faiths before the law, the disestablishment of religion, and the basic separation of the offices and operations of church and state.

He saw those American principles as more advanced forms and norms of religious freedom than Europe had at the time. I think that assessment continues to be apt today. The American experiment in constitutional freedom continues apace. Protection of religious freedom continues to be important. The United States had a period at the turn of the twenty-first century when religious freedom was increasingly viewed as a second-class right, especially when juxtaposed to sexual liberty, and religious freedom took a beating in the legal academy and in some of the federal court cases. But that time seems to have passed. Under the current US Supreme Court, America still embraces and endorses religious freedom in a basic way that Kuyper praised in 1898.

Second, Kuyper emphasized and praised America's commitment to associational liberty, or what he called *sphere sovereignty*. This was the idea that, standing between the state and the individual, there are many other spheres, structures, or institutions of authority and liberty that are important parts of how to order liberty and structure the rule of law in a given society. Kuyper noted that the family, church, corporation, school, union, and other voluntary associations were important places and communities for a person to enjoy liberty. They were bulwarks against state tyranny, important opportunities for the individual to flourish in externally guided but self-chosen ways. That emphasis on nonstate associations and their respective sovereignty or independence from each other, and especially from the state, was a strong emphasis of Kuyper's in 1898, and he saw this, too, as part of the American cultural and constitutional tradition.

While institutional and social pluralism remain part of American public and private life today, things are also changing rapidly. The institutional and denominational church has lost some of its cultural influence and autonomy, and many churches today are more accommodating of secular culture than Kuyper would find congenial. The traditional marital family has become increasingly fragile and fleeting as a fundamental institution in which a person participates naturally and reflexively. American educational institutions, particularly our public or state-run schools, are failing on many scores, and these public schools, since Kuyper's day, have been constitutionally fenced off from much traditional religious instruction, influence, or integration. Kuyper warned that these plural social institutions must remain strong for the individual to have places to flourish, for the state to have a bulwark against encroachment on individuals, and for the rule of law and protection of liberty to be effective. Those warnings of 1898 are even more apt today.

Third, Kuyper praised the American principle of political pluralism. Rather than having a monarchy or a single state or a single governmental structure, he thought it important to have layers of political authority: from the local clan to the village, to the city, to the county, to the state, and then ultimately to the nation. That idea of "orderly federalism," as he called it, was part of early Dutch constitutional structure, forged after the sixteenth-century revolt from Spain. In the Union of Utrecht of 1579, the Netherlands created a confederation of seven provinces, each with constituent towns and villages but together integrated and represented in the Dutch republic, with a representative estates general drawn from the seven provinces in the day. One of Kuyper's heroes, the Calvinist jurist and political theorist Johannes Althusius, in his *Politics* of 1603 and 1614, developed a theory of consociation or symbiotic federalism to support this kind of political pluralism.

Kuyper saw American constitutionalism in the nineteenth century as another expression of that same kind of political pluralism and federalism, and he praised it and argued that it was an expression of Calvinist ideas. His emphasis on that was well chosen. While there were many prototypes for American federalism and political pluralism, the historical Dutch republic was certainly one of them (as John Adams emphasized), as was the political pluralism expressed in the covenantal politics of Puritan New England.

The American tradition of federalism and political pluralism continues apace today. In the century since Kuyper lectured, however, the New Deal expansion of the federal government in the 1930s and thereafter and the rise of the national military state and now the national security state has expanded the American national government to a point that Kuyper would likely find troubling. But Kuyper would likely laud America's ongoing constitutional commitment to federalism in the Tenth Amendment, which reserves to the states all powers not specifically given to the federal government, as well as to the critical role of state and local governments in sharing the governance of the nation.

Fourth and finally, Kuyper praised America's broader commitment to liberties and rights, which he saw as a strong form of traditional Calvinist influence rather than Enlightenment liberal influence alone. In Kuyper's day, citing the religious sources of human rights and liberties was a controversial idea, but it is now more commonly accepted today in American and broader scholarship. Calvinists did, indeed, contribute to the American constitutional law of basic rights and liberties, as did Enlightenment philosophers, Quakers, Anglicans, republican thinkers, and others in shaping America's basic ideas about ordered liberty.

Kuyper did sometimes oversell the Calvinist contribution. Calvinism was only one source of influence on American rights and liberties—and not always the most definitive. Moreover, Kuyper tended to draw a quick and easy line from the sixteenth-century to late nineteenth-century ideas, arguing that rights talk in Calvin's Geneva was the same as the rights talk of the US Constitutional Convention and Congress in 1787 and 1789. That fails to account for the ongoing reforms in Calvinist rights thinking, the important transitions and seams in the tradition that emerged as later Calvinists responded to persecution, genocide, war, the Inquisition, colonial experiences, and more. My 2007 book, *The Reformation of Rights*, and the sequels to that book map these seams and changes in the Calvinist tradition of rights talk from the sixteenth century forward.

Religion and Human Rights

Q: Some of your books have been translated and published in Chinese, including *Religion and the American Constitutional Experiment*; *From Sacrament to Contract: Marriage, Religion and Law in the Western Tradition*; *Law and Protestantism: The Legal Teachings of the Lutheran Reformation*; and *The Reformation of Rights: Law, Religion, and Human Rights in Early Modern Calvinism*. Some of your ideas, particularly about Christianity and human rights, have received studies and debates in Chinese academia. I even use your texts, such as *Law and Protestantism* and *The Reformation of Rights*, in my course on religion and society. In *The Reformation of Rights*, you have stressed the significant contribution of early modern Calvinism to the development of human rights and constitutional law or, more broadly, the religious resources of human rights. You also highlight that the human rights norm needs a human culture. How would you explain the issues that are at stake? In other words, in what circumstances can religion contribute to the understanding and practice of human rights?

Witte: I'm delighted that some of my books are available in Chinese translation, and I'm delighted that Chinese publishers and readers have become so interested in Western history, including the history of topics that are important for the modern world, such as constitutional order, rule of law, ordered liberty, and orderly society. A global conversation about these vital topics is essential to the globalization project.

In turn, it's really important for us in the West to learn from Chinese historians, jurists, philosophers, and others who have written about these same topics and to hear what their venerable traditions of

241

thought—including Confucian, Buddhist, Taoist, and comparably rich traditions—have said about authority and liberty, political and religious power, culture and society, and more. We must constantly learn from each other. Happily, that has begun to happen as more fundamental works by historical and contemporary Chinese scholars are translated into English and as more books emerge comparing Western and Eastern concepts of law, politics, and society. The more we can produce such books in Mandarin and English and other Asian and European languages, the better it will be for all of us.

That said, today it is still hard to have a global conversation about human rights. So many religious and cultural traditions view human rights with suspicion, if not derision. Some are worried that rights are products of Enlightenment liberalism, individualism, and contractarianism or forms of Western colonialism designed to foment division between the West and the rest. Some condemn human rights as mere self-serving fictions that have produced mythical ideals that no person, society, or state can possibly attain. Some worry that human rights are just new weapons in another cold war, used to demonize and defame the other. These criticisms are real, and they have to be considered in any global conversation about rights.

As a lawyer and legal historian, I see rights talk as a common way to define and defend the law's protection, support, limitations, and entitlements of persons and groups in society as well as the proper relationships between political and other authorities and their respective subjects. Rights are not a modern invention, a seductive new form of liberal exotica crafted by Enlightenment philosophers in manifestation of their new secular theories of individualism, rationalism, and contractarianism. Western lawyers since classical Roman and medieval times have used rights ideas and terms as a plain and uncontroversial way of talking about the claims one legal subject could legitimately make against another, the charges that an authority could legitimately impose upon its subjects, and the procedures that were to be followed in these legal interactions.

These rights were—and still are—applied to different areas of law and life. Family laws, for example, protect the reciprocal rights and duties of spouses, parents, and children at different stages of the lifecycle. Social welfare rights speak to the basic human need for food, shelter, health care, and education, especially for vulnerable populations. Free speech and free press laws protect the rights of persons to speak, preach, and publish. Private and public laws protect the person's rights to contractual performance, to property and inheritance, to the safety and integrity of their bodies, relationships, and reputations, along with the procedural means to vindicate these rights when they are threatened or breached by another. Criminal procedural rights are designed to ensure an individual of proper forms of arrest and detention, fair hearings and trials, and just punishments proportionate to specific crimes. Freedom of conscience and the free exercise of religion protect the essential right (and duty) of Christians to love God, neighbor, and self.

As a Christian, I see basic human rights and liberties as natural gifts of God to human beings. The Bible teaches that human beings are created in the image of God. God has given us the gifts of reason, will, and memory; the companionship of other humans ("bone of my bones, flesh of my flesh"); the rights and duties to "be fruitful and multiply," to "dress and keep" the Garden, to govern and use God's creation; the privilege of hearing and obeying God's basic laws for our lives; and the assurance that we will be judged justly for our faults, be asked to bear responsibility for our failures, and yet assured of grace and mercy in the judgments imposed on us. These are some of the basic ontological and anthropological foundations for concepts of human dignity, rights, and relationships, of responsibility, judgment, and reconciliation that lie at the heart of a human rights culture. Other religious and cultural traditions, including many in China, will have their own ontological framing, which will be interesting to compare.

The positive law formulations of human rights set out in international human rights instruments, national constitutions, local statutes and cases, and the like are much more contingent. They are attempts to enumerate specifically what these basic conditions of human lives require or entail. They help create expectations of mutual respect for and from other human beings. They help shape the way that we interact with each other, and with authorities in the state, the church, or the family. They help create procedures for enforcement of rules, for vindication of interests, for protection from abuse, for creation of new relationships and actions. In brief, human rights documents help to map some of the basic forms and norms of a human rights culture.

However they are enumerated, human rights norms and cultures depend upon deeper worldviews to be grounded and guided. Religious communities, among other cultural and philosophical communities, provide some of the grounding and grammar for human rights. Even in postmodern liberal societies, religions help to define the shame and regret, restraint and respect, responsibility and restitution that a human rights regime presupposes. They help to lay out the fundamentals of human dignity and human community and the essentials of human nature, human capacities, and human needs upon which human rights are built. Moreover, religions stand alongside the state and other institutions in helping to implement and protect the rights of persons and communities, especially when the state becomes weak or poorer. Religious communities can create the conditions and sometimes prototypes for the realization of civil and political rights of speech, press, assembly, and more. They can provide a critical, and sometimes the principal, means of education, healthcare, childcare, labor organizations, employment, and artistic opportunities, among other things. And they can offer some of the deepest insights into duties of stewardship and service that lie at the heart of environmental care.

I like to think about human rights as middle axioms of our discourse—halfway between the local civil laws of a particular political community and the higher laws maintained by religious or philosophical communities. This is an idea that Kuyper, as theologian and politician, would have liked. He saw all legal and political structures, including human rights and liberties, as variant from community to community. But he also thought there were certain fundamentals taught to us by higher sources—whether scripture or tradition, creed or confession, that had to be respected by, if not reflected in legal and political structures.

I also like to think about human rights, such as those set out in the Universal Declaration of Human Rights, as a mirror in which every religion and every culture can reflect on itself and see values that may be congenial, complementary, challenging, and sometimes aspirational for them. Every major religious tradition in the twentieth and twenty-first centuries has given its assessment of the Universal Declaration in light of its own texts and traditions and used this exercise both to consider reforms for its own tradition and to offer reforms for the world of human rights. This has been a healthy and productive interaction, bringing much-needed reforms both to religions and to human rights norms in our day. This method of mutual reform is something that Kuyper would have condoned as well.

Q: It is illuminating for us in our context to see in your detailed clarifications about how the religious ideas and religious institutions can make contribution to the understanding of human rights and its practice.

Witte: Religion certainly is one factor or dimension of human rights. It's not the only one, but it's an important one. It provides grounding for human rights. For example, the Christian tradition built a number of its basic teachings of human rights on fundamental ideas of the image of God, which vests each person with inherent dignity; on the fundamental ideas that we are prophets, priests, and kings with natural rights to speak, worship, and rule; on the Ten Commandments, which provide a set of duties and rights that we owe to God and to our neighbor—the duties and rights to worship God, to use God's name properly, to honor the Sabbath in accordance with the First Table of the Decalogue; and the duties and rights to honor our parents and respect our neighbor's marriage, household, life, property, and reputation in accordance with the Second Table. The Christian tradition also emphasizes the special duties that we have to the needy, the widow, the orphan, the stranger, who have rights to be cared for. "As much as you do it to the least of these, you do it to me," Jesus reminds us. Those are fundamental axioms on which to build a rights framework.

Human Rights in the Global Context

Q: When we claim religious implications for human rights culture, how do we evaluate religion and human rights in the global context beyond the West?

Witte: The issue is whether and to what extent do non-Western and non-American traditions think about the role their own religious communities and cultural communities can and should play in the articulation and enforcement of human rights. Here the historian and comparative lawyer in me emphasizes that human rights documents and constitutional bills of rights are not simply commodities that can be exported and imported from one state or region to another. Rights are something that are discovered within and shaped by the soils and souls, the experiences and expectations of the people that put them in place.

Yes, in 1948, the world could and did articulate a Universal Declaration of Human Rights in the aftermath of a world war that had killed sixty million people and featured the horrors of the Holocaust, the gulags, and death camps. The Declaration thus might still provide a useful starting point about the basics of human life and civilization, a common grammar to be considered. But each political community must articulate human rights norms in its own way. No one country provides a paradigm for the rest.

Even the differences between Europe and North America in talking about rights are quite dramatic. There is a much stronger emphasis on second-generation rights in Europe—that is, rights to education, healthcare, economic security, and other social goods—while in the United States, there is a much stronger emphasis on first-generation rights—that is, political rights like the right to vote, speak freely, assemble, receive a fair trial, and so on. There is much greater cooperation of church and state in a number of European countries than in the United States, where separation of church and state is a starting premise. Those are differences in two Western traditions that have grown up side by side, almost as cultural twins.

If you have those kinds of differences across the Atlantic, you can expect even stronger differences when you go to the Global South or the Pacific Rim and see how communities there formulate rights. Such differences in formulating rights across political, religious, and cultural traditions have to be respected. We cannot simply take the Bill of Rights set out in the US Constitution and introduce those to Eastern Europe or Russia after *glasnost* and *perestroika* or set them down in modern China and expect them to work at all, or at least in the same way they work in the United States. Human rights norms don't and can't work that way. A given formulation of rights can provide a people or culture with a point of reference, a set of ideals to be considered, a ground for rethinking their own tradition. But not more.

That said, there are some violations of human beings that are so fundamentally wrong that they cannot be abided, regardless of where they take place. No matter where a person comes from, or what they believe in, horrible offenses like genocide, torture, deliberate starvation when resources are at hand, gratuitous killings, systematic rape, maiming, and the like cannot be countenanced anywhere. The law calls these *malum in se* offenses, evils in themselves, which no country or culture can countenance, regardless of how it formulates its rights talk. Those things simply cannot be done to another human being, and when they are done, citizens must protest and revolt, and other countries must react with appropriate firm measures consistent with modern international law. But on less grave matters, nations and local communities deserve a greater margin of appreciation for how they think about, enumerate, and implement rights.

Witte's View of Human Rights Compared to Nicholas Wolterstorff's

Q: In an interview in South Korea, you strongly recommended Nicholas Wolterstorff's book *Justice: Rights and Wrongs* as "a fundamental rethinking of the rights talk in a justice framework animated by deep Christian vision."[2] The book examines the ideas of a "moral subculture of rights" and "theistic grounding of rights."[3] Would you share how your approach to human rights from a Calvinist perspective shares commonalities with Wolterstorff's studies in rights? And where do you differ? How do you engage each other with respect to Christian involvement in the human rights discourse in general?

---

[2] See "Interview with Professor John Witte, Jr. for the *Worldview* Magazine," July 25, 2019, https://www.johnwittejr.com/uploads/5/4/6/6/54662393/handong_interview_2015.pdf.

[3] See Wolterstorff, *Justice: Rights and Wrongs*.

Witte: I have great respect for Nicholas Wolterstorff, who was a leading philosophy professor at Calvin College when I was there as a student in the late 1970s, before he went on to a distinguished career at Yale Divinity School. Since then, I've had the privilege of working with him on a number of projects, and we have lectured together on occasion as well. His book *Justice: Rights and Wrongs* is a fundamental text, providing a Christian philosophical defense of human rights.

Nicholas is a philosopher; I am a historian. He brings to the task a refined understanding of modern political philosophy, including, notably, Rawlsian liberalism, as well as a refined epistemology and ontology defended in broad biblical, historical, and philosophical terms. I come to the topic as a historian interested in the development of rights talk in the Western tradition.

We share an interest in the understandings of rights and liberties in the Bible and Roman law, in medieval canon law, in early modern Protestant and Catholic circles, and then in the contributions of Enlightenment liberalism. Our projects therefore converge, and Nick draws in some of my work and other people's work that I respect in telling his rights narrative, just as I draw in some of his philosophical reflections on love and rights in drawing out my conclusions. I plan to deal more deeply with his views and those of other modern Calvinists in the sequel to my *Reformation of Rights*.

Nick and I share an understanding that the Bible, while not a textbook of human rights, nonetheless has fundamental ideas in place that are consistent with how we think about rights today. I mentioned those earlier—the Decalogue; the *imago Dei* concept; the need to care for the orphan, the widow, the poor, and the needy; the image of persons as prophet, priest, and king; the notion that we are given freedom as children of God, and as rightful heirs of God's gracious promise of salvation. Nick and I share the idea that these biblical concepts can be translated into rights terms, as various church fathers, medieval scholastics, and early modern Protestants and Catholics all elaborated.

We also share the conviction that human rights are not inventions of the eighteenth-century Enlightenment or the twentieth-century human rights revolution but have deep roots in the Western tradition going back to biblical and classical times. The Western tradition of rights, led by patristic, medieval, and early modern Christians, provided the foundation on which Enlightenment liberalism built. Enlightened liberals, while certainly innovative, did not invent many of the rights we now take for granted; they adopted and adapted these from earlier Christian and classical sources. What Enlightenment liberals did was to place these earlier rights formulations, which were sometimes limited by biblical and Christian theological understandings, into broader and more universal philosophical frameworks. On all these matters, Nick and I converge in our work.

Nick has gone further than I in asking how a contemporary Christian should defend human rights against detractors, both within and without the Christian tradition. That project is still largely ahead for me. I have gone further in trying to answer historians, both within and without the church, who seek to deny the Christian sources and foundations of rights in the West.

Rights skepticism is especially rife in the Protestant world, and Nick answers those critics by showing that rights are actually part of the Protestant tradition. Nick also argues about how a secular or post-Christian or anti-Christian culture can still accept religious formulations of rights, in particular Protestant Christian formulations of rights, and see them as valuable for modern rights discussions rather than as a danger to modern constitutional life. He does so by working out an interesting anthropology of rights based upon the idea that we are all creatures of God, that we enjoy God's love, God's gracious forgiveness of our sins, God's acceptance of us, no matter who we are. And the love that God gives us is a love that all of our neighbors, who are created in the image of God, have to respect in us and we in them. That we are loved and forgiven by God requires that our neighbor look at us and see that same worth in us and respect it. Justice is measured by the extent to which a community respects the worth of all people, and by how much each person in that community respects the worth of his or her neighbor.

Other modern Protestants, particularly Reformed or Kuyperian Protestants, are also at work. One good example is David Little, another brilliant Protestant rights thinker, who focuses not on the inherent good and worth that every person has. He focuses on the opposite—on the deep evils that cannot be done to any person: torture, genocide, cannibalism, child sacrifice, and more. These, for him, provide the template for our most fundamental human rights; they set out the nonderogable, nonnegotiable, nonqualified rights that have to be put in place in every community. His interest is building on the basic right of self-preservation and self-defense that provides the foundation for all other rights. Another, earlier Protestant rights theorist, Swiss theologian Emil Brunner, offered a really interesting idea of rights and justice based in part on his understanding of human nature and its grounding in the natural or created order. And then, of course, we have Kuyper's own formulations, which are an interesting blend of scripture and tradition, old texts and new. Kuyper adds to these formulations a strong emphasis on the rights of the association, especially against an overreaching state.

I find all of those ideas congenial and compatible and will use them to try to articulate a philosophical grounding for rights when I get to the end of my sequels to *The Reformation of Rights*. That first volume traced the sixteenth-to-eighteenth-century story of law, religion, and human rights in early modern Calvinism. I am now at work on the eighteenth-to-twenty-first century story of Calvinist rights talk and reform in the West and will write a concluding chapter, or concluding volume, tentatively titled "Here I Stand: A Protestant Defense of Human Rights for a Post-Christian World."

Human Rights in the Chinese Context

Q: In the Chinese context, there has been rich debate on Confucianism and human rights. Some support their compatibility (for example, in terms of a Confucian emphasis on social and communitarian values, the dignity of the self and person, civility, humane concern, and mutual respect). Still, at least one observer suggests that the human rights debate in China tends to be "political and polemical in character."[4] As a Chinese scholar, I am also hesitant to ask how far our own cultural resources (say, Confucianism) engage in and further contribute to the understanding and development of human rights in China effectively. As a foreign observer and human rights expert, how do you evaluate the cultural aspect of human rights and its implications in the human rights discourse in China?

Witte: Allow me a few necessarily incomplete remarks, some of them echoes of what we discussed before. First, I don't know Confucianism well enough to weigh in on the compatibility/incompatibility dialectics. A book I edited five years ago, called *Religion and Human Rights: An Introduction*, includes a chapter by Joseph Chan. He assesses the compatibility/incompatibility dialectic and then lays out the best case, as he sees it, of how Confucianism can be viewed as compatible with human rights— even if, necessarily, that requires a Confucian to be selective in drawing from the international bill of human rights and critical of some current global formulations of human rights, particularly the more specific rights pressed by affinity groups in recent years.

It's worth noting that the distinguished Confucian scholar Peng-chun Chang was a critical player in the human rights committee that drafted the Universal Declaration of Human Rights in 1948. He worked hard to

---

4   Svensson, *Debating Human Rights in China*, 5. See chapter 8.

show how the wisdom of the Confucian tradition was conducive to and could contribute to twentieth-century human rights formulations. His ideas are worth holding up, too, and I hope his writings have currency in modern China.

Second, as I said earlier, human rights should not be reduced to a single formulation, nor should they be used as weapons in international discourse and diplomacy. Americans and other Westerners cannot insist on one formulation of human rights and hold every other culture to that formulation. This has happened in some diplomatic exchanges with China; it is not productive. That approach does not take sufficient account of the way various cultures inform and implement human rights on the ground. I'm not saying that America is the best example or China the best example of a human rights culture. I am saying that each country and its leadership have to have a bit of epistemic humility about their own formulations and how and whether they fit or don't fit other cultures.

But, third, as indicated earlier, I do think it important for every community around the world, including China, to think about what the world articulated as its Universal Declaration of Human Rights in 1948 and to use that as a mirror in which to reflect upon their own traditions, religions, and cultures. China has gone through massive changes over the last generation and has emerged as a world superpower. As China steps into global leadership, it must also engage global instruments like the Universal Declaration of Human Rights that a badly bruised but united world seventy years ago judged to be essential standards for every nation-state to consider. China must judge its own political actions and social structures in light of these standards and also encourage its own traditions of Confucianism, Buddhism, and Taoism, as well as the growing traditions of Christianity that have emerged in China, to weigh in. That will take time, dialogue, and experimentation, but that will bring its own reforms.

Fourth, regardless of how nation-states like China or the United States judge their own human rights obligations and performance, we academics and religious leaders would do well to articulate the fundamentals of human rights—those fundamental bads and goods that must be a baseline of agreement and of a nation's acceptance into the world community. No nation can systematically torture or starve people nor commit persons to lifetime imprisonment or death without fair trials and procedures. No nation can violate a people's basic freedoms to believe what they wish to believe. No nation can seek to abolish or destroy fundamental institutions like the family or pulverize other such essential associations. There has to be consistent articulation and agreement on these basic fundamentals, and we academics would do well to continue to push for them. The more exotic rights set out in the Universal Declaration of Human Rights and later human rights instruments are less important than the starting points, which include a basic commitment to liberty, dignity, fraternity, and equality; basic protections of due process; basic understandings of institutions and services like education and healthcare that are essential to the protection and organization of a good life and a good society. In that sense, religious leaders can be leaders of the global human rights conversation.

Fifth, it's important to separate discussion of the theoretical foundations of human rights and how we can embrace them from empirical questions of rights or their violation in a given context. A serious diplomatic and academic project of trying to articulate the foundations and fundamentals of a human rights culture in China can and should go on, even if there are continued controversies about particular human rights issues on the ground. We have plenty of human rights violations in America, too, and elsewhere in the West—not least against various racial, religious, cultural, and ethnic minorities and affinity groups. That focus on fundamentals while wrestling with particulars is how the law on the books and the law in action works. That's how theory and practice work. That's how human rights declarations eventually can become human rights deeds as well.

Finally, I hear the frustration that your question reflects about how to be most effective as a Christian and as scholar in China in bringing about reforms. It might help to think through a few different methods and strategies. Sometimes, it helps to translate concepts. If *human rights* is an inflammatory term in China today, maybe talking about justice and fairness is better. If talk of individual freedoms, like freedom of speech, religion, assembly, or press, is controversial, maybe it's better to talk about the communal discourse we all need to learn to live together. If ideas of federalism are seen as too deeply embedded in Western constitutional and covenantal theories, maybe the Chinese context lends itself better to discuss how to live in local community and national community at once and to have efficient and effective authority structures for each community. Finding neutral terms that allow for the conversation about what others might call *human rights* is an important translation exercise for academics.

Providing historical and comparative examples might also help provide comfort for those who are oppressed and inspiration for leaders to change their oppressive way. Religious persecution and repression are nothing new for Christians. Christians faced the lions and the catacombs in Rome. Heretics have been burned at the stake. Protestants and Catholics slaughtered each other with a vengeance in early modern times.

Both French and American revolutionaries were viciously anti-Catholic. And many Christians today face persecution in China and in many other parts of the world. It's helpful to articulate and compare earlier strategies of resistance, resilience, and reconciliation. It's helpful to remember that all those earlier persecutors died, and their persecutions ended, and yet the church lived on. It's helpful to point out how and why these persecutions ended: Rome eventually accepted Christianity as essential for the survival of the empire. The Roman Catholic Church ultimately realized the scandal and ineffectiveness of torture, inquisition, and stake burning and passed criminal procedural protections against them. Early modern Christians eventually learned the fruitlessness of persecuting each other and instead learned to live together while granting religious freedom to all peaceable believers, and Western society flourished as a consequence. China might discover the same thing, particularly as the number of Chinese Christians continues to grow.

Being authentic in Christian identity and witness is also key. The church in China needs, first and foremost, to be not a human rights advocacy group but the body of Christ on earth, which has its fundamental responsibility to abide by scripture, to imitate Christ, to follow the great commission of being disciples, going out to the world and bringing others to Christ, being examples of cruciform living, being ethical. The political or constitutional reforms or human rights agendas that churches have, or the resistance struggles that they lead, have to be part of that authentic mission and ministry, not a substitute for it. As Dietrich Bonhoeffer said in the midst of the church's resistance to the horrors of Nazism, "We must never forget to maintain our essential calling of being a true Christian church first." When churches grow too preoccupied with pushing political agendas, at the cost of being authentic to their own distinct spiritual calling, they endanger themselves.

All that said, advocacy for religious freedom is one facet of living by the admonition of Acts 5:29 that "we must obey God rather than men." And basic legal protection of religious freedom will bring other human rights in its train. The Western Protestant tradition discovered by hard experience that protection of religious freedom for individuals and groups is the foundation of many other civil and human rights for individuals and groups. Having a basic right to freedom of religion eventually produced freedoms of speech, assembly, and publication, rights to parenting, pilgrimage, and education, and other individual rights. Giving a basic right to a religious group to exist as a licit and legal entity eventually provided the foundation for rights to charity, social welfare, holding corporate property, organizing community, enforcing disciplinary structures, and the like. For the church and its members to pursue religious freedom is not to engage in self-service but to lay the foundation for many other human rights.

Q: In China today, there are various cases regarding Christian engagement with human rights issues. Some churches in China adopt a public way of resistance, defending church interests in particular. There is also a group of Christian lawyers who aim to defend and protect civil rights in China. Some Christian intellectuals, including some influenced by Calvinist teachings, are involved in public discourse on political and social issues. Inspired by your work on Christianity and human rights, I am compelled to ponder to what extent these Chinese Christians' efforts can inform and bear certain implications for the progress of "many other human rights" as well as institutional forms in China, which in turn can advance religious and other human rights. Would you, please, offer your observations and ideas in this regard?

Witte: Building on what I just said, in the Western tradition, especially in the Western Protestant tradition, we came to understand that religious freedom is the first right, the foundational right, the cornerstone right on which many other individual and group rights depend. Again, for the church to seek religious freedom is not necessarily just self-serving. It's often the best way to ensure that other human rights also get protected. Churches engaged in the pursuit of religious freedom for all peaceable believers are serving the broader human rights cause.

Calvinism has a strong tradition of rights advocacy based upon protecting the right to religious freedom first. Calvinist rights reformers— Calvin, Beza, Althusius, Milton, and many others into the eighteenth century—all saw religious freedom as the first right because they saw the duty to obey, worship, and honor God and God's law as the first duty of humankind.

But this is not just a historical argument or observation. As we look around the world today, empirical studies of the 198 individual nation-states and independent territories show that when and where religious freedom is well protected, other human rights are also well protected; where religious freedom is compromised, abridged, or destroyed, other human rights topple as well, and grave injustice often obtains. As a consequence, Chinese Christians and others who are pressing for religious freedom are serving a broader and essential human rights cause.

The harder question that Christians have always faced is what to do when the right of religious freedom is not respected. Do we turn the other cheek and become martyrs, as Christ did, and as some martyrs in the tradition have always done? Or do we instead take up arms and fight for God's cause? Do we lead a revolution, at the risk of many thousands of lives and a generation of disruption? Christians over the centuries have developed stages or layers of resistance, individually and corporately, and Calvinists were particularly instructive in setting out these layers or steps.

A first step of resistance is for the individual and family quietly to pray, read the Bible, and worship God in disobedience of the state's law. Having house churches that are not licensed by the state but that provide opportunities for worship, charity, education, and close association with others is how groups embrace this first step of resistance theory. Being faithful in and to those communities, being hospitable to members of those communities, making them "zones of liberty" for proper and right Christian living is critical service and witness. We have examples of house churches already in the New Testament, and they flourished despite their repression by the Roman authorities who called them illicit associations.

A second step of resistance is leaving—exercising the right to emigrate when the local authorities don't allow you to worship in the way that you think is appropriate—and taking your family, labor, taxes, education, expertise, work, and businesses with you to settle in a neighboring area where you are welcome. If enough people leave with all of these goods and services, and especially if they settle in a rival political community, the persecuting authorities at their prior homes will begin to question whether that cost is worth it. Religious persecutors in the past often vacillated between narratives of purity (and consequent repression of dissenters) and utility (relaxing persecution in order to ensure that enough labor, taxes, business, and other good things stay and get done in their community).

A third step of resistance is to push the government by lawsuits, petitions, demonstrations, and grievances—and today also by use of social media—to expose the rights violations, to make them visible to fellow believers who can know they are not alone in the suffering, and to other folks who can take up their cause in prayer, as well as in diplomatic, political, and legal efforts to have the persecution end. Doing that with humility but with insistence is a third step in rights resistance.

A fourth step is building networks and organizations of resistance and revolt. This is not a step to be taken lightly today, for fear of violent reprisal and setback for others. But organizing with other religious freedom and human rights reformers, finding community and common cause with advocacy groups who can litigate, lobby, and mobilize reform efforts from within and without the country short of violence or revolt is a critical step.

For the Calvinist tradition, violent revolt and revolution was always a last resort, to be used only after all these stages of resistance were tried. Even then, the Calvinist tradition insisted on various strong procedural steps. If a repressed community was so chronically, pervasively, and persistently repressed and persecuted that it had no other recourse but to rise up in revolt, Calvin and his followers stressed the need to follow orderly, collective, and constitutionally licit methods. No individual or small group, they argued, could take it upon themselves to make a collective judgment about what the whole community needs and then initiate violent rebellion, possibly triggering a massive reaction by the government in a response that could cost the religious freedom and human rights for everyone. Coordinating resistance with representative leaders from throughout the community was critically important.

One of the keys today is to persuade the state that it is good for them as a state to protect human rights, especially religious freedom. It is important to demonstrate—historically, comparatively, and empirically— that the church has long been and can be a vital ally of the state and can help the state achieve its goals. Many of the things that the state is trying to achieve in education, charity, poor relief, healthcare, fostering public and private morality, and more, the church has and can help it achieve effectively—at the granular level, on the ground, neighborhood by neighborhood, community by community. Granting religious freedom therefore helps the state achieve greater justice, moral order, and public provisioning. The empirical studies that I mentioned about the consequences of protecting religious freedom around the world make it clear that if a state protects religious freedom, it does better in its statecraft and in its service to all citizens.

So the pitch to the state is: if you want to protect the poor, the needy, the widow, the orphan, the stranger, the sojourner; if you want to put in place basic structures of charity, education and social welfare; if you want to foster public morality and political allegiance, you would be better served by giving freedom to religious communities to help you as a state. That will give churches and other religious communities the freedom to discharge what for them are duties to do these things. That leads to much more effective and efficient governance than seeking to suppress these potential allies or to monopolize governance and provision.

Faith, Freedom, and Family

Q: You mentioned earlier the three fundamental aspects of life: faith, freedom, and family. As a way of concluding our conversation, could you please share something more about this from your own understanding of Chinese culture, politics, and society? In other words, is there a difference between these terms in the West and in the East?

Witte: Unfortunately, I can't answer that properly. I don't know enough about the role that faith, freedom, and family play in Chinese culture and cosmology historically and today. What I can say is that in the West, over the past two thousand years, there have been three things that most people will die for—their faith, their freedom, and their family. Their faith: what they believe to be their fundamental obligations toward God. Their freedom: the most essential condition that they need to live out their faith, their love of God, neighbor, and self. Their family: the sacrificial love, even to death, that we have for our spouse, for our children, for our parents and siblings. In the West, faith, freedom, and family are in that sense the most fundamental. These are three things that people will die for, and they are foundational elements of an orderly society and ordered liberty.

I can't judge whether that formula or something comparable is part of Chinese thinking. I suspect that there are at least parallels to that in Confucian and Buddhist and other cultures, and there are certainly expressions of that in the Chinese Christian cultures that I have encountered. I published a book with a couple of colleagues a decade or so ago called *Sex, Marriage, and Family in World Religions*. We had primary texts from Asian Buddhist, Confucian, and other traditions alongside Judaism, Christianity, and Islam. I was struck by how comparable the teachings are about the family as you read across these great world religions. At least at the intellectual level of official teachings, all these religions emphasize the importance of the family for individual and social flourishing. I suspect that is part of Chinese culture and cosmology too.

Q: In the Chinese traditions, we have strong emphasis on the family structure and family-based understanding of community and society. In contemporary China, particularly in urban China, more and more intellectuals have their own individual quest for the meaning of life and search for the ideal of freedom in its various layers. Some of them come close to Christianity. For me, it seems increasingly important for Chinese society and government to take seriously what freedom and order mean for us in our transitional period. I do hope both the East and the West can learn from each other on these common issues.

Witte: Amen! The West certainly has something to learn from the rest of the world, as the West experiences the gradual decline in its own commitments to faith, freedom, and family. Maybe a century from now, our successors will be in a very different kind of conversation. An American may be sitting at a Chinese scholar's desk asking his or her advice about how the Chinese operate with their robust new Christian identity, while the West sits with only the memory and residue of its once-Christian culture.

BIBLIOGRAPHY

Angle, Stephen. *Human Rights and Chinese Thought: A Cross-Cultural Inquiry*. Cambridge: Cambridge University Press, 2002.

Anonymous. "Tenth National Chinese Christian Conference Issued an Initiative on Actively Promoting and Practicing Socialist Core Values." *Chinese Theological Review* 29 (2019): 4–5.

Au, Kin-ming 歐建銘. "Ai yu ren: bijiao tianlike yu zhuxi zongjiao lunli yuanze de yanjiu" 愛與仁: 比較田立克與朱熹宗教倫理原則的研究 ["Love and Ren: A Comparative Study of Paul Tillich and Zhu Xi's Religious Ethical Principles"]. In *Jidu zongjiao yu rujia duitan shengming yu lunli* 基督宗教與儒家對談生命與倫理 [*Christian-Confucian Dialogue on Life and Ethics*], edited by Pan-chiu Lai 賴品超, 177–97. Hong Kong: Center for the Study of Religion and Chinese Society, Chung Chi College, The Chinese University of Hong Kong 香港中文大學崇基學院宗教與中國社會研究中心, 2002.

Bacote, Vincent E. Introduction to *Wisdom and Wonder: Common Grace in Science and Art*, by Abraham Kuyper, edited by Jordan J. Ballor and Stephen J. Grabill, and translated by Nelson D. Kloosterman, 23–29. Grand Rapids: Christian's Library Press, 2011.

Bays, Daniel H. *A New History of Christianity in China*. Chichester: Wiley-Blackwell, 2012.

Bell, Daniel A. Introduction to *A Confucian Constitutional Order: How China's Ancient Past Can Shape Its Political Culture*, by Qing Jiang, edited by Daniel A. Bell and Ruiping Fan, and translated by Edmund Ryden, 1–24. Princeton: Princeton University Press, 2013.

_____. "Preface." In *Confucian Political Ethics*, edited by Daniel A. Bell, ix–xiv. Princeton: Princeton University Press, 2008.

Bellah, Robert N. "Civil Religion in America." *Daedalus* 96, no. 1 (1967): 1–21.

Bennett, John C. "Reinhold Niebuhr's Social Ethics." In *Reinhold Niebuhr: His Religious, Social, and Political Thought*, edited by Charles W. Kegley and Robert W. Bretall, 45–77. New York: Macmillan, 1956.

Berling, Judith A. *A Pilgrim in Chinese Culture: Negotiating Religious Diversity*. Maryknoll: Orbis Books, 1997.

———. "Why Chinese Thought on Religious Diversity Is Important." In *Religious Diversity in the Chinese Thought*, edited by Perry Schmidt-Leukel and Joachim Gentz, 27–37. New York: Palgrave Macmillian, 2013.

Berthrong, John. "Confucianism." In *Encyclopedia of Religious Freedom*, edited by Catherine Cookson, 68–73. London: Routledge, 2003.

Breitenberg, E. Harold, Jr. "What Is Public Theology?" In *Public Theology for a Global Society: Essays in Honor of Max L. Stackhouse*, edited by Deirdre King Hainsworth and Scott R. Paeth, 3–21. Grand Rapids: Eerdmands, 2010.

Brennan, Patrick McKinley. "The Relationship between Sphere Sovereignty and Subsidiarity." In *Global Perspectives on Subsidiarity*, edited by Michelle Evans and Augusto Zimmermann, 49–63. Dordrecht: Springer, 2014.

———. "Subsidiarity in the Tradition of Catholic Social Doctrine." In *Global Perspectives on Subsidiarity*, edited by Michelle Evans and Augusto Zimmermann, 29–47. Dordrecht: Springer, 2014.

Carpenter, Joel A., and Kevin R. den Dulk, eds. *Christianity in Chinese Public Life: Religion, Society, and the Rule of Law*. New York: Palgrave Macmillan, 2014.

Chan, Joseph. "Confucianism and Human Rights." In *Religion and Human Rights: An Introduction*, edited by John Witte Jr. and M. Christian Green, 87–102. Oxford: Oxford University Press, 2012.

———. "On the Legitimacy of Confucian Constitutionalism." In *A Confucian Constitutional Order: How China's Ancient Past Can Shape Its Political Culture*, by Qing Jiang, edited by Daniel A. Bell, translated by Edmund Ryden, 99–112. Princeton: Princeton University Press, 2013.

Chan, Kim-kwong, and Graeme Lang. "Religious Diversity and the State in China." In *The Politics and Practice of Religious Diversity: National Contexts, Global Issues*, edited by Andrew Dawson, 82–98. London: Routledge, 2016.

Chan, Shun-Hing "Civil Society and the Role of Catholic Church in Contemporary China." In *Christianity in Contemporary China: Socio-Cultural Perspectives*, edited by Francis K. G. Lim, 123–37. New York: Routledge, 2013.

Chan, Shun-hing, and Jonathan W. Johnson, eds. *Citizens of Two Kingdoms: Civil Society and Christian Religion in Greater China*. Leiden: Brill, 2021.

Chan, Wing-tsit. "The Evolution of the Confucian Concept Jen." *Philosophy East and West* 4, no. 4 (1955): 295–319.

Chang, P. C. "Chinese Statements during Deliberations on the UDHR (1948)." In *The Chinese Human Rights Reader: Documents and Commentary 1900–2000*, edited by Stephen C. Angle and Marian Svensson, 478–92. New York: Routledge, 2015.

Chao, Jonathan Tien-en 趙天恩. *Zhongguo Jiaohui bensehua yundong 1919–1927: Jidu jiaohui dui xiandai zhongguo fan jidujiao yundong de huiying* 中國教會本色化運動 1919–1927: 基督教會對現代中國反基督教運動的回應 [*The Chinese Indigenous Church Movement, 1919–27: A Protestant Response to the Anti-Christian Movements in Modern China*]. New Taipei: Olive Press 橄欖出版有限公司, 2019.

Chao, T. C. 趙紫宸. "Jidujiao de shehuixing" 基督教的社會性 ["Sociality of Christianity"]. In *Zhongguo jidujiao gonggong shenxue wenxuan*, edited by Ken-pa Chin, 179–92. Hong Kong: Center for Advanced Biblical Studies and Application 研道社, 2012.

Chaplin, Jonathan. *Herman Dooyeweerd: Christian Philosopher of State and Civil Society*. Notre Dame: University of Notre Dame Press, 2011.

_____. "Subsidiarity and Sphere Sovereignty: Catholic and Reformed Conceptions of the Role of the State." In *Things Old and New: Catholic Social Teaching Revisited*, edited by Francis P. McHugh and Samuel M. Natale, 175–202. Lanham: University Press of America, 1993.

Chen, Albert Hung-yee 陈弘毅. "Zhengzhi Ruxue yu Minzhu" 政治儒學與民主 ["Political Confucianism and Democracy"]. *Fazhi yu shehui fazhan* 法制與社會發展15, no. 2 (2009): 3–11.

Chen, Bin 陳彬, and Shining Gao 高師寧. "Dui 'zongjiao shengtai lun' de huigu yu fansi" 對"宗教生態論"的回顧與反思 ["Review and Reflection on the So-Called Theory of Religious Ecology"]. *Daofeng jidujiao wenhua pinglun* 道風基督教文化評論 [*Logos and Pneuma: Chinese Journal of Theology*], no. 35 (2011): 317–35.

Chen, Jo-shui 陳弱水. "Zhongguo lishi shang 'gong' de guannian jiqi xiandai bianxing." 中國歷史上"公"的觀念及其現代變形 ["The Concept of 'Public' in Chinese History and Its Modern Deformations"]. In *Gong gong xing yu gong min guan* 公共性與公民觀 [*Publicness and Citizenship*], edited by Xu Jilin 許紀霖, 3–39. Nanjing: Jiangsu renmin chubanshe 江蘇人民出版社, 2006.

Chen, Ming 陳明. "Rujiao yanjiu xin sikao: Gongmin zongjiao yu zhonghua minzu yishi jiangou." 儒教研究新思考:公民宗教與中華民族意識建構 ["A Reconsideration of Confucianism Studies: Civil Religion and the Construction of Chinese National Consciousness"]. In *Dunkang xiansheng bashi shouchen jinian ji* 余敦康先生八十壽辰紀念集 [*A Tribute to Mr. Yu Dunkang*], edited by Ming Chen, 241–50. Bejing: Shoudu shifan daxue chubanshe 首都師範大學出版社, 2009.

————. "Rujiao zhi gongmin zongjiao shuo" 儒教之公民宗教說 ["On Confucianism as Civil Religion"]. In *Wenhua ruxue: sibian yu lunbian* 文化儒學: 思辨與論辯 [*Cultural Confucianism: Speculative and Deliberative*], 41–51. Chengdu: Sichuan renmin chubanshe 四川人民出版社, 2009.

Chen, Yongtao 陳永濤. "Lunli de jidulun: zhongguo jiaohui shenxue sixiang jianshe zhong jidulun sikao yige keneng de fangxiang" 倫理的基督論: 中國教會神學思想建設中基督論思考一個可能的方向 ["Ethical Christology: A Possible Direction of the Chinese Church's Theological Construction of Christology"]. In *Xinyang zhijian de zhongyao xiangyu: Yazhou yu xifang de zongjiao wenhua jiaoliu guoji xueshu yantaohui wenji* 信仰之間的重要相遇: 亞洲與西方的宗教文化交流國際學術研討會文集 [*Faith/Faithful Encounters: Religion and Cultural Exchanges between Asian and the West—Proceedings from an International Conference*], edited by Xinping Zhuo 卓新平, Judith Berling 伯玲, and Philip Wickeri 魏克利, 165–96. Beijing: Zongjiao wenhua chubanshe 宗教文化出版社, 2005.

Chin, Ken-pa 曾慶豹. "Hanyu shenxue yu xinzuopai de yinni duihua" 漢語神學與新左派的隱匿對話 ["The Hidden Dialogue between Sino-Christian Theology and the New Left"]. *Daofeng jidujiao wenhua pinglun*, no. 41 (2014): 27–51.

————. "Shi shui ba gonggong shenxue yange zuo 'gonggong shenxue" 是誰把公共神學閹割做 "公公神學" ["Who Emasculates Public Theology into 'Eunuch Theology'?"]. *Shidai luntan* 時代論壇, no. 1360 (September 22, 2013): 11 and no. 1361 (September 29, 2013): 11.

————. "Zhongguo jidujiao gonggong shenxue wenxuan xilie zongxu" 中國基督教公共神學文選系列總序 ["General Introduction to Anthology of Christian Public Theology in China"]. In *Zhongguo Jidu jiao gonggong shenxue wenxuan, yi, shehui sixiang pian* 中國基督教公共神學文選一: 社會思想篇 [*Collected Essays on the Public Theology of Chinese Christianity I, Volume on Social Thought*], edited by Ken-Pa Chin, xiii–xxxi. Hong Kong: Center for Advanced Biblical Studies and Application, 2012.

Chow, Alexander. "Calvinist Public Theology in Urban China Today." *International Journal of Public Theology* 8, no. 2 (2014): 158–75.

————. *Chinese Public Theology: Generational Shifts and Confucian Imagination in Chinese Christianity.* Oxford: Oxford University Press, 2018.

————. *Theosis, Sino-Christian Theology and the Second Chinese Enlightenment: Heaven and Humanity in Unity.* New York: Palgrave Macmillan, 2013.

Chow, Christie Chui-shan. "Demolition and Defiance: The Stone Ground Church Dispute (2012) in East China." *Journal of World Christianity* 6, no. 2 (2016): 250–76.

Christensen, David E. "Breaking the Deadlock: Toward a Socialist-Confucianist Concept of Human Rights for China." *Michigan Journal of International Law* 13, no. 2 (1992): 469–514.

Clark, Anthony E. "Introduction: 'China's Christianity' and the Ideal of a Universal Church." In *China's Christianity: From Missionary to Indigenous Church*, edited by Anthony E. Clark, 1–20. Leiden: Brill, 2017.

Clart, Philip. "'Religious Ecology' as a New Model for the Study of Religious Diversity in China." In *Religious Diversity in the Chinese Thought*, edited by Perry Schmidt-Leukel and Joachim Gentz, 187–99. New York: Palgrave Macmillian, 2013.

Cline, Erin. *Confucius, Rawls, and the Sense of Justice*. New York: Fordham University Press, 2012.

Cohen, Paula. *China and Christianity: The Missionary Movement and the Growth of Chinese Antiforeignism 1860–70*. Cambridge, MA: Harvard University Press, 1963.

de Bary, Wm. Theodore, and Tu Wei-ming, eds. *Confucianism and Human Rights*. New York: Columbia University Press, 1998.

de Gruchy, John W. "From Political to Public Theologies: The Role of Theology in Public Life in South Africa." In *Public Theology for the 21st Century: Essays in Honour of Duncan B. Forrester*, edited by William F. Storrar and Andrew R. Morton, 45–62. London: T&T Clark, 2004.

Deng, Zhenglai 鄧正來, and Yuejing Jing 景躍進. "Jiangou zhongguo de shimin shehui." 建構中國的市民社會 ["Constructing Civil Society in China"]. In *Guojia yu shimin shehui: Zhongguo shijiao* 國家與市民社會: 中國視角, edited by Zhenglai Deng, 3–21. Shanghai: Gezhi chubanshe 格致出版社 Shanghai renmin chubanshe 上海人民出版社, 2011.

Dooyeweerd, Herman. "Roots of Western Culture." In *Political Order and the Plural Structure of Society*, edited by James W. Skillen and Rockne M. McCarthy, 265–97. Atlanta: Scholars Press, 1991.

Dorrien, Gary. Introduction to *The Children of Light and the Children of Darkness*, by Reinhold Niebuhr, ix–xxvi. Chicago: University of Chicago Press, 2011.

Duan, Qi 段琦. "Zongjiao shiheng yu zhongguo jidujiao fazhan" 宗教失衡與中國基督教發展 ["The Outbalance of Religious Ecology and Development of Christianity in China"]. In *Sanshinian lai zhongguo jidujiao xianzhuang yanjiu lunzhuxuan* 三十年來中國基督教現狀研究論著選, edited by Huawei Li 李華偉, 492–503. Beijing: Shehui kexue wenxian chubanshe 社會科學文獻出版社, 2016.

Eisenstadt, Shmuel N. "The Protestant Ethic and Modernity—Comparative Analysis with and beyond Weber." In *Soziale Ungleichheit, kulturelle Unterschiede: Verhandlungen des 32. Kongresses der Deutschen Gesellschaft für Soziologie in München*, edited by K. S. Rehberg, 161–84. Frankfurt: Campus Verl, 2006.

Fei, Xiaotong. *From the Soil: The Foundations of Chinese Society*. A Translation of Fei Xiaotong's *Xiangtu Zhongguo* by Hsiang t'u Chung-kuo, with an introduction and an epilogue by Gary G. Hamilton and Wang Zheng. Berkeley: University of California Press, 1992.

Fergusson, David. *Church, State, and Civil Society*. Cambridge: Cambridge University Press, 2004.

Fiorenza, Francis Schüssler. *Foundational Theology: Jesus and the Church*. New York: Crossroad, 1992.

Forrester, Duncan B. *Forrester on Christian Ethics and Practical Theology: Collected Writings on Christianity, India, and the Social Order*. Farnham: Ashgate, 2010.

Frederking, Lauretta Conklin. *Reconstructing Social Justice*. New York: Routledge, 2014.

Frei, Hans. *Types of Christian Theology*. New Haven: Yale University Press, 1992.

Frolic, B. Michael. "State-Led Civil Society." In *Civil Society in China*, edited by Timothy Brook and B. Michael Frolic, 46–67. London: ME Sharpe, 1997.

Gao, Bingzhong 高丙中. "'Gongmin shehui' gainian yu zhongguo xianshi" 公民社會"概念與中國現實 ["The Concept of 'Civil Society' and Realities in China"]. *Sixiang zhanxian* 思想戰線 [*Thought Frontier*] 38, no. 1 (2012): 30–38.

Gao, Shining 高師寧. "Cong shizheng yanjiu kan jidujiao yu dangdai zhongguo shehui" 從實證研究看基督教與當代中國社會 ["Christianity and Contemporary Chinese Society from Empirical Studies"]. *Zhejiang xuekan* 浙江學刊 [*Zhejiang Academic Journal*], no. 4 (2006): 56–62.

———. "Dangdai zhongguo zongjiao san yi" 當代中國宗教三議 ["Three Issues in Contemporary Chinese Religions"]. *Daofeng jidujiao wenhua pinglun*, no. 36 (2012): 17–35.

Gernet, Jacques. *China and the Christian Impact: A Conflict of Cultures*. Translated by Janet Lloyd. Cambridge: Cambridge University Press, 1985.

Goodin, Robert E. *Protecting the Vulnerable: A Reanalysis of Our Social Responsibility*. Chicago: University of Chicago Press, 1985.

Gregg, Benjamin. *Human Rights as Social Construction*. New York: Cambridge University Press, 2012.

Grenz, Stanley J. *The Social God and the Relational Self: A Trinitarian Theology of the Imago Dei*. Louisville: Westminster John Knox Press, 2001.

Grim, Brian J., and Roger Finke. *The Price of Freedom Denied: Religious Persecution and Conflict in the Twenty-First Century*. Cambridge: Cambridge University Press, 2011.

Guo, Qingxiang 郭清香. *Ye ru lunli bijiao yanjiu—minguo shiqi jidujiao yu rujiao lunli sixiang de chongtu yu ronghe* 耶儒倫理比較研究—民國時期基督教與儒教倫理思想的衝突與融合 ["Comparative Study of Christian and Confucian Ethics—Confucian and Christian Ethical Thought's Conflict and Harmony in the Republic of China Period"]. Beijing: Zhongguo shehui kexue chubanshe 中國社會科學出版社, 2007.

Guo, Qiyong 郭齊勇. "Yetan 'zi wei fu yin' yu mengzi lun shun: jian yu liu qingping xiansheng shangque" 也談"子為父隱"與孟子論舜: 兼與劉清平先生商榷 ["'Father and Son Screening Each Other' and Mencius on Shun: A Debate with Qingping Liu"]. *Zhexue yanjiu* 哲學研究 [*Philosophical Research*], no. 10 (2002): 27–30.

Haire, James. "The Place of Public Theology between Theology and Public Policy." In *Contextuality and Intercontextuality in Public Theology*, edited by Henrich Bedord-Strohm, Florian Hohne, and Tobias Reimeier, 39–51. Munster: LIT Verlag, 2013.

Hamilton, Gary G., and Wang Zheng. Introduction to *From the Soil, The Foundations of Chinese Society: A Translation of Fei Xiaotong's Xiangtu Zhongguo*, by Fei Xiaotong, translated by Hsiang t'u Chung-kuo, 1–36. Berkeley: University of California Press, 1992.

Hao, Zhidong, and Yan Liu. "Mutual Accommodation in the Church-State Relationship in China? A Case Study of the Sanjiang Church Demolition in Zhejiang." *Review of Religion and Chinese Society* 5, no. 1 (2018): 26–42.

Hauerwas, Stanley, and D. Stephen Long. "Foreword." In *Basic Christian Ethics*, edited by Paul Ramsey, xiii–xxix. Louisville: Westminster/John Knox Press, 1993.

He, Huaihong 何懷宏. "Zhengyi zai zhongguo: lishi yu xianshi de—yige chubu de silu" 正義在中國: 歷史與現實的——個初步的思路 ["Justice in China: Historical and Contemporary—A Preliminary Approach"]. *Gonggong xingzheng pinglun* 公共行政評論 [*Public Administration Review*], no. 1 (2011): 2–15.

He, Guanghu 何光滬. "Hanyu shenxue de fangfa yu jinlu" 漢語神學的方法與進路 ["Methodology and Approach of Sino-Christian Theology"]. In *Hanyu shenxue chuyi*, 漢語神學芻議 [*Preliminary Studies on Chinese Theology*], edited by Daniel Yeung 楊熙楠, 39–53. Hong Kong: Institute of Sino-Christian Studies 汉语基督教文化研究所, 2000.

Henkin, Louis. "Confucianism, Human Rights, and 'Cultural Relativism.'" In *Confucianism and Human Rights*, edited by Wm. Theodore de Bary and Tu Weiming, 308–15. New York: Columbia University Press, 1998.

―――. "The Human Rights Idea in Contemporary China: A Comparative Perspective." In *Human Rights in Contemporary China*, edited by R. Randle Edwards, Louis Henkin, and Andrew J. Nathan, 7–40. New York: Columbia University Press, 1986.

Hertzke, Allen D. Introduction to *The Future of Religious Freedom: Global Challenges*, by Allen D. Hertzke, edited by Allen D. Hertzke, 3–31. Oxford: Oxford University Press, 2013.

Hildebrandt, Timothy. *Social Organizations and the Authoritarian State in China*. New York: Cambridge University Press, 2013.

Hollenbach, David. "Public Theology in America: Some Questions for Catholicism after John Courtney Murray." *Theological Studies* 37, no. 2 (1976): 290–303.

Howell, Jude 朱迪·豪威爾. "Zhongguo shehui bianyuan qunti de zuzhihua yu gongmin shehui de fazhan" 中國社會邊緣群體的組織化與公民社會的發展 ["The Organization of Marginal Groups and the Development of Civil Society in China"]. In *Gongmin shehui yu zhili zhuanxing: fazhan Zhong guojia de shijiao* 公民社會與治理轉型: 發展中國家的視角 [*Civil Society and Governance Transition: Perspective from Developing Countries*], edited by Mingzhen Liu 劉明珍, 141–53. Beijing: Zhongyang bianyi chubanshe 中央編譯出版社, 2008.

Hsieh, Fu-ya 謝扶雅. "Jidujiao dui jinri zhongguo de shiming" 基督教對今日中國的使命 ["The Mission of Christianity in China Today"]. In *Ershi shiji zhongguo jidujiao wenti* 二十世紀中國基督教問題 [*The Problems of Chinese Christianity in the 20th Century*], edited by Yuming Shaw 邵玉銘, 516–40. Taipei: Cheng Chung 正中書局, 1980.

Huang, Haibo. "Approaching Civil Society under Construction: Protestant Churches in China in 2010, Responsibility and Introspection." In *Yearbook of Chinese Theology 2015*, edited by Paulos Z. Huang, 217–48. Leiden: Brill, 2015.

Huang, Jianbo 黃劍波, and Fenggang Yang 楊鳳崗. "Diaocha baogao: Beifang mou yanhai chengshi jidutu de jiating lunli he gongzuo lunli" 調查報告: 北方某沿海城市基督徒的家庭倫理和工作倫理 ["A Report: One Northern Coastal City's Christian Population's Family Ethics and Work Ethics"]. *Jidujiao wenhua xuekan* 基督教文化學刊 [*Journal for the Study of Christian Culture*], no. 11 (2004): 326–54.

Huang, Yong. "Confucian Love and Global Ethics: How the Cheng Brothers Would Help Respond to Christian Criticisms." *Asian Philosophy* 15, no. 1 (2005): 35–60.

Huang, Yushun. *Voice from the East: The Chinese Theory of Justice*. Translated by Pingping Hou and Keyou Wang. Reading: Paths International, 2016.

Huen, Chi W. 褟智偉. "Gonggong shenxue: Shui de gonggong? you ji shenxue?" 公共神學: 誰的 "公共"? 有幾"神學"? ["Public Theology: Whose 'Public'? How 'Theological'?"]. *Shandao qikan* 山道期刊 [*Hill Road*] 16, no. 1 (2013): 31–63.

Jiang, Qing 蔣慶. *Wangdao zhengzhi yu rujiao xianzheng: Weilai zhongguo xianzheng zhengzhi fazhan de ruxue sikao* 王道政治與儒教憲政: 未來中國憲政政治發展的儒學思考 ["Kingcraft Politics and Confucian Constitutionalism: Confucian Thinking on Political Development for Future China"]. Guizhou: Yangming jingshe 陽明精舍, 2010.

_____. *A Confucian Constitutional Order: How China's Ancient Past Can Shape Its Political Culture*. Edited by Daniel A. Bell and translated by Edmund Ryden. Princeton: Princeton University Press, 2013.

Jiang, Yi-huah 江宜樺. "Huaren shijie fazhan gonggong zhexue de yiyi" 華人世界發展公共哲學的意義 ["The Significance of Developing Public Philosophy in the Chinese-Speaking World"]. In *Gongsi lingyu xintan: dongya yu xifang guandian zhi bijiao* 公私領域新探: 東亞與西方觀點之比較 [*A New Exploration of the Public and Private Spheres: A Comparison between East Asian and Western Perspectives*], edited by Chun-chieh Huang 黃俊傑 and Yi-huah Jiang, 41–54. Shanghai: Huadong shifan daxue chubanshe 華東師範大學出版社, 2008.

Kan, Baoping 闞保平. "Xiandaihua dui Jiaohui de Tiaozhan" 現代化對教會的挑戰 ["The Challenge of Modernization to Church"]. *Jinling shenxue zhi* 金陵神學志 [*Jinling Theological Journal*], no. 2 (1994): 22–29.

Kang, Zhijie 康志傑, and Tao Xu 徐弢. "Dangdai zhongguo jidutu lunli shenghuo de kaocha—yi e xibei mopanshan jidutu shequ weili" 當代中國基督徒倫理生活的考察—以鄂西北磨盤山基督徒社區為例 ["Investigation of Contemporary Chinese Christians' Ethical Lives: Taking Mopan Mountain in Northwest Hubei as an Example"]. *Jidujiao sixiang pinglun* 基督教思想評論 [*Regent Review of Christian Thought*], no. 8 (2008): 295–307.

Kang, Namsoon. *Diasporic Feminist Theology: Asia and Theopolitical Imagination*. Minneapolis: Fortress Press, 2014.

Kang, Xiaogang 康曉光. *Renzheng: zhongguo zhengzhi fazhan de disantiao daolu.* 仁政: 中國政治發展的第三條道路 [*Benevolent Rule: The Third Way of Political Development in China*]. Singapore: Global Publishing 八方文化創作室, 2005.

Kärkkäinen, Veli-Matti. *The Doctrine of God: A Global Introduction.* Grand Rapids: Baker Academic, 2004.

Keller, Perry. "The Protection of Human Dignity under Chinese Law." In *The Cambridge Handbook of Human Dignity*, edited by Marcus Düwell, Jens Braarvig, Roger Brownsword, and Dietmar Mieth, 414–21. Cambridge: Cambridge University Press, 2014.

Kilcourse, Carl S. *Taiping Theology: The Localization of Christianity in China, 1843–64.* New York: Palgrave Macmillan, 2016.

Koesel, Karrie J. *Religion and Authoritarianism: Cooperation, Conflict, and the Consequences.* Cambridge: Cambridge University Press, 2014.

Koppelman, Andrew, and Benjamin Gregg. "Critical Exchange on Human Rights as Social Construction." *Contemporary Political Theory*, no. 13 (2014), 380–86.

Koyzis, David T. "Introductory Essay: Political Theory in the Calvinist Tradition." In *Political Philosophy—Selected Essays*, by Herman Dooyeweerd, 1–16. Grand Rapids: Paideia Press, 2012.

Krumbein, Frédéric. "P. C. Chang—The Chinese Father of Human Rights." *Journal of Human Rights* 14, no. 3 (2015): 332–52.

Küng, Hans. "Shijie lunli zai zhongguo de fazhan shi." 世界倫理在中國的發展史 ["A History of Development of World Ethic in China"]. In *Shijie lunli shouce* 世界倫理手冊 [*A Handbook of World Ethic*], translated by Jianhua Deng 鄧建華 and Heng Liao 廖恒, 1–5. Beijing: Sanlian shudian 三聯書店, 2012.

Kung, Lap-Yan 龔立人. "Gonggong, jiaohui yu xianggang shehui: Gonggong shenxue de xushixing" 公共、教會與香港社會: 公共神學的敘事性 ["The Public, Church, and Hong Kong: The Narrative Nature of Public Theology"]. *Daofeng jidujiao wenhua pinglun*, no. 32 (2010): 85–115.

———. "Jidujiao youpai de gonggong shenxue: Yige pipanxing de yuedu" 基督教右派的公共神學—一個批判性的閱讀 ["Public Theology of Christian Right: A Critical Reading"]. In *Zongjiao youpai* 宗教右派 [*Religious Right*], edited by Lo Wing-sang 羅永生 and Lap Yan Kung, 53–66. Hong Kong: Hong Kong Christian Institute 香港基督徒學會 and Dirty Press, 2010.

Kuyper, Abraham. *Abraham Kuyper: A Centennial Reader.* Edited by James D. Bratt. Grand Rapids: Eerdmans, 1998.

_____. *Lectures on Calvinism*. Grand Rapids: Eerdmans, 1931.

_____. *Pro Rege: Living under Christ the King, Volumes 1 and 2*. Edited by John H. Kok with Nelson D. Kloosterman, translated by Albert Gootjes. Bellingham: Lexham Press, 2016, 2017.

_____. *Sacred Theology*. Lafayette: Sovereign Grace, 2001.

Kwan, Kai-man 關啟文. "Jidujiao lunli yu shisu zhuyi lunli: Yige pipanxing bijiao" 基督教倫理與世俗主義倫理: 一個批判性比較 ["Christian Ethics and Secularist Ethics: A Critical Comparison"]. *Jidujiao wenhua xuekan*, no. 7 (2002): 139–72.

Kwan, Simon Shui-Man 關瑞文. "Shenxue yu shehui jian de hudong: Yi guangyi de chujing shenxue weili" 神學與社會間的互動: 以廣義的處境神學為例 ["Interaction between Theology and Society: The Case of Contextual Theology in the Broad Sense"]. In *Zongjiao yu shehui juese chongtan* 宗教與社會角色重探 [*The Social Role of Religion Reexamined*], edited by Peter T. M. Ng 吳梓明, 113–40. Hong Kong: Center for the Study of Religion and Chinese Society, Chung Chi College, The Chinese University of Hong Kong 香港中文大學崇基學院宗教與社會研究中心, 2002.

Kwok, Pui-lan, and Francis Ching-wah Yip, eds. *The Hong Kong Protests and Political Theology*. Lanham: Rowman & Littlefield, 2021.

Lai, Pan-chiu 賴品超. "Chinese Religions: Negotiating Cultural and Religious Identities." In *Christian Approaches to Other Faiths: An Introduction*, edited by Alan Race and Paul Hedges, 270–88. London: SCM, 2008.

_____. *Guangchang shang de hanyu shenxue: cong shenxue dao jidu zongjiao yanjiu* 廣場上的漢語神學: 從神學到基督宗教研究 [*Sino-Christian Theology in the Public Square: From Theology to Christian Studies*]. Hong Kong: Logos and Pneuma Press, 2014.

Lai, Pan-chiu, and Hongxing Lin 林宏星. *Ru ye duihua yu shengtai guanhuai.* 儒耶對話與生態關懷 [*Confucian-Christian Dialogue and Ecological Concern*]. Beijing: Zongjiao wenhua chubanshe 宗教文化出版社, 2006.

Laliberté, André. "Managing Religious Diversity in China: Contradictions of Imperial and Foreign Legacies." *Studies in Religion/Sciences Religieuses* 45, no. 4 (2016): 495–519.

Lam, Wing-hung 林榮洪. *Zhonghua shenxue wushi nian.* 中華神學五十年 [*Fifty Years of Chinese Theology: 1900–1949*]. Hong Kong: China Graduate School of Theology 中國神學研究院, 1998.

Lee, Siu Chan. "Towards a Theology of Church-State Relations in Contemporary Chinese Context." *Studies in World Christianity* 11, no. 2 (2005): 251–69.

Li, Qiang 李強. "Cong shehuixue jiaodu kan xiandaihua de zhongguo daolu" 從社會學角度看現代化的中國道路 ["The China Path of Modernization from Sociological Perspective"]. *Shehuixue yanjiu* 社會學研究 [*Sociological Studies*], no. 6 (2017): 18–26.

Li, Xiangping 李向平. "Lunli shenfen rentong—zhongguo dangdai jidujiaotu de lunli shenghuo" 倫理 身份 認同—中國當代基督教徒的倫理生活 ["Ethics, Identity, and Identification: Ethical Life among Contemporary Chinese Christians"]. *Tian Feng* 天風 [*Heavenly Wind*], no. 7 (2007): 30–35 and no. 9 (2007): 26–33.

———. "Xinjiao lunli jiqi zhongguo shijian moshi: Yi jidutu qiye wei zhongxin" 新教倫理及其中國實踐模式—以基督徒企業為中心 ["Protestant Ethics and Its Model of Practice in China: Focusing on Christian Enterprises"]. *Daofeng jidujiao wenhua pinglun*, no. 29 (2008): 199–221.

———. "'Zongjiao shengtai' haishi 'quanli shengtai'—cong dangdai zhongguo de 'zongjiao shengtailun' sichao tanqi" "宗教生態" 還是 "權力生態"—從當代中國的"宗教生態論"思潮談起 ["'Religious Ecology'or 'Power Ecology': To Begin with the Trend of the Theory of 'Religious Ecology'"]. *Shanghai daxue xuebao (shehui kexue ban)* 上海大學學報 (社會科學版) [*Journal of Shanghai University* (Social Sciences Edition)] 18, no. 1 (2011): 124–40.

Liang, Zhiping 梁志平, ed. *Zhuanxingqi de shehui gongzheng: Wenti yu qianjing* 轉型期的社會公正: 問題與前景 [*Social Justice in Transitional Period: Problem and Prospect*]. Beijing: Sanlian shudian, 2010.

Liang, Shuming 梁漱溟. *Liang Shuming Quanji 3* 梁漱溟全集三 [*Collected Works of Liang Shuming, Vol. 3*]. Jinan: Shandong renmin chubanshe 山東人民出版社, 1990.

Lim, Francis Khek Gee, ed. *Christianity in Contemporary China: Sociocultural Perspectives*. New York: Routledge, 2013.

Liu, Qingping 劉清平. "Meide haishi fubai? Xi Mengzi Zhong youguan shun de liangge anli" 美德還是腐敗? 析孟子中有關舜的兩個案例 ["Virtues or Corruption? An Analysis of Two Cases on Shun in Mencius"]. *Zhexue yanjiu* [Philosophical Research], no. 2 (2002): 43–47.

———. "On the Possibility of Universal Love for All Humans: A Comparative Study of Confucian and Christian Ethics." *Asian Philosophy* 25, no. 3 (2015): 225–37.

Liu, Xiaofeng 劉小楓. "Zhongguo dangdai lunli zhixu zhong de zongjiao fudan" 中國當代倫理秩序中的宗教負擔 ["Religion's Burden in the Contemporary Chinese Ethical Order"]. *Er shi yi shiji* 二十一世紀 [*Twenty-First Century*], no. 30 (1995): 15–23.

Liu, Yan. "Christian Faith Confessions in the Chinese Jiating Church Context: The Discourse of Sovereignty and the Political Order." In *Christian Social Activism and Rule of Law in Chinese Societies*, edited by Fenggang Yang and Chris White, 289–319. Bethlehem: Lehigh University Press, 2021.

Lo, Ping-cheung 羅秉祥. "Ai yu xiaofa: Duihua yu quanshixing de shenxue lunli xue" 愛與效法—對話與詮釋性的神學倫理學 ["Love and Imitation: A Dialogical and Hermeneutical Theological Ethics"]. 中國神學研究院期刊 [*Journal of China Theology Graduate School*], no. 35 (2003): 67–96.

_____. "*Ren* as Fundamental Motif and the Promise and Problem of a Contextual Theology of an Agape-Ren Synthesis." In *Christianity and Chinese Culture: Proceedings of A Sino-Nordic Conference on Chinese Contextual Theology*, edited by Miikka Ruokanen and Paulos Huang, 102–19. Grand Rapids: Eerdmans, 2010.

Lovin, Robin W. *Christian Realism and the New Realities*. New York: Cambridge University Press, 2008.

_____. "Christian Realism for the Twenty-First Century." *Journal of Religious Ethics* 37, no. 4 (2009): 669–82.

_____. *Reinhold Niebuhr and Christian Realism*. Cambridge: Cambridge University, 1995.

_____. "Reinhold Niebuhr's Realistic Pluralism." *Theology Today* 77, no. 3 (2020): 298–309.

Ma, Li, and Jin Li. "Remaking the Civil Space: The Rise of Unregistered Protestantism and Civil Engagement in Urban China." In *Christianity in Chinese Public Life: Religion, Society, and the Rule of Law*, edited by Joel A. Carpenter and Kevin R. den Dulk, 11–28. New York: Palgrave Macmillan, 2014.

Madsen, Richard. "Confucian Conceptions of Civil Society." In *Confucian Political Ethics*, edited by Daniel A. Bell, 3–19. Princeton: Princeton University Press, 2008.

Marsh, Christopher, and Zhifeng Zhong. "Chinese Views on Church and State." *Journal of Church and State* 52, no. 1 (2010): 34–49.

McClay, Wilfred M. "Reinhold Niebuhr and the Problem of Religious Pluralism." In *Reinhold Niebuhr and Contemporary Politics: God and Power*, edited by Richard Harries and Stephen Platten, 218–33. Oxford: Oxford University Press, 2010.

McConnel, Timothy I. "Common Grace or the Antithesis? Towards a Consistent Understanding of Kuyper's 'Sphere Sovereignty.'" In *On Kuyper: A Collection of Readings on the Life, Work and Legacy of Abraham Kuyper*, edited by Steve Bishop and John H. Kok, 303–16. Sioux Center: Dordt College Press, 2013.

Mcilroy, David H. "Subsidiarity and Sphere Sovereignty: Christian Reflections on the Size, Shape and Scope of Government." *Journal of Church and State* 45, no. 4 (2003): 739–63.

Meeter, H. Henry. *The Basic Ideas of Calvinism.* 6th ed. Revised by Paul A. Marshall. Grand Rapids: Baker, 1990.

Mitchell, Ryan Martinez. "Chinese Receptions of Carl Schmitt Since 1929." *Penn State Journal of Law and International Affairs* 8, no. 1 (2020): 181–263.

Mizoguchi, Yuzo. "Zhongguo sixiang zhong de gong yu si" 中國思想中的公與私 ["Public and Private in Chinese Intellectual History"]. In *Gong yu si de sixiang shi* 公與私的思想史 [*Public and Private in Comparative Intellectual Histories*], edited by Sasaki Takeshi 佐佐木毅 and Kim Tea-Chang 金泰昌, and translated by Wenzhu Liu 劉文柱, 37–87. Beijing: Renmin chubanshe 人民出版社, 2009.

Moltmann, Jürgen. "Christianity and the Revaluation of the Values of Modernity and of the Western World." In *A Passion for God's Reign: Theology, Christian Learning, and the Christian Self*, by Jürgen Moltmann, Nicholas Wolterstorff, and Ellen T. Charry, edited by Miroslav Volf, 23–42. Grand Rapids: Eerdmans, 1998.

———. *God for a Secular Society: The Public Relevance of Theology.* Translated by Margaret Kohl. London: SCM Press, 1999.

———. *On Human Dignity: Political Theology and Ethics.* Translated by M. Douglas Meeks. Philadelphia: Fortress Press, 1984.

Mouw, Richard J. "Kuyper on Common Grace: A Comprehensive Theology of 'Commonness.'" In *Common Grace Vol. 1: The Historical Section*, by Abraham Kuyper, edited by Jordan J. Ballor and Stephen J. Grabill, and translated by Nelson D. Kloosterman and Ed M. van der Maas, xix–xxx. Grand Rapids: Christian's Library Press, 2014.

Muller, William A. *Church and State in Luther and Calvin: A Comparative Study.* Garden City: Anchor Books, 1965.

Nadeau, Randall L. "Divinity." In *The Wiley-Blackwell Companion to Chinese Religions*, edited by Randall L. Nadeau, 369–95. West Sussex: Wiley-Blackwell, 2012.

Nathan, Andrew J. "Sources of Chinese Rights Thinking." In *Human Rights in Contemporary China*, edited by R. Randle Edwards, Louis Henkin, and Andrew J. Nathan, 125–64. New York: Columbia University Press, 1986.

Niebuhr, Reinhold. *The Children of Light and the Children of Darkness.* Chicago: University of Chicago Press, 2011.

———. *An Interpretation of Christian Ethics.* New York: Meridian, 1958.

———. *Love and Justice: Selections from the Shorter Writings of Reinhold Niebuhr.* Edited by D. B. Robertson. Louisville: Westminster/John Knox Press, 1992.

_____. *Moral Man and Immoral Society: A Study in Ethics and Politics.* Eugene: Wipf & Stock, 1998.

_____. "The Relation between Common and Saving Grace." In *Archive Collection: Reinhold Niebuhr Papers (1907–1990).* Archive: Manuscript Division, Library of Congress, United States.

_____. "Theology and Political Thought in the Western World." *Ecumenical Review* 9, no. 3 (1957): 253–62.

Ng, Lee Ming 吳利明. *Jidujiao yu zhongguo shehui bianqian* 基督教與中國社會變遷 [*Christianity and Social Change in China*]. Hong Kong: Chinese Christian Literature Council 基督教文藝出版社, 1997.

Ng, Tze Ming Peter. "Chinese Christianity: A 'Global-Local' Perspective." In *Handbook of Global Contemporary Christianity: Themes and Development in Culture, Politics, and Society*, edited by Stephen Hunt, 152–66. Leiden: Brill, 2015.

Ottati, Douglas F. "A Collaborative Manner of Theological Reflection." In *Theology as Interdisciplinary Inquiry: Learning from the Natural and Human Sciences*, edited by Robin W. Lovin and Joshua Mauldin, 132–61. Grand Rapids: Eerdmans, 2017.

Paeth, Scott. "Jürgen Moltmann and the New Political Theology." In *T&T Clark Handbook of Political Theology*, edited by Rubén Rosario Rodríguez, 211–24. London: T&T Clark, 2020.

Patterson, Eric. "The Enduring Value of Christian Realism." *Philosophia Reformata* 80, no. 1 (2015): 27–39.

Paul, Gregor. "China and Religious Diversity: Some Critical Reflections." In *Religious Diversity in the Chinese Thought*, edited by Perry Schmidt-Leukel and Joachim Gentz, 40–44. New York: Palgrave Macmillian, 2013.

Perry, Elizabeth J. "Chinese Conceptions of 'Rights': From Mencius to Mao and Now." *Perspectives on Politics* 6, no. 1 (2008): 37–50.

Peter, Nosco. "Confucian Perspectives on Civil Society and Government." In *Confucian Political Ethics*, edited by Daniel A. Bell, 20–45. Princeton: Princeton University Press, 2008.

Peters, Ted. "Public Theology: Its Pastoral, Apologetic, Scientific, Political, and Prophetic Tasks." *International Journal of Public Theology* 12, no. 2 (2018):153–77.

Philip and Janice Wickeri 魏克利、魏愷貞. "Yiwei dui pushi shenxue you tuchu gongxian de zhongguo shenxuejia" 一位對普世神學有突出貢獻的中國神學家 ["A Chinese Theologian Making Great Contributions to Ecumenical Theology"]. *Jinling shenxue zhi*, no. 1 (2002): 4–9.

Pieris, Aloysius. "Western Christianity and Asian Buddhism." *Dialogue* 7, no. 2 (1980): 49–85.

Pilgrim, Walter E. "God and/or Casesar." In *God and Country? Diverse Perspectives on Christianity and Patriotism*, edited by Michael G. Long and Tracy Wenger Sadd, 23–53. New York: Palgrave Macmillan, 2007.

Pils, Eva. *Human Rights in China: A Social Practice in the Shadows of Authoritarianism*. Cambridge: Polity Press, 2018.

Qin, Hui 秦暉. "Cong gongtongti benwei dao shimin shehui: Chuantong zhongguo jiqi xiandaihua zai renshi" 從共同體本位到市民社會: 傳統中國及其現代化再認識 ["From Communities to Civil Society: A Reconsideration of Traditional China and Its Modernization"]. In *Guojia yu shimin shehui: zhongguo shijiao*, edited by Zhenglai Deng, 266–78. Shanghai: Gezhi chubanshe/Shanghai renmin chubanshe, 2011.

Qu, Hong. "Religious Policy in the People's Republic of China: An Alternative Perspective." *Journal of Contemporary China* 20, no. 70 (2011): 443–48.

Quanxi Gao 高全喜. "Zhengzhi shenxue yu dangdai zhongguo: Moltamann Beijing guoji zhuanjia duitanhui shilu (I)" 政治神學與當代中國: 莫爾特曼北京國際專家對談會實錄一 ["Political Theology and Contemporary China: In Dialogue with Jürgen Moltmann (I)"]. *Jidujiao wenhua xuekan*, no. 34 (2015): 38–40.

Rankin, Mary Backus. "'Public Opinion' and Political Power: Qingyi in Late Nineteenth-Century China." *Journal of Asian Studies* 41, no. 3 (1982): 453–84.

Rasmussen, Larry, ed. *Reinhold Niebuhr: Theologian of Public Life*. Minneapolis: Fortress Press, 1991.

Ren, Jiantao 任劍濤. "Gongmin zongjiao yu zhengzhi zhidu: Zuowei gongmin zongjiao de rujiao jiangou zhi zhidu tiaojian" 公民宗教與政治制度: 作為公民宗教的儒教建構之制度條件 ["Civil Religion and Political Institution: Constitutional Conditions of Construction of Confucianism as Civil Religion"]. *Tianjin shehui kexue* 天津社會科學 [*Tianjin Social Sciences*], no. 4 (2013): 40–49.

Renaud, Robert Joseph, and Lael Daniel Weinberger. "Sphere of Sovereignty: Church Autonomy Doctrine and Theological Heritage of the Separation of Church and State." *Northern Kentucky Law Review* 35, no. 1 (2008): 67–102.

Reny, Marie-Eve. *Authoritarian Containment: Public Security Bureaus and Protestant House Churches in Urban China*. New York: Oxford University Press, 2018.

Robertson, D. B. Introduction to *Love and Justice: Selections from the Shorter Writings*, by Reinhold Niebuhr, 9–21. Louisville: Westminster John Knox Press, 1992. First published 1957.

Rowe, William T. *Hankow: Conflict and Community in a Chinese City, 1796–1895*. Stanford: Stanford University Press, 1989.

_____. *Saving the World: Chen Hongmou and Elite Consciousness in Eighteenth-Century China*. Stanford: Stanford University Press, 2001.

Ruokanen, Mikka 羅明嘉, and Paulos Huang 黃保羅, eds. *Jidujiao yu zhongguo wenhua* 基督教與中國文化 [*Christianity and Chinese Culture*]. Beijing: Zhongguo shehui kexue chubanshe, 2004.

Sabella, Jeremy L. *An American Conscience: The Reinhold Niebuhr Story*. Grand Rapids: Eerdmans, 2017.

Sagovsky, Nicholas. "Public Theology, the Public Sphere and the Struggle for Social Justice." In *A Companion to Public Theology*, edited by Sabastian Kim and Katie Day, 251–70. Leiden: Brill, 2015.

Sanders, Thomas G. *Protestant Concepts of Church and State: Historical Backgrounds and Approaches for the Future*. New York: Anchor Books, 1965.

Schmitt, Carl. *Political Theology: Four Chapters on the Concept of Sovereignty*. Translated by George Schwab. Chicago: University of Chicago Press, 2005.

Schweiker, William. *Theological Ethics and Global Dynamics: In the Time of Many Worlds*. Malden: Blackwell Publishing, 2004.

Skillen, James W. *The Good of Politics: A Biblical, Historical, and Contemporary Introduction*. Grand Rapids: Baker Academic, 2014.

_____. *God's Sabbath with Creation: Vocations Fulfilled, the Glory Unveiled*. Eugene: Wipf & Stock, 2019.

Skillen, James W., and Rockne M. McCarthy, eds. *Political Order and the Plural Structure of Society*. Atlanta: Scholars Press, 1991.

Spykman, Gordon J. "Sphere Sovereignty in Calvin and the Calvinist Tradition." In *Exploring the Heritage of John Calvin*, edited by David E. Holwerda, 163–208. Grand Rapids: Baker, 1976.

Stackhouse, Max L. "Civil Religion, Political Theology and Public Theology: What's the Difference?" *Political Theology* 5, no. 3 (2004): 275–93.

_____. *Public Theology and Political Economy: Christian Stewardship in Modern Society*. Grand Rapids: Eerdmans, 1987.

Stammers, Neil. "Social Movements and the Social Construction of Human Rights." *Human Rights Quarterly*, no. 21 (1999): 1008–980.

Stamo, David N. *The Myth of Universal Human Rights: Its Origin, History, and Explanation, along with a More Humane Way*. Boulder: Paradigim, 2013.

Starr, Chloë. *Chinese Theology: Text and Context*. New Haven: Yale University Press, 2016.

Stockman, Norman. *Understanding Chinese Society*. Cambridge: Polity Press, 2000.

Svensson, Marina. *Debating Human Rights in China: A Conceptual and Political History*. Lanham: Rowman & Littlefield, 2002.

Sun, Pinghua. *Human Rights Protection System in China*. Berlin: Springer Verlag, 2014.

Tang, Andres S. 鄧紹光. "Gonggong shenxue, shenmeyang de shenxue? Yixie genbenxing de fansi" 公共神學, 什麼樣的神學? 一些根本性的反思 ["Public Theology, What Theology? Some Radical Reflections"]. *Shandao qikan* 16, no. 1 (2013): 3–30.

Tang, Edmond. "The Cosmic Christ—The Search for a Chinese Theology." *Studies in World Christianity* 1, no. 2 (1995): 89–111.

Teets, Jessica C. *Civil Society under Authoritarianism: The China Model*. New York: Cambridge University Press, 2014.

Ting, K. H. (Guangxun Ding) 丁光訓. Ai shi yongbu zhixi: Ding guangxun wenji 愛是永不止息: 丁光訓文集 ["Love Never Ends: Papers by K. H. Ting"]. Edited by Janice Wickeri. Nanjing: Yilin chubanshe 譯林出版社, 2000.

———. *Ding guangxun wenji*. 丁光訓文集 [*Collected Works of Guangxun Ding*]. Nanjing: Yilin chubanshe, 1998.

Tipton, Steven M. "Public Theology." In *The Encyclopedia of Political and Religion*, edited by Robert Wuthnow, 624–28. Washington, DC: Congressional Quarterly, 1998.

Tracy, David. *The Analogical Imagination: Christian Theology and the Culture of Pluralism*. New York: Crossroad Publishing, 1981.

Travagni, Stefania. "A Harmonious Plurality of 'Religious' Expressions: Theories and Case Studies from the Chinese Practice of (Religious) Diversity." In *The Critical Analysis of Religious Diversity*, edited by Lene Kühle, William Hoverd, and Jorn Borup, 150–51. Leiden: Brill, 2018.

Tu, Wei-ming. "Embodying the Universe: A Note on Confucian Self-Realization." In *Self as Person in Asian Theory and Practice*, edited by Roger T. Ames, with Thomas P. Kasulis, and Wimal Dissanayake, 177–86. New York: State University of New York Press, 1994.

Twiss, Sumner B. "A Constructive Framework for Discussing Confucianism and Human Rights." In *Confucianism and Human Rights*, edited by Wm. Theodore de Bary and Tu Wei-ming, 27–54. New York: Columbia University Press, 1998.

Vala, Carsten. *The Politics of Protestant Churches and the Party-State in China: God above Party?* London: Routledge, 2018.

_____. "Protestant Resistance and Activism in China's Official Churches." In *Handbook of Protestant and Resistance in China*, edited by Teresa Wright, 316–30. Northampton: Edward Elgar, 2019.

Van Der Vyver, Johan D. Leuven. *Lectures on Religious Institutions, Religious Communities and Rights.* Leuven: Uitgeverij Peeters, 2004.

VanDrunen, David. "Two Kingdoms in China: Reformed Ecclesiology and Social Ethics." In *China's Reforming Churches: Mission, Polity, and Ministry in the Next Christendom*, edited by Bruce P. Baugus, 199–222. Grand Rapids: Reformation Heritage Books, 2014.

Van Til, Cornelius. *Common Grace and the Gospel.* Phillipsburg: P&R Publishing, 1973.

Van Til, Henry R. *The Calvinistic Concept of Culture.* Grand Rapids: Baker, 2001.

Van Til, Kent A. "Subsidiarity and Sphere-Sovereignty: A Match Made in . . .?" *Theological Studies* 69, no. 3 (2008): 610–36.

Veg, Sebastian. "The Rise of China's Statist Intellectuals: Law, Sovereignty, and Repoliticization." *China Journal* 82, no. 1 (2019): 23–45.

Wagenman, Michael R. *Engaging the World with Abraham Kuyper.* Bellingham: Lexham Press, 2019.

Waldron, Jeremy. *God, Locke, and Equality: Christian Foundations in Locke's Political Thought.* Cambridge: Cambridge University Press, 2002.

Walls, Andrew F. *The Cross-Cultural Process in Chrstian History: Studies in the Transmission and Appropriation of Faith.* Maryknoll: Orbis Books, 2002.

Wan, Milton Wai-yiu 溫偉耀. "Xinxing zhi xue yu xinyue renxing lun" 心性之學與新約人性論 ["School of Mind (xin xing zhi xue) and the Doctrine of Humanity in the New Testament"]. In *Dao yu yan: huaxia wenhua yu jidu wenhua xiangyu* "道" 與 "言": 華夏文化與基督文化相遇 [*Logos and Word: Encounters between Chinese Culture and Christian Culture*], edited by Xiaofeng Liu, 483–97. Shanghai: Sanlian shudian, 1996.

_____. *Shengming de zhuanhua yu chaoba: Wode jidu zongjiao hanyu shenxue sikao* 生命的轉化與超拔: 我的基督宗教漢語神學思考 [*The Transformation and Transcendence of Life: My Thoughts on Sino-Christian Theology*]. Beijing: Zongjiao wenhua chubanshe, 2009.

Wang, Aiming 王艾明. *Tizhi jiaohui yu ziyou jiaohui* 體制教會與自由教會 [*Magisterial Church and Free Church*]. Hong Kong: Center for the Study of Religion and Chinese Society, Chung Chi College, The Chinese University of Hong Kong, 2017.

Wang, Hui 汪暉, and Yangu Chen 陳燕谷, eds. *Wenhua yu gonggong xing.* 文化與公共性 [*Culture and Publicness*]. Beijing: Sanlian shudian, 2005.

Wang, Shaoguang 王紹光, and Jianyu He 何建宇. "Zhongguo de shetuan geming: Zhongguo ren de jieshe bantu" 中國的社團革命: 中國人的結社版圖 ["The Revolution of Chinese Mass Organizations: A Map of Chinese Association Life"]. In *Guojia yu shimin shehui: Zhongguo shijiao*, edited by Zhenglai Deng, 3–21. Shanghai: Gezhi chubanshe/ Shanghai renmin chubanshe, 2011.

Wang, Shida 王世達. "Zongjiao kuanrong: Yizhong guanyu zhongguo gudai zongjiao de wudu" 宗教寬容: 一種關於中國古代宗教的誤讀 ["Religious Toleration: A Misinterpretation of Ancient Religion in China"]. *Shijie zongjiao wenhua* 世界宗教文化 [*World Religious Culture*], no. 2 (2010): 57–61.

Wang, Weifan 汪維藩. "Jidujiao lunli yu dangdai jingshen chongjian" 基督教倫理與當代精神重建 ["Christian Ethics and Contemporary Spiritual Reconstruction"]. *Jinling shenxue zhi*, no. 1 (2008): 61–91 and no. 2 (2008): 26–52.

Wang, Xiaochao 王曉朝. "Gongsi lingyu de huafen dui dangdai zhongguo de lilun yiyi" 公私領域的劃分對當代中國的理論意義 ["The Theoretical Significance of Division of Public-Private Areas for Contemporary Chinese Religion"]. *Zhongguo zongjiao* 中國宗教 [*Religion in China*], no. 8/9 (2008): 32–35.

Watson, Andrew. "Civil Society in a Transitional State: The Rise of Association in China." In *Associations and the Chinese State: Contested Spaces*, edited by Jonathan Unger, 14–47. New York: Routledge, 2015.

Weatherley, Robert. *The Discourse of Human Rights in China: Historical and Ideological Perspectives.* New York: St. Martin's Press, 1999.

Wei, Renlian 隗仁蓮. "Shizijia de zhengzhi shenxue yihouji" 《十字架的政治神學》譯後記 ["Comments on Political Theology of the Cross"]. *Jinling shenxue zhi*, no. 2 (1992): 43–46.

Welch, Claude E., Jr., and Sergio Brian Cruz Egoávil. "China's Rising Power: Economic Growth vs. Freedom Deficit." *Journal of Human Rights* 10, no. 3 (2011): 290–310.

Weller, Robert P. "The Politics of Increasing Religious Diversity in China." *Dædalus* 143, no. 2 (2014): 135–44.

White, Chris, and Fenggang Yang. "A Historical Overview of Chinese Christian Activism: Institutional Change toward Democracy." In *Christian Social Activism and Rule of Law in Chinese Societies*, edited by Fenggang Yang and Chris White, 1–30. Bethlehem: Lehigh University Press, 2021.

Wielander, Gerda. *Christian Values in Communist China*. New York: Routledge, 2013.

Williams, Craig. "International Human Rights and Confucianism." *Asia-Pacific Journal on Human Rights and the Law* 7, no. 1 (2006): 38–66.

Winston, Morton. "Human Rights as Moral Rebellion and Social Construction." *Journal of Human Rights* 6, no. 3 (2007): 279–305.

Witte, John Jr. "The Biography and Biology of Liberty: Abraham Kuyper and the American Experiment." In *Religion, Pluralism, and Public Life: Abraham Kuyper's Legacy for the 21st Century*, edited by Luis E. Lugo, 243–62. Grand Rapids: Eerdmans, 2000.

Wolterstorff, Nicholas. *Justice in Love*. Grand Rapids: Eerdmans, 2011.

_____. *Justice: Rights and Wrongs*. Princeton: Princeton University Press, 2008.

_____. *Religion in the University*. New Haven: Yale University Press, 2019.

_____. *In This World of Wonders: Memoir of a Life in Learning*. Grand Rapids: Eerdmans, 2019.

Wood, James E. *Church and State in Historical Perspective*. Westport: Praeger, 2005.

Xie, Libin, and Haiga Patapan. "Schmitt Fever: The Use and Abuse of Carl Schmitt in Contemporary China." *International Journal of Constitutional Law* 18, no. 1 (2020): 130–46.

Xie, Zhibin. "Between Individuality and Publicness: Christianity in Urban China Since the 1980s." In *World Christianity, Urbanization, and Identity*, edited by Moses Biney, Kenneth Ngwa, and Raimundo Barreto, 241–56. Minneapolis: Fortress Press, 2021.

Xie, Zhibin, Pauline Kollontai, and Sebastian Kim, eds. *Human Dignity, Human Rights, and Social Justice: A Chinese Interdisciplinary Dialogue with a Global Perspective*. Singapore: Springer Singapore, 2020.

Xu, Ben 徐賁. "Zhongguo bu xuyao zheyang de 'zhengzhi' yu 'zhuquanzhe jueduan-'shimite re' he guojia zhuyi" 中國不需要這樣的"政治"和"主權者決斷—"施密特熱"和國家主義 ["China Does not Need Politics and Decesionism as Such—'The Fervor of Schmitt' and Nationalism"]. *Er shi yi shiji*, no. 94 (2006), 26–37.

Xu, Jilin 許紀霖. "Jindai zhongguo de gonggong lingyu: xingtai, gongneng yu ziwo lijie: yi Shanghai weili" 近代中國的公共領域: 形態、功能與自我理解: 以上海為例 ["Public Sphere in Modern China: Its Pattern, Function, and Self-Understanding: Taking Shanghai as an Example"]. *Shi lin* 史林, no. 2 (2003): 77–89.

Xu, Zhiwei 許志偉. "Rujia yu jidujiao de renge guan zhong guanxi de zhongxin diwei" 儒家與基督教的人格觀中關係的中心地位 ["Relationship in Personality of Confucianism and Christianity"]. In *Ruye duihua xinlicheng* 儒耶對話新里程 [*A New Stage in Christian-Confucian Dialogue*], edited by Pan-chiu Lai and Peter K. H. Lee 李景雄, 239–59. Hong Kong: Center for the Study of Religion and Chinese Society, Chung Chi College, The Chinese University of Hong Kong, 2001.

Yang, C. K. *Religion in Chinese Society: A Study of Contemporary Social Functions of Religion and Some of Their Historical Facts.* Berkeley: University of California Press, 1961.

Yang, Fenggang. "Confucianism as Civil Religion." In *Confucianism, A Habit of Heart*, edited by Phliip J. Ivanhoe and Sungmoon Kim, 25–46. Albany: State University of New York Press, 2015.

————. "Cong poti dao jieti: Shouwang jiaohui shijian yu zhongguo zhengjiao guanxi chuyi" 從破題到解題: 守望教會事件與中國政教關係芻議 ["Comments on Shouwang Church Events and the Church-State Relationship in China"]. *The Chinese University of Hong Kong Center for Christian Studies and Christian Study, The Center on Chinese Religion and Culture Newsletter* 香港中文大學基督教研究中心暨基督教中國宗教文化研究社通訊, no. 13–14 (2011): 1–7.

————. "From Cooperation to Resistance: Christian Responses to Intensified Suppression in China Today." *Review of Faith and International Affairs* 15, no. 1 (2017): 79–90.

————. "Market Economy and the Revival of Religions." In *Chinese Religious Life*, edited by David A. Palmer, Glenn Shive, and Philip L. Wickeri, 209–23. New York: Oxford University Press, 2011.

————. "A Research Agenda on Religious Freedom in China." *Review of Faith and International Affairs* 11, no. 2 (2013): 6–17.

Yang, Huilin 楊慧林. "'Lunlihua' de hanyu jidujiao yu jidujiao de lunli yiyi jidujiiao lunli zai zhongguo wenhua yujing zhong de kenengxing jiqi nanti" 倫理化"的漢語基督教與基督教的倫理意義—基督教倫理在中國文化語境中的可能性及其難題 ["Ethicalization of Sino-Christianity and Ethical Significance of Christianity: The Possibility and Difficulties of Christian Ethics in the Chinese Cultural Context"]. *Jidujiao wenhua xuekan*, no. 2 (1999), 223–39.

Yang, Shi 楊适. "Jidujiao yu zhongxi wenhua chuantong zhong de renxing guan" 基督教與中西文化傳統中的人性觀 ["Doctrine of Humanity in Christianity and Chinese-Western Cultural Traditions"]. In *Ruye duihua xinlicheng*, edited by Pan-chiu Lai and Peter K. H. Lee, 175–93. Hong Kong: Center for the Study of Religion and Chinese Society, Chung Chi College, The Chinese University of Hong Kong, 2001.

Yang, Nianqun 楊念群. "Shehui fuyin yu zhongguo jidujiao xiangcun jianshe yundong de lilun yu zuzhi jizhu" 社會福音與中國基督教鄉村建設運動的理論與組織基礎 ["Social Gospel and Theoretical and Organizational Foundation of the Chinese Christian Movement of Rural Construction"]. *Daofeng jidujiao wenhua pinglun*, no. 8 (2010): 253–302.

Yao, Xinzhong. *Confucianism and Christianity: A Comparative Study of Jen and Agape*. Brighton: Sussex Academic, 1996.

———. An *Introduction to Confucianism*. Cambridge: Cambridge University Press, 2000.

Yao, Xinzhong, and Yanxia Zhao. *Chinese Religion: A Contextual Approach*. London: Continuum, 2010.

Yin, Haiguang. "Do You Want to Be a Human Being? (1958)" In *The Chinese Human Rights Reader: Documents and Commentary 1900–2000*, edited by Stephen C. Angle and Marian Svensson, 519–38. New York: Routledge, 2015.

Ying, Fuk-tsang (Fuzeng Xing) 邢福增. "Church-State Relations in Contemporary China and the Development of Protestant Christianity." *China Study Journal* 18, no. 3 (2003): 19–48.

———. "Minjian zuzhi zhengce yu zhongguo jidujiao" 民間組織政策與中國基督教 ["Policy on Nongovernmental Organizations and Christianity in China"]. *Er shi yi shi ji*, no. 114, (2009): 26–37.

———. "The Politics of Cross Demolition: A Religio-Political Analysis of the 'Three Rectifications and One Demolition' Campaign in Zhejiang Province." *Review of Religion and Chinese Society* 5, no. 1 (2018): 43–75.

———. "Zhongguo weiquan yundong yu zhongguo de jidujiao Xinyang" 中國維權運動與中國的基督教信仰 ["Rights Defense Movement and Christian Faith in China"]. *The Chinese University of Hong Kong Center for Christian Studies and Christian Study, The Center on Chinese Religion and Culture Newsletter*, no. 21 (2014): 1–7.

Yip, Francis Ching-wah 葉菁華. *Xun zhen qiu quan: Zhongguo shenxue yu zhengjiao chujing chutan* 尋真求全: 中國神學與政教處境初探 [*Chinese Theology in the State-Church Context: A Preliminary Study*]. Hong Kong: Christian Study Center on Chinese Religion and Culture 基督教中國宗教文化研究社, 1997.

You, Xilin 尤西林. "Xiandaixing yu zhongguo dalu dangdai hanyu shenxue de sixiangshi genyuan" 現代性與中國大陸當代漢語神學的思想史根源 ["Modernity and the Origin of History of Thoughts of Sino-Christian Theology in the Mainland"]. *Daofeng jidujiao wenhua pinglun*, no. 41 (2014): 53–69.

Yu, Jie 余杰. "Zhongguo jiating jiaohui de gongkaihua ji jidutu gonggong zhishifenzi qunti de chuxian" 中國家庭教會的公開化及基督徒公共知識份子群體的出現 ["The Publicization of House Churches in China and the Emergence of Public Christian Intellectuals"]. *The Chinese University of Hong Kong, The Center for Christian Studies and Christian Study Center on Chinese Religion and Culture Newsletter*, no. 6 (2009), 9–11.

Yu, Keping 俞可平. "Zhongguo gongmin shehui: guannian, fenlei, yu zhidu huanjing" 中國公民社會: 觀念、分類與制度環境 ["Civil Society in China: Concepts, Classification, and Institutional Environment"]. In *Guojia yu shimin shehui: zhongguo shijiao*, edited by Zhenglai Deng, 37–61. Shanghai: Gezhi chubanshe/Shanghai renmin chubanshe, 2011.

Yuan, Hao 袁浩. "Zhongguo jidujiao yu bufucong de chuantong: yi mingdao wang, tanghe jiaohui yu shouwang jiaohui weili" 中國基督教與不服從的傳統: 以王明道、唐河教會與守望教會為例 ["Chinese Christianity and Their Tradition of Disobedience: Wang Mingdao, Tanghe Church, and Shouwang Church as Examples"]. *Daofeng jidujiao wenhua pinglun*, no. 44 (2016): 88–122.

Zagorin, Perez. *How the Idea of Religious Toleration Came to the West.* Princeton: Princeton University Press, 2003.

Zhang, Delin 張德麟. "Rujia renguan yu jidujiao renguan zhi bijiao yanjiu" 儒家人觀與基督教人觀之比較研究 ["Comparative Study of the Confucian and Christian Concepts of Humanity"]. In *Dao yu yan: huaxia wenhua yu jidu wenhua* xiangyu, edited by Xiaofeng Liu, 450–82. Shanghai: Sanlian shudian, 1996.

Zhang, Desheng 張德勝. *Rujia lunli yu shehui zhixu: Shehuixue de quanshi* 儒家倫理與社會秩序: 社會學的詮釋 [*Confucian Ethics and Social Order: A Social Interpretation*]. Shanghai: Shanghai renmin chubanshe, 2008.

Zhang, Jian 張踐. *Zhongguo gudai zhengjiao guanxi shi (xia ce)* 中國古代政教關係史(下冊) [*A History of Religion and State Relationship in Ancient China, Vol. 2*]. Beijing: Zhongguuo shehui kexue chubanshe, 2012.

Zhang, Jing 張靜. "Qianyan" 前言 ["Preface"] to *Zhuanxing zhongguo shehui gongzhengguan yanjiu* 轉型中國社會公正觀研究 [*A Study in Viewpoints of Social Justice in Transitional China*], edited by Jing Zhang, 1–9. Beijing: Renmin daxue chubanshe 中國人民大學出版社, 2008.

Zhang, Qianfan, and Yingping Zhu. "Religious Freedom and Its Legal Restrictions in China." *Brigham Young University Law Review 2011*, no. 3 (2011): 783–818.

Zhao, Dunhua 趙敦華. "Jidujiao lunli yu rujia lunli de 'jiuhua' yu 'xinti'" 基督教倫理與儒家倫理的 "舊話" 與 "新題" ["The Old and New Themes in Christian Ethics and Confucian Ethics"]. *Jidujiao wenhua xuekan*, no. 9 (2003), 287–92.

_____. "Xingshan yu yuanzui: zhongxi wenhua de yige qutong dian." 性善與原罪: 中西文化的一個趨同點 ["Human Goodness and Original Sin: A Point of Convergence between Eastern and Western Culture"]. In *Jidu zongjiao yu zhongguo wenhua*, edited by Miikka Ruokanen and Paulos Huang, 3–28.

Zhao, Jun. "China and the Uneasy Case for Universal Human Rights." *Human Rights Quarterly* 37, no. 1 (2015): 29–52.

Zhao, Tingyang. *Redefining a Philosophy for World Governance*. Singapore: Springer Singapore, 2019.

Zhuo, Xinping 卓新平. "'Quanqiuhua' zongjiao yu dangdai zhongguo." "全球化"宗教與當代中國 ["'Global' Religions and Contemporary China"]. Beijing: Shehui kexue wenxian chubanshe, 2008.

_____. "Zhongguo jiaohui yu zhongguo shehui" 中國教會與中國社會 ["Chinese Church and Chinese Society"]. In *Jidu Zongjiao yu Dangdai Shehui* 基督宗教與當代社會 [*Christianity and Contemporary Society*], edited by Xinping Zhuo and Josef Sayer 薩耶爾, 247–53. Beijing: Zongjiao wenhua chubanshe, 2003.

Zuidema, S. U. "Common Grace and Christian Action in Abraham Kuyper." In *On Kuyper: A Collection of Readings on the Life, Work and Legacy of Abraham Kuyper*, edited by Steve Bishop and John H. Kok, 247–86. Sioux Center: Dordt College Press, 2013.

INDEX